Logic Matters

Logic Matters

P. T. GEACH

UNIVERSITY OF CALIFORNIA PRESS
Berkeley and Los Angeles 1972

UNIVERSITY OF CALIFORNIA PRESS
Berkeley and Los Angeles, California

ISBN: 0–520–01851–6
Library of Congress Catalog Card Number: 72–138286

Printed in Great Britain

Ku czci tych co polegli w sprawie Ojczyzny

Preface

I here bring together almost all my English articles that I have previously published and have not already collected or cannibalized in other books. They are arranged not chronologically but topically under various headings, in as good an order as I could devise. I have made many stylistic changes, removed incidental errors, and deleted inessential adverse criticisms of other authors. However, nearly all the articles appear without substantial change. I have added a very few brief afterthoughts in footnotes, under the rubric '(*Note*, 1969)'.

Only one article has undergone more drastic surgery: 'Quantification theory and the problem of identifying objects of reference'. In this one article I rashly put over two unconventional theories: a theory of quantification, inspired by Leśniewski and previously sketched in my book *Reference and Generality*; and a theory of quotation, inspired by K. Reach. The first theory was used in expounding the second, but did not commit me to the second; I was and am much more certain that the first theory is sound than that the second is, and I have much regretted that I prejudiced the first theory's chances of winning acceptance by this way of presenting it. In reprinting the article I have accordingly excised the pages that dealt with quoted occurrences of expressions; these now appear with slight rewriting as a separate article 'Quotation and quantification'.

In the final section of the book, 'Logic in Metaphysics and Theology', the article 'Nominalism' was originally addressed to an audience of Catholic priests: I was urging that the crude logic of the ordinary Scholastic manuals is positively harmful to theological thinking. This article was included because it may possibly interest readers who do not share the author's faith; I must ask such readers' indulgence for my not questioning, but simply assuming, certain highly controversial positions; before my original audience I did not need to argue the truth of these positions, but was concerned to draw out their consequences as I saw them.

My first published article 'Designation and truth', which now stands in section 5, originally bore a Polish dedication; this now appears as a motto for the book. I dedicate this book to the glorious memory of those who died for Poland's freedom, honour, and civilised existence. To those who worked at peril of their lives in Poland's underground Universities, logic and all learning mattered indeed. Life, we are often told, is more than logic; but for these Poles logic was more than life. The survivors of those gallant men and women teach in the Polish Universities today, and the torch is handed on.

P. T. GEACH

University of Leeds
Michaelmas 1969

Contents

Acknowledgements

The articles in this volume originally appeared in the following periodicals and collections. The editors and publishers are gratefully thanked for permission to reprint.

1.1   Journal of the Philosophical Association (Bombay), vol. 5, no. 19–20, 1958
1.2   Ratio, vol. 5, no. 1, 1963
1.3   Analysis, vol. 19, no. 3, 1958–59
1.4   The Monist, vol. 50, no. 3, 1966
1.5   An inaugural lecture delivered at the University of Leeds, 22 January, 1968: printed as a pamphlet, Leeds University Press, 1968, and reprinted in the University of Leeds Review, vol. 12, no. 1, 1969. This is a longer version of a Polish article Nazwy i Orzeczniki, which has since been published in Semiotyka Polska; Państwowe Wydawnictwo Naukowe, Warsaw 1972

2.1   Philosophical Review, vol. 69, no. 3, 1960
2.2   Mind, vol. 77, no. 1, 1968
2.3   Mind, vol. 72, no. 1, 1963
2.4   Analysis, vol. 29, no. 6, 1969–70
2.5   Aristotelian Society Supplementary Volume 30, 1956

3.1   Analysis, vol. 21, no. 3, 1960–61
3.2   Analysis, vol. 22, no. 4, 1961–62
3.3   Analysis, vol. 23, no. 1, 1962–63
3.4   Analysis vol. 24, no. 5, 1963–64
3.5   Journal of Philosophy, vol. 72, no. 1, 1965
3.6   Journal of Philosophy, vol. 72, no. 23, 1965
3.7   Ratio, vol. 7, no. 2, 1965

3.8   Synthese, vol. 19, no. 1/2, 1968–69

4.1   Analysis, vol. 18, no. 1, 1957–58
4.2   Proceedings of the International Congress for Logic, Methodology, and Philosophy of Science, Jerusalem, 1964
4.3   Acta Philosophica Fennica, fasc. 16, 1963
4.4   Journal of Philosophy, vol. 74, no. 20, 1967
4.5   Review of Metaphysics, vol. 23, no. 2
4.6   Księga Pamiątkowa ku czci T. Kotarbińskiego (Fragmenty Filozoficzne, Seria Trzecia): Państwowe Wydawnictwo Naukowe, Warsaw, 1967
4.7   Aristotelian Society Supplementary Volume 32, 1958
4.8   Philosophical Review, vol. 79, no. 2, 1970

5.1   Analysis, vol. 8, no. 6, 1947–48
5.2   Analysis, vol. 10, no. 5, 1949–50
5.3   Analysis, vol. 9, no. 3, 1948–49
5.4   Mind, vol. 58, no. 4, 1949
5.5   Mind, vol. 57, no. 4, 1948
5.6   Mind, vol. 59, no. 4, 1950
5.7   Analysis, vol. 19, no. 6, 1958–59
5.8   (Originally part of 4.3; see Preface)
5.9   Analysis, vol. 15, no. 2, 1954–55

6.1   Philosophical Review, vol. 60, no. 4, 1951
6.2   Philosophical Review, vol. 62, no. 4, 1953
6.3   Philosophical Review, vol. 64, no. 4, 1955
6.4   Mind, vol. 65, no. 3, 1956

7.1   Review of Metaphysics, vol. 21, no. 1, 1967
7.2   Review of Metaphysics, vol. 22, no. 3, 1969

8.1   Philosophical Review, vol. 69, no. 2, 1960
8.2   Philosophical Review, vol. 74, no. 4, 1965

9.1   Analysis, vol. 18, no. 3, 1957–8
9.2   Analysis, supplement to vol. 23, 1963
9.3   Analysis, vol. 26, no. 3, 1965–6

10.1   Sophia, vol. 3, no. 2, 1964
10.2   Proceedings of the British Academy, 1965
10.3   Sophia, vol. 8, no. 2, 1969.

1

Historical Essays

1.1. HISTORY OF A FALLACY

The logical fallacy that I am going to discuss here is one that it is quite easy to see by common sense in simple examples. For all that, it is of great philosophical importance. Anybody can see that from "Every boy loves some girl" we cannot infer "There is some girl that every boy loves"; that from "It is obligatory that somebody should go" it does not follow that "There is somebody who it is obligatory should go", for the obligation that somebody should go may be fulfilled by somebody's volunteering to go when he was not obliged; that there is a natural way of taking "Every one of these books it is possible to read in less than half an hour" and on the other hand "It is possible to read every one of these books in less than half an hour" so that the latter does not follow from the former. In the light of modern logic one might call this the operator-shift or quantifier-shift fallacy, because the difference between the premise and the conclusion fallaciously inferred from it would be symbolized by a difference in relative position between two operators—an existential and a universal quantifier, or a quantifier and a modal operator like "it is obligatory" or "it is possible". But the application of formal logic to statements made in the vernacular has lately been rather blown upon; and I must therefore not assume at the outset that this is the correct description of the fallacy, by calling it the operator-shift fallacy. I shall for the moment christen it the boy-and-girl fallacy, after my first example of it.

The philosophical importance of the fallacy is twofold. First, it has often been committed in famous arguments of great philosophers; it was easy for them to commit it, because in philosophical contexts we cannot see by common sense what might be true, and hence conclude that the premise could be true and the conclusion false, as we can in the simple examples of the fallacy that I began with. Secondly, the logical consideration of this fallacy is one of the best ways of showing what needs modern quantification theory had to satisfy.

To begin with, then, I give examples of our fallacy from philosophical writings.

(i) At the beginning of the *Nicomachean Ethics* Aristotle passes from "We do not choose everything for the sake of something else, for that way one would go on *ad infinitum*, and the pursuit (ὄρεξις) would be empty and vain", to "There is some end of actions which we make an object of will (βουλόμεθα) for its own sake, and everything else for its sake . . . this would be the good and the best" (1094a18-22). It is clear that he thinks himself entitled to pass from: "Every series whose successive terms stand in the relation *chosen for the sake of* has a last term" to "There is something that is the last term of every series whose successive terms stand in the relation *chosen for the sake of*".

(ii) It is pretty clear that Plato's difficulties in the Third Man argument arise as follows. He assumes

(*a*) There is some pre-eminent man to whom and to whom alone any men other than he owe it that they are men. (Following Aristotle, I use "man" as an example of a general term instead of Plato's "large".)

From (*a*) there of course follows:

(*b*) There is a pre-eminent man to whom any men other than he owe it that they are men.

Plato confuses this with:

(*c*) For any men there is a pre-eminent man other than they to whom they owe it that they are men.

And then he soon lands himself in contradiction. For suppose that (*c*) is true. Then for any men A, B, C, . . . there will be a pre-eminent man other than they to whom they owe it that they are men—W, let us say. But since W, A, B, C, . . . are all of them men, there will be another pre-eminent man other than they, X

let us say, to whom they owe it that they are men; so A, B, C,
. . . will owe it that they are men not only to W but also to X. We
can then shew, by repeating the argument, that there is yet
another pre-eminent man Y to whom W, X, A, B, C, . . . owe
it that all of them are men; so that A, B, C, . . . owe it that they
are men, not just to one pre-eminent man W, but to W, to X,
and to Y—indeed, to an infinite series of pre-eminent men. This
is in flagrant contradiction to (*a*), and yet seems to follow logically
from (*a*).

The contradiction arises, not because the regress is infinite,
but at the very first stage: it cannot be true *both* that there is
some pre-eminent man to whom and to whom alone all other
than he owe it that they are men, *and also* that, if a group of men
owe it that they are men to one pre-eminent man W, then they
also owe it to another pre-eminent man X. But the argument
leading to contradiction is invalid; there *are* grave difficulties in
the view that what justifies the application of a general term to a
number of things is their common relation to a pre-eminent thing,
to which that same general term applies, but the Third Man
argument is only a spurious difficulty. This result is of some
interest, in view of the extensive discussion of the argument in
antiquity. I do not think we can be sure whether Plato ever
thought of a way round it.

(iii) Berkeley argues as follows (*Second Dialogue between Hylas
and Philonous*): ". . . sensible things cannot exist otherwise than in a
mind or spirit . . . seeing they depend not on my thought and
have an existence distinct from being perceived by me, *there must
be some other mind wherein they exist* [His italics] . . . I . . . immediately
and necessarily conclude the being of a God, because all sensible
things must be perceived by him." Let us notice the way Berkeley
tells us that his inference follows immediately and necessarily;
when a philosopher talks like this, always suspect a fallacy; when
something really does follow immediately and necessarily, there's
no need to say so.

We may waive the question whether an all-perceiving spirit
would have to be a God; and we may remark that the reference
of "I" "me" "my" is not to Berkeley (or his spokesman Philonous)
in particular but to any finite spirit like us. (I owe this point to
Strawson.) The argument may thus be presented in the following
form:

(*a*) Every sensible thing depends for its existence upon being perceived by some mind.

(*b*) Of no *finite* mind is it true that any sensible thing depends for its existence on being perceived just by *that* mind;

Ergo (*c*) Every sensible thing depends for its existence upon being perceived by some *non-finite* mind.—If we add to (*c*) the premise, which was almost certainly in Berkeley's thought,

(*d*) There cannot be more than one non-finite mind, we may then infer:

(*e*) There is some non-finite mind upon whose perception every sensible thing depends for its existence.

At least, I shall not dispute the inferability of (*e*) from (*c*) and (*d*). To infer (*e*) from (*c*) alone would be, of course, an instance of our fallacy, and I once thought Berkeley was here guilty of it; but Strawson has convinced me that this was probably an injustice.

There is, however, still an instance of our fallacy in inferring (*c*) from (*a*) and (*b*). To show this, I construct a parallel argument in which the fallacy is patent.

(*a′*) Every game depends for its actual existence on being played by some person;

(*b′*) Of no *finite* person is it true that any game depends for its actual existence on being played just by *him*;

Ergo (*c′*) Every game depends for its actual existence upon being played by some *non-finite* person.

And the fallacy here *is* our fallacy; for it is a confusion between a game's having to be played by somebody and there being somebody such that the game has to be played by just *him*—the same confusion as that between "It is obligatory that somebody should go" and "There is somebody who it is obligatory should go". We may notice that, with one (now rare) sense of "depend", we may logically infer from "Every icicle depends on a branch of some tree" and "Of no oak-tree is it true that any icicle depends on its branch" the conclusion "Every icicle depends on a branch of some tree that is not an oak". This shows a radical difference of logic between the two senses of "depend"; failure to observe this may foster the fallacy.

(iv) Many philosophers have used a fallacious argument to prove that all definition must bring us in the end to simple and indefinable terms, and all proof begin with indemonstrable propositions. They fail to distinguish between

(a) In any demonstrative discipline it is necessary to take some terms as undefined and some assumptions as unproved and

(b) In any demonstrative discipline there are some terms that it is necessary to take as undefined and some assumptions that it is necessary to take as unproved.

(v) When mathematicians took infinitesimals seriously, they were prepared to pass from

(a) For any finite length, there is a shorter length

to (b) There is a length shorter than any finite length—i.e. an infinitesimal length.

(vi) In *Ethics* I.17, Scholium, Spinoza says that "nothing can be imagined more absurd or more contrary to the Divine omnipotence" than to deny that God "can effect everything that is within the scope of his power". Here it is important not to let ourselves be made dizzy by the mention of God and omnipotence; the logical point that arises here is the need to distinguish two senses of "*x* can effect everything that *x* can effect"—regardless of whether "*x*" is taken to stand for God. In one sense it would be absurd to deny such a statement about a given being, *x*; in another sense it would not, because the various possibilities open to *x* might not be compossible. One might express the distinction by using for the tautologous assertion about *x* "*x* can effect *anything* that *x* can effect" and for the non-tautologous one "*x* can effect *everything* that *x* can effect". We shall be considering this distinction between "any" and "every" later on. In any event, it is clear that Spinoza is making the same mistake as though one confused "It is possible to read *any* one of these books in less than half an hour" with "It is possible to read *every* one of these books in less than half an hour", which (in rather different words) was one of our examples of the boy-and-girl fallacy.

I think this ought to be enough to show the historical importance of our fallacy. I do not think its frequent occurrence in arguments about high matters like God, infinity, and men's highest good is at all surprising; in such realms paradoxical consequences are so common that, as I said, common sense is no guide. But even in such realms, I believe, logic is a guide; and those who think it is not are estopped from arguing the matter. It is no use saying that in such realms our language becomes 'logically odd'; things are never *odd* in logic, only *different*.

I now come to the logical nature of the fallacy. First, we may

B

observe that the traditional formal logic is wholly incompetent to resolve it. The only traditional rule that even seems to be relevant is the rule that no term may be distributed in the conclusion if it is not distributed in the premises. But in the conclusion "Some girl is loved by every boy" the term "girl" would be called undistributed, and the term "boy" distributed, and the same goes for the premises "By every boy some girl is loved". So even if the doctrine of distribution made coherent sense, as it does not, it would be useless here. Since there are still Colleges of Unreason where the traditional formal logic is taught as the only genuine logic, this is worth pointing out.

One might be inclined to say that in "By every boy some girl is loved" there is no reference to a definite girl, whereas there is such a reference in "Some girl is loved by every boy". But "reference to a definite girl" cannot be being contrasted with "reference to an indefinite girl"; there is no such creature. The phrase ought rather to be "definite reference to a girl"; but of course "some girl" is not a definitely referring expression; on the contrary it is a paradigm case of an indefinite description. That someone who asserted "Some girl is loved by every boy" must mentally refer definitely to a girl, have her definitely in mind, is neither true nor relevant. It is not true, because he might accept the statement (on testimony, say) without having any one girl definitely in mind. It is not relevant: suppose he has Mary in mind whereas in fact not Mary but Jane is loved by every boy; then "Some girl is loved by every boy" will be true although "Mary is loved by every boy" would be false, and hence "some girl" cannot, even for the nonce, be being used to refer to Mary.

I now come on to the treatments of our fallacy by medieval logicians, and the very similar treatment by Russell in his chapter "Denoting" in *The Principles of Mathematics*. Since I do not wish to bother you with irrelevant details I shall not describe any of these ways of treating it, but shall construct a simple theory with a broad similarity to the medieval and Russellian theories. Further, for expository purposes I shall use a simple model in which there are just two boys, John and Tom, and just two girls, Mary and Kate. The complications that arise from a general term's not necessarily applying to a definite list of objects, as "boy" and "girl" do in my model, are not important, because our theory will run into intractable difficulties even within the model.

Our theory distinguishes sharply between statements about *some girl* and statements about *a girl*. I write "$\phi(\quad)$" for the general form of a statement: then "ϕ(some girl)" will be true if and only if "ϕ(Mary) or ϕ(Kate)" is true, but "ϕ(a girl)" will be true if and only if "ϕ(Mary or Kate)" is true. In some contexts the difference makes no odds; it makes no odds whether we say "Tom kissed a girl" or "Tom kissed some girl", for "Tom kissed Mary or Kate" is the same in effect as "Tom kissed Mary or Tom kissed Kate". But "Tom has promised to marry some girl" and "Tom has promised to marry a girl" are quite different; the former corresponds in truth-value to "Tom has promised to marry Mary or Tom has promised to marry Kate", the latter to "Tom has promised to marry Mary or Kate" which is not at all the same thing. (Thus "some girl" is to be restricted to cases where it is proper to ask "which girl?"; this gives a *sort* of sense to saying it has a definite reference.)

Again our theory distinguishes sharply between statements about *any girl* and statements about *every girl*. "ϕ(any girl)" will be true if and only if "ϕ(Mary) and ϕ(Kate)" is true; "ϕ(every girl)" will be true if and only if "ϕ(Mary and Kate)" is true. In some contexts the difference makes no odds; it makes no odds whether we say "Tom kisses any girl" or "Tom kisses every girl", for "Tom kisses Mary and Tom kisses Kate" is the same in effect as "Tom kisses Mary and Kate". But "Tom is free to marry any girl" and "Tom is free to marry every girl" are quite different; the former corresponds in truth-value to "Tom is free to marry Mary and Tom is free to marry Kate", the latter to "Tom is free to marry Mary and Kate", which is not at all the same thing.

Let us call a general term with "a", "some", "any", or "every" prefixed, a *denoting phrase*. So far we have been considering sentence-forms containing only one denoting phrase. Let us now consider some containing two. "Every boy loves some girl" corresponds in truth-value to "Every boy loves Mary or every boy loves Kate", and therefore to "(John and Tom love Mary) or (John and Tom love Kate)". Or we might have argued that it corresponds in truth-value to "John and Tom love some girl", and therefore to "(John and Tom love Mary) or (John and Tom love Kate)"; we get the same result either way. On the other hand, "Any boy loves a girl" corresponds to "John loves a girl and Tom loves a girl", and thus to "(John loves Mary or Kate) and (Tom loves Mary or Kate)"; or again, it corresponds to "Any boy loves Mary or Kate", and thus to "(John loves Mary or Kate) and (Tom loves Mary or Kate)". Thus when "Every boy loves some girl" and "Any boy loves a girl" are construed in the artificial way recommended by our theory, they serve to express the very distinction that the boy-and-girl fallacy makes people ignore. On the other hand, the substitution of "any" for "every", or "some" for "a", or vice versa, will not always make a difference when there are two denoting phrases in the same context; you will easily be able to work it out that there is no difference in the force of the statement produced by putting "any" instead of "every", both times or once only, in "Every boy loves every girl", or by putting "a" instead of "some", both times or once only, in "Some boy loves some girl".

It would be easy to go through our examples of the boy-and-girl fallacy and show that in every case the distinction necessary to resolve it can be expressed in a contrast between "every" and "any", or between "some" and "a". Thus, in the Aristotle case, case (i), we should distinguish between

(a) *Any* series whose successive terms stand in the relation *chosen for the sake of* has a thing as its last terms;

(b) *Some* thing is the last term of *every* series whose successive terms stand in the relation *chosen for the sake of*.

In the Berkeley case, case (iii), we should distinguish between

(a) Every sensible object depends on *a* mind's perceiving it, and (b) Every sensible object depends on *some* mind's perceiving it. And so on. Thus a theory of our type is quite powerful; and this sort of solution to our problem was naturally acceptable to many great logicians. It was the sort of solution generally accepted by medieval logicians; but the solution, and indeed the problem, were forgotten by the fools who dismissed the medieval doctrine of *suppositio* as useless subtlety and substituted for it the barren and sophistical doctrine of distribution. The solution was however re-discovered by Russell; it is interesting to notice that some of the examples he uses are practically identical with ones used to the very same end in Walter Burleigh's *De puritate artis logicae*.

For all that, it is quite easy to show that our theory breaks down. Let us try to interpret "Any boy loves some girl", for example, according to our rules. On the one hand, it ought to correspond in its truth-value to "(John loves some girl) and (Tom loves some girl)", which is tantamount to "(John loves a girl) and (Tom loves a girl)"; but to that "Any boy loves a girl" corresponds in truth-value; so on this account "Any boy loves some girl" ought to be tantamount to "Any boy loves a girl". On the other hand, it ought to correspond in its truth-value to "(Any boy loves Mary) or (any boy loves Kate)", which is tantamount to "(Every boy loves Mary) or (every boy loves Kate)"; but to that "Every boy loves some girl" corresponds in truth-value; so by this argument "Any boy loves some girl" ought to be tantamount to "Every boy loves some girl", not to "Any boy loves a girl". Thus by our rules a certain expression comes out equivalent to each one of the pair that it was the whole aim of our theory to distinguish. This is odd; as I said, in logic nothing can be odd; so our theory isn't logical.

It is not, indeed, true in general that a statement of the form "ψ (any boy, some girl)" can be shown equivalent in truth-value to both of the forms "ψ(any boy, a girl)" and "ψ(every boy, some girl)", which it was the business of the theory to distinguish; this does happen if we interpret "$\psi(—, \ldots)$" as "— loves . . .", but only because of certain things that hold on this interpretation but not generally. If we interpret "$\psi(—, \ldots)$" in *this* way, then "ψ(John, some girl)" is tantamount to "ψ(John, a girl)"; but not if we interpret it as "— has promised to marry . . .", since, as we saw, "John has promised to marry some girl" is quite different in force from "John has promised to marry a girl".

There is, however, as Strawson has pointed out to me, a difficulty that must always arise for "ψ(any boy, some girl)", on any interpretation. (a) Let us begin by using our rule for "any boy"; then "ψ(any boy, some girl)" comes out equivalent in truth-value to "ψ(John, some girl) and ψ(Tom, some girl)". Now let us apply our rule for "some girl"; then "ψ(John, some girl)" comes out equivalent in truth-value to "ψ(John, Mary) or ψ((John, Kate)". Similarly for "ψ(Tom, some girl)". So by this method "ψ(any boy, some girl)" comes out as true if and only if "(ψ(John, Mary) or ψ(John, Kate)) and (ψ(Tom, Mary) or ψ(Tom, Kate))" is true. (b) Let us now begin by using our rule for "some girl"; then "ψ(any boy, some girl)" comes out equivalent in truth-value to "ψ(any boy, Mary) or ψ(any boy, Kate)". Now let us apply our rule for "any boy"; then "ψ(any boy, Mary)" comes out equivalent in truth-value to "ψ(John, Mary) and ψ(Tom, Mary)".

Similarly for "ψ(any boy, Kate)". So our final result makes "ψ(any boy, some girl)" come out equivalent in truth-value to: "(ψ(John, Mary) and ψ(Tom, Mary)) or (ψ(John, Kate) and ψ(Tom, Kate))". Thus our two procedures yield statement-forms related as "(*p* or *r*) and (*q* or *s*)" and "(*p* and *q*) or (*r* and *s*)", which as is obvious by the logic of truth-functions may well differ in truth-value.

It is remarkable how the logicians who held our sort of theory had a blind spot that prevented their seeing this difficulty. One would expect formation-rules to be stated forbidding the awkward sentence-form "ψ(any boy, some girl)": rules to the effect (a) that in a context "ψ(. . . , some girl)", only "every boy", not "any boy", will fit; (b) that in a context "ψ(any boy, —)", only "a girl", not "some girl", will fit. Now medieval logicians did make a distinction corresponding to our distinction between "some" and "a", although there is no indefinite article in Latin; so they did have a rule corresponding to (b); but oddly enough they were not nearly so well aware of the twin distinction between "any" and "every". They accordingly had no rule corresponding to (a), and no tenable account of the (obviously possible) kind of statement which on our conventions appears as "ψ(every boy, some girl)", which, if "every" and "any" are not distinguished, would be forbidden by rule (b). Russell, on the other hand, made both of the distinctions, between "a" and "some" and between "any" and "every", but never noticed that (say) "any boy" and "some girl" cannot be coherently fitted into the same context on his explanations of what they mean; this comes about because when giving examples of sentences containing more than one denoting phrase, he tacitly assumes that the rule for the "some" phrase must be applied before the rule for the "any" phrase, although this nowise follows from his own conventions for the use of denoting phrases; if he had been strict, the difficulty would have struck him at once.

Let us go back to where we found ourselves in a bog. Our trouble was that "Any boy loves some girl" can be expounded in two different ways, according as we take it to be of the form "Θ (any boy)"—when it turns out to be tantamount to "Any boy loves a girl"—or of the form "Λ (some girl)"—when it turns out to be tantamount to "Every boy loves some girl". Now let us suppose that the distinctions we were trying to make between "any" and "every", between "some" and "a", are illusory, but that it makes all the difference whether we predicate of every boy that he loves some girl or predicate of some girl that every boy loves her. In that case our necessary distinction can be expressed by a difference of bracketing—"Every boy (loves some girl)" as opposed to "(Every boy loves) some girl". One might express the matter thus: it makes a difference to the sense of "Every boy loves some girl" whether we take the predicate "— loves some girl" to be formed first and then completed with the denoting phrase "every boy", or rather take the predicate "every boy loves —" to be formed first and then completed with the denoting phrase "some girl". (Contrast the synthesis of a chemical substance: it makes absolutely no difference whether you synthesize the ammonium radical first and add the nitrate radical or the other way around, you get nitrate of ammonium just the same.)

This difference of bracketing works for all our examples. Let me take the Spinoza example, which I found specially difficult to disentangle when I was teaching Spinoza's *Ethics* to undergraduates. We have to distinguish between first forming the predicate "God can effect—" and then completing it with "everything that God can effect", in which case what is asserted about God is trivial; and on the other hand first forming the predicate "effect everything that God can effect", then modalizing this with "can", and finally attaching the subject "God". Using brackets, we distinguish between "(God can effect) everything that God can effect", which is trivial, and "God can (effect everything that God can effect)", which is not. Once again, let us not be bemused by the Name of God, as if it had the power to abrogate logical laws, by a kind of magic that makes everything in the neighbourhood 'logically odd'; there is precisely the same distinction between the trivial truism "(Sixpence will buy) everything that sixpence will buy", and "Sixpence will (buy everything that sixpence will buy)", which would suitably express a greedy child's dream of buying for one single sixpence every article in a shop that is priced at sixpence.[1]

A great medieval logician, William of Sherwood, had this solution in his fingers, only to let it drop. In his *Syncategoremata* he remarks that it makes no difference whether we take "Every man sees every man" as predicating of every man that he sees every

---

[1] In this example "will" is only an idiomatic substitute for "can".

man or that every man sees him; on the other hand it does make a difference whether we take "Every man sees every donkey but Brownie" (a) as asserting of every man that he sees every donkey but Brownie, i.e. that he does not see Brownie but does see every other donkey, or (b) as asserting it of every donkey but Brownie, i.e. denying it of Brownie but asserting it of every other donkey, that every man sees him. (a) and (b) can easily be seen to yield different truth-conditions for the statement. William of Sherwood actually uses such expressions, regarding denoting phrases like "every man" and "every donkey but Brownie", that the one gets into the proposition first and the other arrives later and finds the first already there; his metaphor of a race between denoting phrases to get into the proposition first has the same point as my mataphor of an order of construction; but unluckily he used this idea only *ad hoc* to solve particular problems, not to form any general theory.

I will end this paper by trying to explain the rationale of the modern notation of bound variables. Using something like that notation—I postpone a discussion of any differences—one might write:

"For any boy x, for some girl y, x loves y" *for* "Every boy (loves some girl)"

and "For some girl y, for any boy x, x loves y" *for* "(Every boy loves) some girl."

Let us now see what constructions in the vernacular most closely correspond to this use of letters. We may most profitably compare

"For any boy x, for some girl y, x loves y"

to: "It is true as regards any boy that there is a girl such that he loves her"

and "For some girl y, for any boy x, x loves y"

to "There is a girl such that it is true as regards any boy that he loves her".

The pieces of the vernacular and of the symbolic sentences stand in close correspondence. "For any boy x" is rendered by "it is true as regards any boy that"; "for some girl y", by "there is a girl such that"; the variable "x" bound by "for any boy x", by the pronoun "he" whose antecedent is "any boy"; the variable "y" bound by "for some girl y", by the pronoun "her" whose antecedent is "a girl". It is very important to notice that the relation of bound variables to the binding operator in symbolism *strictly* corresponds to the relation of pronoun to antecedent in the vernacular. I may perhaps give another example for a different sort of operator: "$\lambda x(2x^2)$" means precisely "the function of a number that twice *its* square is"; and here the grammatical relation of "its" to the antecedent "a number" *strictly* corresponds to the binding of the "x" in "$2x^2$" by the operator "λx". Quine has rightly drawn attention to this relation between pronouns and bound variables, which incidentally greatly helps in the teaching of symbolic logic; criticisms of his view are mere mistakes. (Frege also, though he disliked the word "variable" as a source of many muddles, classified together as "indefinite indicators" the letters that would now be called bound variables in symbolism and the pronouns of the vernacular in the uses I have just discussed.)

One last word. In my above example of quantificational symbolism, I used a restricted rather than an unrestricted quantifier: e.g. "for any boy x", instead of "for any x" followed by "if x is a boy, then . . . " I think this is not merely a matter of notation, but raises an important problem for the philosophy of logic. But that cannot be discussed here; nor would my view on that matter, whether right or wrong, make any difference to what I have said here.

1.2. ARISTOTLE ON CONJUNCTIVE PROPOSITIONS

I shall begin by expounding the classical doctrine of the conjunctive proposition. This doctrine is to be found already full-fledged in the medieval discussions of copulative propositions; it is not, as some people seem to fancy, the creation of modern symbolic logic. It may be stated as follows:

(I) For any set of propositions there is a single proposition that is their *conjunction*, they being its *conjuncts*. (Henceforth, instead of "conjunction" in the grammatical sense, I shall use "connective" to avoid confusion.)

(II) The conjunction of a set of propositions is true iff (i.e. if and only if) each one of them is true, and false iff some one of them is false. It therefore always has a truth-value, given that its conjuncts all have truth-values.

(III) Like any other proposition, a conjunction may occur as an unasserted part, e.g. as an *if* or *then* clause, of a longer proposition.

(IV) Conjunctive propositions frequently occur in ordinary discourse: "*καί*" and other words in Greek, "et" and other words in Latin, and "and" in English, are connectives that serve as signs of conjunction in very many ordinary sentences.

This doctrine is sometimes disputed, but only, I think, through confusion (indeed, I think a logical error of this sort can never be anything but confusion). Mill denied (I), on the score that to call a conjunction a kind of proposition is like calling a street a kind of house or a team of horses a kind of horse.[1] His error was probably the result of an error about (III) as well; if conjunctions occurred only as asserted propositions, there might be some case for regarding a conjunction as a mere aggregate of propositions, not a proposition; but this account will not cover "*p* and *q*" as it occurs in "*p* and *q*, or else *r*" or in "if *p* and *q*, then *r*". Similarly, when Strawson tells us[2] that the dot used by logicians to form conjunctions has a role rather like the full stop; this just illustrates the very common failure of philosophers to take the unasserted occurrences of propositions into account.

(II) and (IV) together imply that very often in ordinary discourse propositions strung together with "and" form a proposition whose truth-value is determined by those of its conjuncts. This also Strawson would apparently deny, on the score that "we do not string together at random" the propositions we conjoin with "and"—"there is some further reason for the *rapprochement*".[3] He seems to think that 'that for the sake of which we conjoin' has of itself an influence on the logical force of the conjunction. But our reasons for putting an "and" between two propositions form no part of what we propound in the resulting conjunction. Formal logicians do not put a dot between any old propositions —they have reason to do so when they do; on Strawson's view, then, it ought to be impossible for the propositions thus formed to be bare conjunctions satisfying (I) to (IV) above—they ought to have their truth-value affected by 'that for the sake of which' the logician frames them. Apparently Strawson is not willing to go so far.

[1] *System of Logic*, book I, chapter IV, section 3.
[2] In his *Introduction to Logical Theory*, p. 80.   [3] Ibid., p. 81.

Assuming the classical theory of conjunctive propositions to be the truth, I shall now inquire how far Aristotle had grasped this truth. Before going into details, we can see a general reason why he hardly could grasp it perfectly. The classical theory uses the idea of propositional truth-values; and I doubt whether Aristotle had this idea. Of course it does not matter at all that he has no word for truth-value; that word is no more than an abbreviation for the verbiage "truth or falsity, as the case may be", and the medieval logicians contrived to formulate the classical theory without any such handy term of art. What I suspect is that when Aristotle speaks of propositions as true and false, he is muddling together two quite different pairs of contrary notions.

There are two sorts of truth which Aristotle at any rate failed to distinguish explicitly: the truth of propositions, and the truth of predications. To each of these is opposed a corresponding sort of falsehood. A proposition is true (or false) *tout court*; a predicate is true (or false) *of* something. If every proposition could be satisfactorily analysed as a single predication, with one subject and one predicate, the relation between true or false predication and a true or false proposition would be so simple that my distinction between them would hardly seem worth making a fuss about. For a proposition with subject "*S*" and predicate "*P*" is true or false according as "*P*" is true or false of the thing(s) called "*S*"; this would need to be made more precise—if "*S*" is taken to be not a singular but a general term, then its quantification must be taken into account—but such details are not our present concern.

The important fact is that not every proposition admits of subject-predicate analysis. This is most obvious for disjunctions: "*p* vel *q*" is true iff one of the propositions "*p*" and "*q*" is true, and "*p* aut *q*" is true iff one of these propositions is true and the other is false. (I use Latin words as connectives in order to dodge the idiotic but seemingly perennial dispute as to the 'proper' meaning of "or" in ordinary language.) These truth-conditions are quite different in kind from those of a simple predication; the truth-value of the complex proposition is here specified by—in mathematical language, given as a function of—the truth-values of its constituents, and is at least not directly determined by some predicate's being true or false *of* something.

Modern logicians have in fact sometimes written as though the truth of a proposition could always be determined in relation to the truth-values of simpler propositions, and as though the use of a connective like "aut" or "vel" could be sufficiently specified by its building propositions out of propositions in a truth-functional way. It is, however, easy to produce counter-examples. "Every S is P aut Q" is not a disjunction of two propositions: it is true iff the predicate "P aut Q" is true of each thing called "S", and "P aut Q" is true of an object b iff one and only one of the predicates "P" and "Q" is true of b. In some instances, then, we have to explain a proposition's being true or false in terms of predicates' being true or false *of* things; and even when a proposition is truth-function-ally derived from simpler propositions, these simpler propositions will themselves have truth-conditions that relate to predicational truth. Thus if we get down to bedrock we have to state truth-conditions in terms of predicates rather than propositions; for every proposition contains at least one predicate, whereas not every proposition is analysable into simpler propositions. No wonder then that in his fundamental researches concerning the concept *true*, Tarski had to take the concept *true of* as basic, under the style "satisfaction"; as Aristotle would put it, Tarski was "so to speak compelled by Truth itself".

So much justification there is for taking truth of predication as the fundamental sense of the word "truth". But "truth" as attributed to propositions has a different sense, related to the fundamental one (as Tarski has likewise explained) in a rather complicated way; and if we do not keep the two senses clearly apart, we shall run into confusion.

Now Aristotle did nothing to keep these two senses apart; indeed, in various passages where he discusses truth and false-hood, he pretty clearly has in mind only simple predications—that is to say, the case in which it is easiest and least harmful to confuse the two sorts of truth. For example, in *De interpretatione* c.6 he is concerned to show that propositions pair off into 'antiphases' in which one member is true and the other false; he is content to argue that an affirmative predication (κατάφασις) is expressible iff the corresponding negative predication (ἀπόφασις) is so, and that one can assert and can deny that something applies (ὑπάρχει) both when it does apply and when it does not—this verb being his regular technicality to signify a *predicate's* applying to something. Here, then, he can have had in mind only simple predications. Aristotle never considers the truth or falsity e.g. of disjunctions, and never asks what sort of proposition would pair off with a disjunction in an antiphasis; raising this question must surely have driven him to explicitly recognizing conjunctions as propositions, for the only proposition with which "p vel q" would pair off in an antiphasis is "not p and not q". Moreover, the truth-value of a disjunction, as we saw, does not relate directly to predicational truth or falsehood; and so considering the truth-value of disjunctions almost forces upon one the distinction between propositional and predicational truth; similarly, if conjunctions as wholes have truth-values assigned to them.

Did Aristotle, then, consider and explicitly reject the claim of conjunctions to be regarded as true or false propositions? I shall try to show that in his earlier logical work he did so, but later changed his mind. As regards evidence of his earlier view, we have to be cautious; various passages that might seem to be relevant are not really so. First, there are various passages where Aristotle discusses what we may call the fusion of predicates. "Is white" and "is a man" fuse neatly into "is a white man" (whatever scruples we may have about a white man's being ἕν τι); but "is good" and "is a cobbler" do not fuse into "is a good cobbler", nor can "is a dead man" be regarded as a fusion of "is dead" and "is a man", since a dead man is not a man. (See e.g. De interpretatione c. xi) This problem is interesting, but does not now concern us; we are concerned only with the proposition "Socrates is good and Socrates is a cobbler", not with its relation to "Socrates is a good cobbler"; and the fact that this last proposition does not split up into "Socrates is good" and "Socrates is a cobbler" does nothing to show whether these two propositions can be formed into one conjunctive proposition by simply putting an "and" between them.

Again, in De interpretatione c. viii Aristotle considers what we are to say about the truth of predications whose subject-term is a single word (Aristotle uses "ἱμάτιον"; I shall use "morse") arbitrarily chosen to mean man and horse. He concludes by a two-part argument that such a term cannot legitimately be introduced as a subject of predication. (i) If the supposition that "morse" means: man and horse implies that we could call a thing "a morse" iff it were both a man and a horse, then "morse" is not a name of anything; and a predication with "morse" as subject οὐδὲν σημαίνει, signifies nothing.—This view as to empty subject-

terms is highly disputable, and I think there is evidence that
Aristotle does not always adhere to it. Anyhow, a predication
with such a compound term as subject would in no case be a conjunctive proposition; for example, if "*S*" means "lawyer (and)
politician", neither "Every *S* is a scoundrel" nor "Some *S* is an
honest man" can be analysed as a conjunction of the predications
got from it by substituting first "lawyer" and then "politician" for
"*S*". So this part of Aristotle's argument is quite irrelevant.

The second part, however, looks rather more relevant. (ii) If
a predication with "morse" as subject is an intended equivalent to
combining the two predications with "man" and "horse" as
subjects, then of the two sides of an antiphasis we shall not necessarily get one true and one false.—Aristotle does not spell out this
argument for us, but it is clearly valid, and does show that "morse"
cannot thus be understood. For "Some morse is white" will be
true iff some man is white *and* some horse is white; "No morse is
white" will be true iff no man is white *and* no horse is white; we
can thus specify a possible case, e.g. the case where no man is
white but some horse is white, in which we should not have one
side true and the other false in the antiphasis "Some morse is
white.—No morse is white". Thus "Some morse is white" is not
a well-formed proposition. But the conjunction "Some man is
white and some horse is white" is not thereby shown not to be a
proposition—unless one were assuming that every proposition can
be expressed as a single predication. On the evidence, we should
not ascribe this further, unjustified, assumption to Aristotle.

In *Sophistici elenchi*, however, Aristotle explicitly denies that a
conjunction is a true or false proposition. He calls it "the ruin of
discourse" (176a) to answer either "Yes" or "No" to a question of
the form "Is it the case that *p* and *q* and *r* . . . ?"—even if such an
answer may seem harmless because it so happens that the conjuncts are all true or all false. A modern logician would not be
embarrassed how to answer, even when the conjuncts had different
truth-values; the right answer is "Yes" iff each single conjunct is
true and "No" iff some one conjunct is false; if anybody infers
from the answer "No" that all the conjuncts are false, he is simply
muddle-headed.

Aristotle in this passage treats "Are Coriscus and Callias at
home?" as though it were an instance of "Is it the case that *p* and
q?" But this is not the very same proposition as "Coriscus is at

home and Callias is at home"; in general, "d and b are $P(s)$" is to be distinguished from "d is (a) P and b is (a) P". To be sure, if the latter form were open to exception, as Aristotle thought, then so would the former be; but there are instances where predicating "P" in the plural of d and b together might be regarded as illegitimate even though "P" in the singular could be truly predicated of d and b severally. As I have argued elsewhere,[1] the back of the Third Man argument in the Parmenides could be broken even if we conceded that the term "great" can be truly predicated of *great* itself ($αὐτὸ τὸ μέγα$) and also truly predicated of the many great things ($τὰ πολλά μεγάλα$), provided that we denied the licence to infer from this that "great" in the plural ("$μεγάλα$") can be truly predicated of *great* itself and the many great things *together* ($αὐτὸ τὸ μέγα καὶ τἆλλα τὰ μεγάλα$ may not be rightly called $πολλὰ μεγάλα$ or $πάντα μεγάλα$). Perhaps Plato intended us to take this way out of his paradox. Similarly I suspect—though I have failed to find any text saying just this—that a medieval theologian who said predications concerning God were 'analogical' would disallow the inference from "God is wise (*sapiens*) and Plato is wise" to "God and Plato are wise (*sapientes*)". What makes very good logical sense of disallowing such inferences is the fact that if d is P and b is P, or again if d is P and a is a set of Ps, then we cannot infer that "P" in the plural is predictable of a set containing just d and b, or just d and the members of a; for it depends on your set theory whether you allow that there is such a set at all.

However, if "d" and "b" are taken to be names of two animals, then we may waive such objections to the equivalence e.g. of "d and b are blind" with "d is blind and b is blind". Aristotle has a perversely ingenious argument to show that even in this sort of case propositions of the form "d and b are $P(s)$" are ill-formed; if he were right, the conjunction "d is P and b is P" would have to be rejected too. The argument occurs at 168a in the Sophistici elenchi; it runs as follows, if we fill up some steps that Aristotle makes tacitly:

(1) "Is blind" means "is of a nature to see but has not sight"; so "are blind" means "are of a nature to see but have not sight".

(2) If d and b are of a nature to see, either they have sight or they have not sight.

<hr />

[1] 'The Third Man Again', *Philosophical Review*, 65 (1956), p. 72.

(3) If d and b are of a nature to see but have not sight, then (by step (1)) they are blind.

(4) Hence, if d and b are of a nature to see, either they both have sight or they are both blind.

(5) If d has sight and b is blind, d and b are of a nature to see.

(6) Hence, if d has sight and b is blind, either they both have sight or they are both blind; which is absurd.

Aristotle's suggested way out of the absurdity is to ban altogether such plural questions as "Are they of a nature to see?", 'Are they blind?' This drastic surgery is unnecessary; Aristotle has simply been deceived by a fallacy of 'figure of speech'. In Greek, the phrase "μὴ ἔχοντα ὄψιν", predication of which I have rendered above by "have not sight", can be construed in two ways: as the plural of "μὴ ἔχον ὄψιν", in which sense it would be truly predicable of a set of things iff not one of them had sight; and as the negation of "ἔχοντα ὄψιν", in which sense it would be truly predicable of any set iff it were not a set of things that had sight —i.e. iff not every one of the set had sight. The phrase "have not sight" has a corresponding ambiguity, which was my reason for using it. To make step (2) correct, "have not sight" must be taken as predicating of a set the negation of "have sight", i.e. as meaning "do not all of them possess sight"; to make step (3) correct, this phrase must be taken as predicating "has not sight" of each member of a set.

The *Analytica priora* in its existing form is generally regarded as later than the *Sophistici elenchi*, and the modal logic as a later insertion within the main body of the *Analytica priora*. It is thus not surprising that in this work we find an inchoate recognition of conjunctive propositions, which becomes more explicit in the modal sections; but Aristotle's treatment of conjunctions is vitiated even here by serious logical errors.

The first passage we have to consider is *An. pr.* 57 a 37–b 18. What does Aristotle mean by the words "ἔστι μηδενὸς ὄντος ἀληθοῦς τῶν ἐν τῷ συλλογισμῷ τὸ συμπέρασμα ὁμοίως εἶναι ἀληθές, οὐ μέντοι ἐξ ἀνάγκης"? The last two words are often used by Aristotle for a conclusion's necessarily following from premises; so some scholars have held that Aristotle was stating that a true conclusion cannot logically follow from false premises. This logically illiterate view certainly cannot be Aristotle's; in fact, he expressly shows that a true conclusion may follow from "wholly false" premises, i.e. propositions whose contraries are true; his example is "If every man is a stone and every stone is an animal, then every man is an animal" (53 b 31 seqq.). Moreover, both "If every horse is an animal and no stone is an animal then no horse is a stone" and "If no horse is an animal and every stone is an animal then no horse is a stone" are valid syllogisms (55 b 11 seqq.); and here the same conclusion follows both from a pair of true premises and from their "wholly false" contraries.

Ross has suggested that we should take "ἐξ ἀνάγκης" in our passage not as referring to the logical necessity by which one proposition follows from another, but as signifying the necessitation of one fact by another: "the same fact cannot be a necessary consequence both of another fact and of the opposite of that other".[1] But even if we suppose that when "*p*" and "*q*" are (short for) true propositions, the phrases "the fact that *p*" and "the fact that *q*" have entities called 'facts' corresponding to them, there will then be no such entity answering to the phrase "the fact that it is not the case that *p*"; the opposite of a fact is not itself a fact, and so cannot stand in a relation of 'necessitation' to a fact if this relation (whatever if may be) is always a relation between facts.

Moreover, Ross is quite clearly anachronistic in ascribing to Aristotle a metaphysic that admits "facts" as entities. Of course the phrase "τὰ πράγματα" in Aristotle may often be rendered by the general phrase "the facts"; but the idea of a principle of individuation for πράγματα, corresponding to modern discussions of when the fact that *p* is the same fact as the fact that *q*, is simply not to be found in Aristotle's works; and moreover there is no Greek construction in Aristotle, say "τόδε τὸ πρᾶγμα, ὅτι...", corresponding to the construction of the words "the fact" with a *that* clause. The passage we are discussing anyhow contains nothing like a word for "fact".

Indeed, facts came to be counted among the entities in the philosopher's world only after the construction whereby "the fact", or its synonym in another language, is put in apposition with an indirect-statement clause had spread like the pox from one European language to another, largely by way of journalism. This happened at the end of the last century; only then did philosophers come to postulate facts as individual entities,

[1] *Aristotle's Prior and Posterior Analytics*, p. 436.

C

answering to the phrases so formed. Once stated, the philosophy of facts flourished mightily, especially in Cambridge. It is an amusing self-betrayal of this philosophy's journalistic origins when Wisdom says: "The *Strand Magazine* often uses the word 'fact' and nobody makes any bother; in this book the word will be used in those ways in which it is used in the *Strand*."[1]

It seems clear to me that use of the construction "the fact that . . . " is always a sign of a proposition's not yet having been sufficiently analysed for logical purposes. Analysis of an asserted proposition containing this construction will always produce a pair of assertions, one answering to the *that* clause; e.g. if we had the assertion:

(7) Smith was surprised at the fact that Brown's wife left him

this would split up into a pair of assertions:

(8) Smith heard with surprise that Brown's wife left him.

(9) Brown's wife did leave him.

Notice that this analysis applies only to assertoric formulas,[2] and does not amount to analysing a proposition containing "the fact that" as a conjunction. For if there were a single proposition asserted in our example (7), tantamount to the conjunction:

(10) Smith heard with surprise that Brown's wife left him, and Brown's wife did leave him

then the assertion of:

(11) If it is not the case that Smith was surprised at the fact that Brown's wife left him, then Smith was in collusion with her lover

would turn out equivalent to the assertion of:

(12) If it is not the case that both (Smith heard with surprise that Brown's wife left him) and (Brown's wife did leave him), then Smith was in collusion with her lover.

But plainly this is wrong; the right analysis of (11) as an assertoric formula would be into a pair of assertions, one the assertion of (9) as before, and the other the assertion of:

(13) If it is not the case that Smith heard with surprise that Brown's wife left him, then Smith was in collusion with her lover. This may help to clarify the reason why a conjunction is not to be regarded as a mere pair of propositions; for by way of contrast an

---

[1] J. Wisdom, *Problems of Mind and Matter* (Cambridge, 1934), p. 20.
[2] I use this phrase as an abbreviation for "formulas of sentence-form used with assertoric force".

assertoric formula with "the fact that" in it *is* a double-barrelled assertion, not the assertion of a conjunction.

The ontology of facts is thus 'a dream of our language'— perhaps even to be called a nightmare. (We must be thankful that the legitimate locution "it is not the case that . . . ", and the perverse locutions like "The case of thunder here and now is a case of rain here and now" that were employed by the silly people who wanted to 'reduce' hypotheticals to categoricals, did not give birth to an ontology recognizing 'cases' as entities.) In any event, this ontology, even if it were coherent, is not to be fathered upon Aristotle; its origins are traceably quite different.

If we allow for the concision of Aristotle's style, we may fairly render the puzzling sentence I quoted on p. 20 thus: 'On the supposition that neither premise of a syllogism is true, it is still possible that the conclusion is true; but the conclusion does not then follow necessarily, sc. *from* this supposition of the premises' being both false'. Let us suppose "If p and q, then r" to be (an abbreviation for) a valid syllogism with false premises; Aristotle is telling us that in this case "r" does not follow from "It is false that p and false that q"; i.e. that "If not p and not q, then r" is never a valid syllogism on any interpretation of "p, q, r" that makes "If p and q, then r" a valid syllogism. On this view of his doctrine, Aristotle has not switched without notice from syllogistic necessity to the 'necessitation' of 'facts'; he is stating a metatheorem of his syllogistic. I shall now give an elementarv proof that this metatheorem is indeed correct; a *reductio ad absurdum* of the supposition that "If p and q, then r" and "If not p and not q, then r" could ever both be read as valid syllogisms, for the same reading of "p, q, r".

First, "p" and "q" cannot both be read as universal; for then "not p" and "not q" will both come out as particular, and "If not p and not q, then r" will be invalid.

Secondly, "p" and "q" cannot both be read as affirmative; for then "not p" and "not q" will both come out as negative, and "If not p and not q, then r" will be invalid.

The remaining possibility is that just one of the premises be universal and just one affirmative, the conclusion being in any case particular and negative. Without loss of generality we may assume "p" to be the universal premise. We now get two sub-

cases: (a) "*p*" is an *E* proposition, so that "*q*" is an *I* proposition;
(b) "*p*" is an *A* proposition, so that "*q*" is an *O* proposition.

(a) Since both *E* and *I* propositions are simply convertible, it
does not matter which figure we assume our syllogism to be in;
let us take the second figure. From the conjunction of an *E–I*
pair, "No *X* is *Y* and some *Z* is *Y*", we get the conclusion "Not
every *Z* is *X*". But from the conjunction of the contradictories of
this pair, "Some *X* is *Y* and no *Z* is *Y*", we get in the same mood
and figure not this conclusion but only "Not every *X* is *Z*".

(b) The only valid moods with *A* and *O* as premises and *O*
as conclusion are *Baroco* and *Bocardo*. In *Baroco*, a premise-conjunction "Every *X* is *Y* and not every *Z* is *Y*" yields a conclusion
"Not every *Z* is *X*"; the conjunction of the contradictories, "Not
every *X* is *Y* and every *Z* is *Y*", yields only the quite different
conclusion (again in *Baroco*) "Not every *X* is *Z*".—In *Bocardo*, a
premise-conjunction "Not every *Y* is *X* and every *Y* is *Z*" yields
a conclusion "Not every *Z* is *X*"; the conjunction of the contradictories, "Every *Y* is *X* and not every *Y* is *Z*", yields only the
quite different conclusion (again in *Bocardo*) "Not every *X* is *Z*".

This completes our proof; but we must carefully notice how
restricted our result is. We have not shown that no interpretation
of "*p*, *q*, *r*" turns both "If *p* and *q*, then *r*" and "If not *p* and not
q, then *r*" into valid formulas; we have only shown that this holds
if the three propositions symbolized are all traditional categoricals,
with three 'terms' among them all. The slightest relaxation of
this condition, and our result no longer holds; for example, both
of the following formulas are valid:

If not every *Y* is *X* and every *Y* is *Z*, then it is not the case both
that every *X* is *Z* and that every *Z* is *X*.

If every *Y* is *X* and not every *Y* is *Z*, then it is not the case both
that every *X* is *Z* and that every *Z* is *X*.

Here the conclusion follows from each of two premise-conjunctions, related to each other as "*p* and *q*" is to "not *p* and not
q"; and it is only by arbitrary delimitation that "it is not the case
both that every *X* is *Z* and that every *Z* is *X*", or for short "the
*X*s are not the same as the *Z*s", is not among the forms of proposition recognized as allowable forms of (premise or) conclusion in
the syllogism.

Let us now examine Aristotle's own proof of his metatheorem.
We may conjecture that after an exhaustive examination of valid

160 G269
C. 1

forms had shown him that the metatheorem does always hold, he looked for a proof not resting on such exhaustion of possibilities. He had a strange prejudice, as appears in the *Analytica posteriora*, against proofs that work by exhausting all the possibilities; he calls them "sophistical"—74 a 28. Aristotle arbitrarily represents the premises of a valid syllogism by "A is white" and the conclusion by "B is large"; accordingly, he represents the supposed syllogism in which the conclusion follows from the supposition that the premises of the original syllogism are *not* true as follows:

(14) If A is not white, then B is large,

and the valid syllogism itself is represented by:

(15) If A is white, then B is large.

(15) yields by contraposition

(16) If B is not large, then A is not white;

and finally, (16) and (14) yield by the step Aristotle calls διὰ τριῶν —hypothetical syllogism—the conclusion:

(17) If B is not large, then B is large.

Aristotle calls (17) absurd. Critics have rightly pointed out that a proposition of the form "If not p, then p" need not be absurd; we may in fact use a step "If not p, then p", in order to reach "p" itself (e.g. in geometry; "If AB and CD are not parallel, then they are parallel; *ergo*, AB and CD *are* parallel"). But this criticism overlooks the fact that "B is large" does not go proxy for any old proposition, nor indeed for a proposition at all, but for a schematic conclusion of a syllogism, like "Every X is Y". Aristotle claims to have shown that if we have two valid syllogistic schemata with premise-conjunctions related to each other as "p and q" and "not p and not q", then, if both could yield the formal conclusion "Every X is Y", we should be committed to the *general* validity of the formula "If not every X is Y, then every X is Y"; and this is indeed absurd. (Similarly when a conclusion is E, I, or O, rather than A.)

The proof Aristotle gives is in fact fallacious for quite a different reason—a defect in his doctrine of conjunction. In representing the premises by a single proposition, "A is white", which can be true or false, Aristotle is implicitly admitting—and rightly so—that a conjunction is a proposition. But if "A is white" represents the premise-conjunction "p and q", then "A is not white" cannot represent "not p and not q", it will instead represent "not both p and q". Aristotle's proof thus fails; he fell

into error because his recognizing conjunctions as propositions
was only implicit, and so he never really considered the question
what is the contradictory of a conjunction.

In the still later stage of Aristotle's thought represented in his
modal logic, conjunctions are explicitly recognized as propositions. Here, Aristotle takes the decisive step of using the letters
"*A*" and "*B*" as propositional variables (a stupendous invention),
and explicitly tells us that "*A*" may represent the two premises
together. He then formulates the following metatheorems:

(18) If, if *A* is the case, it follows that *B* is the case; then, if *A*
is possible, it follows that *B* is possible.

(19) If the premises are *A* and the conclusion *B* (sc. in a valid
syllogism), then if *A* is necessary it follows that *B* is necessary.
(18), at 34 a 5, amounts to saying that if "If *p* and *q*, then *r*" is used
to represent a valid formula, then "If possibly (*p* and *q*), then
possibly *r*" will also represent one; and (19), at 34 a 22, amounts
to saying that similarly "If necessarily (*p* and *q*), then necessarily
r" will represent a valid formula. These metatheorems of modal
syllogistic logic are unexceptionable. Moreover, since "necessarily
(*p* and *q*)" is tantamount to "(necessarily *p*) and (necessarily *q*)",
(19) can indeed be used, as Aristotle uses it, to generate a valid
syllogism *de necessario* from a valid syllogism *de inesse*; i.e., from a
valid syllogism "If *p* and *q* then *r*" we may derive the corresponding syllogism "If necessarily *p* and necessarily *q* then
necessarily *r*".

We get into trouble only over (18). A proposition "possibly
p and possibly *q*" is in general a weaker proposition than is
"possibly (*p* and *q*)", correspondingly interpreted; so although the
validity of "If *p* and *q*, then *r*" would mean that "If possibly (*p* and
q), then possibly *r*" came out valid for the same reading of the
propositional letters, this does not imply that "If possibly *p* and
possibly q, then possibly *r*" is a valid syllogism *de possibili* derivable
from the original syllogism *de inesse*. Aristotle did, however, make
this false inference; in recognizing conjunctions as propositions,
he did not consider carefully enough the effect of modalizing a
conjunction with "possibly". There are of course many passages,
in non-logical works, where Aristotle makes the common-sense
distinction between things' being severally possible and their
being possible together; e.g. *De caelo* 281 b 16. But Aristotle was

only the first of many logicians to use in formal work a procedure that he would and did instantly reject in concrete examples.

In the revised version of Łukasiewicz's *Aristotle's Syllogistic* there is formulated a modal system in which "possibly *p* and possibly *q*" would imply "possibly both *p* and *q*", so that the mistake I ascribe to Aristotle would be no mistake after all. But in spite of his logical virtuosity, Łukasiewicz's modal system is useless for the exposition of Aristotle; for in that system all propositions of the form "necessarily *p*" are to be rejected; and so are all propositions stating a contingency—"possibly *p* and possibly not *p*" will be tantamount to the obvious absurdity "possibly both *p* and not *p*". It shows an insobriety of judgment to have offered this as a likely interpretation of Aristotle; this child of Łukasiewicz's old age deserves only exposure.[1]

In this paper I have largely been engaged in exposing Aristotle's mistakes; this may have given the impression that I think "Aristotle was not a very good logician". I actually once heard an Oxford professor express this sentiment; to my mind it would be only a shade less fatuous to say Aristotle *was* a 'very good' logician; for Aristotle was *the* logician, the author, as he could boast, of the very first treatise of formal logic—and apart from formal logic there could be no such thing as logic. He was well aware that his work very likely contained many mistakes; it is not his fault that an 'Aristotelian' logic which was not his so long held up progress; and we cannot refuse him what he modestly claims at the end of the *Organon*—"indulgence for the defects of the treatise, and for its achievements much thanks".

1.3. RUSSELL ON MEANING AND DENOTING

Mr. Searle's article[2] has shown the odd irrelevance of Russell's criticisms of Frege in the famous paper 'On Denoting'. I here offer an explanation of the oddity: Russell had excusably, but wrongly, conflated Frege's distinction between *Sinn* and *Bedeutung* with his own distinction between what an expression 'means' and what it 'denotes', as expounded in *The Principles of Mathematics* (hereafter *PM*). The occurrence of this conflation is clear from Russell's explicit statement that the two theories are 'very nearly

[1] Op. cit. (O.U.P., 1957), pp. 156, 170, 174.
[2] *Analysis* 18.6, June 1958, pp. 137 ff.

the same'[1]; and also from a fact remarked by Mr. Searle—that in expounding Frege's alleged theory Russell uses the term "denoting complex", which is not Frege's term at all, but echoes a technicality of the *PM* theory, the term "denoting concept". Church, apparently supposing that all Russell was doing was to recommend certain translations of Frege's "*Sinn*" and "*Bedeutung*", professes to be just following Russell in rendering "*bedeuten, Bedeutung*" as "denote, denotation"; Church's authority is likely to give the confusion longer life. (His way of rendering Frege's terms is anyhow undesirable; what the general term "man" denotes would ordinarily be taken to be individual men, whereas for Frege the *Bedeutung* of "man" is not many men, but one concept.)

As I said, Russell's conflation of Frege's theory with the *PM* theory was excusable. In many contexts, "meaning" would be the natural English for "*Sinn*"; and again what the definite description "the King of England in 1905" would be said by Russell to 'denote' is the same as what Frege would say is the *Bedeutung* of the description—*viz*. Edward VII. The apparent parallelism between Frege's theory and the *PM* theory may be succinctly expressed as follows: A proposition (*Gedanke*) that corresponds to a sentence with a definite description in it will have the meaning (*Sinn*) of that description as a constituent part, but will not be *about* that meaning, but *about* the object that the description denotes (*bedeutet*).

We get, however, a more fruitful and less misleading comparison of the two theories if we rather set beside each other Russell's *PM* use of "mean" and Frege's use of "*bedeuten, Bedeutung*". We then get the following results: What is 'meant' (*bedeutet*) by a sentence has as parts what the significant bits of the sentence 'mean' (*bedeuten*).[2] For Frege, an indicative sentence is always *about* these *Bedeutungen* of the significant bits of the sentence; Russell in *PM* says the same thing concerning what is 'meant' by the significant bits of sentences, *with the exception of 'denoting' phrases*, a 'denoting' phrase being a general term prefaced with "the", "a", "every", "any", "some", or "all". Russell's use of "about" is, however, further complicated by the following restriction: A sentence is not to be regarded as being 'about' the

[1] Cf. the reprint of 'On Denoting' in *Logic and Knowledge* (ed. R. C. Marsh; Allen and Unwin, 1956): first footnote on p. 42.

[2] Cf. *Philosophical Writings of Gottlob Frege* (ed. Geach and Black; Blackwell, 1952), p. 65.

concept 'meant' by its predicate or the relation 'meant' by its
verb; e.g. "Socrates is wise" is not 'about' the concept *wise*, and
"Socrates excels Plato" is not 'about' the relation *excels*. But in
each case there will be a logically equivalent sentence—e.g., "*wise*
is an attribute of Socrates", "*excels* relates Socrates to Plato"—
which *is* 'about' the concept or relation in question. (*PM* § 48).
For present purposes the restriction is unimportant.

For both Russell and Frege a proper name 'means' its bearer;
a general term 'means' a predicative entity—a concept; a relative
term 'means' a relation. These similarities justify us in rejecting
Russell's later equation of his "denote" to Frege's "*bedeuten*"; on
the contrary, it is clear that when Frege enquires what the
Bedeutung of an expression is, and when Russell in *PM* asks what it
'means', the question is essentially the same, and the answers they
give are often the same. The fact that to these questions Russell
(in *PM*) and Frege *sometimes* gave divergent answers is not of
itself proof that the questions were different. (Apart from the
divergence here discussed, about denoting phrases, there is a
divergence as to when two sentences 'mean' the same thing: in
PM, it is when they convey the same supposition; for Frege, it is
when both are true or both false.)

Frege's distinction between *Sinn* and *Bedeutung* was largely (I
think entirely) derived from puzzles about indirect-speech clauses;
no such considerations are used in *PM* to justify the distinction
between meaning and denoting. The sort of argument we do
find is that in "I met a man" the phrase "a man" does not 'mean'
the man I met—'an actual man with a tailor and a bank-account
and a public-house and a drunken wife' (*PM* 56); and no such
argument is to be found in Frege. In fact, if we equate Russell's
"mean" and Frege's "*bedeuten*", then nothing in Frege's theory
will correspond to Russell's "denoting". Russell's motive for his
own distinction was clearly his 'robust sense of reality'—his
laudable dislike of such Meinongian monstrosities as the round
square and the indefinite man.[1]

If we confine our attention to definite descriptions, the *PM*
theory of denoting may be stated as follows:

(1) To the general term *following* the "the" there answers a

---

[1] (*Note* 1969) His conscience in such matters was not so tender as it later became;
'combinations' that are 'neither one nor many' are not all that much better than
round squares! Cf. *PM* §§ 59, 75, 88.

concept, as what is 'meant'; and so the sentence containing the definite description is in any event analysable as making an assertion *about* this concept. Thus it never happens that a sentence fails to be about anything at all, not even when it contains a definite description (or other denoting phrase) that denotes nothing. (Russell says, however, that sentences containing vacuous denoting phrases must be 'rejected', apparently as false: *PM* § 73).

(2) The concept *A* is however not what is 'meant' by the *whole* phrase "the *A*"; what is 'meant' by "the *A*" is a peculiar sort of entity—a *denoting concept* or (in 'On Denoting' only) *denoting complex*.

(3) A denoting concept is always part of what is 'meant' by a sentence that contains the corresponding definite description; but the sentence is not in general *about* the denoting concept.

(4) There are, however, contexts in which a definite description is so used that the assertion is made about the denoting concept 'meant' by the definite description; in these contexts there is no 'denoting'. An example would be: "*The even prime* is not a number but a denoting concept". Clearly, though, this is not the ordinary use of definite descriptions.

(5) With the ordinary use of a definite description, we are talking not about the denoting concept that it 'means', but about the object it describes (supposing it is not a vacuous description): e.g. "The King of England in 1905 was bearded" is about Edward VII.

(6) The fundamental denoting-relation holds between a non-linguistic denoting concept and an object, e.g. between the denoting concept *the even prime* and the number 2; a denoting *phrase* 'denotes' an object secondarily, by 'meaning' the denoting concept that primarily 'denotes' the object.

This historical background enables us to understand Russell's later statements that definite descriptions are 'incomplete symbols' with no 'meaning'. The opinion seems to prevail in some quarters that Russell thought, or half thought, that his Theory of Descriptions reduced the entities described to mere 'logical fictions', and that this was why he said descriptions had no 'meaning'. It would be admitted that this involves a gross confusion; but some people are willing to ascribe confusion as gross as this to Russell, rather than suspect it is their own.

What Russell was in fact doing was to hark back to his own
PM theory. Definite descriptions have no 'meaning' in the sense
that we need not postulate a piece of meaning, a logical unit,
answering to a definite description in the way the denoting concept
was supposed to. In fact, when

"The King of England in 1905 was bearded"
is analysed as

"For some x, x, and nobody other than x, reigned over
England in 1905, and x was bearded",
the sentence-fragment that is left when the predicable "was
bearded" is removed no longer forms a syntactical unity, as "The
King of England" did; so the temptation to postulate a unified
piece of meaning that should correspond to this sentence-fragment
no longer arises.

Considered as criticisms not of Frege, but of Russell's own *PM*
theory, the arguments in 'On Denoting' take on quite a different
force and relevance. Whether they are valid I shall not here try to
determine. It is unfortunate that Russell, like Aristotle, so often
distorts others' thought into his own mould; readers of 'On
Denoting' will find it best simply to ignore his use of Frege's
name.

1.4. PLATO'S *EUTHYPHRO*

AN ANALYSIS AND COMMENTARY

The *Euthyphro* might well be given to undergraduates to read
early in their philosophical training. The arguments are apparently simple, but some of them, as I shall show, lead naturally on
to thorny problems of modern philosophy. Another benefit that
could be gained from reading the *Euthyphro* is that the reader may
learn to be forewarned against some common fallacies and debating tricks in moral disputes.

We may pass rapidly over the pages in which the stage is set
for the discussion (2a-3e). Socrates and Euthyphro meet outside
the office of the King Archon, where each has to put in an
appearance respecting a legal action. Socrates tells Euthyphro
how he is being prosecuted for impiety. Euthyphro is pained but
not surprised; his own speeches in the Ecclesia are ridiculed when
he speaks of things divine; no doubt Socrates' well-known divine
sign has roused popular prejudice.

With some reluctance, if we may judge by the form of his answers ("I'm prosecuting.—People will think me crazy.—It's an old man; he won't fly away.—It's my own father.—For murder"), Euthyphro tells Socrates what his own cause is. Socrates is naturally astounded: surely then the victim must be some other member of the family, or Euthyphro would never have started the prosecution (3e-4b).

Euthyphro replies that whether the victim belongs to your own family or not does not really matter; what matters is whether the man was wrongfully killed. Then he tells the story. The man who died was a dependent of Euthyphro, a farm labourer on the family estate in Naxos. In a drunken brawl he quarrelled with and killed one of the household slaves. Euthyphro's father, after having the killer tied up and thrown in a ditch, sent off to ask the authorities in Athens what was to be done—and then put the matter out of his mind. It was no concern of his if the fellow died. Before an answer came back from the mainland, the prisoner had in fact died from hunger, cold and his bonds. Euthyphro felt he could not sit at his father's fireside and table as if nothing had happened; to the indignation of all his family, he thought himself obliged to prosecute his father; only so could he or his father be made clean of blood-guiltiness. The family protested that in fact the father had not murdered anybody; even if he had, the man was himself a killer and not worth considering; anyhow, it is impious for a son to prosecute his own father. This only shows, says Euthyphro, how little his relatives understood piety and impiety (4b-e).

Since the attitude of Euthyphro's relatives in the matter was likely to be shared by others and since Euthyphro knew that his own religious attitude attracted derision rather than respect, we may suppose Euthyphro to be well aware that his father would not in fact be in any serious legal danger; the prosecution is just a gesture. What sort of gesture? Some commentators call it superstition: even an accidental death—and this is practically the case in hand!—would bring on the man who caused it a contagious defilement, and Euthyphro is going through the proper motions to cleanse this away from the house. Others, just like Euthyphro's relatives, morally condemn him for making such a fuss, especially with his own father involved.

An unprejudiced reading shows that Euthyphro is not represented as merely superstitious about a ritual contamination; what upset Euthyphro was the way his father "was heedless and made little of the man, even if he should die." How far Euthyphro was from making a fuss about nothing comes out in the fact that in quite a number of civilized jurisdictions a man who acted like Euthyphro's father would be held guilty of a serious crime.

Euthyphro is represented as an earnest and simple believer in the old traditional religion of the Hellenes. To him, therefore, the defence of a poor man's case may well have seemed a religious duty: Zeus of the Suppliant was there to hear the cry of the poor man with none to help him, and to punish those who walked in blind pride. Moreover, Euthyphro says, had not Zeus himself punished his own father's wicked deeds?

Euthyphro's genuine belief in the old legend is something Socrates finds it hard to stomach (5e-6c), but he does not try to shake it. Instead, he adopts a line of argument that we find paralleled in many dialogues. If Euthyphro really knows that his own action is pious, then he must be able to say what is pious; he must not just give examples of pious actions, like his own action or again the punishment of sacrilegious robbery, but say "what kind of thing it is that makes *whatever* is pious to be pious" (5d and 6d).

We need not here enter upon the vexed questions whether language like the piece I have just translated (6d 10-11) is meant to imply a full-blown theory of Forms, and whether we are to ascribe such a theory to the historical Socrates. Let us rather concentrate on two assumptions Socrates makes: (A) that if you know you are correctly predicating a given term "T" you must 'know what it is to be T' in the sense of being able to give a general criterion for a thing's being T; (B) that it is no use to try and arrive at the meaning of "T" by giving examples of things that are T. (B) in fact follows from (A). If you can already give a general account of what "T" means, then you need no examples to arrive at the meaning of "T"; if on the other hand you lack such a general account, then, by assumption (A), you cannot know that any examples of things that are T are genuine ones, for you do not know when you are predicating "T" correctly.

The style of mistaken thinking—as I take it to be— that comes from accepting these two assumptions may well be called *the Socratic fallacy*, for its *locus classicus* is the Socratic dialogues. Its influence has, I think, been greater even than that of the theory of

Forms; certainly people can fall into it independently of any theory of Forms. I have myself heard a philosopher refuse to allow that a proper name is a word in a sentence unless a 'rigorous definition' of "word" could be produced; again, if someone remarks that machines are certainly not even alive, still less able to think and reason, he may be challenged to define "alive". Both these controversial moves are clear examples of the Socratic fallacy; and neither originates from any belief in Forms.

Let us be clear that this *is* a fallacy, and nothing better. It has stimulated philosophical enquiry, but still it is a fallacy. We know heaps of things without being able to define the terms in which we express our knowledge. Formal definitions are only one way of elucidating terms; a set of examples may in a given case be more useful didactically than a formal definition.

We can indeed see in advance why a Socratic dialogue so often ends in complete failure to elucidate the meaning of a term "T". If the parties to a discussion are agreed, broadly speaking, about the application of a term, then they can set out to find a criterion for applying it that shall yield the agreed application. On the other hand, if they agreed on the criterion for applying the term, then they can see whether this criterion justifies predicating "T" of a given example. But if there is no initial agreement either on examples of things that certainly are T or on criteria for predicating "T", then the discussion is bound to be abortive; the parties to it cannot know what they are about—they do not even know whether each of them means the same by saying "T". Any profit they gain from the discussion will be *per accidens*; *per se* the discussion is futile.

How harmful the rejection of examples may be we see from the *Theaetetus*. Theaetetus, asked what knowledge is, gives some instances of knowledge—geometry and shoemaking and the various crafts. Socrates objects that these are only examples, and he wants to know just what knowledge *is*. To give examples, each of which is the knowledge *of* so-and-so, is to miss the point —as though, asked what clay was, one mentioned potter's clay, brickmaker's clay, and so on (146d-147a). But of course any knowledge *is* knowledge *of* so-and-so; and a correct definition would have to run "Knowledge of so-and-so is . . . ", with the "so-and-so" occurring over again in the *definiens*. Moreover, the definition "Knowledge is sense-perception" could have been dismissed at once by looking to Theaetetus' examples of knowledge. I am sure that imbuing a mind with the Socratic fallacy is quite likely to be morally harmful. Socrates, let us suppose, starts chatting with an ingenuous youth and says he has been puzzled about what injustice is. The youth says "Well, that's easy; swindling is unjust." Socrates asks him what swindling is; no, examples will not do—a formal definition is required. Failing that, we don't know, do we?, what swindling is, or that it is unjust. The dialogue, we may suppose, ends in the usual *aporia*. The ingenuous youth decides that perhaps swindling is not unjust; he turns to ways of villainy, and ends as one of the Thirty Tyrants. After all, a number of Socrates' young men did end that way.

Pressed for a formal definition, then, Euthyphro comes out with this one: "The pious is what is liked by the Gods, the impious what is not liked" (6d 10). As in English, so in Greek, we must not take the negative word in the second clause for a bare negation: "not liked", here, = "disliked".

The next argument Socrates uses has force only *ad hominem*; it explicitly depends on Euthyphro's traditionalist belief that stories about the quarrels of the Gods are literally true. What then, Socrates asks, do *men* quarrel about? For questions of fact—accountancy, measurement, weighing—there are agreed decision procedures. It is precisely questions of fair or unfair, right or wrong, that are undecidable and lead to quarrels. If, then, the Gods do quarrel, presumably they too quarrel about such questions; actions that one God thinks just another thinks unjust, and so they quarrel. Thus one and the same action may be both God-loved, and thus pious, and God-hated, and thus impious. Moreover, if we assume the truth of the traditional stories, different Gods may be expected to view with very different eyes acts like Euthyphro's: the chastisement of parents. Euthyphro's appeal to the example of Zeus is thus neatly turned against him (7b-8b).

This passage is of some historical interest; it may well be the first appearance in Western philosophy of the distinction between factual questions, for which there is a definite and accepted decision procedure, and moral questions, for which there is no such procedure. To my mind, this distinction is none the better for being an old one.

It very often happens that people who have no relevant disagreement about what ought to be done in given circumstances nevertheless quarrel bitterly, even go to law, because they disagree about the facts of the case. And of course they need not be irrationally ignoring some well known decision procedure; there may be no such procedure. The only eye-witnesses of an incident may grievously differ as to what happened, because men's observation and memory are both fallible; there is then no agreed decision procedure to settle the matter once for all. It is mere thoughtlessness when a modern writer tells us that any purely factual premise of moral reasoning must admit of definite tests (not themselves involving evaluation) for determining its truth or falsity.

So much for the decidability of factual questions; what about the undecidability of moral questions? Socrates just asserts this —or at least wins Euthyphro's assent to it by leading questions. There are many arguments now used to defend the position by prominent moral philosophers, which I have not space to discuss. We ought in any case to notice that the extent of moral disagreement both within and between civilized societies is often grossly exaggerated. As we may learn from Hobbes, no commonwealth will hold together without a great deal of moral consensus; if everyone made up his own morality by 'free decision' and, as in the Book of Judges, every man did that which was right in his own eyes, then society would disintegrate. Between societies, too, there is a great deal of moral consensus, covered by the phrase "the comity of nations". Moral disagreements often do lead to enmity and conflict; but people who conclude from this that they *could* not be rationally resolved "argue as ill, as if the savage people of America should deny there were any principle of reason so to build a house as to last as long as the materials, because they never saw any so well built" (*Leviathan*, c. 30).

There is a reason why moral arguments often are inconclusive and lead only to quarrels: namely, people may start a moral disputation when, as regards one of the key terms, they are not initially in agreement *either* on a class of instances to which it applies *or* on criteria for applying it. I remarked just now that in that case disputants are pretty well bound to get at cross purposes. But of course such frustration of the purpose of discussion may come about for any sort of term, not just for an ethical term. In general, people cannot even use a term to express disagreement unless they are agreed on a lot of the judgments they would express

with that term; for example, people cannot even disagree about
an historical character, because they will not manage to refer to
one identifiable person, unless they would agree on a good deal
of what to say about him. There is no reason to think things are
otherwise for a term "T" whose meaning is 'evaluative'; unless
people have a great deal of moral consensus about judging actions
to be T, they cannot sensibly use "T" to express moral disagreement. Recent moral philosophers have devoted far too much
attention to moral disagreements and perplexing situations and
the alleged freedom to make up a morality for yourself; if instead
they had concentrated on moral consensus, we might by now
understand the rationale of that a lot better.

We ought not, then, to be impressed by the argument Socrates
presents; it limps on both legs. Factual questions are not necessarily decidable; moral questions have not been shown to be
essentially undecidable.

All the same, weak as his position is on this abstract issue,
Socrates has a strong case *ad hominem* against Euthyphro; if Greek
stories were literally true, as Euthyphro believes, then it would be
all too likely that the Gods would take opposite sides about
Euthyphro's action. Euthyphro does not attempt to defend
himself on this, his really weak point; and Socrates does not press
the attack further home.

Euthyphro protests, however, that all the Gods will agree that
wrongful homicide must be punished. Socrates makes short work
of this: everybody, God or man, will agree that homicide is to be
punished if it is wrongful; but when is it wrongful? That is just
where disagreements arise (8b-e).

This short passage of the dialogue illustrates a trap into which
an unwary man of decent principles may fall when arguing.
Euthyphro says that *wrongful* killing is odious to God and man;
and Socrates gets him in one move by saying: What killing is
wrongful? In our time, we should more likely have A saying
that the act he protests against is wrong because it is murder; his
adversary B will then extract from him an admission that murder
—unless the word is a legal term of art—is just wrongful killing;
so that A has said no more than that the act is wrong because it is
wrong. This move by Socrates, or by a contemporary B, is
merely eristic; worthwhile discussion can only start if that feature
of the act which Euthyphro, or A, really is objecting to is brought
out into the open and carefully considered.

D

Socrates has no intention of doing any such thing. Instead (9a-b) he appeals to class prejudices. Has a man been wrongfully killed when he is a *serf*, who killed somebody's slave, was tied up by the slave's master, and 'happened to die first' before the master could ask the authorities what to with him? Ought a son to prosecute his own father over such a man? Will all the Gods agree that the killing is wrongful and the prosecution righteous?

Euthyphro says he could make it plain that his cause is just, if only the judges would hear his reasons; "I suppose you find me slower of understanding," says Socrates—and does not ask what Euthyphro's reasons may be. Instead, he says in effect: "I *give* you that *all* the Gods hate what your father did; I waive the point about one God's hating what another God loves; if you like, say that the pious is what *all* the Gods love and the impious is what *all* the Gods hate, so as to be sure that the same act is not both pious and impious. Even so, will your account of piety and impiety stand?" (9c-e).

The next stage of the dialogue (10a-11b) purports to refute the thesis that *pious* is the same as *loved by the Gods*, regardless of whether "the Gods" means "all the Gods" or "some Gods". The general scheme of the argument is plain. Euthyphro is got to agree that the following pair of propositions is true:

(1) What is pious is loved by the Gods because it is pious

(2) What is God-loved is God-loved because it is loved by the Gods

and the following pair false:

(3) What is God-loved is loved by the Gods because it is God-loved

(4) What is pious is pious because it is loved by the Gods.

Now we get (3) from (1) by putting "God-loved" instead of "pious", and (4) from (2) by the reverse substitution; so (3) and (4) ought both to be true if *God-loved* and *pious* were the same; "but in fact it is quite the opposite," so *God-loved* and *pious* cannot be the same.

The principle underlying the argument appears to be the Leibnizian principle that two expressions for the same thing must be mutually replaceable *salva veritate*—so that a change from truth to falsehood upon such replacement must mean that we have not two expressions for the same thing. Of course it would be anachronistic to see here a formulation of the Leibnizian principle; but it is not anachronistic to discern a *use* of the principle; any more than it is anachronistic to call an argument a syllogism in *Barbara* when it antedates even Aristotle, let alone Peter of Spain. Though some forms of argument have been invented by logicians, many existed before there was any science of logic; and this is no bar to logical classification of them *ex post facto*.

The validity of arguments using Leibniz's principle is one of the most thorny points in recent philosophical discussion. It is well known both that such arguments are liable to break down in contexts that are not securely extensional, and that propositions formed with "because" give us non-extensional contexts. Indeed, the following pair of expressions, as used by a man X on a given occasion, need not be propositions agreeing in truth-value:

(5) I hit him because he was the man who had just hit me

(6) I hit him because he was my father

even if the term "father of X" were coextensive with the term "man who had just hit X (on the occasion in question)". So the truth of (1) and (2) and the falsehood of (3) and (4) would perhaps not allow of our concluding that pious actions and men are not the same classes as God-loved actions and men; as the truth of (5) and falsehood of (6) do not warrant us in concluding that the man who had just hit the speaker was other than his father.

A reader may be inclined at this point to make Mill's distinction: what the argument does validly derive from its premises is that "God-loved" and "pious" have a different *connotation*, even if they *denote* the same men and actions. But have we the right to ascribe any such distinction to Plato? I doubt if any such distinction is anywhere even clearly exemplified, let alone formally expounded.

Using more Platonic language, the reader might suggest that *God-loved* and *pious* are supposed to be different Forms. But surely, for Plato, there could not be a Form *God-loved*. Rather, the view we are meant to adopt is that "loved by all the Gods", unlike 'pious', answers to no Form whatsoever. Being God-loved is something that the pious 'has done to it'; there is no reason to suppose that "God-loved" expresses what something *is*, in that sense of "what so-and-so *is*" which would mean, for Plato, that we are laying hold of a Form.

It is possible that the present argument is supposed to prove

that the two terms "God-loved" and "pious" differ in *application*;
for at the end of the dialogue Euthyphro is supposed to have
contradicted his own previous admission by saying that pious acts
are dear to the Gods, loved by the Gods (15a-c). If what the
present argument is meant to prove were what some would
express nowadays by saying that two terms differ in *connotation*,
this criticism of Euthyphro by Socrates would be an unfair
debating trick. But we need not impute deliberate unfairness; we
need only suppose that at this stage in philosophical thought the
different kinds of difference in meaning were not well sorted out.
We could scarcely be confident that they are really well sorted out
even today.

Let us now look at the way the premises of the argument are
reached. It is accepted by Euthyphro without demur that (1) is
true and (4) false. The truth of (2) and the falsehood of (3) are
deduced by a tricky argument, relating to passive verbs in general.
Plato of course could not use a grammarian's terms of art; they
hardly existed when he wrote, and it would have spoiled the
dialogue to introduce them if they had existed. So he has to make
Socrates convey the general principle to Euthyphro by a series of
examples; from these, Euthyphro is meant to get the application
of the principle to the verb "to love" in particular.

Here we come up against a linguistic obstacle. Taking "ϕ
pass." as representing the ordinary inflected third-person singular
passive of a verb, and "ϕed" as representing the passive participle
of the same verb, we may say that what Plato gives us are a series
of examples in which these two propositions are contrasted:

(7) A thing ϕ pass. because it is ϕed

(8) A thing is ϕed because it ϕ pass.

The successive interpretations of "ϕ" are "to carry", "to drive"
"to see", and finally "to love". But as regards the first two, it is
extraordinarily hard to make out what the point is. In Greek, the
expressions I have schematically represented as "ϕ pass." and "is
ϕed" are of course different; but in English both are naturally
rendered by the ordinary present-tense passive form. One might
try using the plain passive for the "ϕ pass." form and a periphrastic
expression for the "is ϕed" form; for example, one would get
some such pair as this:

(9) A thing is carried because *carried* is what it is.

(10) Because a thing is carried, *carried* is what it is.

But this is just whistling in the dark; we just do not know how Plato conceived the difference between the forms I provisionally translate "so-and-so is carried" and *"carried* is what so-and-so is", nor why it is supposed to be obvious that (10) is true and (9) is false.

Fortunately there is no need for us to try and solve this problem; for the supposed parity of reasoning between "carried" and "loved" just does not exist. Socrates is made to treat both as examples of "what things have done to them". We get the same assimilation in the *Sophist* (248d-e), where the Eleatic Stranger argues that being known is something the Forms "have done to them" (the same Greek verb is used as in the *Euthyphro*) and they therefore are not wholly changeless. But this assimilation is certainly wrong; among grammatically transitive verbs, verbs like "know", "love" and "see" are logically quite different from verbs expressing that something is shifted or altered.

We need not try to delineate this difference, which has been the theme of much recent philosophical writing. It will be enough to concentrate on the peculiar use of "because" in one of the premises of the main argument:

(11a) What is pious is loved by the Gods because it is pious.

The conjunction "because", and the corresponding word in Greek, occur in a lot of logically different sorts of propositions. To avoid confusion, I shall slightly rephrase (11a):

(11b) What is pious is loved by the Gods in respect of being pious.

This way of speaking—that something is the object of an attitude *in respect of* this or that characteristic—is one that I owe to Mc-Taggart (*The Nature of Existence*, vol. ii, Section 465). Following close in his footsteps, I shall try to show the difference between propositions like (11b) and ordinary causal propositions.

The most obvious difference is that a person can have an attitude towards something in respect of its being X when the thing is not X but is mistakenly regarded by him as being X; I may e.g. admire a man in respect of his courage when he was in fact a great coward —and then his courage cannot be a cause or part-cause of my admiration. What is a cause or part-cause of my admiration is his *being believed by me* to be courageous; which is quite different from his being courageous, even if he is. And I certainly do not admire people in respect of *this* characteristic—

being believed by myself, rightly or wrongly, to be courageous is not a characteristic that I find admirable. No doubt the Gods would never falsely believe a man to be pious who was in fact impious; but we could still draw the distinction—the Gods would love him in respect of his piety, not in respect of his being *known to the Gods as* a pious man; that would only be the cause of the Gods' loving him, not the characteristic in respect of which they loved him.

Let us now rephrase (3) in the same style:

(12) What is God-loved is loved by the Gods in respect of being God-loved.

If (11b) is true, as Euthyphro surely wishes to say, and (12) is false, then "pious" and "God-loved" must somehow differ in meaning—in fact, there must be a big difference. And surely (12) is false; nobody, God or man, can love a thing simply *for*, in respect of, being loved by himself. Similarly, nobody can fear a thing simply *for* its being fearful to him; if the Church approves the Bible *for* being inspired, then "being inspired" cannot simply mean "approved by the Church"; and so in general. The principle illustrated by the falsehood of (12) does seem to be both sound and sufficient to serve as a premise in the way Plato intended. Failing a rigorous account of verbs of attitude (intentional verbs, as they are now sometimes called), we cannot quite clearly see the rationale of this principle; all the same, it surely *is* a sound principle.

The remainder of the dialogue is of less interest. Socrates gets over to Euthyphro, with some difficulty, the idea that though anything pious is just, it does not follow that everything just is pious; he does this by the 'You might as well say' technique familiar to readers of *Alice*—you might as well say that if all shame is fear, all fear is shame, or that if everything odd is a number, every number is odd (12a-d). We thus get the question: What sort of just acts are pious? Euthyphro replies: Those which concern the service of the Gods rather than men (12e).

Socrates professes himself unable to understand this answer. Huntsmen serve, or look after, hounds, drovers look after cattle, and so on ; presumably this consists in helpful actions, actions that are for the betterment of that which is served. Then is piety aimed at the betterment of the Gods? Euthyphro of course protests that this is not at all the kind of service he meant; rather, we serve the Gods as slaves their masters (13a-d).

Socrates does not reject this answer, but raises further questions about it. The work of a subordinate is ordered to the particular end of his master; for a doctor the servant's work will be directed towards health, for a shipwright towards voyaging, for an architect towards building, and so on. What then is the magnificent work of the Gods in which we play a subordinate role as their servants? Or at least, what is the chief end of this work, as victory is the general's chief end and winning food from the soil is the farmer's? (13e-14a).

Euthyphro cannot answer this question; and we should notice that he is not logically committed to doing so. If men are the slaves of the Gods, then by obeying them men will fulfil the Gods' ends, whatever these may be; but men can know that without knowing in what particular the Gods' ends are. "The servant knoweth not what his lord doth"; and Euthyphro would account himself only a servant, not a friend, of the Gods.

Instead of answering the question, then, Euthyphro states which actions specially constitute giving the Gods their due: prayers and sacrifices and the like. The answer is seriously meant, and deserves to be taken seriously if any theological discourse does. We may notice that for Aquinas the virtue of 'religion' is the part of justice that gives to God what is specially due to him, and that he conceives the characteristic acts of 'religion' as Euthyphro does. There are, of course, serious objections that can be raised about the rationale of acts like prayer and sacrifice. Socrates raises none of these; his retort is, as commentators say, 'playful'. At that rate, piety would be a skill of bargaining with the Gods ("If you choose to call it that", Euthyphro interjects), and the bargain is a bad one for the Gods, since only we and not they are benefited (14b-15a).

Euthyphro says, as he has said before, that of course our pious acts cannot benefit the Gods; they are acts of honour and courtesy (*charis*) that *please* the Gods. At this point Socrates charges him with going back to the old rejected explanation of pious acts as acts that the Gods love. The charge, as I said, need not be deliberately sophistical, but at least is far from having been logically made to stick. We may see this quite simply if we use the Mactaggartian apparatus of 'in respect of' that I introduced just now. Though the Gods cannot be pleased by an act in respect of its being pleasing to the Gods, they logically could be pleased by an act in respect of its *being intended* to be pleasing to them, as human parents are by the acts of their children. And Euthyphro's act in prosecuting his father could be pleasing to the Gods both as an act of human justice and as an act of piety; both in respect of its avenging a poor man's wrong, and in respect of its being intended to please the Gods.

Socrates presses Euthyphro to try again to define piety; surely he would not have ventured, without knowing what piety is, to . . . . Here Euthyphro has to listen again to Socrates' appeals to conventional prejudices—including the class prejudice against a 'serf fellow'. But he has heard enough, and says he is too busy for further talk. The commentators seem to agree that the dialogue ends with a moral victory for Socrates. I should prefer to think that, to use Bunyan's language, Mr. Right-Mind was not to be led a-wandering from the straight path.

1.5. HISTORY OF THE CORRUPTIONS OF LOGIC

An Inaugural Lecture 1968

Since I had no predecessor in this Chair of Logic at the University of Leeds, I take the opportunity of paying a long over-due tribute to the memory of my father, George Hender Geach. He was an undergraduate at Trinity in the great Cambridge days before the two wars—the days of Russell and Whitehead, Neville Keynes and W. E. Johnson, Moore and McTaggart. On his retirement from the Indian Educational Service he devoted himself to starting his son off on the right foot in philosophy by making me read, and discussing with me, the works of all these great men. I could scarcely have had a better start.

The history of logic begins with Aristotle, who could proudly say that he had written the very first treatise on formal logic. I may summarize what I am going to say in one sentence: Aristotle, like Adam, began right, but soon wandered into a wrong path, with disastrous consequences for his posterity.

Adam's state before the Fall is a matter of theological speculation; but Aristotle's first logical ideas can be described with reasonable certainty. Aristotle's logic, from first to last, was mainly a theory of the subject-predicate relation; and the view of predication he began with was a development of one sketched by Plato in the *Sophist*. Plato there put forward the view that the simplest form of proposition is composed of two heterogeneous elements, a noun (*onoma*) and a verb (*rhema*); for example, "Man walks", "Theaetetus flies". A string of nouns, like "man lion", or of verbs, like "runs walks", is on the other hand not intelligible discourse at all.

In his early work, the *De Interpretatione*, Aristotle took over this Platonic terminology, and with it the Platonic view as to the analysis of the simplest possible propositions. But the rendering of *onoma* and *rhema* as "noun" and "verb", which fits Plato's few examples well enough, would not very well fit in with the way Aristotle explains and illustrates his use of the terms. *Onoma* may naturally be rendered "name"; for *rhema* I propose the rendering "predicable", since Aristotle's explanation of the term includes the clause that a *rhema* "is always a sign of what is said about something else".

Aristotle, like Plato, clearly intended these two classes—*onoma* amd *rhema*, name and predicable—to be mutually exclusive. For one thing, in explaining the terms he tells us that predicables have tense and names do not. We may indeed doubt whether all predicables have tense: predications in arithmetic and geometry do not appear to be significantly tensed. But at least it is *often* sensible, as regards what is predicated of a thing X, to ask whether the predication does apply, did ever apply, or will some time hence apply, to the object X. On the other hand, the relation of a name to what it names never allows of such temporal qualifications. If a schoolboy is asked for the date of Augustus' birth, it is mere cheek for him to reply "Please, Sir, he wasn't called Augustus then"; once the name "Augustus" has come into use, it relates to Augustus throughout his career, and still serves to name him though he is long dead.

Aristotle thus seems to have hit upon a differentia that serves to distinguish at least those names and predicables that ralate to temporal objects. Later in his exposition, Aristotle brings out a more general and fundamental distinction: in order to negate a proposition, we can negate the predicative part, but not the name that stands in subject position. Surface grammar might well mislead us here; in a pair like "A man sneezed—Not a man sneezed (or No man sneezed) "we seem to be negating a proposition by forming a negative subject-term, "no man" or "not a man". Greek grammar is here even more deceptive than English, for in a phrase like "no man", "no" is rendered by an inflected adjective agreeing with its noun. But Aristotle was not deceived, and we should not be; to take "no man" or "not a man", in such an example, as a negated subject-term, is simply a logical howler, one that in my experience beginners often commit. I have sometimes found bogus syllogisms like the following useful in dispelling this grammatical mirage:

> I am no horse man;
> No horseman could clear that fence;
> *Ergo*: I could clear that fence.

I have spoken of "man" as a possible subject-term, and thus, by implication, as a name; here I am simply following Aristotle, who in turn follows Plato, in counting some common nouns like "man" as names along with proper nouns like "Theaetetus".

An important requirement of Aristotle's about names is that names must be syntactically simple—must not have any parts with a significance of their own. This requirement also seems entirely reasonable. The logical role of a name is simply to refer to its bearer, and it can do that without having any parts where separate meanings matter: "The Silent Woman" or "Help the Poor Struggler" may convey associations by its verbal structure, but this structure is quite irrelevant to the role of the expression as the name of a public house. To this Aristotelian doctrine of the logical simplicity of names Russell and Wittgenstein reverted after the doctrine had lain neglected for more than two millennia; and Wittgenstein added the important argument that a complex sign can relate to things only by the mediation of the other signs that go to its make-up, whereas a name relates to its bearer directly, and therefore a name not only need not but cannot have parts that signify on their own account. (Russell and Wittgenstein certainly had different metaphysical views from Aristotle, and indeed from one another, about what there was in the world to be named; but this is not at all matter of present concern.)

All the doctrines of the *De Interpretatione* that I have so far stated appear to me to be true, and I have argued for them at length in published works. But I cannot accept Aristotle's further requirement that a *rhema* too must be syntactically simple; I can see no reason to abide by this. To name a thing we need only a single word; but if we need to say something complicated about a thing, then the *rhema*, the predicative part of the sentence, will have to be complex in its syntactical structure. I can only conjecture why Aristotle set up this postulate: he may have had the programme, when he wrote the *De Interpretatione*, of analysing every complex proposition as a molecular compound, *syndesmos*, of simple propositions containing one name and one simple *rhema* apiece.

If Aristotle ever had such a programme, he must soon have convinced himself that it would not work. Examples will readily have occurred to him, such as "Socrates loves Theaetetus" and "Any man either wakes or sleeps", which are quite irreducible to any *syndesmos* of one-name, one-*rhema* propositions like "Theaetetus sleeps". At any rate, Aristotle certainly did later on drop the requirement that a single subject-predicate proposition must have a syntactically simple predicative part. He changed his mind on this point after writing the *De Interpretatione* and before composing his greatest logical work, the *Prior Analytics*.

Unfortunately, Aristotle abandoned at the same time other positions he had held in the *De Interpretatione*. He lost the Platonic insight that any predicative proposition splits up into two logically heterogeneous parts; instead, he treats predication as an attachment of one term (*horos*) to another term. Whereas the *rhema* was regarded as essentially predicative, 'always a sign of what is said of something else', it is impossible on the new doctrine for any term to be essentially predicative; on the contrary, any term that occurs in a proposition predicatively may be made into the subject-term of another predication. I shall call this "Aristotle's thesis of interchangeability"; his adoption of it marks a transition from the original name-and-predicable theory to a *two-term* theory. And since the term shifted from predicate to subject position could be syntactically complex, Aristotle dropped the requirement that a subject of predication must be a syntactically simple name.

Aristotle's going over to the two-term theory was a disaster, comparable only to the Fall of Adam. What kept Aristotle from seeing he had gone wrong was the spectacular success of his theory of syllogism. In a syllogistic argument as described by Aristotle, we have as premises two categoricals (that is, predicative propositions) with a 'middle term' occurring in both of them, and these yield as a conclusion a third categorical whose terms are the remaining two terms of the premises. Simple combinatorial considerations then show that in any syllogism of this structure at least one term must appear as subject-term of one categorical and predicate-term of another. There is nothing obviously wrong with this if one does not look beyond the theory of syllogism; and the excitement of having constructed a powerful and beautiful theory will have blinded Aristotle to the shakiness of its foundations.

All the same, the foundations were shaky. Of course, I am not saying that the concrete examples of valid syllogisms given by Aristotle are in fact invalid arguments; but his analysis of these arguments is defective and confused. It is logically impossible for a term to shift about between subject and predicate position without undergoing a change of sense as well as a change of role. Only a name can be a logical subject; and a name cannot retain the role of a name if it becomes a logical predicate; for a predicate purports to give us what holds good or does not hold good of an individual, but a name just serves to name or refer to an individual. (Of course a name can be *part* of a predicable, as "Socrates" is part of the predicable expression "taught by Socrates".) Nor can names shade off by fine degrees into predicables, as some people have fancied; as though there were a scale, with strongly referential and weakly descriptive terms at one end and strongly descriptive terms at the other end. As I once heard Wittgenstein say, all logical differences are big differences; in logic we are not making *subtle* distinctions, as it were between flavours that pass over into one another by delicate gradations.

Aristotle himself recognized that at any rate proper names cannot be predicated, not really (*haplōs*) predicated. And he had some scruples even about applying the interchangeability thesis to common names: Can "This timber is white" really be turned round into the form "This white is timber"? There are also other signs that Aristotle's Fall did not plunge him into total depravity. We might have expected him to recognize as terms of predication only nouns or noun-phrases, which could grammatically be either subjects or predicates, and to employ schemata like "*A* is

B" to represent predication. In fact Aristotle carefully avoids using schemata like "A is B" or "Some A is B"; his standard expression is rather "B applies (*hyparchei*) to (some) A". And sometimes he even deliberately constructs, as interpretations of such schemata, sentences in which we do not find the grammatical form: noun-phrase, copula, noun-phrase. In the very first chapter of the *Prior Analytics* Aristotle gives the example "There is a single science of (a pair of) contraries"; in a later chapter he fits this to the schema "A applies to B" by putting $B = contraries$, $A = there being a single science of them$. And in this latter place Aristotle emphasizes that on this analysis the predication does not mean that contraries *are* there being one science of them, but rather that *it is true to say of* contraries that there is one science of them. All this is splendid; but it makes nonsense of Aristotle's interchangeability thesis. For, with this reading of the letters, only "A applies to B" makes sense, not also "B applies to A"; anything like "it is true to say of there being a single science of them that it is contraries" (or "that they are contraries") is simply gibberish.

The *Prior Analytics* supplies in fact quite a number of such counter-examples to the interchangeability thesis; but once committed to the two-term theory of predication, Aristotle could not see the point of his own examples. In later logicians the choice of example became more restricted, less likely to provoke awkward questions. To quote Wittgenstein again: on an unbalanced diet of examples our thinking develops deficiency diseases.

Ordinary language allows a word to shift around between a naming and a predicative use; for all that, we can distinguish such uses even in the vernacular—we need not translate our sentences into a special symbolism. When a general term, say "philosopher", occurs in our propositions as a name, it relates directly to individual philosophers; and accordingly, we can state the conditions for a proposition's being true (for short, its *truth-conditions*) by giving other propositions in which the individual philosophers are severally mentioned by name. For example, "Socrates taught a philosopher" is true just in case one or another proper name of a philosopher written after "Socrates taught . . . " yields a true proposition. But it is quite different when a general term occurs in predicate position. No replacement of the term "philosopher" by the mention of individual philosophers is at all relevant to the truth-conditions of "Socrates was a philosopher" or of "Alcibiades became a philosopher". Let us not be distracted by the thought that "Alcibiades became a philosopher" is false; for the point I am making can be made just as well over the true proposition "Lord Home became prime minster"; no mention of individual prime minsters, like Harold Macmillan and Harold Wilson, is at all relevant to the truth-conditions of this. To be sure, Lord Home then became Sir Alec Douglas-Home; but this is not logically relevant either, and in affirming this I am not saying which prime minister Lord Home became; I am only saying that he then came to be known by a different name, not that when he became prime minister he became himself for the first time—and he certainly did not then become some prime minister other than himself, say Winston Churchill.

"Alcibiades became a philosopher" is not the only sort of proposition where the term "philosopher" occurs, but mention of individual philosophers is irrelevant to the truth-conditions. Another sort of proposition for which this holds good is:

"Philosopher" means by etymology "lover of wisdom".

In both sorts of proposition the term "philosopher" is used in a special logical role, not in the role of serving to talk about actual philosophers. In careful logical writing the use of the word "philosopher" to talk about the word itself is distinctively marked by the insertion of quotes; it would conduce to logical clarity if the predicative use of "philosopher", as in "Alcibiades became a philosopher", were likewise marked with some other special sign. In both cases it is neither here nor there to observe that ordinary people have got on well enough without such a sign for a good long time; for that matter, ordinary Polish people do instinctively distinguish the predicative use of a term, by using a case-ending. Whether we choose to remark it or not, the change between subject and predicate use of a general term, like the shift from directly using a word to talking about the word, involves a logical gear change; and we do well to develop a sensitive ear for such gear changes, lest we jam our gears by our clumsiness.

Those who have accepted the interchangeability thesis, from Aristotle onwards, have not always done so with complete good faith; the protests of a repressed logical conscience have shown themselves in curious symptoms. One such symptom is the repugnance felt towards arguments in the so-called fourth figure of the syllogism. Aristotle recognized some such arguments as sound but excluded them from his systematic account of syllogistic forms; and in later logicians, too, these arguments have rarely enjoyed parity of esteem with other arguments. The grounds given for this invidious distinction have been various, and all very bad. But to borrow Aristotle's own phrase, I think it is a matter of people being compelled by Truth herself. For the logical gear change of which I have just spoken, the shift of a term from subject to predicate position, or the other way round, occurs *three times over* in any fourth-figure argument, but only once in any other Aristotelian syllogism; so the fourth figure really does not belong in the same formal scheme with the other three—though holders of the interchangeability thesis have no right to say so, and were only aware of a vague discomfort that they tried to rationalize. Sometimes there were even more violent symptoms of repression; Keynes cites an author who loads the fourth figure with abuse as though it were a personal enemy, comparing it, among other things, to the drunken Helot whom Spartan fathers used as an object lesson in the virtue of sobriety.

Aristotle's fall into the two-term theory was only the beginning of a long degeneration. Aristotle never rejected the distinction between an expression's *naming* an object and an expression's *being truly predicated of* an object, though of course his theory committed him to saying that one and the same expression could stand now in one relation, now in the other. But it is a natural further step to identify *naming* with *being predicable of* and to declare explicitly that the two terms of a categorical are two names. So we pass from the *two-term* theory to the *two-name* theory. This two-name theory is best known in England from John Stuart Mill's *Logic*; Mill explicitly calls terms "names", and speaks of *many-worded names* when he means syntactically complex terms. And Mill's term "denoting" simply embodies the fundamental confusion of the two-name theory between the relations *being a name of* and *being predicable of*.

Mill was not a very subtle or hard-working formal logician; his main interests lay elsewhere. The two-name theory has had a long history and much stronger representatives than Mill. It was the predominant logical theory of the Middle Ages, and was expounded by such great men as William of Ockham and Jean Buridan; though there was a minority party of logicians who insisted that naming and predicating were radically distinct, and this minority had the support of Aquinas. In our own time the two-name theory has been given a new lease of life by Polish logicians, notably by Stanisław Leśniewski. Great logical subtlety has sometimes been shown in developing the theory. It would be unjust to call this subtlety futile, but I do call it misdirected. The two-name theory is like the theory that planetary motion has to be reduced to uniform circular motion. Mill's version of the theory is like a crude astronomy in which each planet moves in a simple circular orbit round the Sun; its breakdown is manifest. By increasing the number of logical devices we get something like Copernicus' astronomy, which by assuming a considerable complexity of circles would fit the facts with few notable discrepancies. But just as Kepler could sweep away this complexity at the price of introducing a more sophisticated geometrical construction—an ellipse instead of a circle—so we get a simpler and more powerful logical theory if we distinguish names and predicables from the outset.

Let us briefly consider some of the special troubles of the two-name theory. If what is predicated has to be a name, we get one or the other of two awkward consequences. We may find ourselves recognizing as names what by any decent standard are not names, like "on the mat", "going to the fair". Or we may insist that a predicate-term be properly dressed as a noun-like phrase, that it be 'put into logical form', before we will recognize it as a term, or as a predicate, at all. "Brutus stabbed Caesar" clearly says, predicates, something about Brutus and also something about Caesar. A man who has good logical perceptions will see this directly from the meaning of the sentence. But a two-namer cannot officially recognize that a predication is there at all until he has before his eyes the appropriate pair of names, say "Brutus" and "stabber of Caesar" or "Caesar" and "one stabbed by Brutus". Of course, he then owes us an explanation of how such many-worded names as "stabber of Caesar" and "one stabbed by Brutus" may be formed from "Brutus stabbed Caesar". I believe Polish two-name logicians have tackled these problems of forming and introducing many-worded names; but for the most part the art of 'putting into logical form' has been simply a drill without clear rationale, like school grammar.

If a proposition consists of two names, it must also contain a linking element to hold them together; remember Plato's point that a mere string of names does not make up an intelligible bit of discourse. Two-name logicians in fact assign such a linking role to the grammatical copula, in English the verb "is" or "are". This was a further departure from Aristotle, who held that a proposition may consist simply of two terms. (The verb "applies to" in the schema "A applies to B" was meant only to give a sentence a lecturer can pronounce, not to supply a link between "A" and "B".) And so there arose many perplexities as to the import of the copula.

For the two-name theory, the copula has to be a copula of identity. For, in its pure form, the two-name theory says that an affirmative proposition is true because the subject and predicate terms name one and the same thing: "Socrates is a philosopher" is true because one of the individuals named by the common name "philosopher" is also named by the proper name "Socrates". But it is easy to slide away from this position. On the two-name theory, the common name "philosopher" is here used as name of every philosopher. But if we express this carelessly in the form

The term "philosopher" denotes all philosophers

then it is easy to slide over to the view that what "philosopher" denotes, the denotation of the term, is not any and every philosopher, but rather the class of all philosophers.

By this slide the rake's progress of logic that I have described reaches its last and most degraded phase: the *two-class* theory of categoricals. The subject and predicate terms are now said to denote two classes. (The terms are often also said to *be* two classes; for the writers who hold the two-class theory are mostly very neglectful indeed of the distinction between sign and thing signified.) In our proposition "Socrates is a philosopher", the subject-term is treated as standing for a one-man class: I shall return to this point shortly.

A further confusion in the two-class theory was the muddled doctrine of 'distribution'. I have elsewhere criticized this doctrine at length and must now just briefly illustrate its muddles. We are told that in "Socrates is a philosopher" the term "philosopher" *denotes* the class of all philosophers, but *refers to* just a part of the class. We are not told, and had better not enquire too narrowly,

E

which part of the class is then being referred to; nor yet how a term's referring to a class is different from its denoting a class.

Logic in this last stage of decrepitude is called "traditional logic", and it is mendaciously claimed that these doctrines have held the field continuously since the time of Aristotle. In some Colleges of Unreason this sort of logic is called "logic" *tout court*, and either is the only logic taught or at least is a piece of examination material that must be mastered before any other logic is studied. Some bad old textbooks are still selling in their fiftieth or sixtieth thousand. It is as though flat-earth geography were still a compulsory subject.

Between such logic and genuine logic there can only be war; what fellowship has light with darkness? A training in the two-class logic inculcates bad habits of thought that a training in modern logic later on cannot always eradicate. Those who get such a training grow up and write logic books in which the old stuff is presented as a legitimate though minor part of logical theory; and so the sorry business goes on.

Sometimes bungling attempts are made to mend the errors in two-class logic. I mentioned just now that the singular term "Socrates" is taken to denote a one-man class. Now indeed that relation of Socrates to the class of philosophers which holds good if Socrates is a philosopher is quite different from the relation of the class of logicians to the class of philosophers if every logician is a philosopher. The relation of member to class is quite different from the relation of sub-class to class; a committee of Parliament is not a member of Parliament. So it was certainly a mistake on the part of the older logic books to confound the two relations together by treating Socrates as a one-man class, and it is well that newer books should point out the mistake.

That is: it *would* be well, if only the correction of this mistake did not commonly go with another equally bad mistake. For the newer books tell us that "is" means different things in "Socrates is a philosopher" and "Every logician is a philosopher"; that the first "is" is a copula of class-membership and the second a copula of class-inclusion. Of course this ambiguity is a mere illusion; the predicable expression "is a philosopher" means exactly the same in both propositions, just as "errs sometimes" means exactly the same in "Socrates errs sometimes" and in "Every logician errs sometimes"; and here there is no copula to pin the ambiguity upon.

The whole problem comes about because of the successive corruptions of logic that I have been describing. Aristotle neither had nor needed any theory of the copula; a proposition just consisted of a subject and a predicate. In the two-name theory a copula was needed to stick names together and keep them from being just an unintelligible catalogue; but since on this theory we got a true affirmative predication by sticking together two names of *the same* thing, no need was felt for varieties of copula. The idea that different varieties of copula are needed comes from the fundamental mistake that is introduced in the two-class theory: the belief that in predicating we are joining with a copula the names of *two different* things somehow related—the names of two classes, or of an individual and a class.

Certain categorical propositions can be made out equivalent *as wholes* to propositions affirming relations of classes; for example the propositions:

(1) Socrates is a philosopher

(2) Every logician is a philosopher

are respectively equivalent to the propositions:

(3) Socrates is a member of the class *philosophers*

(4) The class *logicians* is a sub-class of the class *philosophers*

But if you have a pair of equivalent propositions, it does not follow that you can slice up each of the two and then assert equivalences between the successive slices. Supposing that this does follow might be called the *segmentation fallacy*. We are prone to the segmentation fallacy because, in the first elementary foreign-language lessons we have, we do learn to pair off bits of the foreign sentences with bits of an English sentence and conversely. But, of course, not all translation works like that. We must not correlate (1) and (3), (2) and (4), like this:

(1) Socrates	is	a philosopher
(3) Socrates	is a member of	the class *philosophers*
(2) Every logician	is	a philosopher
(4) The class *logicians*	is a sub-class of	the class *philosophers*

For surely "every logician" is not at all equivalent to "the class *logicians*"—and, even if it were, why is "the class *philosophers*" made

out equivalent not to "every philosopher" but to "a philosopher"?
Moreover, if we try another way of translating (2), namely:

(5) Every logician |is a member of| the class *philosophers*

and then segment this in the way I have shown, the result is that
"is" in (2) gets paired off with "is a member of", just like "is" in
(1), and the alleged ambiguity of "is" vanishes.

I have deliberately made this instance of the segmentation
fallacy less plausible than I might have, for I have used the singular
form "Every so-and-so is . . ." rather than the plural form "All
so-and-sos are. . . .". With the transition from the two-name to the
two-class analysis, there in fact went historically a change-over
from logical examples in the singular number (almost invariably
so in the medieval two-name logicians) to examples in the plural
number. There was nothing inherently vicious in this change; it
was always taught that "All Ss are P" is true in cases where there
is just one S and it is P, so "All Ss are P" as conventionally used
did not differ in force from the older "Every S is P". But this
segmentation fallacy is thus made more plausible, as we may see:

(6) All logicians	are	philosophers
(4) The class *logicians*	is a sub-class of	the class *philosophers*

It is much more plausible to equate "all logicians" with "the class
logicians", and "philosophers" with "the class *philosophers*", than to
equate "every logician" with "the class *logicians*" and the dissimilar
phrase "a philosopher" with "the class *philosophers*". More
plausible, but no more justifiable; for if "All logicians are . . . " is
understood distributively, as here it must be, then it does not
differ logically, but only grammatically, from "Every logician
is. . . . "

The segmentation fallacy becomes a regular habit of mind for
many people who are early made to learn how to 'put propositions into logical form' in the bad old traditional way. Another
bad mental habit often picked up from the same training is the
way of thinking that Frege called mechanical or quantificatious
thinking: *mechanische oder quantifizierende Auffassung*. I have used a
rude made-up word "quantificatious" because Frege was being
rude; "quantificational" and "quantifying" are innocent descriptive
terms of modern logic, but they are innocent only because they

are mere labels and have no longer any suggestion of quantity. But people who think quantificatiously do take seriously the idea that words like "all", "some", "most", "none", tell us *how much*, how large a part, of a class is being considered. "All men" would refer to the whole of the class *men*; "most men", to the greater part of the class; "some men", to *some* part of the class *men* (better not ask which part!); "no men", finally, to a null or empty class which contains no men. One can indeed legitimately get to the concept of a null class—but not this way.

I have not time to bring out in detail how destructive of logical insight this quantificatious way of thinking is. I shall just offer one proof of its incoherence. Imagine me for the moment to be addressing a quantificatious thinker. "You say that the phrase "some men" in subject position regularly stands for some sub-class or other of the class *men*. Naturally you would not say that the phrase stands for the same sub-class all the time; but what I want to know is whether you say it continues to stand for the same class in the course of a single short syllogistic argument. If you don't lay down a rule that the reference of the phrase does stay fixed in this way, you will make the following argument invalid:

> Some men are philosophers
> All philosophers can control their temper
> *Ergo*: Some men can control their temper

For without this rule "some men" in the conclusion would possibly refer to a different class of men from "some men" in the premise; and then the syllogism would be invalid, just as a syllogism containing a proper name would be invalid if the name meant a different person in the premise and the conclusion. Obviously, though, you want this syllogism to be valid; so you need the rule that, just as a man's proper name in a syllogism must continue to name the same man, so "some men" in a syllogism must continue to stand for the same class of men. But then the following syllogism would be valid:

> Some men smoke hashish
> Some men study logic
> *Ergo*: Some who study logic smoke hashish

For "some men" would refer to the same class of men each time;

and so the syllogism would be valid, just as it would be if I had listed the same men in both premises instead of saying "some men". Clearly, though, this syllogism is invalid, and you can no more accept it as valid than I can. The only way out is for you to drop the whole idea that "some men" is ever used to stand for a class consisting of some men."

I have imagined myself addressing somebody who is used to thinking quantificatiously; but if I were really addressing such a person my hopes of getting the message over to him would be very slender—his early training would have filled his brain with too much noise. And, unhappily, quantificatious habits of thought can persist in spite of a good training in modern logic; that is why it is important for a young student to start right and never pick up bad logical habits.

In a reputable textbook of modern logic I once came across a shocking specimen of quantificatious thinking. Before presenting it to you, I must supply some background. In ordinary affairs we quite often need to talk about kinds of things that do not exist or about which we do not yet know whether they exist or not; and this applies to ordinary scientific discourse as well—I once saw a lengthy chemical treatise with the title 'Nonexistent Compounds'. Accordingly, logicians need to lay down rules for propositions with empty subject-terms. The convention generally adopted is that when the subject-term is empty, ostensibly contrary categorical propositions are taken to be both true; for example, if there are no dragons, "All dragons are blue" and "No dragons are blue" are both true. This convention may surprise you, but there is nothing really against it; there are other equally consistent conventions for construing such propositions, but no consistent convention can avoid some surprising and even startling results.

Now my author was trying to show the soundness of this convention, and to secure that, came out with the following argument. (I shall for convenience stick to my "dragon" example; the author's example was more long-winded, but not relevantly different.) "If there are no dragons, the phrases "all dragons" and "no dragons" both refer to one and the same class—a null or empty class. Therefore "All dragons are blue" and "No dragons are blue" say the same thing about the same class; so if one is true, the other is true. But if there are no dragons to be blue, "No dragons are blue" is true; therefore, "All dragons are blue" is also true." I know the argument sounds like bosh; but don't you be fooled—it *is* bosh. Let me repeat: I am not saying that all talk about the null class is bosh. But this argument is exactly the same sort of bosh as the schoolboys' fallacy:

Any normal dog has one more tail than no dog
No dog has two tails
One more tail than two tails is three tails
Ergo: Any normal dog has three tails

Only, nobody would take this argument seriously, and a competent logician was convinced by the other argument. So it just shows what persistently harmful ways of thinking can be picked up from the bad old logic.

Thus far I have painted in very sombre colours the history of the subject I teach; of course this picture is very one-sided. In many universities and many countries, good logic is a subject of active research; though other places are still plunged in Egyptian or Cimmerian darkness. The restitution of genuine logic is due to two men above all: Bertrand Russell and Gottlob Frege. To Frege we owe it that modern logicians almost universally accept an absolute category-difference between names and predicables; this comes out graphically in the choice of letters from different founts of type for the schematic letters or variables answering to these two categories. Bertrand Russell re-emphasized this point; and he added a denial that significantly many-worded expressions can ever have the logical role of naming; Frege had still allowed many-worded names.

This was the central thing in Russell's famous Theory of Descriptions. "The Mayor of Cambridge" does not *name* a certain man, as "The Duke of Cambridge" names a certain public house; logic can ignore the internal structure of the one phrase, but not of the other. For from the premise

The Mayor of Cambridge is honest

we may pass to the conclusion

Cambridge is a place whose Mayor is honest;

but it would be a bad joke to pass from

The Duke of Cambridge sells good beer

to

Cambridge is a place whose Duke sells good beer.

"The Duke of Cambridge" is, if you like, a many-worded name; but just on that account, just because this is a many-worded *name*, logic not only can but must ignore the occurrences of "Duke" and "Cambridge" within it; whereas the occurrences of "Mayor" and "Cambridge" in "the Mayor of Cambridge" are logically essential. Or again, to adapt an example of Quine's, from the premise

The broker who hires Joseph hires no negroes

we can logically infer "Joseph is not a negro"; but if "the broker who hires Joseph" were a name, it would be logically one and undivided, and the conclusion about Joseph would no more be logically inferable than it is inferable with "Theodore hires no negroes" as the only premise, supposing "Theodore" to be the broker's name. A description like "the Mayor of Cambridge" or "the broker who hires Joseph" may well appear to be (so to say) a prefabricated unit that we can make enter into the structure of our propositions without needing to consider its own internal structure, so long as we have once satisfied ourselves that it is properly put together. But all sorts of examples show that this prefabricated-unit view of descriptions will not work.

The development of logic inaugurated by Frege and Russell is often called symbolic or mathematical logic. These titles sometimes lead to misconceptions, which I must try to remove. If what makes logic symbolic is the use of patterns or schemata of reasoning rather than concrete examples, with letters taking the place of actual terms, then Aristotle's own logic was already symbolic logic; in fact the word "schemata" is his own word. The use of shorthand symbols instead of words like "all" and "not" is of no fundamental importance; a scientific article does not come under a different discipline if it is dictated to a stenographer. And it is simply false that modern logic cannot be applied to arguments in the vernacular about ordinary topics, but only to mathematics and mathematical physics and so on. Careless talk on these matters by the friends of modern logic has unfortunately sometimes given aid and comfort to her enemies: to those who want to make out that for ordinary reasonings the old logic still holds the field, and to those who simply do not like a serious attempt to clarify our reasonings anyhow.

But in spite of all enemies modern logic grows and flourishes; we have reaped such a harvest of discoveries that in the words of the hymn we may "boast More blessings than our father lost". And thanks to Russell and Frege, most of the logical insights that were lost by Aristotle's Fall have been recovered; but not, to my mind, quite all of them. As I said, Aristotle's *De Interpretatione* recognized as belonging to the category of names not only proper nouns like "Socrates" but also certain common names like "man". This simple and natural view was rejected by Frege and Russell, for reasons that I do not find convincing; and most modern logicians have followed Frege and Russell in this matter; the only important exceptions are those Polish logicians to whom I referred previously, who have misguidedly devoted their energies to a rigorous and sophisticated refashioning of the two-name theory. What we still have not got is a formal theory that recognizes the status of some general terms as names without blurring the distinction between names and predicables. Success in stating such a theory would be Paradise Regained.

2

Traditional Logic

2.1. DISTRIBUTION: A LAST WORD?

In this note I shall ignore any philosophical objections to the doctrine of distribution considered as a semantical theory of the denotation and reference of terms. Before that doctrine need be even considered as a semantical theory, we should have to be certain that the formal rules of inference relating to distributed terms are correct; for the whole point of the semantical theory—of making the distinction between cases where a term refers to every one of the objects it denotes and cases where it refers to only some of them—is to supply a rationale and intuitive justification for the rules. If the rules are inconsistent, this task is futile.

Let us, then, state the rules quite formally. All we need to know about "distributed" in that case is what terms it applies to, namely, the subject terms of universal, and the predicate terms of negative, categoricals. Any other terms will be undistributed.

A conversion will be an inference from a categorical p to a categorical q such that

(i) the subject term of p (or q) is the predicate term of q (or p);

(ii) the quality (affirmative or negative) of p and of q is the same.

By the doctrine of distribution, the conversion is valid if and only if

(iii) no term is distributed in q unless it is distributed in p.

It is easily verified that, by these rules, "SaP" and "SiP" both have the converse "PiS"; "SeP" has the converse "PeS"; and

"*SoP*" has no converse, because the term "*S*" in the predicate would have to be distributed, by (ii), and undistributed, by (iii).

An obversion will be an inference from a categorial *p* to a categorical *q* such that

(i) *p* and *q* have the same subject term, but the predicate terms of *p* and *q* are contradictories;

(ii) the quality of *p* is opposite to the quality of *q*.

By the doctrine of distribution, the obversion is valid if and only if

(iii) the subject term of *q* is not distributed unless that of *p* is.

We may easily verify—using a prime, as Keynes does, to form contradictory terms—that by these rules we may infer "*SaP′*" from "*SeP*", "*SeP′*" from "*SaP*", "*SiP′*" from "*SeP*"or from "*SoP*", and "*SoP′*" from "*SaP*" or from "*SiP*". These are all the valid obversions.

We thus get into no trouble if we use the doctrine of distribution to state necessary and sufficient conditions for a conversion or an obversion to be valid. But it has long been known that trouble does arise if we consider inversion. An inversion is an inference from a categorical *p* to a categorical *q* such that

(i) *p* and *q* have the same predicate term, but the subject terms of *p* and *q* are contradictory;

(ii) the quality of *p* is opposite to the quality of *q*.

Now, by the doctrine of distribution the inversion will be valid *only* if

(iii) the predicate term of *q* is not distributed unless that of *p* is.

And by this rule the inversion whereby we pass from "*SaP*" ("*P*" undistributed) to "*S′oP*" ("*P*" distributed) will be invalid. Yet by our rules we may validly pass from "*SaP*" to "*SeP′*", from "*SeP′*" to "*P′eS*", from "*P′eS*" to "*P′aS′*", from "*P′aS′*" to "*S′iP′*", and from "*S′iP′*" to "*S′oP*".

This is not a decisive argument against the doctrine of distribution; for it rests upon the medieval 'from first to last' rule, that if a chain of inference consists of links severally valid the whole chain is valid; and some may agree with Fitch in allowing exceptions to this rule—so that, in order to know whether a conclusion was proved, we should need to check not only whether, but also how, the premises had been proved. But this is a significant departure from the familiar idea of formal proof, and I do not know if the friends of distribution would be willing to make the departure. Anyhow, they must choose between the 'from first to last' rule and the doctrine of distribution.

Neville Keynes deals with this old crux for the doctrine of distribution by saying that "$S'oP$" follows not from "SaP" alone, but from that *plus* a tacit existential premise "not everything is P" in which "P" would be distributed (*Formal Logic*, 4th ed., p. 139 f.). But now consider the following interpretation of the four traditional categorical forms:

"SaP" is read as

$$"S= \wedge \cdot P= \wedge \cdot v \cdot S=V \cdot P=V \cdot v \cdot S \neq \wedge \cdot P \neq V \cdot S \subset P".$$

"SeP" is read as

$$"S= \wedge \cdot P=V \cdot v \cdot S=V \cdot P= \wedge \cdot v \cdot S \neq \wedge \cdot P \neq \wedge \cdot S \cap P= \wedge ".$$

"SiP" is read as

$$"S= \wedge \cdot P \neq V \cdot v \cdot S \neq V \cdot P= \wedge \cdot v \cdot S \cap P \neq \wedge ".$$

"SoP" is read as

$$"S= \wedge \cdot P \neq \wedge \cdot v \cdot S \neq V \cdot P=V \cdot v \cdot \sim (S \subset P)".$$

This interpretation preserves the square of opposition, and all and only those valid syllogisms which are traditionally so regarded. It renders valid all and only those conversions, and (if we have negative terms) all and only those obversions, which the doctrine of distribution would make out to be valid. It also contains the Łukasiewicz axioms "SaS" and "SiS". The universe is assumed to be nonempty, so that $V \neq \wedge$, but the terms may be empty and may be universal.[1]

On this interpretation the inference from "SaP" to "$S'oP$" *is* a valid inference. Moreover, to exclude Keynes's defence, no added premise is needed; and the great unnaturalness of the interpretation is irrrelevant. For the question is whether the doctrine of distribution affords a formal test of validity. By constructing a system in which the usual relations of categoricals are maintained, but nevertheless an inference condemned by the doctrine of distribution is valid, I have shown that the doctrine of distribution is useless even as a mechanical test of validity.

[1] This interpretation was already proposed by Jaśkowski in *Studia Societatis Scientiarum Torunensis*, Section A, Bd. 2 Heft 2 (1950), 77–90 (reviewed in the *Journal of Symbolic Logic*, XVII, 1952, 268). A similar interpretation was proposed by H. B. Smith in the *Journal of Philosophy*, XXI (1924), 631–633. I owe these references to Professor Alonzo Church.

2.2. TOMS ON DISTRIBUTION

In a recent discussion note[1] Mr. Eric Toms argues in defence of the traditional rule that the predicate-term in an O proposition is distributed. Toms uses a familiar pattern of argument; it is worth while to show why it fails.

If we tighten up Toms's own exposition a little (he oscillates between using plain "*P*" as a term of categoricals and using "member of *P*" instead), the thesis Toms tells us he is going to prove is this:
(1) For any given readings of "*S*" and "*P*", there is a reading of "*Q*" such that "Some *S* is not *P*" entails "Every *P* is *Q*".
And he rightly takes this to be the test I state (as a sufficient condition) for the distribution of the predicate-term "*P*" in "Some *S* is not *P*"; his argument does not call in question this test. In applying the test, we must indeed not treat a necessary proposition as being entailed by every proposition; otherwise, as Toms himself remarked in a letter to me, this test for distribution would make any term "*T*" in any categorical distributed, because "Every *T* is *T*" would be entailed. But many logicians, including myself, would so use "entails" that not every proposition entails a necessary proposition.

However, as readers of his discussion note may easily check, Toms, arguing after the fashion of distributionist logicians,[2] in fact only proves the following:
(2) For any given readings of "*S*" and "*P*", the truth of "Some *S* is not *P*" entails that there is a reading of "*Q*" such that "Every *P* is *Q*" is true.
It is easy to confuse (1) and (2), but they are quite different; and an argument concluding to (2) is no proof of (1), and therefore is no support for traditional doctrine. The difference between (1) and (2) is parallel to the difference between the two following:
(3) For any given readings of "*S*" and "*P*", there is a reading of "*X*" as a singular term such that "Some *S* is *P*" entails "*X* is *P*".
(4) For any given readings of "*S*" and "*P*". the truth of "Some *S*

---

[1] *Mind*, lxxiv (1965), 428–431.
[2] I have found similar arguments in elementary logic books by Wesley Salmon, Irving Copi, and others; nobody that I know of has given us an argument any better than Toms gives.

is P" entails that there is a reading of "X" as a singular term such that "X is P" is true.

(3) answers to (1), and (4) to (2); obviously (3) cannot be derived from (4), for (4) is true and (3) is false; similarly, (1) cannot be derived from (2).

In fact, even if I *gave* Toms proposition (1), which he has not proved, it would do the doctrine of distribution no good. For if (1) showed that "P" in "Some S is not P" is distributed, then by parity of reasoning the truth of the following proposition would show that "P" in "Some S is P" is distributed, so that the distinction of distributed and undistributed terms vanishes:

(5) For any given readings of "S" and "P", there is a reading of "Q" such that "Some S is P" entails "Every P is Q".

And (5) is easily proved: take "Q" to mean "thing that either is an S or is different from some P". Toms can scarcely say this interpretation is ruled out, since he himself accepts "something other than X" as a proper kind of term. Moreover, the entailed proposition "Every P is Q" does not on this interpretation come out as one that is anyhow necessary, like "Every P is P".

Observe that this reading of "Q" does not introduce an empty term 'surreptitiously', in a way Toms could disallow; "Q" so read will certainly be non-empty if "S" is read as non-empty. I should think not all distributionist logicians would wish to follow Toms in rejecting empty general terms. There are, I think, very good reasons for not rejecting them. If they have to be admitted, then the argument in the second part of his note is useless as a defence of distributionist logic.

Toms says "a general breakdown in the doctrine of distribution" would be "serious": why, and for whom?

2.3. STRAWSON ON SYMBOLIC AND TRADITIONAL LOGIC

Some readers of Strawson's *Introduction to Logical Theory* may have been struck, as I have, by a systematic difference between his treatment of the modern (truth-functional and quantificational) logic and of the traditional pseudo-Aristotelian logic. (It looks as though Strawson would let the traditional logicians steal the horse, but not let the modern logicians look over the hedge, as regards departures from ordinary language.) I shall not try to explain this difference, nor shall I draw any conclusion from it as regards Strawson's general attitude in logical theory; I shall merely establish that it is a fact.

(1) How far do the logical constants of a formal system correspond to the use of certain expressions in ordinary language? In answering this question, Strawson painstakingly brings out divergences between truth-functional connectives and the nearest ordinary-language analogues (pp. 79–93). Even in "the identification of 'and' with '.' there is already a considerable distortion of the facts" (p. 79); and even for cases where only a very stupid pupil would try to transcribe "and" into symbols with ".", we are warned that such transcription would be illegitimate (*cf.* the examples on p. 80).

On the other hand, the only divergence that Strawson recognises between the uses of "all" and "some" in the traditional "All *S* is *P*" and "Some *S* is (not) *P*" and the ordinary-language uses of the same words is that " 'some', in its most common employment as a separate word, carries an implication of plurality" (pp. 177 f.) (I am not sure what this "implication of plurality" is: whether, *e.g.*, for the example "Some metal is lighter than water" the implication would be that there is more than one metal, or that there is more than one metal lighter than water; a back-reference to p. 165 f. suggests the latter interpretation. And, as often happens for philosophers' assertions about the common use of words, one may feel tempted to dispute the assertion; but I resist the temptation.)

Now in fact there are other divergences. It would admittedly be odd to say "(Not) all John's children are asleep" if John had no children; and accordingly Strawson insists that an assertion or denial that all John's children are asleep 'presupposes' a statement that there exist children of John's (p. 175). He does not remark, however, that the use of a sentence like this would be equally odd if in fact John had only one child or even only two children; and he gives no reason for thus exclusively attending to a 'presupposition' of non-emptiness, rather than of non-singularity or non-duality, on the part of the term "child of John". Indeed, by implication Strawson denies that the oddity I have just discussed exists; for he expressly says that "with the reservation noted above" (concerning "some") his account of the matter "gives the constants of the system just the sense which they have in a vast group of statements of ordinary speech" (p. 178).

(2) Strawson raises difficulties over the entailment of "*p* or *q*" by "*p*", on the score that "*p*, *ergo p* or *q*" is not a "logically proper step"; "the alternative statement carries the implication of the speaker's uncertainty . . . and this implication is inconsistent with the assertion" of the first alternative (p. 91). It is needless for us to discuss whether these difficulties have any substance; it ought, in any case, to be clear that there is a very similar oddity or difficulty over the inference-pattern "All *S* is *P*, *ergo* some *S* is *P*", since the assertion that *some* are very often carries with it the implication of the speaker's uncertainty as to whether *all* are. But *this* inference-pattern is a part of the traditional formal logic; and Strawson claims, on behalf of his own way of reading the traditional forms, that "it enables the whole body of the laws of the system to be accepted without inconsistency" (p. 178); moreover, in the passage where he expressly mentions the "all" —"some" entailment (p. 158), he gives us no hint that this entailment is at all open to exception.

(3) Strawson raises a number of objections to the symbolic rendering of "There was at least one woman among the survivors" in quantificational form:

(A) $(\exists x)$ (x is a woman. x was among the survivors)
He first considers what we got if we read "$(\exists x)$ (x . . . x . . .)" as "There *is* at least one person who . . . and who . . ." (his italics). On this reading the formula is alleged "at least to suggest that the person is alive at the time the sentence is uttered. . . . Changing the . . . 'is' to 'was' will not help; it will merely prompt the question 'What became of her then? Has she changed her sex' " ? (pp. 150 f.). The natural rejoinder that we ought not to read "$(\exists x)$ (x . . .)" as "there *is* (etc.)", with an emphatic present-tense "is", is met with the argument that surely "the question of time-reference" does arise "when we speak of persons and incidents".

I do not think much of these difficulties. What a formula suggests, what question it prompts, is not relevant to a logician; for in these respects logically equivalent formulas may differ. Again, since the verbs following "$(\exists x)$" are tensed, it is not clear why "$(\exists x)$" need also be so in order to give the whole formula a time-reference. But however this may be, the rendering of our ordinary-language expression in a traditional I schedule, *viz.*

(B) Some woman is a person who was among the survivors, generates parallel difficulties. "Some woman is . . ." suggests that we are speaking of a woman now living; and worries about the propriety of the expression if there had been a change of sex are at least as relevant here as they are for (A). Strawson, however, refuses to concern himself with the problems of fitting tensed statements into the traditional four-fold schedule; this schedule gives us only "representative patterns" which need not be "strictly exemplified" (p. 153).

(4) Strawson is concerned at the (alleged) fact that only a few sentences of ordinary language, beginning with "rather strained and awkward phrases", give us formulas to which quantification theory can be straightforwardly applied (p. 147); and he elaborately argues that twisting sentences around so as to make the theory applicable does not just give us clumsy English but leads to philosophical errors as well (pp. 148 f., 185 ff.). Now to be sure Strawson does at one point mention the fact that if we turn sentences into one or other of the four categorical forms "the results would be, as English, often clumsy and sometimes absurd" (p. 153); but he does not display this clumsiness and absurdity in any actual example; and he never considers the possibility that the traditional manipulations may lead to philosophical errors— his harshest judgment on the traditional logic of categoricals is that it is "very limited" (p. 192). He does not remark the extreme grammatical oddity of the traditional "All S is P" for most readings of "S";[1] and this oddity at least is not philosophically innocent. The wrong idea that a universally quantified subject-term stands for the whole class of Ss[2] can be put across where that term has the form "every S" or "all Ss": but how much the illusion is helped by using "all S"!

(5) The undeniable extent of formal parallelism between "$\supset$" in symbolic logic and "if . . . then" in ordinary language (cf. pp. 86–87) does not in Strawson's eyes at all justify, or even excuse, our reading "$\supset$" as "if . . . then". On the other hand, the class of statements to the effect that Socrates is such and such has a certain formal parallelism to the class of statements to the effect that every man is such and such; e.g. within either class we may reach

---

[1] How did this odd form originate? Was it a mistranslation of "Omne S est P", which should of course be "Every S is P"? And who introduced it?

[2] On the nature of this error cf. the chapter 'The Doctrine of Distribution', in my book *Reference and Generality*. See also p. 56 of this volume.

F

the member with "P" for predicate as a conclusion from the member with "M" for predicate and the further premise "Every M is P". Now Strawson *does* regard this partial formal parallelism as showing that the traditional logic was "not absurd" in classifying statements to the effect that Socrates is such and such as universal affirmatives (p. 181).

I have not here tried to appraise Strawson's general doctrine as to the relation between formal logic and ordinary-language arguments. It will be enough to say that that doctrine affords no grounds for treating the traditional syllogistic logic as raising fewer or less radical problems of application than the modern calculi of truth-functions and quantifiers. In one place Strawson seems to recognise that he may have given a false impression:

> Some of the foregoing sections may appear to wear the guise of a defence of the traditional system. But the appearance is, at least in part, misleading . . . it would be mistaken in fact, and in principle, to present the traditional system as succeeding in an enterprise in which the modern logic fails, or *vice versa* (pp. 193 f.).

I am afraid this disclaimer will not have remedied the false impression. Many readers will vaguely think Strawson has *proved* that the traditional system with all its faults is philosophically less misleading than the new-fangled one. Those Colleges of Unreason where the pseudo-Aristotelian logic is presented as the only genuine logic, and those lecturers who would like to teach the philosophy of logic without having to learn any modern logic, may well thus have been supplied with a pretext for supine ignorance.

2.4. CONTRADICTORIES AND CONTRARIES

A pair of contradictory predications, "Fa" and "$\sim Fa$", may legitimately be taken as the results of attaching contradictory predicates, "F" and "$\sim F$", to a common subject; but if we rewrote this pair as "aF" and "$\sim aF$", we could not regard them as the results of attaching a common predicate to a pair of contradictory subjects, "a" and "$\sim a$". Elsewhere I have appealed to this consideration among others in order to show that names (possible logical subjects) and predicables (possible logical predicates) are necessarily different in category, and that we must reject the traditional idea of a 'term' that can shift from predicate to subject position without change of sense.[1] The doctrine of 'terms' is, of course, Aristotle's doctrine in the *Prior Analytics*; but in his earlier work *De Interpretatione* he had himself recognized the difference between names (*onomata*) and predicables 'signifying what is said of something else' (*rhemata*).

In this earlier Aristotelian view, common nouns like "man" and proper nouns like "Socrates" are alike counted as names, as possible subjects of predication. I have defended this thesis;[2] but it may well seem to jeopardize the category-distinction between names and predicables. A friendly critic in fact suggested in correspondence an ingenious rejoinder to my argument that contradictory propositions can be obtained only by negation of a predicable, never by negation of a name. In traditional logic, he pointed out, we may obtain a pair of *contrary* propositions either by negating a subject-term or by negating a predicate-term; in fact, by the traditional rules both the pair:

No non-*P* is *S*—No *P* is *S*

and the pair:

Every *S* is *P*—Every *S* is non-*P*

are equivalent to the pair of contraries:

Every *S* is *P*—No *S* is *P*

This seems to show that the sense of a proposition may after all be reversed by attaching negation either to a subject-term or to a predicate-term; and that we cannot differentiate predicables from names on the score that such reversal of sense can be made only by negating a predicable.

This argument assimilates contrary and contradictory opposition; but the two kinds of opposition differ much more radically than the traditional 'square' suggests. Contradictory, *i.e.* ordinary, negation is a proposition-forming operator on propositions; we cannot coherently think of contrary negation this way. For we may speak of *the* contradictory of a proposition, since no proposition has two (non-equivalent) contradictories; but a proposition may well have more than one contrary in the square-of-opposition

[1] See my *Reference and Generality* (Cornell University Press, 1968), p. 32f.
[2] *Ibid.*, pp. 40–46, 178–180, 188f.

sense of the word. Consider the proposition "Every cat detests every dog". If we read this as an instance of "Every A is F", what is the contrary proposition "No A is F"? There is no determinate answer. If we take this interpretation of the schematic letters:

A=cat; — is F=— detests every dog

then we get "No cat detests every dog"; but if we take the equally legitimate interpretation:

A=dog; — is F=every cat detests —

we get "(There is) no dog every cat detests". A moment's thought shows these two 'contraries' of "Every cat detests every dog" are not logically equivalent.

Let us now consider the contradictory of "Every A is F": the schema "Not every A is F". If we apply the two interpretations already given we obtain two verbally different contradictories for "Every cat detests every dog" *viz.* these respectively:

Not every cat detests every dog

(It is) not *every* dog (that) every cat detests

But these *are* logically equivalent, though the equivalence is not obvious at first glance. So contradictory opposition is a matter of a proposition-forming operation upon propositions; but contrary opposition is not. As has been noticed by other writers,[1] when contrariety is explained in connexion with the square of opposition the account is often very confusing; I think one source of the confusion is a failure to realise this essential difference between contrary and contradictory opposition. And since a reputable modern logician[2] has written of a contrariety-operator upon propositions, I am not demolishing a straw man in attacking the idea.

If a general term does indeed function as a name, as a logical subject, when inserted in the empty places of "Every — is F" "Some — is F", "Only a — is F", *etc.*, then we may regard such incomplete expressions as predicables, which are formed from the predicable "— is F" by the operators "every", "some", "only", *etc.* And then we may explain contrariety as a relation not between propositions, but between a pair of predicables "Every—is F"

[1] *E.g.* David A. Sanford on 'Contraries and Subcontraries', *Noûs*, II.1, February 1968.
[2] See Storrs McCall, 'Contrariety', *Notre Dame Journal of Formal Logic*, *VIII*, 1 and 2, April 1967, pp. 121–132.

and "No — is F". Naturally on this explanation not every predicable will have a contrary; but we may speak of *the* contrary of any predicable that has a contrary at all.

We cannot use this notion of contrary predicables to refashion a sense for "*the* contrary of a proposition". Our previous cat-and-dog example is enough to show why: more than one predicable with a contrary can sometimes be extracted from one and the same proposition P, and in that case there may be non-equivalent propositions obtained from P through replacing a predicable with its contrary. This sometimes happens without our considering a different general name as logical subject: from "Every man loves every man" we may extract the two predicables "Every — loves every man" and "Every man loves every — ", and the respective results of re-attaching the contraries of these to "man" as logical subject will be:

No man loves every man
(There is) no man every man loves

which of course are not logically equivalent.

Contradictory negation may be thought of either as operating upon entire propositions or as operating upon predicables; contrariety can be treated as an operator only upon predicables, not upon entire propositions. Contradictory negation of the predicate is demonstrably not equivalent to any operation upon the subject-term; is some operation upon the subject-term equivalent to the operation of replacing a predicable by its contrary? We can soon show that this is not so either. If it were so then this would have to be a theorem:

(1) Every A is F iff no NA is F

for some reading of "N" as a name-forming operator on names. By (1) we should have:

(2) If every A is F or G, no NA is F or G

(3) If no NA is G, every A is G

Now whatever is F, is F or G; and whatever is G, is F or G. Hence we have:

(4) If every A is F, every A is F or G

(5) If some NA is G, some NA is F or G

(6) If no NA is F or G, no NA is G—contraposition of (5).

By reasoning 'from first to last', as medieval logicians says, (4), (2), (6), and (3) yield:

(7) If every A is F, every A is G,

which is absurd. So the reversal of sense by a contrariety-operator can be effected only at the predicate-end of a proposition, not at the subject-end. This result does not depend on a wilfully chosen definition of "contrariety"; (1) is unacceptable as a theorem no matter how we apply the word "contraries". Here again, as with contradictory negation, there is an operation on predicables to which there corresponds no operation upon names; the category-difference between names and predicables comes out once more, even though we are explicitly considering general names.

2.5. THE LAW OF EXCLUDED MIDDLE

The forms of the Law of Excluded Middle to which I shall devote most of my discussion are the following:

(A) For any x, either x is F or x is not F.

(B) For any predicate P and any object x, either P or its negation is true of x.

(A) and (B) may respectively be called a *logical* and a *semantical* form of the Law; for the semantical expression "true of" occurs in (B), but (A) uses only logical expressions—"for any . . . ", "either . . . or . . . ". The word "predicate" as used in (B), and as I shall use it in the rest of this paper, means a certain feature of language; the schematic letter "F" in (A) goes proxy for an arbitrary predicate *used as such*, whereas to get an instance of (B) one would replace the letter "P" by a *quotation* of a predicate; thus:

For any x, either x is white or x is not white:

For any object x, either the predicate "white" or its negation is true of x.

(A) and (B) seem to be close to the historically earliest formulations of the Law, in Aristotle's *De Interpretatione*. For most purposes we may treat (A) and (B) as equivalent; I shall ignore trivial complications about languages too poverty-stricken to contain negations of all the predicates they contain.

It may at first sight appear that (A) and (B) are less fundamental than the more general forms of the Law:

(C) Either p or not p.

(D) Every statement either is itself true or has a true negation. In fact, however, (A) and (B) employ simpler notions, and raise fewer problems, than (C) and (D). When we compare the two logical forms of the Law, (A) and (C), or again the two semantical forms, (B) and (D), we observe that the negation used in (A) and mentioned in (B) is predicate-negation, whereas that used in (C) and mentioned in (D) is propositional negation. Now though propositional negation has been made familiar by modern logic, it is a rather sophisticated notion. In ordinary language it is rather rare to negate a statement by prefixing a sign of negation that governs the whole statement; negation is almost always applied primarily to some part of a statement, though this often has the effect of negating the statement as a whole. (The virtual absence of propositional negation from 'ordinary language' might supply the worshippers of that *idolum theatri* with one more reason for demanding that arguments in ordinary language shall be deemed to be exempt from the rules of formal logic.)

The negation Aristotle was interested in was predicate-negation; propositional negation was as foreign to ordinary Greek as to ordinary English, and he never attained to a distinct conception of it. The Stoics did reach such a conception, but in doing so they violated accepted Greek usage; their use of an initial οὐχί at the standard negation must have read just as oddly as sentences like "Not: the Sun is shining" do in English. The view that there is a univocal negation operating upon statements was explicitly denied by the authors of *Principia Mathematica*, who held that negation could not be introduced once for all as a primitive term, but must be defined recursively for the various types of statements; in particular, they held that the the propositional negation of "For every x, Fx" must be defined as "For some x, not Fx"—defined, that is, in terms of the predicate-negation applied to "F".

Again, though this is not clear at first sight, the notion of truth expressed by "true of" in (B) is a simpler notion than the notion of propositional truth used in (D). This fact comes out in

Tarski's work on the 'definition' of truth for formalised languages; he found himself compelled (*quasi ab ipsa veritate coactus*) to begin, not with propositional truth, but with the 'satisfying' of a propositional function—essentially the same idea as is expressed by "true of" in (B). For in 'defining' truth recursively you cannot in general define the truth of complex propositions by that of simpler ones (because in general complex propositions do not split up into simpler ones); but in any proposition some prositional function is used, and propositional truth can be adequately defined when once the 'satisfying' of the propositional functions concerned has been defined. It seems to me, incidentally, that in the present century enquiries as to 'the nature of truth' have very often started off on a wrong track because people have considered propositional truth rather than the truth signified by "true of"; they have looked for a complex *in rebus* (a subsistent true proposition, or a fact) answering to the statement-complex, whereas the important relation to have considered was that of a predicate to the thing it is truly predicated of.

Semantical formulations of the Law of Excluded Middle often use the term "false" as well as "true", omitting explicit mention of negation.

For any predicate P and any object x, P is either true of x or false of x.

Every statement is either true or false.

I cannot see that there is any advantage in such formulations. Negation needs to be explicitly discussed in any case; and I think we lose nothing by talking about a negation's being true instead of using the term "false". Indeed, taking the formulations with "false" in them as the standard formulations of our Law might strengthen a widespread mistake: that the negation of a statement is a statement that that statement is false, and is thus a statement *about* the original statement and logically secondary to it. It may help us here to remember that there are negative commands, and that this negation obviously cannot be explained in terms of falsehood; "Do not open the door!" is a command on the same level as "Open the door!", and does not mean (say) "Let the statement that you will open the door be false!" The logical priority of affirmation to negation will be directly refuted later on in this paper; falsehood will not need to be discussed again.

My reason for writing (A) with a quantifier at the beginning

—"For any x, x . . ."—instead of simply having "x" as a schematic letter—"Either x is F or x is not F"—was that the latter form of the Law might occasion difficulties over the substitutions allowed for "x". There are notorious problems, which I shall not discuss, about what happens if we substitute vacuous proper names, or inapplicable definite descriptions; roughly speaking, I think the solution of these problems is just a matter of tidying-up. An older, and, I think, a more serious problem is: Why may we not substitute "every man" for "x"? Aristotle remarks that although "Is Socrates wise?—No.—Then not wise" is all right, nevertheless "Is every man wise?—No.—Then not wise" is all wrong. (*De Int.* 20*a*, 25–30). But he hardly shows why there is this difference; and I do not think he could have explained it in terms of his own doctrines. On his view, both in "Socrates is wise— is not wise" and in "Every man is wise—not wise" we have contradictory predicates attached to a common subject. A modern reader may glibly explain that we get values of the propositional functions "x is wise" and "x is not wise" only when "Socrates" is substituted for "x", not when "every man" is substituted; but that only shifts the difficulty. For we now want to know why the substitution for "x" is allowable only when it yields as clauses of the disjunction values of these functions— why some substitutions are ruled out although the clauses arrived at by the substitutions make perfectly good sense.

Let us compare the genuine contradictories "Every man is wise—not every man is wise" and "Socrates is wise—Socrates is not wise". We observe that whereas in the second pair "is wise", the predicate, is negated, in the first pair the negation governs "every man". This may perhaps suggest that in the first pair "is wise" plays a part comparable to that of the common subject "Socrates" in the second pair; and that "every man", "not every man", are to be compared to the contradictory predicates "is wise", "is not wise" in the second pair—that as these serve to make contradictory assertions about Socrates, so "every man" and "not every man" serve to make contradictory assertions about that which the predicate "is wise" stands for. And we might try to show that this is indeed the right way of looking at things by writing down circumlocutory equivalents of our first pair: "Wisdom is possessed by every man; wisdom is possessed by not every man." (Such circumlocutions, however, have dangers of their own. "Wisdom" must not be assumed to be a singular term with a reference on its own account, like"Socrates"; it has significance as part of the phrase "wisdom is possessed by —", which just means "—is wise".)

However this may be, it ought to be clear that "every man" is not a name, like "Socrates"; it is neither a name of *every man* (a name that each man bears in addition to his personal name), nor yet a proper name of some τρίτος ἄνθρωπος, *individuum vagum*, or *unvollständiger Gegenstand*. Whereas we may have some trouble over specifying the substitutions for the schematic letter "*x*" in "Either *x* is *F* or *x* is not *F*", it ought to be clear that the quantification in "For any *x*, either *x* is *F* or *x* is not *F*" does not cover an object named "every man". But of course no formulation can be made secure in advance against all the varied types of philosophical perversity.

For some reason the Law of Excluded Middle has the appearance of being a more substantial assertion than other logical laws. In disputation, people have the odd way of asserting with great emphasis, as a premise of the argument, a particular case of the Law: "*Either* so-and-so *or* not so-and-so. If so-and-so, then . . . , and if not so-and-so, then . . . ." Now of course this emphatically uttered premise can in no wise advance the argument; whatever follows from "Either *p* or not *p*" and "If *p*, then *q*", and "If not *p*, then *r*" would follow from the last two premises by themselves. In his lectures Wittgenstein used to say that at this point of an argument we ought to look out for a fallacy; while the hearer's attention is fixed upon the tautological premise, the sleight of hand is performed where he is not looking. When he realizes that he has been tricked, he will very likely suspect fallacy at the wrong place; supposing as he does that the emphasized premise is an important stage of the argument, he may well conclude that the Law of Excluded Middle allows of exceptions.

The apparent substantiality of the Law partly derives from a mistaken view of negation. Verbally, the negation of a predicate is more complex than the predicate itself, since it contains an added "not"; this has often led people to think that the understanding of the negative predicate includes something over and above the understanding of the affirmative predicate—viz. the understanding of negation. They regard "Either Evelyn is a male or Evelyn is *not* a male" as a substantial and dubitable assertion, because half-consciously they are taking it to be something like "Either Evelyn is a male or Evelyn is *daughter of* a male"; just as in this assertion the meaning of "daughter" comes in as well as that of "male", so in the former assertion we have a predicate combining the meaning of "male" and "not".

But the understanding of "not male" is no more complex than that of "male": they go inseparably together—*eadem est scientia oppositorum*. A predicate may be represented by a closed line on a surface, and predicating it of an object be represented by placing the point representing the object on one or the other side of this line. A predicate and its negation will then clearly be represented by one and the same line; and there can be no question of logical priority as between the inside and the outside of the line, which inseparably coexist. There will, indeed, be a well-marked difference, when the line is drawn on a plane, between the definite area inside it and the indefinitely large area outside it; this feature of the representation may have led to, or confirmed, the idea that a negative predicate is in some way unlimited or indefinite as compared with the affirmative predicate. But the asymmetry of the two sides disappears if we imagine a closed line drawn on the surface of a globe; for even if I said that whichever of the two areas bounded by the line is the smaller shall be called the inside, the Equator (or any great circle) would then not have an inside and an outside (though of course it would have two sides); anyhow, the relative size of the two areas plainly has no logical importance. Of course a predicate cannot really be any more definite than its negation is; the one is exactly as sharply defined as the other. We may use the globe-representation to dispose of the view that negation is an asymmetrical relation between predicates, enabling us to pick out one predicate of a pair as affirmative and the other as negative.

We must *a fortiori* reject the view that a negative predication needs to be backed by an affirmative one—that we are not justified in predicating the negation of P unless we can predicate some Q which is positive and incompatible with P. What positive predication, we might well ask, justifies us in saying that pure water has no taste? Again, when I say there is no beer in an empty bottle, this is not because I know that the bottle is full of air, which is incompatible with its containing beer; as compared with knowing there is no beer left, the positive predication that the bottle is full of air is a recondite bit of scientific information, which I do not need in order to know there is no beer left.

There is indeed often *an* asymmetry between P and its negation. Let us call P an *identifying* predicate when the phrase "the same (thing that is)" prefixed to P expresses a criterion of identity for a thing. Thus "man" is an identifying predicate, and so is "number"; for we know what to make of "the same man" and "the same number". Now I think that when P is an identifying predicate its negation never is one. "I saw again today the same man as I saw yesterday" has no longer a clear sense if we replace "man" by "non-man"; we cannot make anything of "the same non-man". It is, if possible, even less clear what could be meant by "the same non-number". Perhaps it is natural, when one of a pair of contradictory predicates is an identifying predicate, to call that one positive and its negation negative. This test of positiveness, however, works only in special cases; very often neither of the contradictories is an identifying predicate. We can do nothing with either "the same thing that is either red or round" or "the same thing that is neither red nor round"; nothing with either "the same thing in my room" or "the same thing not in my room."

Even if this or some other asymmetry does hold between contradictory predicates, the asymmetry does not arise from negation itself. As our globe-representation showed, contradictory predicates are one another's negations; there is no way of separately representing a predicate and its double negation in this model. The Law of Double Negation has been doubted for much the same reasons as the Law of Excluded Middle; double negation, like single negation, looks like an added piece of meaning, in which the sense of the original predicate is (in Frege's phrase) wrapped up. The new, doubly negated predicate may apply to the same objects as the original predicate; but surely it has a different sense—and then how can we after all be sure that it has the same application? The right rejoinder is just to deny that the doubly negated predicate has got a different sense.

It will be well to notice here the interrelation of certain logical laws. Let us allow "neither . . . nor—" as a convenient linguistic variant of "not: either . . . or—". By the Law of Contradiction, a thing must not be both not-F and not not-F; and by one of de Morgan's Laws (which has given nobody any worry) we may transform "both not-F and not not-F" into "neither F nor not-F". So a thing must not be neither F nor not-F; so, cancelling out the "not" with the "neither . . . nor . . . " by the Law of Double Negation, it must be either F or not-F—the Law of Excluded Middle. This is specially relevant to a three-valued logic that retains the Law of Double Negation and the relevant de Morgan Law; exceptions to the Law of Excluded Middle can then be allowed only if exceptions to the Law of Contradiction are also allowed—a much less popular concession.

People have tried to maintain (sometimes appealing to three-valued logic) that of a pair of contradictory predictions relating to a future contingency neither need be true. (Sometimes they say that neither need be *determinately* true; but this qualification, though it may make their doctrine easier to swallow, is quite devoid of sense.) Oddly enough, they claim as a precedent the famous chapter IX of Aristotle's *De Interpretatione*. In fact, Aristotle expressly rejects the idea of such a breakdown of our Law (*op. cit.* 18b, 18–20). Moreover, he supplies a strong argument against the idea. What it is now true to say that a thing will be, it will be true to say that it is or has been; so, if it is now true to say of Jones that he is neither going to be hanged tomorrow nor not, then tomorrow it will be true to say of him that he neither has been hanged nor has not; and this sort of result, Aristotle says, is absurd (*op. cit.* 18b, 22–25).

In fact, too, it is useless to bring in a three-valued logic, in which the prediction of contradictories may have the same, 'neuter', truth-value. For if we get the same truth-value by predicating P and by predicating its negation, then we shall get the same truth-value by predicating P and its negation as conjoint (or alternative) predicates as we get by predicating P and P as conjoint (or, as the case may be, alternative) predicates—i.e. the same as we get by just predicating P. So if "Jones will be hanged tomorrow" has the same truth-value as "Jones will not be hanged tomorrow", then both will have the same truth-value as "Jones will be both hanged and not hanged tomorrow" and again as "Jones will be either hanged or not hanged tomorrow". This is not at all the way we intend our statements in the future tense to be taken.

Another alleged counter-example to the Law of Excluded Middle is the sort of predicate that 'presupposes' the application of another predicate. I say that P presupposes Q when, if Q is not true of an object x, the question does not arise whether or not we ought to predicate P of x, and thus neither P nor its negation is true of x. Thus, it might be alleged that only for an object of which the predicate "animal" is true does the question arise whether or not we should apply the predicate "hungry" to it; of other objects neither the predicate "hungry" nor the predicate "not hungry" will be true. "Hungry" and "not hungry" would thus be predicates presupposing the predicate "animal". This relation of presupposition is quite different from entailment; for if "hungry" entailed "animal" then "not animal" would entail "not hungry", whereas the presupposition-relation would require that if the predicate "not animal" is true of anything, then *neither* "hungry" *nor* "not hungry" is true of that thing. Alleged relations of presupposition are sometimes used to mark out category-differences between predicates; thus, it might be argued that because "hungry" presupposes "animal", these are predicates in different categories.

It may well be right to use this idea of presupposition in describing the actual use of predicates in ordinary language; but I cannot see that it has much significance for the philosophy of logic. Suppose that the relation alleged does indeed hold between "hungry" and "animal" in ordinary usage. Let us now introduce an artificial predicate "hungery": "hungery" is to be true of just what "hungry" is true of, "not hungery" is to be true of whatever "not hungry" is true of and also of whatever "animal" is not true of. Surely the new word will allow us to say whatever we wanted to say with the old word; and it cuts out some troublesome restrictions on the use of the old word (troublesome to a formal logician, that is). As for the alleged category-difference between "hungry" and "animal": if there is still such a difference between "hungery" and "animal", then the account of category-differences in terms of presuppositions is inadequate; and if "hungery" used instead of "hungry" no longer has any category-difference from "animal", then the difference never was philosophically important anyhow.

Sometimes, when a logician wishes to establish the necessity of a type-distinction, he resorts to a very peculiar manoeuvre. He constructs a formula in which the type-distinction in question is ignored; then, using this formula, he constructs a proof that of some object the predicate P is true if and only if its negation is true; then he concludes that the formula he started with is nonsensical, and accordingly that the type-distinction ignored in the formula is necessary. Another logician, disliking the type-distinction, may now make the rejoinder that the reason why P is truly predicable if and only if its negation is so, is that in this particular case the Law of Excluded Middle breaks down and there is an object of which neither P nor its contradictory is true; predication of P is, however, not devoid of sense.

In such disputes I think both sides are wrong. How can you use a formula in a pretended logical proof as though it had sense, with a view to proving that it has no sense? This is not at all like a valid *reductio ad absurdum*; you can make a false assumption for the sake of argument, but not a meaningless one. If any derivation contains a meaningless formula, the derivation itself has no sense either, let alone its being valid. But abandoning the Law of Excluded Middle is not the right way out of the difficulty. If it needs to be proved that P is true of x if and only if the negation of P is so, then, although the argument has made it appear that the two contradictory predications have the same truth-value, there is no reason to suppose that they have the same sense; on the contrary, one will be demonstrable from the other only with the aid of an added premise. It will then be this added premise that should be doubted, rather than the Law of Excluded Middle.

Let us take the example of Russell's paradox. To predicate "is a member of itself" and "is not a member of itself" of a given object will never have the same sense, even if that object is supposed to be the class of classes that are not members of themselves. We cannot show even that the two predications have in this case the same truth-value, unless we assume the premise that there is some class x of which any class y is a member if and only if y is not a member of itself. Russell's paradox might be used as a *reductio ad absurdum* of this assumption; it cannot be used to show that the assumption is meaningless, as containing a meaningless predicate "member of itself"; nor can it be used to establish an exception to the Law of Excluded Middle.

Sometimes, however, we seem to see that, if sense there be, opposite predications must have the same sense, not just the same truth-value. The recourse of rejecting some suppressed premise is then denied us. Some logicians perhaps would say that among the exceptions to the Law of Excluded Middle there are some that are actually synonymous with their own contradictories. I shall not here discuss how reasonable this would be.

It is hard to offer unexceptionable examples of paradoxically synonymous contradictories, but I will do my best. Suppose we use "the property F is a property of x" as a form of expression synonymous with "x is F". If we now suppose that "x is (not) a property of x" is a form of expression that makes sense, then "x is (not) a property of itself" will be a synonymous form of expression. Then "the property *not a property of itself* is not a property of itself" will be synonymous with "the property *not a property of itself* is a property of the property *not a property of itself*". (We read "F" in our first synonym as "not a property of itself", and "x" as "the property *not a property of itself*".) But the latter statement in turn will be synonymous with "the property *not a property of itself* is a property of itself", the contradictory of our original statement.

Again, suppose we lay down the following definition: The result of writing a predicate P in quotes followed by "is heterological" is to have the same sense as the result of writing P in quotes followed by the negation of P. For example, ' "is an obscene expression" is heterological' is to have the same sense as ' "is an obscene expression" is not an obscene expression'. This definition would make ' "is heterological" is heterological' synonymous with ' "is heterological" is not heterological'.

Synonymy is a rather treacherous subject; it is fortunate that the sort of paradox just illustrated is not necessary to establish type-distinctions. Let us consider the type distinction between numbers and numerical functions (those whose arguments and values are numbers). We could not establish this distinction by saying that an equation between a number and a numerical function ("8=the square of") is nonsense, or that a functional sign standing in its own argument-place ("the square of the square of") is nonsense. For if by our existing conventions these expressions have simply not yet acquired a sense, then that is no reason why we should not devise a suitable sense for them. Consider how mathematicians devised a sense for zero, negative, and fractional exponents. For an integral exponent, "x^m" may be taken to mean "the result of multiplying 1 by x, m times over";

we might then say that 1 multiplied by x 0 times over is just 1, but it would be manifest nonsense to speak of multiplying 1 by x a negative or fractional number of times. Nevertheless mathematicians have devised a way of taking exponentiations that fits all exponents impartially.

There already *is* a place in our language for "8 = the square of"; as a sentence-fragment, which, when we complete it by adding the name of a number at the end, serves to assert that 8 is the square of that number; or again we may use it in such a statement as "There is no integer that 8 is the square of". So reading "8=the square of" as a statement (even one to which the Law of Excluded Middle did not apply) would not be supplementary to our existing conventions but inconsistent with them. Similarly "the square of the square of" already makes good sense by our existing conventions, only what it stands for is not a value of the function *square of*, but rather the function *fourth power of*. It is not meant that the one function is the square of the other function, but rather that, for any argument x, the value of the one function is the square of the value of the other; and to try to treat the one function as the square of the other would again positively contravene our existing use of signs.

Reasonings like these can establish, I believe, that certain type-distinctions are necessary and not arbitrary, for example, Frege's distinction between concept and object. However this may be, recognizing a type-distinction is always a way of *dis*-allowing exceptions to the Law of Excluded Middle; it does not commit us to answering some questions with a third answer on a level with "yes" and "no", but rather entitles us to tell the people who ask them to shut up—perhaps before the question is well out of their mouths. "Is the concept *concept not falling under itself* —?" "Shut up!" (The form of question, however it was meant to be completed, would violate the distinction between concept and object.)

I know of no serious objection to the Law of Excluded Middle, except the one arising over vague predicates—predicates that allow of border-line cases. It is only this sort of vagueness that is logically important. There are of course cases where vagueness hangs over a statement as a whole, as in much popular writing about religion, morals, politics, etc. Such vague statements will, however, hardly be alleged as counter-examples

G

to the Law of Excluded Middle in a form relevant to statements as whole, i.e. (C) or (D); it is clear at once that it is waste of time for logicians to consider them professionally. It is another matter when we ask whether the Law holds in the form (A) or (B) when we take P to be, or interpret the predicate-letter "F" as representing, a vague predicate; especially as it may be plausibly argued that every empirical predicate has some degree of vagueness. This sort of vagueness is one that logic cannot afford to ignore.

It may be objected at the outset that logic cannot deal with such vagueness either, without a radical change of character; for how can vague predicates have precise logical properties? But I see no more reason to hold that the logic of vague predicates must itself be vague, than that who drives fat oxen must himself be fat. Logic, in Wittgenstein's phrase, must not be bargained out of any of her rigour; and a valuable remark of his in an unpublished work that I have been allowed to quote shows how we can certainly ascribe some precise logical properties to a vague predicate. To represent a vague predicate P, we draw two concentric boundary-lines, A and B; P will be definitely true of what lies inside the inner boundary, and the negation of P, of what lies outside the outer boundary. "There would be an indeterminate zone left over; the boundaries A and B are inessential to the concept defined. The boundaries A and B are as it were just the walls of the forecourt. They are drawn arbitrarily where it is still possible to draw a firm line.—It is like walling off a bog; the wall is not the boundary of the bog, it merely surrounds it while itself standing on firm ground. It shows that there is a bog inside, not that the bog is just as large as the walled-off area." The two boundaries would thus stand concentrically on the firm ground, the bog of vagueness lying wholly between them.

It might appear that second-order vagueness arises over the drawing of the boundaries; but this is not so. If x is even doubtfully inside the inner boundary, P will be true of it; if x is even doubtfully outside the outer boundary, the negation of P will be true of it. So Wittgenstein's diagrammatic representation shows that even a vague concept can have precise logical properties, not infected with any second-order vagueness. This conclusion really ought not to shock us. Even if "oak" and "elephant" are both vague predicates, it is perfectly clear and certain that no oak-tree is an elephant; something that has even a doubtful claim to the predicate "oak" is certainly no elephant.

I hold, then, that developing a logic of vague predicates is certainly a task for logicians, and not one that can be seen in advance to be an impossible one. But the task cannot be undertaken in this paper: and I am not prepared to anticipate whether the allowing of exceptions to the Law of Excluded Middle would here turn out to be useful.

3

Theory of Reference and Syntax

3.1. RYLE ON NAMELY-RIDERS

'I proceed. "Edwin and Morcar, the earls of Mercia and Northumbria, declared for him: and even Stigand, the patriotic archbishop of Canterbury, found it advisable—" '
'Found *what*?' said the Duck.
'Found *it*' the Mouse replied rather crossly: 'of course you know what "it" means.'
'I know what "it" means well enough, when *I* find a thing,' said the Duck: 'it's generally a frog or a worm. The question is, what did the archbishop find?'
Alice in Wonderland, c.ii.

I shall here critically examine the doctrine of reference put forward by Professor Ryle in his article 'Heterologicality'.[1] I shall try to show that this doctrine is inadequate, and that the alleged proof that we cannot rightly ask whether "heterological" itself is heterological is fallacious. I shall not in the least be concerned with Grelling's paradox itself, and my remarks have no bearing on its solution. "—is heterological" means "— (is an epithet that) lacks the property which it stands for"; my discussion will relate not to the terms "property" and "stands for", whose use would have to be examined if I were concerned with Grelling's paradox as such, but to the logical role of the pronoun "it".

---

[1] *Analysis* 11.3, 1951: reprinted in *Philosophy and Analysis*, Blackwell, 1954.

The crucial passage of Ryle's discussion[1] is the following one. (For the sake of clarity, I have taken the liberty of slightly altering the format of the passage.)

"If unpacked, the assertion that "heterological" is heterological would run:

"heterological" lacks the property for which it stands, namely, that of lacking the property for which it stands, namely, that of lacking. . . .

No property is ever mentioned, so the seeming reference to such a property is spurious."

The procedure of unpacking that Ryle employs goes on the principle that a 'referring expression' calls for a 'namely-rider'; and in applying the principle he assumes that the phrase "the property for which it stands", at both its occurrences in the unpacking, is a 'referring expression'. Now as regards the first line of Ryle's unpacking:

(1) "heterological" lacks the property for which it stands

the demand for a namely-rider seems natural and legitimate: namely, which property? For which property does "heterological " stand?

Let us, however, go more slowly. It may be conceded that in the proposition:

(2) "heterological" lacks the property for which "heterological" stands

the last six words are an expression that calls for a namely-rider. And the pronoun "it" in (1) may well seem to be merely, as we may say, a *pronoun of laziness*—a grammatical dodge to avoid inelegant repetition of words. If this were correct, the last six words of (1), no less than those of (2), would be an expression that called for namely-rider.

It is questionable, though, whether "it" in (1) is a mere pronoun of laziness. We may see this if we contrast this "it" with what is indubitably a mere pronoun of laziness: the pronoun "that", at both its occurrences in Ryle's unpacking, is a mere elegant variation, to avoid repeating the words "the property".

[1] P. 51, in the reprint of the article.

(For logical purposes, repetition is more perspicuous than elegant variation; so in the sequel I shall speak as though Ryle's unpacking had actually contained "the property" instead of these occurrences of "that"). But "it" in (1) is not mere elegant variation. For if we consider the predicates in (1) and (2), namely:

(3)— lacks the property for which it stands
and (4)— lacks the property for which "heterological" stands

respectively, it is clear that (3) and (4) are not at all the same. (Indeed, on the face of it, since (3) is an expansion of "is heterological", (3) is true of just those epithets of which (4) is *not* true; that is precisely what gives rise to Grelling's paradox.)

Two things may hinder us from seeing this point. First, it seems clear that (1) says the same as (2)—if either sentence can be successfully used to say anything. And if two propositions coincide in import, we may be tempted to infer that by removing their subject we get two predicates that coincide in import. But this is just a fallacy. "Smith shaves Smith" says the same as "Smith is shaved by Smith"; but the predicates "—shaves Smith" and "—is shaved by Smith" are quite distinct in their import.

Secondly, it may be thought that (3) is an ambiguous predicate, whose import varies according to which logical subject we supply as antecedent to "it"; in that case, (3) as occurring in (1) might after all coincide in import with (4). This impression can be removed if we consider a paraphrase of (3) from which the pronoun "it" has disappeared, e.g.:

(5)—(is an epithet that) at once (unambiguously) stands for and lacks some property or other.

It is most important to see that (3) is *not* ambiguous in the way just alleged. If (3) had such ambiguity, then we might indeed suppose that "the property for which it stands" occurs in (3) as a referring expression that calls for a namely-rider; it would refer to now one, now another, property, according to the antecedent we supplied for "it". But if (3) is not thus ambiguous, we cannot ascribe a shifting reference to this phrase; and we clearly cannot ascribe to the phrase a *constant* reference either, for then it would have to refer to the same property in all occurrences of (3), e.g. in:

(6) "German" lacks the property for which it stands,
and (7) "obscene" lacks the property for which it stands.

We must therefore deny that "the property for which it stands" when it occurs as part of the predicate (3) *ever* refers to a specifiable property; the demand for a namely-rider is quite illegitimate.

The reader may find this argument pedantic. I have admitted that the last six words of (2), as opposed to those of (1), are an expression that calls for a namely-rider; well, would not Ryle's argument go over just as well if (2) rather than (1) had been the first line in his unpacking of the assertion that "heterological" is heterological? Let us see. The unpacking would begin with:

(2) "heterological" lacks the property for which "heterological" stands,

and the namely-rider that would be supplied is:

(8) namely, the property of lacking the property for which it stands.

Now, whereas in a way "it" in (1) was replaceable by "heterological" in quotation marks, no such replacement is possible for "it" in (8). (8) is tantamount to:

(9) namely, the property of being an epithet lacking the property for which it stands

in which the antecedent of "it" is not a mention of "heterological" but is "an epithet". In regard to (9), the question "namely, which property? which property does it then stand for?" is as silly as the Duck's enquiry given above; of course, different (heterological) epithets stand for *different* properties, not for some one property. If "it" in (8) were replaceable by mention of "heterological", as "it" in (1) was, then indeed the old demand for a namely-rider would arise all over again, and we should get the regress that Ryle supposes. In fact the regress never gets started.

A further example ought to show how tricky the pronoun "it" is, and how unreliable is the notion of a referring expression that calls for a namely-rider. In the proposition

(10) The only man who ever stole a book from Snead made a lot of money by selling it

the first ten words certainly seem to call for a namely-rider; and there would be no obvious incongruity in supplying one, say "(namely Robinson)". But the first ten words of (10) can hardly be treated as a referring expression; for they cannot be replaced *salva veritate* by some other style of referring to the same man. From (10) and

(11) Robinson is the only man who ever stole a book from Snead

we certainly cannot infer

(12) Robinson made a lot of money by selling it.

For (12) is not as it stands an intelligible proposition at all. We cannot escape trouble by substituting for "it" in (10) and (12) the phrase "a book", which is the grammatical antecedent of "it" in (10). The inference from (11) and the modified (10) to the modified (12) would indeed then raise no trouble; but the modified (10) has quite a different force from (10) as it stands—"it" in (10) is not a pronoun of laziness.

The logic of pronouns with antecedents was extensively studied by medieval logicians in their chapters *de suppositione relativorum*; the term "*relativa*" covered *all* pronouns with antecedents, like "it" in this article, and not only *grammatically* relative pronouns. This medieval treatment of pronouns was inconclusive; and modern logicians have rather neglected the subject. The most important modern treatment is that of Quine, who has repeatedly pointed out the relation between pronouns of this sort and bound variables in logistic notation.[1] My aim in this note has been to show the need for a detailed and thorough discussion of *relativa*; and to deprecate the lazy assumption that such pronouns, or phrases containing them, can be disposed of by calling them "referring expressions" and asking what they refer to.

3.2.   NAMELY-RIDERS AGAIN

Father FitzPatrick's article[2] gives me a welcome opportunity to try and clear up certain points about pronouns, referring expressions, and namely-riders. I do not think I need discuss his argument about "heterological", in which he seeks to shew that Ryle was after all right in considering ' "heterological" is hetero-

---

[1] Cf. in particular the passages referred to s.v. "pronoun" and "cross-reference" in the index to his *Word and Object*.
[2] ' "Heterological" and Namely-riders', *Analysis* 22.1 (October 1961).

logical' to be a pseudo-proposition because an attempt to state its truth-conditions gets us into a vicious circle. I am not concerned to deny this conclusion; as I said in my original article,[1] I am not primarily concerned with the puzzle about "heterological" at all; what interested me was Ryle's alleged proof, which essentially appealed to the logical properties of certain 'referring expressions', and I questioned his right to apply this term to some of the expressions. Now the 'referring expressions' in question do not figure in FitzPatrick's proof, which is formulated with the aid of quantifiers; so, whether or not he has established Ryle's conclusions about "heterological", he has done nothing here to support Ryle's view of referring expressions.

It will be more profitable to discuss my other example. Here I was arguing that Ryle's concept of a referring expression is not by any means clear-cut, not even when it is congruous for an expression E to have a namely-rider added to it; E may demonstrably have no reference. For instance, it is quite intelligible to say:

(1) The only man who ever stole a book from Snead (namely Robinson) made a lot of money by selling it;

but if we drop the namely-rider and substitute "Robinson" for the phrase composed of the first ten words in (1), then what we get, namely

(2) Robinson made a lot of money by selling it

is no longer an intelligible proposition; so we cannot after all regard the ten-word phrase as just another way of referring to Robinson. The reason why (2) is no longer an intelligible proposition is, of course, that "it" has been deprived of the antecedent "a book" which it had in (1); and though we get an intelligible proposition if we replace "it" in (2) by "a book", this does not help, for to make the same substitution in (1) would completely alter the sense of (1).

FitzPatrick's reply to this argument is in effect that I have tacitly appealed to a principle, Leibniz's law about substituting designations *salva veritate*, which notoriously admits of exceptions. The point is well taken. But the usually recognized exceptions to Leibniz's law occur when we replace one designation of a thing

[1]Article 3.1 in this collection.

by another in direct or indirect quotations, in modal contexts, or with intentional verbs like "wants". No such troubles, on the face of it, arise over the predicative expression "—made a lot of money by selling it". Moreover, though (2) is not itself an intelligible proposition, it can easily be made into part of one if we supply "it" with an antecedent; and in such a proposition, e.g.

(3) Whenever he stole a book, Robinson made a lot of money selling it,

we may clearly substitute for "Robinson" any alias by which the police knew Robinson, without changing the truth-value. It thus seems a decidedly *ad hoc* manoeuvre to assume a breakdown of Leibniz' law in this context; we should rather conclude that the ten-word phrase in (1) is not, after all, a mere alternative designation of Robinson.

Finally, I should like to enunciate a principle about reference. The reference of an expression in a proposition must always be somehow specifiable independently of that proposition's truth-value. To put it another way: If a question has to be answered "yes" or "no", the reference of expressions in that question must be somehow specifiable independently of which is the right answer. (We can see that this *is* just another way of putting it, if we reflect that any proposition can be turned into such a question by inserting it in the blank of "Is it the case that . . . ?")

The following paralogism, a modified form of one constructed by Buridan, shows the necessity of the principle. 'Let us agree that in "Is A a donkey?", "A" shall stand for you if the right answer is "yes", and for Brownie, the donkey on the village green, if the right answer is " no". Then if the right answer is "yes", you are a donkey; if it is "no", Brownie is not a donkey. Therefore, either you are a donkey or Brownie is not a donkey. But Brownie *is* a donkey; *ergo*, you are a donkey'. Buridan says, as we might expect, that such a stipulation as to the reference of "A" is inadmissible; the reference of "A" must already be fixed somehow, independently of whether the proposition containing "A" that we are considering is true or false. And plainly Buridan is right; in logic as elsewhere, Russell's epigram holds good— not all wisdom is new, neither is all folly out of date.

Some of our contemporaries clearly have not grasped Buridan's principle; I strongly suspect FitzPatrick has not. For FitzPatrick says (p. 22) that (1) is "about a particular book"; so "Robinson sold a book that he stole from Snead" would presumably likewise be about a particular book. But if Robinson never did steal a book, this latter proposition would be false; and which particular book would it then be about?

Naturally, if the right answer to

(4) Is Robinson the only man who ever stole a book from Snead?

is "yes", then the reference of "Robinson" may be truly stated thus:

(5) "Robinson" stands for the only man who ever stole a book from Snead.

But (5) cannot possibly be the only way of specifying the reference of "Robinson" in (4); otherwise, an affirmative answer to (4) would be implied if we merely asked the question, and this is absurd.

3.3. WHAT ARE REFERRING EXPRESSIONS?

If in a given context a string of words has not a certain logical role, this does not mean that the string of words is never used in that role. For example there is absolutely no contradiction in speaking of the proposition "Jones has a car" and yet denying that this string of words has the role of a proposition in the context:

(1) Jones has a car and Jones's daughter drives it.

In fact, I think this denial is forced upon us, because (1) cannot be reached by any such procedure as interpreting "p" in a schema "p and Jones's daughter drives it"—this 'schema' is ill-formed. And it is quite clear that, although "There is a car that belongs to Jones" is a proposition, nevertheless in the context:

(2) There is a car that belongs to Jones and is driven by Jones's daughter

the same string of words has not the role of a proposition; for it is even more obvious that "p and is driven by Jones's daughter" is not a well-formed schema. Since a string of words capable of forming a proposition may or may not actually form one when embedded in a context, we need criteria for recognizing genuine occurrences of a proposition within propositions; such criteria are fairly well known.

Similarly, if a string of words is potentially a referring expression, it does not follow that the words actually play this part in a given context; and it is reasonable to ask for criteria. The referring role of an expression may be held to be modified or suspended in contexts involving modal words, intentional verbs, or quotation; where such complications do not occur, it ought on the face of it to hold good that any two expressions whose role is merely to refer to one and the same object are interchangeable *salva veritate*. I produced an example in which an ostensibly referring expression was not replaceable even *salva congruitate* by the proper name of the object ostensibly referred to, and this although there were none of the complications just mentioned; and I argued that in this example the ostensibly referring expression had not really any such role. It is no answer to imply that the referring role of the expression is obvious, and still less to protest that other examples would have revealed no discrepancy; discrepancies are just what logicians, like accountants, are paid to find out.

I am not all that much concerned to find a reliable test for referring expressions. The term "referring expression" is an Oxford philosophers' term of art which has never been properly explained, and perhaps never could have been. What various Oxford philosophers will call "referring expressions" are to all appearance a lot of logically heterogeneous expressions; it is not mere perversity to doubt whether there is some one recognizble role, referring, which all of them perform alike. If anyone wishes to use this term of art (as I *in propria persona* do not), then let him explain and justify his use. In particular, he should tell us whether he accepts or rejects the criterion of replaceability *salva veritate* (or even the weaker criterion of replaceability *salva congruitate*) by a proper name of the object supposedly referred to: does this state a necessary condition for an expression's genuinely occurring as a referring expression? If not, what is his criterion?

The proposition:

(3) The only man who ever stole a book from Snead made a lot of money by selling the book

raises just the same problems as my own example, which had "it" instead of "the book". The role of "the book" in (3) is not to point at a particular book in the environment, but to point back to the antecedent phrase "a book"; and this was precisely the role of "it" in my example. And if we substitute "Robinson" for the initial ten-word phrase, the result:

(4) Robinson made a lot of money by selling the book

is quite on all fours with my own example:

(5) Robinson made a lot of money by selling it.

In both (4) and (5) we have an expression, "the book" or "it", whose role is to look back to an antecedent, but which here is deprived of an antecedent. Like (5), (4) is not ill-formed, merely not a proposition; either could be made into part of a proposition by prefixing e.g. "Whenever he stole a book", so as to supply an antecedent; but no such part of a proposition is itself a proposition. For this reason, (4) and (5) are certainly not 'intelligible propositions'; that is to say, they cannot be understood as propositions —unless indeed "the book" or "it" is read as pointing to some known object instead of looking back to an antecedent, and of course such a shift in mode of significance cannot be made in an inference without equivocation. The sense in which (3) likewise may fail to be an 'intelligible proposition' is quite different and quite trivial; it is of no interest to logic that someone who heard (3) said, but did not know who Snead was, would fail to catch on.

3.4. REFERRING EXPRESSIONS AGAIN

In the present article I am going to consider the equivalence between the following propositions:

(1) The only man who ever stole a book from Snead made a lot of money by selling it

(2) The only man who ever stole a book from Snead made a lot of money by selling the book that he stole from Snead.

This equivalence between (1) and (2) turns out to throw light on various important points in the theory of reference.

One matter that arises is the definition of my term "pronoun of laziness". By my original definition, this term would apply only to a pronoun that goes proxy for a repetition of its grammatical antecedent. But I now think this definition was too narrow; I would extend the term to cover any pronoun used in lieu of a repetitious expression, even when that expression would not be just the same as the pronoun's own antecedent. In (1) the pronoun "it" is clearly not going proxy for a second occurrence of "a book", so it is not a pronoun of laziness by the original definition; but we might naturally take it to have merely the role of avoiding the repetitive phrase "the book that he stole from Snead" at the end of (2), and then it would be a pronoun of laziness by the wider definition.

We might well use instead of "pronoun of laziness" the linguists' term "anaphoric substitute". This term has the added advantages that "anaphoric substitute for" is handier than "pronoun of laziness going proxy for", and that besides pronouns it covers other expressions which are used to avoid repetitions. But linguists are blunting the edge of their own tool, because of their logical clumsiness; they use "anaphoric substitute" for pronouns whose logical role is not merely that of avoiding repetition. For example, a linguist will tell us that in

(3) John put on his hat and Jim did too

"did" is an anaphoric substitute for "put on his hat", and "his" for "John's ".[1] The first statement is all right, but the second is misleading; for the predicates "— put on his (own) hat" and "— put on John's hat" are quite different, even if they happen to be attached to "John" as subject; we can see this from the difference between (3) and

(4) John put on John's hat and Jim did too.

If "it" in (1) does just go proxy for "the book that he stole from Snead", then it looks as if (1) were not any sort of counterexample to a referring-expression theory of definite descriptions and pronouns. For since (as I once said) repetitiousness is logically more perspicuous than elegant variation, the logic of (1) would have to be elucidated by that of (2). Now surely in (2) the initial ten-word phrase is replaceable, *salva veritate*, by any designation of the book-thief, let us say by "Robinson"; and the

---

[1] See Charles E. Hockett, *A Course in Modern Linguistics* (The Macmillan Co., New York, 1962), pp. 253–4, who has an essentially similar example.

final seven-word phrase, by any designation of the book Robinson stole from Snead. So there appears no *prima facie* case for denying either phrase to be a referring expression; and "it" in (1) would have the same reference as the phrase in (2) for which it goes proxy.

We ought not, however, to be so easily convinced that "it" in (1) does just go proxy for the final seven-word phrase in (2); this does not follow from the equivalence of (1) and (2), and to think it does follow is to commit a fallacy. If *as wholes* the propositions UVW and UXY have the same content, it is not therefore licit to infer that V means the same as X and W means the same as Y, and it need not even be the case that U in UVW and U in UXY mean the same. For example, the proposition

(5) All cats are mortal

is equivalent to either of the following:

(6) All cats are a class included in all mortals

(7) All cats are the same class as some (class of) mortals.

Accordingly, someone might try to make out that in (5) "are" is a copula of class-inclusion, corresponding to "are a class included in" in (6), and that "mortal" means "all mortals"; someone else might maintain that in (5) "are" is a copula of identity, corresponding to "are the same class as" in (7), and that "mortal" means "some (class of) mortals". Of these attempts to make out bits of (5) equivalent to bits of (6) and (7), either is as plausible as the other; but both cannot be right, so both are wrong. Moreover, "All cats" is used collectively in (6) and (7), when it is tantamount to "The class of all cats", but distributively in (5), where "All cats are"="Each cat is".

I shall similarly maintain that, though (1) and (2) as wholes are equivalent, "it" at the end of (1) is not just short for the seven-word phrase at the end of (2); and even, that the ten-word phrases at the beginning of (1) and (2) have different logical roles. To see the actual roles in (1) of the ten-word phrase and the pronoun "it", consider the following parallel example:

(8) The woman whom every true Englishman most reveres is his mother.

The eight-word phrase at the beginning of (8) could in another context have the role of a definite description; but clearly it has no such role in (8) itself, since (8) does not imply that all true Englishmen have the same mother. Moreover, "his" in (8) is not going proxy for "every true Englishman's". We need to notice that what Russell calls the scope of "every true Englishman" runs right to the end of (8); (8) as a whole is a proposition to the effect that every true Englishman is . . . , as we may see from the paraphrase:

(9) It holds good as regards every true Englishman that the woman whom he most reveres is his mother

Similarly, in

(10) The man who stole a (certain) book from Snead made a lot of money by selling it

the scope of "a (certain) book" runs to the end; i.e. (10) is a proposition to the effect that a (certain) book is . . . , as we see from the paraphrase:

(11) As regards some book, the man of whom it holds good that this was a book he stole from Snead made a lot of money by selling it.

(11) as a paraphrase of (10) is strictly parallel to (9) as a paraphrase of (8); and the role of the dangling pronouns, "his" in (8) and "it" in (10), is elucidated by the way they work in (9) and (11).

We still have not an acceptable analysis of (1); for the use of "The *only* man who ever . . . " precludes our taking the initial ten-word phrase in (1) to mean the same as "The man who stole a (certain) book from Snead" in (10). All the same, the relation of the dangling pronoun "it" to its antecedent "a book" is pretty clearly the same in (1) as in (10). I think the right account of the initial ten-word phrase in (1) is that it neither simply means the same as "The only man who ever stole *any* book from Snead", as it does in (2), nor simply means what "The man who stole a (certain) book from Snead" means in (10), but rather corresponds in force to a combination of the two: "The man who stole a (certain) book from Snead, in fact the only man who ever stole any book from Snead". Accordingly, an adequate analysis for (1), on the same lines as (11) for (10), can be stated as follows:

(12) As regards some book, the man of whom it holds good that this was the book he stole from Snead *and that nobody else ever stole a book from Snead* made a lot of money by selling it.

Suppose for the sake of argument that I were quite wrong about this example, and that "it" in (1) were after all a mere substitute for "the book that he stole from Snead" in (2). Even then, the referring-expression account of that phrase would come to grief. For this phrase could have a determinate reference only if "he" within the phrase had one. Now let us consider the predicate occurring in (2):

(13)—made a lot of money by selling the book that he stole from Snead.

If "he" in this predicate has a fixed reference, then we can specify who is meant by "he" regardless of which subject the predicate is attached to; and this must be wrong, because in

(14) Robinson made a lot of money selling the book that he stole from Snead

"he" is replaceable *salva veritate* by "Robinson", whereas in:

(15) Wilkinson made a lot of money by selling the book that he stole from Snead

"he" is replaceable by "Wilkinson". But "he" in (13) is not just a pronoun of laziness, differently replaceable according to context; for (13) occurs as an *unequivocal* predicate in both (14) and (15), and also in:

(16) Nobody (ever) made a lot of money by selling the book that he stole from Snead

where no sensible replacement of "he" by a 'referring expression' could be suggested. It is surely clear from this that "he" in (13) just has not the job of referring to a specifiable person; neither, then, is it the job of "the book that he stole from Snead" in (13) to refer to a specifiable book.

I applaud Strawson's remark that "the logic of ordinary speech provides a field of intellectual study unsurpassed in richness, complexity, and the power to absorb".[1] But this field can be a

---

[1] *Introduction to Logical Theory*, p. 232.

H

profitable one only if it is strenuously worked over with adequate tools and techniques. I said before that I do not regard as in any way adequate a technique aimed at spotting 'referring expressions' and determining what they refer to.

3.5. ON COMPLEX TERMS

In the traditional logic an expression of the form "D that is P" (consisting of a common noun with a 'defining' relative clause attached) is a term in good standing and may be freely taken as the interpretation of a general-term letter in logical schemata. It is very easy, however, to find cases in which such expressions cannot be coherently construed as complex terms, and to show that our first intuitive judgments about the matter are quite unreliable.

Let us first consider the following pair of inferences:

(A) (1) Any thing that counts as the personal property of a tribesman is suitable to offer to a guest by way of hospitality.
(2) One thing that counts as the personal property of a tribesman is that tribesman's wife.
(3) So she is suitable to offer to a guest by way of hospitality.

(B) (4) Any woman whom every tribesman admires is beautiful by European standards.
(5) One woman whom every tribesman admires is that tribesman's wife.
(6) So she is beautiful by European standards.

Argument (A) is plainly a valid inference. There are indeed logical problems about (A): as to the role of "that tribesman's wife" in one premise, and as to the way that "she" in the conclusion attaches to this antecedent in the premises. These problems are interesting but not of present concern; for in these respects there is no difference between (A) and (B). What we have to consider is why (A) should be valid and (B) invalid. If in both (A) and (B) the general-term-plus-relative-clause were a genuine and unambiguous term, then there could be no logical difference between (A) and (B) to account for only one's being valid.

The easy way out is to say that in (B) "woman whom every

tribesman admires" is in fact ambiguous, and has a different force in the two premises. If people are required to say what this different force is, they come out (as I have found by actual questioning) with something like this: 'In (4) "every tribesman" means "all the tribesmen", but in (5) it means "each tribesman".' (Or perhaps, if they want to display knowledge of logical terminology: 'In (4) "every tribesman" is taken collectively, and in (5) distributively.') This attempt to make out an ambiguity is a complete failure: for in fact we could replace "every tribesman" by "each tribesman" both in (4) and in (5) without altering the force of these premises. Moreover, it would much more easily be argued that the expression "thing that counts as the personal property of a tribesman" occurs ambiguously in (1) and (2); for we could replace "a tribesman" by "some tribesman" without altering the force of (1), but this substitution is not possible in (2); so if an 'ambiguous middle term' were what made (B) invalid, (A) would equally be invalid.

In the cases that we have been considering, the context in which a *"D* that is *P"* phrase occurred contained a pronoun— the pronoun "that" of "that tribesman's"—whose antecedent was not the general term *"D"*, but was buried inside the relative clause attached to *"D"*. If in (A) and (B) alike we replace "that tribesman's wife" by "the girl Olalla", the pair of arguments we get are quite on all fours with each other and both plainly valid; so the backward-looking pronoun "that" may after all seem to be the source of our difficulty. These dangling pronouns, as Quine calls them, create difficulties in other examples as well, such as the following:

(7) Any person who borrowed a book from Snead eventually returned it.

(8) Some person who borrowed a book from Snead never returned it.

(9) The man who had an elder brother before anyone else had was murdered by him.

In each of these propositions, the predicative expression attached to the complex term is not as it stands a well-formed one-place predicable.

A solution that readily suggests itself is to regard the dangling pronouns as being, in my jargon, pronouns of laziness—devices to avoid repetitious language. Surely "it" in (7) is short for "any book that he borrowed from Snead"; "it" in (8), for "some book that he borrowed from Snead"; and "him" in (9), for "his own elder brother". In that case, (7), (8), and (9) might respectively be read as instances of the schemata "Any A is Q", "Some A is Q", "The A is Q", "A" being read each time as a complex general term; for we shall get each time an acceptable predicative expression as the reading for "—is Q", e.g., the predicable "—was murdered by his own elder brother".

I think this solution raises difficulties of its own, but for the present I waive these; for it is easy to find similar examples where no solution on these lines is possible, or at any rate none readily suggests itself. Consider the proposition:

(10) Almost every person who borrowed a book from Snead eventually returned it.

The difficulty that interests me has nothing to do with any uncertainty as to what proportion there has to be to justify us in saying "almost every"; for we can remove this by stipulating that the form "Almost every A is Q" is to mean (what in any case is its minimum meaning) "More As are Q than are not". Given this understanding of "almost every", our question is: if we read "A" in "Almost every A is Q" as "person who borrowed a book from Snead", can we find a reading of "—is Q" as a one-place predicable that will yield the sense of (10)? The problem becomes even worse when we have more than one dangling pronoun, as in:

(11) Almost every person who borrows a book from a friend eventually returns it to him.

I have argued elsewhere[1] that the apparent unity of a complex term "D that is P" is delusive; that such a phrase has no more logical unity than, say, "Plato was tall" has in the context "The philosopher whose most famous pupil was Plato was tall"; that the logical structure of sentences containing such phrases becomes clear only when the phrases are analyzed away. If this view were accepted, neither argument (A) nor argument (B) above would contain a complex general term, ambiguous or unambiguous, as its middle term; the difference of (A) and (B) as regards validity

[1] In my book *Reference and Generality* (Ithaca, N.Y.: Cornell Univ. Press, 1962), pp. 115–123, 148–149.

would be due to differences in logical structure that came out only when the "*D* that is *P*" expressions were removed by paraphrase.

It may already have occurred to some readers that the puzzle about (B) could be resolved by considering the different scope of "every tribesman" in (4) and (5). In (4), the scope is only the clause "whom every tribesman admires"; in (5), it is the whole proposition (that is to say, the whole proposition is one to the effect that every tribesman . . .). But this explanation does not conflict with mine; for if you say that the scope of "every tribesman" is not confined to the clause "whom every tribesman admires", then you are in effect saying that upon logical analysis the unity of the phrase "woman whom every tribesman admires" breaks up.

We might, however, suppose that when the scope of "every tribesman" in "woman whom every tribesman admires" *is* confined to the relative clause, as it is in (4), the phrase is a genuine logical unit, a legitimate reading of a general-term letter in a logical schema. And then we might attempt the following explanation of why (A) is valid and (B) is not: 'In (A), a "*D* that is *P*" phrase occurs twice over as a genuine logical unit, and thus serves as a middle term; in (B), there is only one genuine occurrence of such a phrase as a complex term.' But (A) and (B) cannot be distinguished like this. For the scope of "a tribesman" in (2), like that of "every tribesman" in (5), is the whole proposition; (2) says as regards a tribesman (i.e., *any* tribesman) that one thing that counts as his personal property is his wife, just as (5) predicates of every tribesman that one woman whom he admires is his wife. So if the long scope of "every tribesman" in (5) means that the "*D* that is *P*" phrase containing these words is not a genuine logical unit, then the long scope of "a tribesman" in (2) gives us the same result about the "*D* that is *P*" phrase there. Once again, intuitive first impressions as to when such phrases are logical units turn out to be quite unreliable; this thought may remove some of the initial prejudice against my view that such phrases never are genuine logical units.

I admit my view of complex terms is paradoxical; and nothing I have said here goes to show that nevertheless it is true. But I end by quoting and making my own some words of Russell's, written in defence of his own similar view that 'denoting phrases' cannot be understood by themselves as logical units, but only via radical paraphrase of the propositions in which they occur. "I will only beg the reader not to make up his mind against the view —as he might be tempted to do, on account of its apparently excessive complication—until he has attempted to construct a theory of his own on the subject. . . . This attempt, I believe, will convince him that, whatever the true theory may be, it cannot have such a simplicity as might have been expected beforehand".[1]

3.6.　COMPLEX TERMS AGAIN

My views on the eliminability of complex terms[2] have encountered some criticism, published and unpublished. Critics have argued that it is possible to devise a symbolic language with structures in it corresponding to the complex terms of the vernacular, and have even sketched for me new symbolisms that effect this. There is of course no need to invent symbolism in order to make the point; quite familar symbolic representations already exist for complex terms of the forms "the A that is P" and "the class of As that are P". I myself argued[3] that the *renvoi* of pronoun to antecedent in such complex terms has a close symbolic parallel —the binding of a variable to an operator. The same thing holds for the complex terms of functional abstraction: compare "λx $(2x^2+1)$" with "this function of *a number*: twice *its* square plus one".

What I maintained about complex terms was not that they cannot be introduced, but that they can always be eliminated. In the vernacular, the relative pronoun that seems to bind a complex term together can always be dispensed with; some other pronoun, accompanied by one or another connective, can always take its place, and then the unity of the complex term dissolves like a mirage. For certain examples, such as I gave in my article, the dissolution of the complex term is very obviously called for; in discussing these, Mr. Bacon[4] is obliged to admit that part of the

---

[1] 'On Denoting'; reprinted in *Logic and Knowledge* (ed. R. C. Marsh; Allen and Unwin, 1956).

[2] See my book *Reference and Generality* (Ithaca: Cornell Univ. Press, 1964), pp. 115–122; and my article 'On Complex Terms', 3.5 in this collection.

[3] *Reference and Generality*, p. 111.

[4] 'A Simple Treatment of Complex Terms', *Journal of Philosophy*, 62, 12 (June 10, 1965): 330.

complex term is 'dissected out' under logical analysis. Here is yet one more example:

(1) Only a woman who has lost all sense of shame will get drunk.

A person who asserts (1) is by no means implying that a man, as opposed to a woman, will not get drunk; so we cannot regard (1) as obtainable by reading "*B*" in "Only a *B* will get drunk" as the complex term "woman who has lost all sense of shame". Plainly the right way to construe (1) is this:

(2) A(ny) woman will get drunk only if she has lost all sense of shame.

The "Only . . . who . . ." of (1) can be replaced by a connective and a pronoun, "only if she"; and the apparent unity of the complex term has vanished.

Correspondingly, I require that complex terms in a symbolic language should be definitionally eliminable; the variables that are bound to operators in the terms will come to be bound to quantifiers, and only quantifiers and connectives will appear in the final result. This requirement is met by well-known systems, e.g., Quine's *ML*. Moreover, in formulas of *ML* complex terms are differently eliminated according to their immediate context; the complex term corresponding to "the class of *Ps*" will be differently eliminated according as it flanks an identity sign, precedes the epsilon of class membership, or follows the epsilon.[1] For the sort of context last mentioned, Quine gives an eliminative definition that may be paraphrased in the vernacular as follows: "*y* belongs to the class of *Ps*" becomes "For some class *x*, *y* belongs to *x*, and if anything belongs to *x* it is *P*". Of course this quite destroys the unity of the term answering to "the class of *Ps*".

If somebody wishes to construct a formalized language that will refute my view of complex terms, it will not be sufficient for the language to contain structures analogous to ordinary-language complex terms, nor even for the language to lack the *ML* sort of eliminative definitions; he must also ensure that no such procedures of elimination can consistently be added to the language

[1] *Mathematical Logic* (Cambridge, Mass.: Harvard Univ. Press, 1951), pp. 133, 136, 140. Cf. *Reference and Generality*, pp. 118, 120 f.

as rules of inference. Nobody has come near meeting this condition.

3.7. LOGICAL PROCEDURES AND THE IDENTITY OF EXPRESSIONS

I shall here try once more to say what I mean by "logical procedures", and by the term "order of occurrence" as applied to such procedures. In using these terms I of course did not mean processes occurring in some temporal order in the mind or brain. Nor yet did I mean the sort of transformations studied by linguists like Chomsky. I feel confident—and others who have studied both Chomsky's work and mine are of the same opinion—that there is much mutual relevance between the two lines of research. But Chomsky and I are, so to say, tunnelling from opposite sides of the hill. I have good hopes that our tunnels will meet in the middle; for the present I shall go on digging my own tunnel.

A logical procedure is best regarded as a sort of function: its values will be expressions of some definite category, and its arguments too will belong to some definite category or categories (according as it is a one-place or a many-place function). Thus, negation is a logical procedure: propositional negation takes propositions as its arguments and values, predicative negation takes predicables as its arguments and values. Supplying the name "Peter" as a logical subject is a logical procedure: this is a function that takes a one-place predicable as its argument and yields a proposition as its value. And so on.

This already shows how the order of logical procedures is to be defined. "P is applied before Q in getting the expression E' from the expression E" means: "There is an expression E'' that is the value of P for argument E, and E' is the value of Q for E'' as argument". Thus, I say that in "All philosophers are not perceptive" the operation of supplying a one-place predicable with the quasi-subject "all philosophers" precedes that of negation: this means that the proposition is to be read as the negation of "All philosophers are perceptive", which is itself first got as the result of supplying the quasi-subject "all philosophers" to the one-place predicable "— (is) perceptive". (I should maintain that supplying this quasi-subject is itself a matter of performing two logical procedures in succession: first, there is an operation generating the one-place predicable "all —s are perceptive" from the one-place predicable "— is perceptive;" secondly, "philosopher" is supplied as a subject to the predicable formed by the first procedure. But this disputable piece of analysis will not be required in the sequel.)

It is thus obviously quite out of place to consider which part of a proposition is first to get uttered or written down. In "All philosophers are not perceptive" "not" follows "all philosophers", in "Not all philosophers are perceptive" this order is reversed; but in either example negation is the final proposition-forming procedure, carried out upon a proposition which itself results from the logical procedure of inserting "all philosophers" as a quasi-subject. It is quite uninteresting for my inquiry whether in a given language there is a tendency for the subject or quasi-subject of predication to come early in the sentence. Anyhow, in very many examples there is no expression that can be logically picked out as *the* subject or quasi-subject; there is none in "Tom loves Mary", nor in "Some boy loves some girl". (There is of course one grammatical subject, but that again is logically uninteresting.) This does not mean that subject-predicate analysis is inapplicable to these examples, only that there is no *one* such analysis: e.g. "Tom loves Mary" is both the result of supplying "Tom" as subject to "— loves Mary" and the result of supplying "Mary" as subject to "Tom loves —". (Cf. *Reference and Generality*, p. 28 f.)

It is no more puzzling that we may get different propositions by applying the same logical procedures in a different order, than that twice (two plus four), i.e. twelve, is a different number from (twice two) plus four, i.e. eight; and in neither case is the difference a matter of the time-order in which things are thought or said or written down. General philosophical difficulties could indeed be raised about the idea of a function, but I shall not need to go into them here. In concrete examples, like the numerical one I have just given, it is clear enough what difference is made by applying functions in a different order; and our right to recognize such differences is not at all jeopardized by general philosophical puzzles about functions.

What I have not made clear is the criterion of identity for the expressions that are arguments and values of the functions that I call "logical procedures"; it is a lot harder to supply such a criterion, for a natural language, than it is to identify numbers. An expression, as I am using the term, is not to be identified by saying which words come in which order. For one thing, trivial differences of word order are to be ignored: "All philosophers are not perceptive" and "Not all philosophers are perceptive" are alike to count as the negation of "All philosophers are perceptive"; similarly, "Wenn die Erde rund ist, so ist die Erde rund" counts as the result of substituting "Die Erde ist rund" for "p" in "Wenn p, so p". More important, an expression may fail to occur at all, even though the right words occur in the right order. Even superficial school grammar would not count the sentence "Plato was bald" as occurring in the sentence:

(1) The philosopher whose most eminent pupil was Plato was bald.

And if (1) were translated into an inflected language, we might get a nominative-case form of Plato's name immediately preceding the rendering of "was bald", but not in the least counting as the grammatical subject of this predicate. We thus need anyhow to distinguish between genuine and spurious occurrences of expressions in sentences; sometimes the distinction is hard to draw.

Consider this example:

(2) A Cambridge philosopher smoked a pipe and drank a lot of whisky.

This contains an apparent occurrence of the proposition:

(3) A Cambridge philosopher smoked a pipe.

And clearly the connection between (2) and (3) is not a mere play upon words, like that between (1) and "Plato was bald"; for (3) logically follows from (2). But we cannot take (3)'s following from (2) as an instance of the valid scheme "p and q; ergo, p". For how could we interpret "q" in this schema? Perhaps as "He drank a lot of whisky" or "That philosopher drank a lot of whisky". "This amounts to reading (3) as short for:

(4) A Cambridge philosopher smoked a pipe and he (or: that philosopher) drank a lot of whisky.

But now how can we treat the string of words following "and" in (4) as a proposition with a truth-value? We could do this only if "he" or "that philosopher" had a definite reference; and in this context the subject-term has no assignable reference.

This becomes exceedingly clear if we state a supposition about the relevant facts—a *casus*, as medieval logicians would say. Suppose that both X and Y were pipe-smoking Cambridge philosophers, and that Y drank no whisky at all, whereas X drank a lot. With this *casus*, (3) will be unambiguously true; so if we read (4) as a conjunctive proposition, it will have the same truth-value as its second conjunct, the true proposition (3) being its first conjunct. But this second conjunct will be true or false according as we fix upon X or Y as the reference of the subject-term. And so we might find ourselves trying to determine the truth-value of (4) by asking whom a man would have in mind when he uttered or wrote down the sentence (4); for (4) by itself does not show whether X or Y or a third philosopher was meant.

Such psychologizing is not really necessary. Given our *casus*, (4) is as unambiguously true as (3) is; there *was* a Cambridge philosopher, namely X, who both smoked a pipe and drank a lot of whisky. It does not matter one iota if the man who asserted (4) had Y in mind rather than X, or again had hopelessly muddled up the two men; what he *said* was true, even if not all his thoughts were true.

The position, then, is this: Given our *casus*, (4) is unambiguously true. But if we read (4) as a conjunctive proposition, and regarded the grammatical subject of the second conjunct as a "singular referring expression", then (4) would not be unambiguously true; it would be true if this subject-term referred to X, false if the term referred to Y. What we ought to conclude is that (4) cannot be read as a conjunctive proposition. So the clause following "and" is not a proposition, with "he" or "that philosopher" as its subject-term; this grammatical subject is not a logical subject, and it is a mere mistake to ask whom it refers to.

There is no logical objection to rephrasing (2) in the guise of (4); (2) and (4) differ only rhetorically. But neither (2) nor (4) is a conjunctive proposition, and the occurrence of (3) within them is a spurious one. There is, however, no puzzle as to how (3) is inferable from (2). For in (2) just as in (3), the predicable "— smoked a pipe" does genuinely occur; it occurs in (2) as one conjunct of the predicable "— smoked a pipe and drank a lot of whisky"; "and" here serves to form a predicable out of two predicables, not a proposition out of two propositions. And (3) logically follows from (2) simply because whatever such a conjunctively formed predicable applies to (say, a Cambridge philosopher) is something that each one of its conjuncts applies to.

The very term "predicable" testifies to the difficulties that arise over recognizing expressions of this category and eliminating spurious occurrences of them; for I devised that term just because predic*ables* have other ways of occurring in propositions than as predic*ates*. The predic*able* "— smoked a pipe" occurs both in (2) and in "Russell smoked a pipe"; but only in the second example do I call this expression a predic*ate*, for only here is a predication formed simply by attaching it to a subject. In (2), "— smoked a pipe" is not attached on its own account to a subject or quasi-subject, but occurs as part of a compound predicable. Here it is easy to recognize our predicable in its different occurrences; in other cases, recognition is more difficult.

The occurrence of the same words in the same order is neither a necessary nor a sufficient condition for the occurrence of one and the same predicable. It is not a necessary condition; for we may certainly recognize the same predicable as occurring in "Wolfe Tone cut Wolfe Tone's throat" and "Castlereagh cut Castlereagh's throat", or again in "5 is divisible just by 5 and 1" and "3 is divisible just by 3 and 1". Each of these pairs can of course be reformulated so that we get a common predicable consisting of the very same words each time, e.g. "— cut his own throat" and "—is divisible just by itself and 1". But this move will be licit only if there is already a recognizable common predicable; and that may be, and has been, disputed. Somebody has in fact argued as regards my second pair of examples that they do not contain a common predicable as they stand—that the one does not predicate of 3 just what the other predicates of 5—and that accordingly the derivative forms with "itself" do not contain a common predicable either, at least not one of the same category as 'ordinary' predicables like "— is odd".[1] If we reject the conclusion, we must also reject its premise; and this commits us to recognizing a common predicable where there is not an

---

[1] See *Analysis*, vol. 12 (1951–2), no. 4, pp. 77–84. This writer sought to explain the difficulties of prime-number theory by the 'extra-ordinary' character of the predicate "— is prime". The explanation was anyhow wrong: for, as Quine remarked, "prime" is definable without any use of reflexive pronouns, e.g. as "having just two divisors".

extractable string of words that form the predicable. The identity of predicables that do contain reflexive pronouns is itself not an identity of strings of words; for in English (though not e.g. in Polish) the reflexive pronoun is inflected so as to agree with its antecedent in gender, number, and person ("himself", "yourselves"), and logically this variation makes no difference to a predicable.

Neither is a common string of words sufficient for us to have occurrences of one and the same predicable. The predicable that occurs twice over in:

(5) Every man loves Smith and every man loves Brown

only has a spurious occurrence in:

(6) Every man loves himself.

For we can see that (6) could be true even if the predicable "every man loves —" did not apply to anybody at all—what this predicable may be true of is just irrelevant. Again, consider the following sentence:

(7) A hat in this Store will fit any head!

which we may imagine displayed in the hat department of a multiple store. This would naturally be so taken as to be true if and only if the predicable "a hat in this Store will fit—" (understood of the store in question) applied to any (adult male human being's) head. In that case, though there is a string or words occurring both in (7) and in:

(8) Tarnhelm will fit any head

there is no one-place predicable common to both. For whereas (8) is true just in case the predicable "— will fit any head" is true of the hat called "Tarnhelm", it is quite irrelevant to the truth-condition for (7)—if (7) is taken in its more likely meaning—what this predicable is true of, and even whether it is true of anything at all. The predicable would genuinely occur in (7) only if (7) were read as saying of some hat in the store that it would fit just any head; this is a less likely claim to be made and anyhow quite different from the one I have considered.

The string of words in (7) that must be regarded as only a spurious occurrence of a predicable would be parsed as the predicate in ordinary school grammar; and though of course "every man loves —" is not a grammatical predicate, (6) might be mistaken for an affirmative predication of this, since it might be given as an answer to the question "Whom does every man love?" The test I have been using to pick out spurious occurrences of predicables may be formulated thus: if a predicable seems to be affirmatively predicated in a proposition, but the question what the predicable applies to is in fact irrelevant to the truth-conditions of the proposition, then this occurrence of the predicable is spurious. This test is of course meant only for extensional contexts (contexts in which predicables applying to the same things are intersubstitutable *salva veritate*); and even for such cases it is insufficient. For not only does "some man hates —" appear to be affirmatively predicated in each of the following, since either might be an answer to "Whom does some man hate?":

(9) Some man hates himself
(10) Some man hates every man

but moreover both of these must be false if there is nobody that "some man hates —" is true of. Thus our test fails to show that the predicable "some man hates —" occurs only spuriously in (9) and (10); for it *is* relevant to their truth-conditions what this predicable applies to.

All the same, we *can* disqualify these apparent occurrences of "some man hates—", by constructing a *casus*, a logically possible set-up. Let us suppose the following propositions to hold good in our universe of discourse: (9), (10), and furthermore:

(11) Anyone whom some man hates, some man fears; and conversely.

(12) No man fears himself.

It follows from (12) that both of the following propositions are false:

(13) Some man fears himself.
(14) Some man fears every man.

On the other hand, the truth of (11) would make "some man fears —" and "some man hates —" intersubstitutable *salva veritate* in extensional contexts; and "some man fears —" has a genuine (and extensional) occurrence in (13) if and only if "some man hates —"

has a genuine (and extensional) occurrence in (9); (14) stands in just the same relation to (10). Thus (13) and (14) appear to be inferable from (9) and (10) respectively; so our *casus* would give us a false conclusion following from true premises—unless we say, as we must, that there are only apparent \ occurrences of "some man hates —" in (9) and (10), and of "some man fears —" in (13) and (14). The strings of words occur, but not the predicables.

There is much more to be said about the identification of predicables, propositions, and expressions of other categories. (As regards predicables, the *dictum de omni* principle is a powerful tool for weeding out spurious occurrences; see *Reference and Generality*, pp. 83–94, 135–6). At any rate I can claim to have brought out some of the problems and taken some steps towards a solution.[1]

3.8. QUINE'S SYNTACTICAL INSIGHTS

Jokes about "no man" as a name are now some three millennia old; an understanding of the syntactical difference between such a phrase and a name is both much more recent and much less available. To take "no man" as naming, or even referring to, *some* man appears patently contradictory; but many beginners in logic take "no man" as referring to non-men (each of whom, admittedly, is *no man*), or again to a null class of men; and the second mistake has been known to appear in textbooks too. On either view "no man" would be something like a name, only not a name of a man. And what about "some man"? Certainly this is not some man's name (to christen a child "Some Man" would merely create homonymy); but it causes us no shock (many of us) if we read that at least in some of its uses this phrase *refers* to some man. I shall not pursue this question through the copious recent literature. Propositions about *referring to* are there framed in a material too malleable and ductile to bear any argumentative strain.

If we turn from recent 'philosophical logic' to recent grammar, things are not much better. The sophistications of a

---

[1] In this article I try to throw more light on some of the matters Mr. L. J. Cohen has raised in his review of my work *Reference and Generality* (*Ratio* VII/1); he kindly let me see this review before its publication.

computer age overlie ideas that might come straight out of Dionysius of Thrace and Priscian; indeed, Chomsky has expressly said that "by and large the traditional views are basically correct, so far as they go". Proper names and phrases like "some man" are alike called Noun Phrases—whatever virtue there may be in the capitals—and are regarded as belonging to the same substitution class.

Let us fasten upon this notion. It is quite true that we may substitute a phrase like "some man" for a proper name in a sentence and still have a syntactically coherent string of words; as a medieval logician would say, the substitution goes through *salva congruitate*. But Quine has emphasized that all the same the substitution makes a syntactical difference. Genuine names give us no headaches about *scope*. For example, the sentence:

(1) Copernicus was a perfect fool if and only if the Earth is flat

may be read as the result of first attaching the predicable "—was a perfect fool" to "Copernicus" as subject, and then joining the sentence so formed to the sentence "The Earth is flat" with the connective "if and only if"; but it may equally well be read as the result simply of attaching to the subject "Copernicus" the complex predicable:

(2) — was a perfect fool if and only if the Earth is flat

In this sort of case we have, not a syntactically ambiguous string of words, but simply a single syntactical structure that can be analysed in two different ways; and without such possibility of multiple analysis, logic would, as Frege said, be hopelessly crippled.

If we substitute "some astronomer" for "Copernicus", the case is quite altered: we now have a syntactically ambiguous string of words, which is really (like, say, "Drinking chocolate is nice") not one sentence but two. The difference may be brought out by bracketing, thus:

(3) (Some astronomer was a perfect fool) if and only if (the Earth is flat)

(4) Some astronomer (was a perfect fool if and only if the Earth is flat).

To see what the difference amounts to: the string "if and only if the Earth is flat" may as a whole be regarded as an operator like negation. Indeed, since the Earth is not flat, this operator is materially equivalent to negation, in extensional contexts like the ones we have here. (3) and (4) thus correspond respectively to "It is not so that some astronomer was a perfect fool" and to "Some astronomer was not a perfect fool", between which pair there is a clear logical difference.

This, then, is the *first* of Quine's syntactical insights that I want to bring out: the difference between genuine proper names, which give us no scope trouble, and these phrases, which do give it (cf. *Methods of Logic*, p. 83 ff.). Quine himself rather blurs the difference elsewhere by regarding proper names as abbreviated definite descriptions; for, taught by Russell, we know that definite descriptions give rise to scope trouble that has to be removed by some convention, and the same must be true of any word that is short for a definite description. I do not wish to go into this view of proper names; I shall simply say that I think Quine's first account of proper names, as essentially scopeless, is correct, and I deplore its supersession in later sections of *Methods of Logic*.

It will be handy to have in the sequel a term for expressions like "some astronomer", "each man", etc., formed from a substantival general term *plus* an applicative in W. E. Johnson's sense—a word like "some", "any", "each", "just one", "almost every", etc. I shall speak of *applicatival* phrases. The 'referring phrases' of my *Reference and Generality* are a certain sub-class of applicatival phrases. (As I said in introducing this term, the epithet "referring" was meant to describe the role of such phrases according to the theories I was examining, rather than according to my own view of the matter.)

Applicatival phrases are not the only sort of expression for whose syntax a consideration of scope is necessary. For example, the string "young and foolish or wicked" may be read in two ways as a complex adjective formed out of adjectives; the difference is of course a matter of the scopes of the binary operators "and" and "or"; this is shown by bracketing— "(young and foolish) or wicked", "young and (foolish or wicked)". Such ambiguities supply many tedious examples in medieval collections of *sophismata*; the ambiguity gets explained clearly enough, but one misses a bracketing notation that would make the explanations

I

superfluous. Quine remarks that there actually exist in ordinary language ways of showing unambiguously the scope of conjunction: "either both young and foolish or wicked" vs. "both young and either foolish or wicked". To use an old bit of jargon, these are cases of tmesis; each of "both . . . and . . ." and "either . . . or . . ." is a logically indivisible binary operator, one piece being put before the first argument and the other between the two arguments.

Applicatival phrases are similar in syntax to quantifiers in ordinary quantification theory; indeed, some of them may be directly rendered by quantifiers, if we are willing to complicate our logic with restricted quantification (somewhat in the style of the notation Quine sketches out in *Mathematical Logic*, p. 67). This brings me to Quine's *second* syntactical insight: the pronouns whose antecedents are applicatival phrases correspond *strictly* in their syntax to variables bound by quantifiers.

The light this throws on the syntax of language will be seen more and more clearly by anyone who works out examples. For lack of this light, the medievals who discussed *relativa*—pronouns with antecedents—were groping in the dark despite all their ingenuity. Let us consider how such puzzles as theirs arise.

(5) Socrates owned a dog, and it bit Socrates

A medieval would treat this as a conjunctive proposition, and enquire after the reference (*suppositio*) of the pronoun "it"; I have seen modern discussions that made the same mistake. For mistake it is. If we may legitimately symbolize (5) as "$p \wedge q$", then a contradictory of (5), correspondingly symbolizable as "$\neg p \vee (p \wedge \neg q)$", would be:

(6) Socrates did not own a dog, or else: Socrates owned a dog, and it did not bite Socrates.

But (5) and (6) are not contradictories; a moment's thought shows they could both be true. So "$p \wedge q$" is an inept schema to represent (5).

Contrary to what has been suggested (even in print) for similar cases, it makes not a farthing's difference if in (5) and (6) we substitute "the dog" or "that dog" for "it". Any one of these three expressions, in *some* contexts of utterance, could serve as subject of the predicable "bit Socrates", so as to yield a proposition with a truth-value; but here, not one of them could. For no definite dog is before the reader's eyes, or is brought by the sentence before his mind's eye, to supply a reference for this subject-term. And "the" and "that" must be parsed, like "it", not as demonstratives but as *relativa*, looking back to "a dog".

The right solution is to take "a dog" (="some dog") as the main operator of (5); (5) is the result of replacing the schematic letter "*F*" in "*F* (a dog)" by this actual predicable:

(7) Socrates owned —, and — bit Socrates

where both blanks are to be filled the same way if a logical subject is supplied. Compare what we get using restricted quantification:

(8) (Ex) dog ((Socrates owned x) $\wedge$ (x bit Socrates))

In (8) the unfortunate appearance of there being a proposition "Socrates owned a dog" as one conjunct has quite disappeared; if we slice (8) before the "$\wedge$", the result is ill-formed, having an unpaired parenthesis:

(9) (Ex) dog ((Socrates owned x)

whereas "Socrates owned a dog" answers to "(Ex) dog (Socrates owned x)".

In logical symbolisms of the ordinary sort, quantifiers are not the only variable-binding operators: there are also operators that form designations, and as regards these also we may follow Quine in noticing the parallelism between the binding of variables by operators and the pronoun-antecedent relation. For example, this symbolism for a function:

(10) $\lambda x(2x^2 + 3x^3)$

may fairly be rendered in the vernacular:

(11) this function of a number: twice its square *plus* thrice its cube

And here the binding of "x" in "x^2" and "x^3" to the operator "λx" is reflected by the relation of "its" in "its square" and "its cube" to "a number". If we use a more explicit notation for (10):

(12) $\hat{y}\hat{x}(y = 2x^2 + 3x^3)$

and compare this with the vernacular:

(13) that function of a number which is equal to twice its square *plus* thrice its cube

then as before, the binding of "x" (here, to "$\hat{x}$") is reflected by the relation of "its" to "a number", and the binding of "y" to "$\hat{y}$" is reflected by the relation of the pronoun "which" to "that function".

As regards logical symbolism, Quine has followed Russell in emphasizing a *third* syntactical insight: that all such complex designations are eliminable by definition. This is the sort of definition that Russell called definition in use: the complex designation is not itself replaced by another string of symbols of which it is an abbreviation, but we show how to replace strings of which that designation is part, and this *definiens* does not contain a syntactically coherent part representing the designation. For example, in *Mathematical Logic* notation:

(14) $w\epsilon\hat{x}(x=y)$

is defined to mean:

(15) $(\exists z)\, (w\epsilon z.\, (x)\, (x\epsilon z.\, \supset.x=y))$

where "z" is the earliest term, *not* occurring in the *definiendum*, from the infinite alphabet of variables. Clearly we cannot pick out from (15) a syntactically coherent sub-string corresponding to "$\hat{x}(x=y)$". And the elimination of a complex term will be differently carried out according to its context—e.g. according as the term follows the epsilon of class-membership or precedes it. The final result of eliminating such complex terms will be formulas in which the only variable-binding operators are quantifiers, and the only other operators are sentence connectives.

When he comes to consider the vernacular, however, Quine has not scrutinized with due scepticism the traditional view that a phrase of the form "*A* that is *P*", with or without a definite article prefixed, is a syntactically coherent complex term; on the contrary, he seems to accept this view. The only disturbance of ordinary English that he considers here is the "such that" device: e.g. changing "man who killed his own brother" into "man such that he killed his own brother". The point of this analysis is to divide up the two roles played by an ordinary relative pronoun: it both serves to introduce a relative clause and looks back to an antecedent. In the analysed form, the first role is played by "such that", the second by "he". But failing a clear account of "such that" itself, we are not much better off than Russell was when in *Principles of Mathematics* he declared this concept to be *sui generis*. Quine himself describes as 'peculiar' the use of pronouns in "such that" clauses (sc. pronouns with antecedents *outside* these clauses); as in the example:

(16) I am driving a car such that I bought it from you.

(Cf. *Word and Object*, p. 114.) But I cannot see this use of "it" is any more peculiar, or indeed any other, than the use of "it" in the example:

(17) I am driving a car and I bought it from you

In quantifier notation we cannot even represent (16) and (17) differently. It suggests itself that the real role of "such that" is to be a *pro-connective*, going proxy for various other connectives[1] (here, for "and").

In any case, it is very easy to find examples in which the traditional view of "*A* that is *P*" or "*A* such that is it *P*" as a syntactically coherent noun phrase completely breaks down. One such example is the following:

(18) A boy who was only fooling her kissed a girl who really loved him.[2]

On the noun phrase view, (18) would be a substitution instance of "A *B* kissed a *C*", obtained by putting actual (complex) general terms in place of the schematic letters. But it is quite impossible to say which class of boys the replacement of "*B*" would have to cover, and which class of girls the replacement of "*C*" would have to cover, in order to bring out the intended sense of (18).

Again, consider the pair of sentences:

(19) The one woman whom every true Englishman honours above all other women is his mother

---

[1] I use the word "connective" rather than the usual grammatical term "conjunction", to avoid any risk of confusion with the logicians' use of "conjunction" for a particular kind of truth-functional complex.

[2] I adapt this example from a sentence devised by Susumu Kuno, itself cited in a mimeographed paper by James McCawley of the University of Chicago. I am in general much indebted to McCawley for the stimulation of this paper and of many discussions.

(20) The one woman whom every true Englishman honours above all other women is his Queen.

In (20) it is tempting to construe the string "woman whom every true Englishman honours above all other women" as a general term "A"; but we surely cannot do this in (19), or else (19) would imply that the one and only A is the mother of each true Englishman. The noun phrase theory cannot resolve the difficulty.

As it happens, traditional grammar itself contains an alternative account of defining relative clauses. Since this account is regularly taught in English schools to pupils learning Latin prose composition, I shall for short call it the *Latin prose* theory. By this theory, the relative pronoun of a defining clause is treated as a fusion of a connective with a bound pronoun: for example, in the Latin sentence:

(21) Rex legatos misit qui pacem peterent

the relative pronoun "qui" represents the words "in order that they" of the English translation:

(22) The king sent ambassadors in order that they might ask for peace

The subjunctive mood of "peterent" is then accounted for as required by the connective "ut", "in order that", that is here buried in the relative "qui". Such amalgamations of a pronoun with a connective frequently occur in Latin where there would be two separate words in English; learning when to effect them is one of the tricks you learn in order to get a good mark for your Latin prose.

What I call the Latin prose theory of relative clauses is the theory that in a defining relative clause we should regularly try to split up the relative pronoun into a connective and a bound pronoun—which connective it is will depend on the context. This theory can deal with almost all the puzzling cases I have been discussing, and very simply at that.

Let us start with the sentence:

(23) A boy kissed a girl, and she really loved him, but he was only fooling her.

Intuitively, this is a paraphrase of (18), and we can indeed show

how on the Latin prose theory it is actually transformable into (18). By amalgamating "and she" into "who", we get:

(24) A boy kissed a girl who really loved him, but he was only fooling her

Although the string of words "girl who really loved him" gives us a strong impression of syntactical coherence, we have already seen good reason why this impression may be illusory; and the words in (23) that get transformed into this string, namely "girl, and she really loved him", are clearly not a syntactically coherent expression of any category. (The pronoun "she" is indeed here bound to "girl", but that is not enough for the syntactical coherence of the whole string.) If we now wish to repeat the procedure, we have a choice: "but" may be amalgamated with "he" or with "her" in the clause following it. If we amalgamate "but . . . her" into "whom", we at once obtain the acceptable English sentence:

(25) A boy kissed a girl who really loved him, whom he was only fooling.

If on the other hand we amalgamate "but he" with "who", making no other alterations, we get:

(26) A boy kissed a girl who really loved him, who was only fooling her.

This is perhaps not impossible, but slightly deviant—simply because the second "who" is so far separated from its antecedent "a boy". By fitting the final relative clause snugly up against this antecedent, we get (18) over again.

Similarly with the example:

(27) The one woman whom every true Englishman honours above all other women is his mother (his Queen).

Passing over minor details, we can see that (27) is not just paraphrasable by, but actually derivable from, the following:

(28) Every true Englishman honours one woman above all other women, and that is his mother (his Queen).

Here again, though the transformation is not quite so simple, we see that "whom" of the derived sentence corresponds to a pronoun plus connective, "and that", in the underlying sentence; and the pronoun "that" is a bound pronoun—bound, as "whom" was, to the antecedent "one woman". The striking difference between (19) and (20) now turns out to have nothing to do, after all, with the syntax of the relative clause; it is simply a matter of the scope of applicatival phrases. (28) read with "his mother" at the end, which corresponds to (19), is "F (every true Englishman)", where "F ( )" is proxy for:

(29) — honours one woman above all other women, and that is —'s mother.

On the other hand, (28) read with "his Queen" at the end, which corresponds to (20), is "G (one woman)", where "G( )" is proxy for:

(30) Every true Englishman honours — above all other women, and — is his Queen.

The Latin prose theory of defining relative clauses thus enables us to deal with cases that the noun phrase theory cannot manage at all. We must surely accept the Latin prose theory as covering part of the field and as giving the only tenable explanation for that part.

For some particular cases, the Latin prose theory certainly appears much less natural than its rival; but even here the two theories are in competition. If we consider the sentences:

(31) Any man who drives a car dislikes the police
(32) Some man who drives a car dislikes the police

it may well seem most natural to apply the noun phrase theory and treat "man who drives a car" as a complex general term equivalent to "motorist". But even in a case like this we are not compelled to accept the noun phrase theory; the Latin prose theory gives the following as the underlying forms:

(33) Any man, *if he* drives a car, dislikes the police
(34) Some man drives a car *and* (*he*) dislikes the police

A correspondent has raised the objection that (31) is 'about' motorists only, whereas (33) is 'about' all men; and again, that (31) is 'confirmed' only by police-hating motorists, whereas (33) is 'confirmed' also by men who do not drive cars and of whom, therefore, it holds good (vacuously) that if they drive cars, they detest the police. But to my mind neither the theory of "about", nor yet the theory of confirmation, is in a satisfactory enough state for these objections to have any bite to them.

The one sort of case I know where the noun phrase theory seems to have the advantage over the Latin prose theory comes in a rather outlying field of logic: *pleonotetic* logic, as it might be called—the logic of majorities. Let us lay down for simplicity the convention that 'almost every' propositions shall be true if the predicate is true of a *bare plurality* of the things covered by the subject-term. (This is of the same order as the regular minimizing interpretation of "some".) Now consider:

(35) Almost every man who drives a car dislikes the police

The noun phrase theory gives the correct truth conditions for this: (35) is true just in case "Almost every motorist dislikes the police" is true. But clearly neither of the following is equivalent to (35):

(36) Almost every man, *if he* drives a car, dislikes the police
(37) Almost every man drives a car *and* (*he*) dislikes the police

It would take me too far into pleonotetic logic to deal with this objection; I think it can be dealt with. Meanwhile, I may remark that examples from pleonotetic logic pose nasty problems for any theory of relative clauses. There is no obvious paraphrase, or account of the syntax, e.g. for the sentence:

(38) Almost every man who borrows a book from a friend eventually returns it to him.

I know of no way to show which classes of book-borrowers (38) is comparing numerically; I do not know even whether (38) is syntactically coherent. There are surprises about syntactical coherence. The following sentence (I owe it to James McCawley) is syntactically incoherent:

(39) Tom and Bill respectively kicked and punched each other,

for by the usual rules for "respectively" it would yield the nonsense:

(40) Tom kicked each other and Bill punched each other.

But replacement of "each other" by "the other one of that pair", which might seem trivial, in fact restores syntactical coherence. Similarly, we cannot be sure that (38) is syntactically coherent because it becomes so if we delete "almost". With this I must leave the problem as an exercise to the reader.

The Latin prose theory of complex terms in the vernacular is an application to the vernacular of Quine's programme for eliminating the means of forming such terms from the primitive apparatus of symbolic logic. This programme was indeed originally Russell's; but Quine has shown how to avoid the inelegancies, and even mistakes, that spoiled Russell's own execution of the programme. I hope others will be encouraged to perfect the work for vernacular languages too.

A *fourth* syntactical insight of Quine's, by which I have several times been guided in this article without drawing attention to it, is the extremely useful notion of introducing a predicable as interpretation of a schematic letter. This notion is clearly explained and illustrated in *Methods of Logic* (p. 131 ff.) and I need not paint the lily. I add only that this notion is needed in explaining the syntax of quite simple sentences. Here is an example of medieval vintage:

(41) Any proposition or its contradictory is true.

Traditional grammar is impotent here. If we take "or" to join "any proposition" and "its contradictory"; or if, equivalently, we take "is true" to be 'understood' after "proposition" (to speak more modishly, if we take "is true" to be deleted by a transformation); then we make (41) tantamount to something beginning:

(42) Any proposition is true, or . . .

And this is clearly wrong; for a correct paraphrase of (40) need nowise contain as one disjunct the falsehood "Any proposition is true". If on the other hand we take "or" to join "proposition" and "its contradictory", then by accepting (41) as true we let ourselves in for this 'syllogism':

(43) Any proposition is a proposition or its contradictory
     Any proposition or its contradictory is true
Ergo: Any proposition is true.

The right account is very simple: (41) is got from "*F* (any proposition)" by taking "*F* ( )" to be:

(44) — or —'s contradictory is true.

That is, (41) is true just in case (44) is true *of* any and every proposition.

It is matter for regret that insights such as I have discussed are little esteemed by some linguists; that modern textbooks still repeat old nonsense, about sentences' splitting up exhaustively into clauses, and pronouns' going proxy for what would be repetitious language. (The latter view was already thoroughly refuted by medieval examples.) But the bad old traditional logic is already dead, though it won't lie down; and the bad old traditional grammar is surely doomed too. Here as elsewhere Quine has done much against the Kingdom of Darkness.

4

Intentionality

4.1. ON BELIEFS ABOUT ONESELF

If we are attempting a formal treatment of certain problems—
e.g. Moore's paradox about saying and disbelieving, or the
question what it is for one assertion to commit somebody to
another assertion—we may well find ourselves using the symbolism "x believes that Fx", or something essentially like this. Now
there are difficulties here; what are we to take as substitution-
instances of "x believes that Fx"? Can we, in the first place,
obtain substitution-instances of it by writing an actual predicate
for the "F" and a designation of a person for both occurrences of
"x"? This will hardly do. For, if the logic of "x believes that
Fx" is not to be intolerably complicated, we want the following
'Leibniz' law of identity to hold as a logical truth:

(A) If x is the same person as y, and x believes that Fx, then
y believes that Fy.

Now of course we can assert as a logical truth:

(B) If Philip's worst enemy is the same person as Philip, and
Philip's worst enemy believes that Philip's worst enemy is dead,
then Philip believes that Philip's worst enemy is dead.

But we certainly cannot assert as a logical truth what would,
on our present assumption, be a substitution-instance of (A):

(C) If Philip's worst enemy is the same person as Philip, and
Philip's worst enemy believes that Philip's worst enemy is dead,
then Philip believes that Philip is dead.

(C) is obtained from (B) by substituting "Philip" for "Philip's worst enemy" in the consequent; although the antecedent contains the conditional clause "Philip's worst enemy is the same person as Philip", this substitution is not warranted thereby, since it is made within *oratio obliqua*.

We could, however, maintain the logical truth of (A) by a different reading of "*x* believes that *Fx*", according to which a substitution-instance of "*x* believes that *Fx*" would be, not "Philip's worst enemy believes that Philip's worst enemy is dead" but rather "Philip's worst enemy believes that *he himself* is dead" —"he himself" being an *oratio obliqua* proxy for the first-person pronoun of *oratio recta*. For now a substitution-instance of (A) would be e.g.:

(D) If Philip's worst enemy is the same person as Philip, and Philip's worst enemy believes that he himself is clever, then Philip believes that he himself is clever.

And this is indeed logically true.

This solution requires that it should be legitimate to treat "—believes that he himself is clever" as a definite, univocal predicate, no matter what subject we attach it to. I have myself no objection to such predicates, containing what classical grammarians call an indirect reflexive pronoun; though those who think there is something fishy even about predicates containing direct reflexive pronouns, like "—is divisible only by itself and unity", will *a fortiori* suspect these. But if we say of a number of people that each of them believes that he himself is clever, what belief exactly are we attributing to all of them? Certainly they do not all believe the same proposition, as "proposition" is commonly understood by philosophers. I hope this note may provoke more discussion of this class of predicates.

4.2. A MEDIEVAL DISCUSSION OF INTENTIONALITY

In this paper I shall critically examine the way a fourteenth-century logician, Jean Buridan, dealt with certain puzzles about intentional verbs. The class of verbs I shall be considering will all be expressions that can be completed into propositions by adding two proper names; the class will include, not only ordinary transitive verbs, but also phrases of the verb-preposition type like "look for" or "shoot at", and furthermore constructions

like "hopes—will be a better man than his father" or "believes—
to be a scoundrel", which turn into propositions as soon as we
add mention of who hopes or believes this and about whom he
does so. In modern grammar, the term "a verbal" rather than
"a verb" is used for this wider class; following a suggestion of
Professor Bar-Hillel, I adopt this term.

In either or both of the proper-name places that go with such
a verbal, it is possible, without destroying the propositional
structure (*salva congruitate*, as medieval logicians say), to substitute
a phrase of some such form as "some *A*" or "every *A*" or "the
(one and only) *A*"; the letter "*A*" here represents a simple or
complex general term which is grammatically a noun or noun-
phrase. The peculiarity of certain verbals that presently concerns
us comes out when such a phrase formed from a general term
stands in object position, in a construction "*b* F'd an *A*" or the
like. One example in Buridan himself is "I owe you a horse".
Here one would quite naturally distinguish between owing a
particular horse—the handing over of that very horse would be
part of the bargain—and 'just' owing *a* horse. Whatever we are
to make of this distinction, it is clear that what the customer wants
is a real live horse; not a possible horse, or an indefinite horse
that is literally not all there. (Buridan does have some very
dubious passages in which he quantifies over *possibilia*, such as
possible horses and possible men; he has, for example, a doctrine
that when a general term "*A*" stands as subject to a modalized
predicate, it is 'ampliated' or stretched so that it relates to possible
*A*s as well as actual *A*s. On this view, to use an example formally
similar to Buridan's own, "Some man is necessarily damned"
would be exponible as "Some actual or possible man is necessarily
damned", which appears to draw the sting of the doctrine of
reprobation. Anyhow, when it's a question of owing a horse
Buridan will not bring in possible horses.)

It may well appear equally out of place to bring into the
picture such intentional entities as the senses of expressions; the
sense of the term "horse" is assuredly not something whose
possession would content a man when he is owed a horse. All
the same the sense, or as Buridan calls it the *ratio*, given us by an
object expression really is somehow involved when the verbal is
an intentional one; Buridan says the object expression *appellat
suam rationem*, where we may perhaps render the verb "*appellat*"

(perhaps the most obscurely and multifariously employed of all medieval semantic technicalities) by saying the expression 'calls up' or 'evokes' its own *ratio*. Buridan's main point is in any case clear: that the truth-value of a sentence whose verbal is an intentional one may be changed if we change the *ratio*, the sense, given in the object expression, even if this expression still relates to the same thing in the world. This point is clearly correct, as many of Buridan's examples show; thus, if a body is both white and sweet and I see it, I may truly say "I have discerned something white by my sense of sight", but not "I have discerned something sweet by my sense of sight".

Can't I, though, say I have discerned something sweet by my sense of sight, if the body I have discerned is in fact sweet? Well, it's better to say "There is something sweet that I have discerned by sight" if this is the case I have in mind. This means, according to Buridan, that the sweet thing is something which my sense of sight discerns under some *ratio* or other, not at all necessarily under the *ratio*: sweet—this *ratio* comes in only *sub disiunctione ad alias rationes*, as one possible alternative *ratio*.

Buridan here observes a tendency of Latin idiom, which comes out in much the same way in English: when a verbal is intentional, an object phrase is differently construed when it preceeds the main verb that is a part or the whole of this verbal, and when it follows that verb. In general, taking "to F" as representative of an intentional verbal, we shall distinguish between the forms "*b* F's an *A*" and "There is an *A* that *b* F's". The latter form if construed in the spirit of Buridan will mean "There is some actual *A* of which it holds that *b* F's it under some *ratio* or other"— possibly, though, under some other *ratio* than that of being an *A*. (In Buridan's Latin examples there are no words corresponding to "there is" and "that" in the form "There is an *A* that *b* F's"; this difference between English and Latin idiom is obviously trivial). Of course this distinction of word order is not *strictly* observed in ordinary English or Latin; we have to consider what is actually meant in the case under consideration. An instructive example, to which I shall presently return, is one I borrow with slight alteration from John Austin: "I saw a man born in Jerusalem" *versus* "I saw a man run over in Oxford". But we may very well decide for present purposes to stick to Buridan's convention of word order, as a way of marking the distinction he quite properly wishes to draw.

Buridan rightly regards the inference from "There is an A that b F'd" to "b F'd an A" as an invalid form; for if "There is an A that b F'd" is true, the general term represented by "A" need not give us the aspect of *ratio* under which such an A was the object of b's F'ing. Further, he assumes that from "b F'd an A" we may infer "There is something that b F'd". In fact, as we shall presently see, he assumes more than this; and even this much is doubtful. But we may use this assumption to show how Buridan's theory looks in terms of modern quantification theory. The intentional verbal represented by "to F" would answer, not to a two-termed relation between a person and an object of his F'ing, but to a three-termed relation between a person, an object of F'ing, a *ratio*; the forms "b F'd an A" and "There is an A that b F'd" would respectively come out as:

For some z, b F'd z under the *ratio*: A

For some z, and for some w, z is an A, and b F'd z under the *ratio* w.

It may be helpful to work out in this way the concrete example from John Austin that I mentioned just now. "I saw a man run over in Oxford" would come out as:

For some z, z is a man and I saw z in Oxford under the *ratio*: run over,

and "I saw a man born in Jerusalem" would come out as:

For some z, z is a man and z was born in Jerusalem and, for some w, I saw z under the *ratio* w.

Buridan's analysis, seen in this light, already raises one severe difficulty. The form with the term preceding the intentional verbal essentially involves quantifying over *rationes*. Now I am not at all impressed by rhetoric about mysterious entities, by questions in the peculiar (anti-) metaphysical tone of voice 'But what *are* they?'; it is all right to quantify over entities if you can supply a sharp criterion of identity for them. The paradigm of this is Frege's sharp criterion of identity for numbers. But for *rationes* we can get out of Buridan no hint of such a criterion. He gives us many examples of *rationes* he takes to be patently different, like the *ratio*: white and the *ratio*: sweet; but we have not even one example of the same *ratio* differently expressed, from which we might divine a criterion of identity. This lacuna makes Buridan's account schematic at best.

A more serious defect is Buridan's acceptance of the inference from "*b F'd an A*" to "There is an *A* that *b F'd*". Notice that this would still be unacceptable even if we let pass the inference to "There is something that *b F'd*"; for this does follow from:

For some z, *b F'd* z under the *ratio*: *A*

but there is still no obvious necessity that what is *F'd* under the *ratio*: *A* should in fact be an *A*. And in concrete examples Buridan's pattern of inference, from the form 'with the term after' to the form 'with the term before', often seems patently invalid. He himself chooses examples that look all right, e.g. from "I see something white" to "There is something white I see", or from "I recognize somebody coming" to "There is somebody coming whom I recognize". But of course we may not pass from "James is looking for a universal solvent" to "There is a universal solvent James is looking for"; we may not even pass from "Geach is looking for a detective story" to "There is a detective story Geach is looking for", because the premise is compatible with my not having been looking for 'a particular' detective story.

Even among the examples Buridan himself supplies, there are some that hardly favour his thesis. Suppose poor old Socrates is a competent astronomer immured in a dungeon where he cannot tell night from day. Then Buridan is willing to pass from the premise "Socrates knows some stars are above the horizon" to the conclusion "There are some stars Socrates knows are above the horizon". You naturally ask which stars Socrates knows are above the horizon; Buridan has a ready answer—the ones that are. To be sure, it is in a rather attenuated sense that the constellation Aries (say) is then known by Socrates to be above the horizon: namely, not in respect of the complex *ratio* expressed by "Aries is above the horizon", but only in respect of the one expressed by "Some stars are above the horizon". But at least Buridan can hardly be forced to pass from premises that would in this case be true to a conclusion that would in this case be false. Although in his view *one* true answer to the question "Which stars does Socrates know are above the horizon?" might be "There is the constellation Aries that Socrates knows is

K

above the horizon", he can on his own principles disallow the inference from this to "Socrates knows that the constellation Aries is above the horizon"; this shift of the term, *from* before the main-verb part of the verbal "knows that—is above the horizon" *to* after that verb, is just what Buridan disallows, as we saw. And Buridan's motive for wishing to pass to the conclusion "There are some stars that Socrates knows are above the horizon" is that even the abstract knowledge expressed in "Some stars are above the horizon" ought in his eyes to latch on to some actual, and therefore definitely specifiable, stars.

This example is rather a cheat, though, because Buridan is trading on a pecularity of the verb "to know". What you know is so; if Socrates knows some stars are above the horizon, then some stars are above the horizon, and we may ask which ones are. But suppose Socrates believes some lizards breathe fire—not being so good a zoologist as an astronomer. May we pass to the conclusion "There are some lizards that Socrates believes breathe fire"? and if so, which lizards are these? Certainly not the ones that do breathe fire, for Socrates' belief is false. Moreover, it may be impossible to find any principle for picking out, from among actual lizards, the ones Socrates believes to breathe fire. Buridan often resorts, when faced by such an embarrassing choice, to a parity-of-reasoning argument; what is true of some so-and-so, if there is no reason to think it is true of one so-and-so rather than another, must be true of each and every so-and-so. We should then have to pass on from "There are some lizards that Socrates believes breathe fire", to the further conclusion "As regards each lizard, Socrates believes that it breathes fire". From this, indeed, we could not on Buridan's principles infer "Socrates believes that each lizard breathes fire"; Socrates' belief would latch on to each and every lizard, but only *via* the complex *ratio* expressed by "Some lizards breathe fire". Still, in Buridan's own words, *videtur durum*, it seems tough to swallow.

I now come on to a similar puzzle of Buridan's own, in which his own principles raise severe difficulties. A horse dealer, he supposes, currently owns just three thoroughbreds, Brownie, Blackie, and Fallow. The customer accepts the dealer's promise "I will give you one of my thoroughbreds", but the dealer fails to deliver, and denies that he owes the purchaser anything. "If I owe you any horse", he argues, "I must owe you either Brownie or Blackie or Fallow; they're the only horses I have, and you can't say I owe you some other horse, let us say H.M. the King's charger. Now what I said didn't relate specially to Blackie rather than Fallow, or the other way round; what goes for one goes for the other; and similarly for Brownie. So either I owe you all, Brownie and Blackie and Fallow, or I owe you not one of them. You'll surely not have the nerve to say I owe you all three, when I only said I'd let you have one; so I don't owe you even one. *Good* morning."

Part of the trouble Buridan has in saying what is wrong with the horse-coper's argument comes from his accepting the inference from "I owe you a horse" to "There is a horse I owe you"; and we have seen reason to doubt the validity of the rule by which Buridan has to allow this step. But even without this inferential move, Buridan can give the horse-coper a longer run for his (or rather his victim's) money. Even if in general we cannot validly pass from "*b* F's an *A*" to "There is an *A* that *b* F's", it seems plausible to accept this particular instance of a term-shifting inference: "I owe you something: *ergo*, there is something I owe you". And we can consistently accept it without accepting Buridan's invalid rule; many philosophers seem to think that any instance of an invalid form is an invalid argument, but this is a gross logical error. Let us then have our horse-coper arguing again. "If I owe you a horse, then I owe you something. And if I owe you something, then there is something I owe you. And this can only be a thoroughbred of mine: you aren't going to say that in virtue of what I said there's something else I owe you. Very well then: by your claim, there's one of my thoroughbreds I owe you. Please tell me which one it is".

Buridan has an ingenious way out of the difficulty. It can be said that *x* is owing by me to *y* if and only if by handing over *x* to *y* I should be quits with him (*essem quittus*). Now whichever thoroughbred (*bonus equus*) *x* may be, if the horse-coper hands over *x* to the purchaser then they are quits. Buridan concludes that, whichever thoroughbred *x* may be, the dealer owes *x* to the customer. This goes even for H.M. the King's charger; for if the horse-coper bought or were given this horse, he could be quits with his customer by handing it over, as he could not be if he had not handed over exactly what was owing.

We can now clear up the 'parity of reasoning' argument about the three horses the dealer already has. It is true of Brownie, and it is true of Blackie, and it is also true of Fallow, that this is a horse the dealer owes his customer. So, considering just Brownie and Blackie, we may in a sense say these are two horses the dealer owes. But Buridan rightly warns us to avoid confusing collective and distributive predication; it is not that there are two horses together which the dealer owes, but that of each one of the two it holds good that he is a horse the dealer owes. Moreover, by Buridan's general principle we may not pass from "There are two horses the dealer owes" to "The dealer owes two horses"; that would call up the *ratio*: two horses, which did not come into the dealer's original promise. Similarly, from "Brownie is a horse the dealer owes" we may not infer "The dealer owes Brownie"; this would be true only if the dealer's original promise had called up the *ratio* expressed by the name "Brownie", as *ex hypothesi* it did not.

It is with great reluctance that one faults Buridan's brilliant argument, securing obvious justice for the customer without bending the laws of logic. All the same, the inference from "I owe you something" to "There is something I owe you" cannot be let pass unchallenged. No doubt many an investor in the Post Office Savings Bank has inferred from "The Post Office owes me something" to "There is something the Post Office owes me"; his thought is "The Post Office has it all stacked up somewhere —*aes alienum*, other people's brass—and some of it's mine". The inference is invalid, and the conclusion is false; and the mistake is far from trivial—as those unscrupulous politicians were well aware who made use of this false impression in their highly successful propaganda to the effect "The Socialists were going to take *your* money out of the Savings Bank and pay it over to the unemployed".

This difficulty is not confined to the present example; there are, I think, very many instances in which from "*b* F's an *A*" or "*b* F's something or other" we may by no means infer that there is an identifiable something-or-other which *b* is F'ing. On this point Buridan's theory stands in need of radical reconstruction. I think I can see in part how such a reconstruction would be possible; but there are difficulties that still remain.

Let us take the example "Geach was looking for a detective

story". On an analysis which closely followed Buridan this would come out as:

> For some *x*, Geach was looking for *x* under the *ratio*: detective story.

But this would have the unwelcome consequence that, even when I was 'just' looking for *a* detective story, there was some identifiable *x*—not necessarily a detective story, to be sure—that I was looking for. We need rather a dyadic relation between Geach and a *ratio*: "Geach was-looking-for-something-under the *ratio*: detective story", where I have hyphenated the words of the verbal to show that logically it is just one indivisible relative term.

We may achieve considerable clarification if we expand this analysis to:

> Geach was looking for something under the *ratio* evoked (*appellata*) by the expression "detective story"

and then treat "was looking . . . by" as a single relative term, which we may abbreviate to "was *L*'ing". We now have a verbal flanked by a name of a person and a quotation, rather than by a name of a person and designation of a *ratio*. The dodge, suggested to me by Professor R. Montague, avoids our difficulties about quantifying over *rationes*; we may now analyse "There is a detective story Geach was looking for" as:

> For some *x*, *x* is a detective story, and, for some *w*, *w* is a description true just of *x*, and Geach was *L*'ing *w* (Geach was-looking-for-something-under-the-*ratio*-evoked-by the definite description *w*).

Here we quantify over forms of words, whose criterion of identity, if not completely clear, is a lot clearer than that of *rationes*.

A similar method suggests itself for dealing with problems of what may be called *intentional identity*. In a way parallel to the Buridan convention we may distinguish between "There is a poet whom both Smith and Brown admire" and "Smith and Brown both admire the same poet"; the latter would cover the case where both Smith and Brown are victims of the same literary fraud as to the existence of a poet, as well as the more normal case where they both admire (say) Wordsworth's poetry. Let us use the expression "*AP*" as short for "admire as a poet someone conceived under the *ratio* evoked by"; then "There is a poet whom both Smith and Brown admire" would come out as:

> For some *x*, *x* is a poet and, for some *w*, *w* is a description true just of *x*, and both Smith and Brown *AP w*

whereas "Smith and Brown both admire the same poet", taken as conveying only intentional identity, would come out in the simpler form:

> For some *w*, *w* is a definite description, and Smith and Brown both *AP w*.

Unfortunately, the line of solution we have been following leads us into difficulties. Suppose we use *"D'd"* as short for the verbal "dreamed of someone under the *ratio* expressed by". Then in our present view we should have to paraphrase "There is a red-head Harris dreamed of" as:

> For some *x*, *x* is a red-head and, for some *w*, *w* is a description true just of *x*, and Harris *D'd w*.

Now suppose we take *w* to be the description "the fattest woman in the world". The paraphrase would be true if Harris dreamed of the fattest woman in the world and the fattest woman in the world is in fact a red-head; but the proposition paraphrased might then quite well be false, because in Harris's dream there may have been no red-head, and the fattest woman he saw in his dream may have been as bald as an egg. (I owe this counter-example to my pupil Mr. David Bird.)

I hope this paper shows why modern logicians still need to take medieval logicians seriously. In great measure their problems are ours; for some of these, like the problems of *suppositio*, modern logic provides adequate solutions, but there are other problems, about modal and intentional contexts for example, that are still wide open; and the talent that was shown by medieval logicians in wrestling with their problems demands our deepest admiration.

4.3. QUANTIFICATION THEORY AND THE PROBLEM OF IDENTIFYING OBJECTS OF REFERENCE

In practical affairs, and particularly in the law, men often have to consider the question who was meant, or who was being referred to, in a given document or on a given occasion. While preparing this paper I read a news item in some such words as these: "Cronin allegedly made derogatory remarks in his article about American women in general and about one unnamed woman in particular; Mrs. Supanich contends that she was the unnamed woman". This claim might be expressed in a proposition of the following form:

(1) Mrs. Supanich is the one and only woman x such that Cronin said in his article that x was a so-and-so.

Similarly, in the law of inheritance and the law of contract there are disputes as to the truth of propositions like these:

(2) Ralph de Vere is the person x such that the testator's express intention was that x should inherit the business.

(3) P. G. M. Hutchinson is the person x such that the plaintiff believed that x was buying the car.

Clearly in these propositions we have (definite-description) operators outside an indirect-speech construction binding variables within the construction. This notoriously raises grave difficulties. Can such a formula as:

(4) The testator's express intention was that x should inherit the business

be taken as a reading of "Fx" in a quantificational schema? Ordinarily the interpretations of "Fx" would be confined to such predications concerning x (concerning whichever object we take x to be) as held good of x, or failed to hold good of x, under whatever name we chose. Shakespeare tells us that a rose by any other name would smell as sweet; I shall speak of the context of "x" in "x smells sweet" as a Shakespearean context. The context of "x" in (4) is not Shakespearean. Let us suppose that the testator, the rich plebeian great-uncle of Ralph de Vere, regards

Ralph de Vere as a snob and a wastrel, and accordingly makes his will in favour of Ralph Jenkins, the grocer's assistant; but that, unknown to the testator, Ralph Jenkins is none other than Ralph de Vere himself, whose social position obliges him to exercise his inherited commercial talents under an alias while supposedly on holiday. In this case (4) will yield a true or a false proposition according as "x" in (4) is replaced by "Ralph Jenkins" or by "Ralph de Vere"; so even the question whether Ralph Jenkins *alias* de Vere is or is not an x satisfying (4) appears unanswerable —let alone, whether he is the one and only such x.

Proper names are logically simpler to deal with than other singular designations, for they have no (logically relevant) internal structure and no difficulties arise as to how much of a proposition is the 'scope' of a proper name. It is surprising, therefore, that we get difficult non-Shakespearean contexts in which proper names of the same person are not interchangeable *salva veritate*. On the other hand, our problems are going to be simplified by leaving out of consideration the replaceability (*salva veritate*) of a definite description by another definite description, or a proper name, of the same individual. When such wider interchangeability of designations obtains, contexts are often called extensional. Some contexts that are not thus extensional are yet Shakespearean. For example, the context of "Caesar" in

(5) It is (logically and) chronologically possible that Caesar should have been the father of Brutus

is a Shakespearean one. Whether Caesar was born in time to beget Brutus obviously does not depend on what name we call Caesar. But this context is not extensional; if Caesar did not in fact beget Brutus, then this fact could be written into some definite description C that described Caesar, and then the replacement of "Caesar" by C might turn truth into falsehood.

We might try to use the two forms of words:

(6) The testator expressly intended that Ralph de Vere should inherit the business.

(7) Ralph de Vere was (a person) expressly intended by the testator to inherit the business

to mark a logical distinction between a Shakespearean context of the proper name, (7), and a non-Shakespearean one, (6); in our imaginary situation, (6) would be false and (7) true. This distinction corresponds to Quine's distinction between 'opaque' and 'transparent' uses of the verb "believe" [*Word and Object*, pp. 145, 147–150], which would be respectively exemplified in:

(8) It was believed by the testator that Ralph de Vere was hardworking
(9) Ralph de Vere was (a person) believed by the testator to be hard-working.

In my terminology, the proper name would have a non-Shakespearean context in the supposedly false proposition (8) and a Shakespearean context in the supposedly true proposition (9).

What we now need is a logical account of the relation borne by (7) to (6) and by (9) to (8), which should show how the later member of each pair is inferable from the earlier. It is tempting to hold that (7) and (9) are analysable as tantamount to two ways of interpreting the following schema:

(10) For some x, Ralph de Vere is none other than x, and Fx.

"Fx" would be read as (4) to yield an analysis of (7); to get an analysis of (9) we should read "Fx" as "It was believed by the testator that x was hard-working". The context of "Ralph de Vere" does seem to be thus made securely Shakespearean; but the immediate context of "x" that is used as a reading of "Fx" is in either case non-Shakespearean: this makes it uncertain how (10) should be construed, and whether (10) is in truth validly inferable from "F (Ralph de Vere)" with "F" thus read.

I think the obstacle to an understanding of (10) is the assumption that "For some x, ... x ..." must mean "There is an object x such that ... x ...." This assumption runs us into trouble even for some Shakespearean contexts. We can however interpret (10) on quite other lines: a proposition (abbreviated as) "For some x, Fx" would then be true if each free occurrence of "x" in the context (abbreviated as) "Fx" *could* be so replaced by one and the same proper name as to yield a true result.

The main objection to my way of reading quantifiers is that there are many interpretations of "F" for which "For some x, Fx" comes out true even though nobody has bothered to give proper names to the objects covered by the predicate abbreviated to "F"; but in such cases there are no proper names that can take the place of "x" in "Fx" and yield a true proposition. To bring in "possible" proper names, moreover, would threaten to make quantificational logic depend on modal logic; surely modal words cannot have an essential place in the semantical rules for using plain quantifiers. To refute this objection, I show how the 'possibility' of replacing variables by proper names comes out if we formulate the inference-rules for quantification theory in a natural-deduction style. There will then be four inferential moves involving quantifiers:

UI, universal instantiation: we pass from a line universally quantified to a similar line devoid of the initial quantifier, say from "$(x)\ Fx$" to "Fw".

IE, instantial existentiation[1]: we pass from a line to a similar line prefaced with an existential quantifier, say from "Fw" to "$(\exists x)\ Fx$".

EI, existential instantiation: we pass from a line existentially quantified to a similar line devoid of the initial quantifier, say from "$(\exists x)\ Fx$" to "Fw".

IU, instantial universalization[1]: we pass from a line to a similar line prefaced with a universal quantifier, say from "Fw" to "$(x)\ Fx$".

We need consider only the first three of these moves; for if we assume the usual rules connecting negation and the quantifiers, a direct proof using IU can always be replaced by an indirect proof using EI. To take a simple example: Quine's derivation of "$(x)\ (\exists y)\ Fxy$" from "$(\exists y)\ (x)\ Fxy$" in *Methods of Logic* (p. 160) goes thus:

*(i)	$(\exists y)\ (x)\ Fxy$		
*(ii)	$(x)\ Fxz$	(i)	z — by EI
*(iii)	Fwz	(ii)	— by UI
*(iv)	$(\exists y)\ Fwy$	(iii)	— by IE
*(v)	$(x)\ (\exists y)\ Fxy$	(iv)	w — by IU

The 'flagging' of the letters "z" and "w" in the proof enables us to check that we have observed certain restrictions imposed by Quine on the moves IU (UG in Quine) and EI. A proof with the same 'flagging', using only EI and not also IU, might run thus:

---

[1] I borrow the nomenclature for these rules from an anonymous note in *Analysis*, vol. 23, p. 48.

$*$(i) $(\exists y)(x)\,Fxy$
$*$(ii) $(x)\,Fxz$ (i) z — by EI
$**$(iii) $-(x)(\exists y)\,Fxy$
$**$(iv) $(\exists x)-(\exists y)\,Fxy$ (iii),   with "$(\exists x)-$" for "$-(x)$"
$**$(v) $(\exists x)(y)-Fxy$ (iv),   with "$(y)-$" for "$-(\exists y)$"
$**$(v) $(y)-Fwy$ (v) w — by EI
$**$(vii) $-Fwz$ (vi)   — by UI
$**$(viii)$(\exists x)-Fxz$ (vii)   — by IE
$**$(ix) $-(x)\,Fxz$ (viii), with "$-(x)$" for "$(\exists x)-$"
$*$(ix) $-(x)(\exists y)\,Fxy \supset$ $*$(ix) — conditionalizing
           $-(x)\,Fxz$
$*$(xi) $(x)(\exists y)\,Fxy$ (ii),   (x)

It is clear that any valid proof using IU can thus be turned into one using only EI. This is advantageous, for the rationale of IU is less easily grasped than that of the other three moves.

In our formulations of UI, IE, and EI, the letter "w" in the line "Fw" that we used illustratively has the role of an *ad hoc* proper name. This is obvious as regards UI and IE: the line "Fw" is inferred from "$(x)\,Fx$", or again has "$(\exists x)\,Fx$" inferred from it, just as though "w" were a name. The rationale of EI is a little more complicated: a subsequent line of proof follows from "$(\exists x)\,Fx$" iff it follows from a line "Fw" but does not itself contain the dummy singular term "w". The premise "$(\exists x)\,Fx$" gives us what is supposed to be true in some instance; we make believe that we can actually cite an instance w, and then, if a conclusion follows from this make-believe citation of an instance, "Fw", regardless of which instance w may be, that conclusion is deemed to follow from "$(\exists x)\,Fx$". Thus, since quantification theory can be formulated in this natural-deduction style, it necessarily gives us 'possible' proper names, namely the dummy letters like "w" used in natural deduction as if they were proper names.

This deprives of all philosophical significance Quine's neo-Russellian treatment of proper names as disguised descriptions. Such treatment fails on another count too; for a description, the question arises how much of its context counts as its 'scope', whereas no such question can arise for proper names. For example, in (5) above:

(5) It is (logically and) chronologically possible that Caesar should have been the father of Brutus

it is all one whether we take the 'scope' of "Caesar" to run over the whole proposition or to be confined to the that-clause; but if we replaced "Caesar" by a description C, and into C we had written it in that he did not beget Brutus, the truth-value of the result would be affected by the 'scope'. With the shorter 'scope', we should get a that-clause expressing a logical impossibility, and thus the whole proposition would be false; with the long 'scope', we should be predicating of somebody described *inter alia* as not having begotten Brutus that nevertheless he was born in time to have done so, and this would be true. It is remarkable that Quine himself has noticed the freedom of 'genuine names' from troubles about 'scope', and the inescapability of such troubles for descriptions, in the very work in which he seeks to reduce proper names to descriptions [*Methods of Logic*, p. 84 and p. 221].

It follows from the account of quantifiers I gave that a predicate-letter like "F" occurring in a quantificational schema can be interpreted by any Shakespearean context. For I specified that a proposition schematically represented as "$(\exists x)\,Fx$" was to be true if each free occurrence of "x" in the context represented by "Fx" could be so replaced by one and the same proper name as to get a true result; correspondingly, "$(x)\,Fx$" will be true if any possible replacement of "x" at all free occurrences in the context represented by "Fx" by one and the same proper name would yield a true result. These explanations are geared to the explanation of the moves UI, EI, and IE in terms of dummy proper names. It will not matter if the Shakespearean context used to interpret "Fx" contains some intentional occurrences of "x".

It is clear, indeed, that with these explanations IE and UI will be valid moves even without the restriction to Shakespearean contexts. EI, on the other hand, is not a securely valid move except under this restriction. For a given interpretation of "F", "$(\exists x)\,Fx$" will come out true if it is possible to preserve truth when we drop the quantifier and substitute some proper name for "x"; but if we replace "x" by an arbitrary letter, say "w", used as a dummy proper name, and then deem that inferences from "Fw" are to be regarded as inferences from "$(\exists x)\,Fx$", the arbitrary choice of this letter presupposes that if what "Fw" says is true, it holds good of the object named "w" under whatever other name, i.e. that "F" represents a Shakespearean context of "w". IU must be subject to this same restriction upon its validity as EI.

Thus, if we shift to non-Shakespearean ways of reading our schematic letters, the rules of natural deduction do not all still hold good; but our way of reading quantifiers still gives a sense to quantified propositions. As Frege would say, we have specified their truth-conditions, and therewith their sense, namely the sense of: Such-and-such conditions are fulfilled. Moreover, given any non-Shakespearean context, we can specify a corresponding Shakespearean context. For from a line "Fw" we may move to "$w=w$. Fw", and from this again, by IE, to "$(\exists x)(w=x.\ Fx)$"; this last formula gives us a Shakespearean context for "w", and the moves by which it is inferred from "Fw" are valid, whether or not we read "F" as a Shakespearean context.

This justifies our previous suggestion that "w is (a person) expressly intended by the testator to inherit the business" may be treated as a Shakespearean context of "w", obtained from the non-Shakespearean context "The testator expressly intended that w should inherit the business", and construable as follows:

(11) For some x, w is the same person as x, and the testator expressly intended that x should inherit the business.

We can now discuss the logic of those identifying propositions which gave us our original problem. Let us take the example:

(12) P. G. M. Hutchinson is the person x such that x was believed by the plaintiff to be buying the car.

To construe the definite description in a logically coherent way, we must regard the context of "x" in (12), "x was believed by the plaintiff to be buying the car", as a Shakespearean context; it will be related to the non-Shakespearean context "the plaintiff believed that x was buying the car" in the way just explained. We can then say that (12) is true if both of the following are:

(13) For some x, P. G. M. Hutchinson is the same person as x, and the plaintiff believed that x was buying the car.

(14) It is not the case that, for some x, P. G. M. Hutchinson is not the same person as x, and the plaintiff believed that x was buying the car.

For, just in case (13) and (14) are both true, we shall have the predicate "for some x, — is the same person as x, and the plaintiff believed that x was buying the car" holding true of P. G. M. Hutchinson (under whatever name) and not of anybody else.

Now in the actual case that supplied my example[1] the plaintiff was deceived by a rogue using the name of the respectable P. G. M. Hutchinson. (13) is then clearly true, as we can see by dropping the quantifier and substituting "P. G. M. Hutchinson" for "*x*"; we then get a true proposition from which (13) follows by IE. But it is not clear whether (14) is true or false; for *ex hypothesi* we cannot refute (14) by producing an actual proper name of the rogue, known to the plaintiff, such that we should get a true proposition by inserting it in the blanks of:

(15) P. G. M. Hutchinson is not the same person as — and the plaintiff believed that — was buying the car.

There is, however, obviously nothing to prevent a man's being given an *ad hoc* proper name. The plaintiff and her sisters correctly identified the rogue, during their encounter with him, as being one and the same man all the time: let us call the man so identified "*A*"—or better, let "*A*" correspond to the way the plaintiff and her sisters thought at the time of 'the man', sc. of one and the same man. Then the insertion of this *ad hoc* name "*A*" in the blank of (15) brings out a true counter-example to (14); so (14) is false, and therefore so is (12); nobody involved is *the* person whom the plaintiff believed to be buying the car. This appears a reasonable ground for holding the contract of sale void, as the Court of Appeal did hold by a majority.[2]

4.4. INTENTIONAL IDENTITY

A well-known epigram might serve both as a motto for this paper and (at least arguably) as a serious example of its topic. For if a speaker asserts:

(1) I saw a man on the stair yesterday at time t_1, and I saw him (the same man) on the stair again today at time t_2

in such a sense that it would be compatible with his also saying:

(2) No man but me was on the stair either yesterday at time t_1 or today at time t_2

[1] *Ingram* v. *Little* (1961) 1 Q.B. 31.
[2] I am indebted to my colleague Mr. Hudson, of the Faculty of Law at the University of Birmingham, for notice of this case and others, and for stimulating discussions.

then the identity he means to ascribe in (1) to the man on the stair is what I am calling intentional identity, rather than actual identity. I am sure that in fact this is a proper example of what I shall be discussing; but the intentionality of the verb "to see", though I think it can be established, is bound up with matters of controversy that I do not wish to touch upon here; so I pass quickly on from seeing to believing.

Etymology is more often a hindrance than a help in philosophy, but in this case it may be a help to remember the metaphor that underlies the words "intention" and "intentional": "*intendo arcum in* . . .", "I draw a bow at . . ." For a number of archers may all point their arrows at one actual target, a deer or a man (real identity); but we may also be able to verify that they are all pointing their arrows the same way, regardless of finding out whether there is any shootable object at the point where the lines of fire meet (intentional identity). We have intentional identity when a number of people, or one person on different occasions, have attitudes with a common focus, whether or not there actually is something at that focus.

Suppose a reporter is describing an outbreak of witch mania, let us say in Gotham village:

(3) Hob thinks a witch has blighted Bob's mare, and Nob wonders whether she (the same witch) killed Cob's sow.

Quine has distinguished *opaque* and *transparent* ways of construing indirect-speech clauses, but neither sort of construction will give an appropriate sense to (3). For if the indirect-speech clauses in (3) are construed opaquely, then each clause must stand on its own syntactically; this is graphically shown by Quine's way of enclosing such clauses in square brackets; and Quine forbids syntactical liaisons, like the binding of variables, to cross this barrier. But on the face of it we have in (3) a pronoun, "she" or "the same", bound to an antecedent, "a witch", that lies outside the clause containing the pronoun; so unless this *prima facies* can be discounted (and I shall presently consider some possible ways of doing that), the clauses in (3) cannot be construed opaquely.

(In speaking, as I have just done, of a pronoun as being bound to its antecedent, I am deliberately adopting a jargon that serves to express an important syntactical insight of Quine's: that *certain* uses of pronouns correspond very closely to the bound variables of symbolic logic and that the relation of these pronouns to their antecedents corresponds to the binding of variables by quantifiers and other operators. I know that some philosophers and some linguists are opposed to Quine's view, but I am disposed to attach far more weight to the way the view is confirmed by the detailed working out of numerous and varied examples, such as occur in Quine's works and mine. In previous writing I have used the medieval term "relative pronouns"; but I now think it is awkward, except in writings on the history of logic, to divest this term of its familiar grammatical sense; and I propose that the familiar jargon of binding, scope, and so on should be extended from symbolic language to appropriate pieces of the vernacular.)

On the other hand, there is no obvious way of construing the indirect speech in (3) transparently. We might try:

(4) As regards some witch, Hob thinks she has blighted Bob's mare, and Nob wonders whether she killed Cob's sow.

But (4) would express (what the speaker took to be) the *real*, not the intentional, identity of a witch; and (unlike the wise men of Gotham) our reporter might mistakenly believe that there are no witches (not just that spells against livestock are ineffectual, but that nobody ever casts them); in that case he might, and could with consistency, assert (3) and deny (4). Nor do we fare any better with something like:

(5) As regards somebody, Hob thinks that she is a witch and has blighted Bob's mare, and Nob wonders whether she killed Cob's sow.

For (5) would imply that Hob and Nob had some one person in mind as a suspected witch; whereas it might be the case, to the knowledge of our reporter, that Hob and Nob merely thought there was a witch around and their suspicions had not yet settled on a particular person.

The difference between (3) and (4) corresponds to a difference that was much discussed by Jean Buridan and illustrated with numerous examples; (3) and (4) correspond respectively to the first and the second member of such pairs as the following:

(6) I owe John a horse
(7) There is some horse that I owe John

(8) John wants a stamp

(9) There is some stamp that John wants

The difference is gropingly brought out by saying "Just *a* so-and-so, not necessarily a definite so-and-so" for examples like (6) and (8), and "I mean a definite so-and-so" for examples like (7) and (9). Similarly, it would be quite natural to insert the adjective "definite" before "witch" in (4), or again after "somebody" in (5). No clue is to be found here to the real logical difference; for of course witches, horses, and stamps do not come in two species, the definite ones and the indefinite ones. Frege indeed remarked that "referring to an indefinite so-and-so" often really means "referring indefinitely to a so-and-so", and we might try to interpret similarly the phrase "a definite so-and-so"; but there is no *definite* reference made by the "some" phrase in (4), (7), or (9), so this is no clue either. Buridan's own attempt to characterize the difference is made in hopelessly obscure terminology. He speaks of the object phrase in propositions like (6) and (8) as calling up, *appellans*, a certain *ratio*. But the criterion of identity for a *ratio* remains quite obscure; and the semantical term *"appellatio"* neither has a consistent technical use in medieval logic generally (different authors use it differently), nor is carefully explained in Buridan's own text. The most one can say is that *appellatio* of a *ratio* in Buridan is *something like* a term's having *ungerade Bedeutung* in Frege—but of course Frege's theory is very obscure too.

All the same, I am strongly inclined to think that Buridan was here after an important logical distinction—and that the *same* difference of logical structure is involved in all these contrasted pairs; for it is easy to catch on to what the intended difference is and transfer the learning to a fresh example; we have not got to learn it anew for each intentional verb or context. Only at present we (or I at least) are not able to say what the difference is. We are in the same position as the medievals were in about the contrasted pairs they used to show the differences between *suppositio confusa* (the first members of the following pairs) and *suppositio determinata* (the second members):

(10) In order to see, I need an eye

(11) There is an eye that I need to see with

(12) There always has been a man alive

(13) There is a man who has always been alive

L

This difference can be clearly explained in modern logic as a difference in the order of application of two quantifiers or other operators. We have no such clear view of the other problem. Even the difference between this pair:

(14) Hob thinks some women are witches
(15) There are some women Hob thinks are witches

is not *clearly* explicable in terms of a difference in scope for the quantified phrase "some women":

(16) Hob thinks that, as regards some women x and y, x and y are witches
(17) As regards some women x and y, Hob thinks x and y are witches

For Quine has raised some difficulties about the quantification in (17) and the like; though others (Hintikka, Prior, and myself) argue that they need not be insuperable. But (3) raises an even worse difficulty: a pronoun in one indirect-speech clause is on the face of it bound to a quantified phrase in *another* such oblique context; the scope of the quantified phrase thus seems *both* to lie wholly within the earlier oblique context *and* to cover something in the later context. I cannot even sketch a structure of operators that would make good logical sense of this; I go on to consider a couple of ways of evading the difficulty.

First, it might be suggested that "she" in (3) ought not to be glossed as "the same witch", but should rather be regarded as an anaphoric substitute (what I have called a pronoun of laziness) to avoid repetitious language; (3) would then be a substitute for something like this:

(18) Hob thinks a witch has blighted Bob's mare, and Nob wonders whether the witch who blighted Bob's mare killed Cob's sow.

This suggestion is easily dismissed: for our reporter might be justified in asserting (3) if he had heard Hob say "The witch has blighted Bob's mare" and heard Nob say "Maybe the witch killed Cob's sow", even if Hob had not thought or said anything about Cob's sow nor Nob about Bob's mare. Of course our reporter would somehow have to know that when they used the words "the witch" Hob and Nob *meant to refer to the same person*. But this would not necessarily mean his knowing that there was some ('definite') person to whom they both meant to refer; rather, the italicized phrase is itself yet another example of our problematic intentional identity.

This in fact points up the importance of intentional identity as a problem in the philosophy of logic. We very often take ourselves to know, when we hear the discourse of others, that they are meaning to refer to some one person or thing—and that, without ourselves being able to identify this person or thing, without our even being certain that there really is such a person or thing to identify. What we are claiming to know in such cases —let alone, whether the claim is justified—must remain obscure so long as intentional identity is obscure.

There is another objection to this proposed method of analyzing away an intentional identity in (3). Although I see no reason to doubt that:

(19) The witch who blighted Bob's mare killed Cob's sow

is analyzable as:

(20) Just one witch blighted Bob's mare and she killed Cob's sow

it seems doubtful whether these two are mutually replaceable *salva veritate* in a context like "Nob wonders whether". If we prefix "Nob wonders whether" to (19), the result seems to be analyzable, not as:

(21) Nob wonders whether (the following is the case:) just one witch blighted Bob's mare, and she killed Cob's sow

but rather in some such way as this:

(22) Nob assumes that just one witch blighted Bob's mare, and Nob wonders whether she (that same witch) killed Cob's sow

It is not easy to be sure about this, because it is easy to confound the analysis (21), which I have just rejected, with the following:

(23) Nob wonders whether just one witch blighted Bob's mare and (Nob wonders whether) she killed Cob's sow

Objections to (23) as an analysis of "Nob wonders whether the witch who blighted Bob's mare killed Cob's sow" naturally do not carry over to (21). (If the words in parentheses are omitted, as they might easily be, from (21) and (23), we get a verbally identical sentence that could mean either; hence the likelihood of confusing the two.) But even allowing for this, I think (22) is the right sort of analysis rather than (21). Now if so, the analysis of the second conjunct in (18) would introduce intentional identity over again; for (22) manifestly does so—"she" or "that same" is bound to an antecedent, "just one witch", in another oblique clause. In that case (18) is quite useless as a way of getting rid of intentional identity.

This objection to (18), if it is sound, also serves against another possible way of trying to deal with (3): namely, to say that (3) is true just in case the following is true for *some* suitable interpretation of "*F*":

(24) Hob thinks that the (one and only) witch that is *F* has blighted Bob's mare, and Nob wonders whether the witch that is *F* killed Cob's sow

For supposing we have such a reading of "*F*", we should have exactly the same difficulty over the second conjunct of (24) as over the second conjunct of (18): it looks as though intentional identity, which was to be analyzed away, recurs in the analysis.

There is further trouble about (24). On the face of it, if (24) *is* true for some suitable reading of "*F*", then (3) is true; there are, I think, some difficulties about this, but I waive them. Anyhow, it is very doubtful whether the converse holds; whether, if (3) is true, (24) is true for some suitable reading of "*F*". For, as I said, the truth of (3) could be established (in a suitable set of background circumstances) if Hob said "The witch has blighted Bob's mare" and Nob said "Maybe the witch killed Cob's sow" —provided that, in using the phrase "the witch", Hob and Nob meant to refer to the same person. Now is it in truth necessary, if Hob and Nob are to mean to refer to the same person as "the witch", that they should both have some one definite description actually in mind, or even, one producible from each of them by a suitable technique of questioning?[1] This appears to me to stand

---

[1] (*Note*, 1969) The consideration I had here in mind was that in purporting to refer to a given person, Hob or Nob may have more than one definite description 'of that person' that he might produce; consequently, Hob and Bob might 'refer to her' with the same description in mind, and likewise Bob and Nob, but not Hob and Nob.

or fall with the corresponding theory, held by Russell and by Frege (cf. his article 'Der Gedanke'), that any ordinary proper name is used equivocally if it does not go proxy for some *one* definite description; and in spite of these great names, such a theory seems to me extremely ill-founded and implausible.

I have only stated a problem, not tried to solve it; it seems to me interesting and important. It surely brings out how much is obscure in the logic of quite simple constructions of ordinary language. Strawson has spoken of ordinary language as a maze whose paths we tread unhesitatingly. "Maze" suggests something in a gentleman's formal garden, with neat box hedges and a discoverable plan; to my mind it would be better to speak of a clearing in a jungle, whose paths are only kept free if logicians work hard with the machete, and where he who does not hesitate may none the less be lost.

4.5. THE PERILS OF PAULINE

"Pauline" is the name to be used in this paper for the one and only girl Geach dreamed of on N-Night, i.e., the last night of 1963. (To avoid uninteresting complications, we assume that Geach had only one dream on N-Night.) There are then the following (exclusive and exhaustive) possibilities about Geach's dream on N-Night; he may have dreamed of

A	B	C
just one girl:	more than one girl:	no girl at all
1. a real live girl	1. two (or more) real girls	
2. a dead girl	2. just one real girl, but also one or more imaginary girls	
3. an imaginary girl	3. no real girl, but several imaginary girls	

It may be seen from the foregoing that Pauline's existence is multiply jeopardized; or rather, that my right to use "Pauline" as a name, the way I said I was going to, is very doubtful, for I agree with Parmenides that one cannot name what is not there to be named. The words I have used to describe Pauline's various perils are full of what Ryle aptly called "systematically misleading

expressions"; but we need not worry about that for the moment—
enough for now if the words succeed in bringing the various cases
before our minds—and we can tidy up our language as we come
to see things more clearly.

I must emphasize that old-time or recent philosophical discussions of dreaming have nothing to do with the case. I might
just as well have introduced the name "Pauline" in connection not
with the dream I had on N-Night but with the *risqué* story I told
on N-Night at a New Year's Eve party; *mutatis mutandis*, the whole
discussion would carry over, since we get the same set of distinct
possibilities for what my *story* (instead of my dream) could have
been about.

It might well seem as though my using "Pauline" as a name
raised no difficulties in case A–1. But even for this case philosophers have had worries that would be relevant. John Austin
seems to have held that naming is a momentous act, which not
just anyone casually can perform; it would take the right person
in the right circumstances using the right performative formula;
and I am not at all sure that he would have counted me as a validly
ordained namer, or my baptismal formula for Pauline as a valid
sacramental form. Well anyhow, I claim the right to *refer to* any
young lady of my acquaintance *by* the name "Pauline" for the
course of this discussion; and I think the difference between such
use of a name *pro hac vice* and the more official conferment of a
name is only of legal or anthropological, not of logical, importance.

Russell would say "Pauline" is not a real name for anybody
not acquainted with the object named. I agree that the use of
proper names has some dependence on being acquainted with the
object named, so long as the acquaintance meant is the ordinary
sort of acquaintance, say my acquaintance with Łukasiewicz or
with Warsaw. What I take the dependence to be I shall say in a
moment. But in Russell's sense of the word 1 can only be
acquainted with, and therefore can only mention by name,
objects that are present to me at the time of speaking, as Warsaw
and Łukasiewicz are not. This view I reject. It is indeed essential
to the role of a name that the name can be used in the presence of
the object named as an acknowledgement of its presence. But
equally essential to the name's role is its use to talk about the
named object *in absentia*. We are not condemned to carry about
with us sacks of objects to talk about, like the sages of Laputa.

I do indeed think that for the use of a word as a proper name there must in the first instance be someone acquainted with the object named. But language is an institution, a tradition; and the use of a given name for a given object, like other features of language, can be handed on from one generation to another; the acquaintance required for the use of a proper name may be mediate, not immediate. Plato knew Socrates, and Aristotle knew Plato, and Theophrastus knew Aristotle, and so on in apostolic succession down to our own times; that is why we can legitimately use "Socrates" as a name the way we do. It is not our knowledge of this chain that validates our use, but the existence of such a chain; just as according to Catholic doctrine a man is a true bishop if there is in fact a chain of consecrations going back to the Apostles, not if we know that there is. When a serious doubt arises (as happens for a well-known use of the word "Arthur") whether the chain does reach right up to the object named, our right to use the name is questionable, just on that account. But a right may obtain even when it is open to question.

In case A–1, I think, a real live girl could be identified by the description "the one and only girl Geach dreamed of on N-Night" if I was then, at least mediately, acquainted with her. In that case I should be warranted in using her ordinary name, and therefore also warranted in Humpty-dumptyishly replacing it *pro hac vice* by the name "Pauline". Whether I *am* justified no human being can say; for I am quite unable to remember what I dreamed on N-Night, and nobody else can remember my telling this at the time. But if the conditions are fulfilled I *am* justified, even if I don't know it. And I choose the example partly to unscramble Russell's unholy mixture of sound logic with dubious epistemology.

Russell's transition from "A genuine proper name must name something" to "Only a name that *must* name something is a proper name" is of course just a howler in modal logic; here he paid dear for his lifelong neglect of the subject. (There is just the same howler here as in passing from "What you know must be so" to "Only what *must* be so is really known".)

I introduced the use of the proper name "Pauline" by way of the definite description "the one and only girl Geach dreamt of on N-Night"; this might give rise to the idea that the name is an abbreviation for the description. This would be wrong. A proper name can never be logically tied to just one definite description; so long as we agree in a good many of the judgments we make using a certain proper name, we can use that name for communication. And there is no one judgment, mentioning a peculiarity of Pauline, such that agreement on *it* is indispensable; in particular, not the one that would be expressed by "Pauline is the one and only girl of whom Geach dreamed on N-Night". If I told you a lot of things about Pauline under that name, and then suddenly remembered that my dream of her had occurred not on N-Night but the night before, I'd have to withdraw this definite description of Pauline, but I need not stop using the name. Frege called mathematical signs like "π" proper names; and in this respect "π" really is like a proper name; for "π" can be joined in an equation to any number of complex mathematical expressions, and is not shorthand for one of these expressions rather than another.

I have developed these points about case A–1, so as to make clear certain views about proper names that I shall assume in dealing with the other cases. Case A–2, I think, presents no special logical difficulty; I shall return to it shortly; it will turn out not to differ in any logically important feature from case A–1. Case A–3 is quite different from these two cases. If case A–3 obtains, I have not successfully attached the name "Pauline" to an imaginary girl; I simply have not attached the name "Pauline" to any girl at all—I have only put up a show of doing so.

Some may feel a need to describe case A–3 in terms of imaginary girls; if so, I invite them to compare case A–3 with Case C. Does the definite description by which I introduced the name "Pauline" in case A–3 after all describe a girl, only an imaginary girl, not a real one? But then: can the girl I dreamed of on N-Night be more imaginary, less of an existent, if I never even dreamed of a girl on N-Night, than if I did dream of one but she was imaginary? If anyone says that in case A-3 the girl did exist 'in my dream', then I reply that at that rate in case C the girl does exist right now 'in my discourse'—and with the prestige of *present* rather than *past* existence at that! We do well here to heed the still small voice that whispers "Bosh!"

I allow no such entities as imaginary girls in my universe of discourse; and, by the same token, no such entities as false Gods either. The only way to clear thinking on such matters is the

Parmenidean 'way of truth': there is just what there is. If there is a God, there are not also other nonexistent gods; if there is no God, equally there are no false or nonexistent gods. And what is not cannot be named—any more than you can christen a baby, bell, or battle-ship that is not there to be christened.

We can however—and here I disagree with Parmenides— discourse about what did exist but does exist no longer. After all, we can talk about absent friends, and an absent friend may die without our hearing of it; this sad event may alter the truth value of what we say about our friend, but assuredly it cannot make our remarks about him not to be propositions with a truth value at all. And this is how I deal with case A–2.

But now suppose people are trying to discourse about a man who never was: the case imagined in G. K. Chesterton's story 'The Absence of Mr. Glass'. To the persons of the story, it appeared quite reasonable to discourse about Mr. Glass by name so long as he was merely regarded as absent from the scene and as possibly having been murdered. It came out, however, that as Father Brown put it, Mr. Glass was absent not just from the scene but from the Nature of Things; even the name "Mr. Glass" was a mishearing of a conjurer at his practice, "One two and three; damn it! missed a glass", as if he had been wrangling with a man called Glass about money. After this discovery there could be no question of anyone's using "Mr. Glass" as the subject of predicates any more. A detective who did use "Mr. Glass" as though it could be a subject of predicates would not be actually naming a man who happened to be imaginary rather than real, but only acting as if he had named a real man and said things about him; he would not actually be managing to name anybody or to state anything.

Some philosophers—perversely, to my mind—are now willing to say that there are imaginary, fictional, etc., men as well as real men, and that these can be and are named with just the same right as real men. This postulation, as Russell would say, has all the advantages that theft has over honest toil. If it is not true of any identifiable real girl that she is the girl I dreamed of last night, then it just is not true of any girl that I dreamt of her. "From this enquiry keep your thoughts far off," said Parmenides. Let us go back to the honest toil of seeing how we can redescribe such occurrences as worshipping an imaginary God, or dreaming of an imaginary girl, without admitting that there are imaginary gods and girls.

Our troubles arise from what is called the intentionality of verbs like "to worship" and "to dream of". The term "intentional verb" is, I must admit, not a well-understood logical technicality like "transitive relation"; it is usable in philosophical discussion only because quite a number of philosophers would apparently agree pretty well on which verbs it applies to. For present purposes, we may offer the following criterion for the intentionality of a verb "to V": whatever is V'd, is V'd *as* having certain characteristics; a proposition to the effect that a thing is V'd may have its truth value changed by our changing the description of the thing which is V'd, for the new proposition may tell us that the thing is V'd under another aspect. For example, "to inhabit" is not an intentional verb, but "to pick out", in some of its uses, is one. Alaska being both the coldest and the least populous State of the U.S., "X inhabits the coldest State" and "X inhabits the least populous State" must be true or false together; but "Procedure P picks out the coldest State" and "Procedure P picks out the least populous State" at least *could* be so understood that one might be true and the other false, if e.g., procedure P mentioned only temperature records not population statistics; and with this understanding of the propositions, the verb "picks out" is intentional—the difference of truth value arises because it matters what Alaska is picked out *as*, whether *as* the coldest State or *as* the least populous State.

I shall now attend to a general feature of intentional verbs, excellently discussed by the medieval logician Jean Buridan. I take as my example one that I gave you just now—the verb "to look for". The sentence "I am looking for a detective story" has two possible senses: these could be brought out by saying "Well, he may mean that what he's looking for is a definite detective story, or that it's just *a* detective story that he's looking for." I say the two senses could be brought out this way; Heaven only knows why such an explanation works. After all, any detective story is a definite detective story; and on the other hand any detective story is just *a*, that is, just some one, detective story. (Once at a meeting I heard a man criticize Medawar's *Mind* review of Teilhard de Chardin by saying Medawar was after all only *one* biologist; I muttered to my neighbour that Medawar would be hard put to it to be *two* biologists.) Or if being just *a* detective story means having only the attributes implied in being that, then *no* detective story is *just* a detective story, and no sane man would look for such a chimera. The distinction intended is easy to see, but hard to express appropriately.

Now there is a certain tendency, both in English and in medieval Latin, to mark just this kind of distinction by putting the object expression now before, now after, the verb. Buridan proposed that we should always mark the distinction in this way. In our example, the form "There is a detective story I was looking for" corresponds to the case where I was looking for 'a definite' detective story; by contrast, the form "I was looking for a detective story" would be restricted to the case where I was *just* looking for *a* detective story. And if the detective story I looked for was printed (suitably enough) in Baskerville type, then "There was a detective story printed in Baskerville type that I was looking for" would be true but "I was looking for a detective story printed in Baskerville type" would be false—I'd not know how to look out for Baskerville type.

The like goes for intentional verbs in general. Even if we suppose my father to have been the one and only man I descried coming on a given occasion, "I descried a man coming" will not yield "I descried my father", for I may not have descried the man coming *as* my father; but on Buridan's convention it will then be all right to say "It was my father that I descried". Similarly, one would say "In Oxford I saw a man run over" but "It was a man born in Jerusalem that I saw". Or again, on occasions when I ask a postmaster for a 3d. stamp I could truly say "I want a 3d stamp, but it is not true of any 3d stamp that I want *it*"; it would be natural here to put in the word "definite" before the second occurrence of "3d stamp"—"it is not true of any definite 3d stamp . . ."—but this epithet is uninformative and logically superfluous. Notice that in none of these cases does the distinction marked by Buridan's convention even seem to consist in or involve a distinction between real and imaginary detective stories, men, or postage stamps; my wanting the stamps for example may relate to a sheet of 3d stamps on the counter under my eyes, not in the least to imaginary stamps. So if I use the Buridan convention as a device for redescribing cases that may seem to involve dream girls or imaginary gods, I am not smuggling in again what I reject.

Buridan is of course canonizing, for logical purposes, what is no more than a tendency in ordinary language; there are many exceptions—one might quite naturally say both "I saw a man born in Jerusalem" and "I saw a man run over in Oxford". But such use of canonical forms is the first step in puzzling out the logic of a class of propositions. The form "*A*s are *B*", with which ordinary discourse is often content, has to be spelled out in traditional logic as "All *A*s are *B*" or as "Some *A*s are *B*"; and these forms are in fact both used in logic contrary to ordinary usage in some cases—"All *A*s are *B*" when there is only one or only two *A*s, "Some *A*s are *B*" when there is only one *A* or again when in fact all *A*s are *B*. Such artificial stream-lining of usage is a practice to which there is no objection in principle; it helps to make things clear; and if people protest in the name of ordinary language, they are probably the sort of people who don't want things made clear.

We can now see how to banish dream girls and imaginary gods. Instead of saying "Last night I dreamt of a girl, but she was only an imaginary girl", we might say "Last night I dreamt of a girl, but it is not true of any girl that I then dreamt of her". To insert "real"—"it is not true of any real girl"—is natural, but logically needless; there are no girls but real girls. The case is quite parallel to one I gave just now: "I want a 3d stamp on that sheet, but it is not true of any 3d stamp on that sheet that I want it"; and in that case there is no question of real *versus* imaginary stamps. We deal with "worshipping an imaginary God" in just the same way as with "dreaming of an imaginary girl".

I say, then, that there is a reference for the would-be name "Pauline" just in case there was one and only one *real* girl (living or dead) rightly identifiable as a girl I dreamed of on N-Night. This happens in case B-2, as well as in cases A-1 and A-2; for in case B-2 the real girl I dreamt of on N-Night is *the* girl I dreamt of on N-Night; imaginary girls are not competitors for this title, for they are not there to compete. In all my other cases the definite description I supplied is vacuous, and my attempt at, or show of conferring the name is ineffectual. In case B-1, where two real girls are involved, neither is *the* girl of my dream, and my conferment of the name is, as lawyers say, void for uncertainty.

Intentional verbs give rise to difficulties not only about existence but also about identity. For example: what is it for two men to be worshippers of the same God? The problem becomes harder, not easier, on the supposition that there is no God, or no such God as the two men worship. In saying "the same God", one purports to identify a God; and how can one do that if there is no God in question to be identified? Yet on the other hand surely Hannibal and Hasdrubal did worship the same God, namely Baal. But we who say this do not thereby accept the existence of Baal; how then are we using the term "Baal"? How can we name what on our showing is not there to be named?

Here as before we could well introduce a Buridan-type distinction applied to objects of intentional verbs like "to worship". We could appropriate, for the purpose of expressing the necessary distinction, the two sentences:

Hannibal and Hasdrubal worshipped one and the same God.
It was one and the same God that Hannibal and Hasdrubal worshipped.

Only the second proposition would then involve the real identity of a God; the other, I shall say, involves only *intentional identity*. (A number of arrows may be aimed the same way even though there is nothing shootable there for the arrows to be aimed at, but only empty air.)

Now ordinary proper names correspond, or purport to correspond, to a *real* identity. A narrative of events in which, say, "Pauline" is used straightforwardly as a proper name could be replaced by one in which, where "Pauline" occurred in the original story, one said "a certain girl" the first time and "the girl" (sc. "the *same* girl") each other time; those who previously did not know the girl Pauline even by name would lose nothing by this substitution. In parallel fashion, we could have quasi-names corresponding to merely *intentional* identity. Suppose we hear of a man who dreams of the same girl night after night, as happened in a story of H. G. Wells; for convenience of conversation, we may say he dreams of Petronella every night, without either committing ourselves to the view that there is a real live girl he is dreaming of, or meaning that the name "Petronella" is the name he gives the girl in his dreams. For us, "Petronella" is then functioning not as a name but as a quasi-name.

Dictionaries list some words that were actually introduced into the language as quasi-names, unlike "Petronella" which would have had a previous use as a name of a real live girl. It has sometimes happened that members of one group, speaking contemptuously about the religion of another group who 'all worship the same God', have used a quasi-name "N" and said "They worship N" without any implication that the word I here represent by "N" is what the worshippers of N themselves use in their religious discourse. "Baphomet", "Termagaunt", "Mumbo Jumbo", and perhaps "Beelzebub" as used by the Jews, are examples of such quasi-names.

This possibility of introducing quasi-names may seem to give some sort of reality to the dream girl, Petronella, and the false God, Mumbo Jumbo: as though what I have called quasi-names were really names, only of second-grade entities. But no such thing need be assumed. These quasi-names were introduced only in object position after intentional verbs; the use of them as logical subjects of predication neither is explained, nor could be justified, by this introduction. (A word intended to be used as a proper name is simply a different word from a word intended to be used as a quasi-name, even if they look and sound the same; I shall return to this point in a moment.) To say assertorically "Wewena, Chuckery, and Cousheda all worship the same God, Mumbo Jumbo" nowise commits one to allowing questions as to what may be said of this God whom Wewena, Chuckery, and Cousheda worship.

One might of course say "Mumbo Jumbo is invisibly enthroned upon a black stone in the jungle"; but this is an easily understood brachylogy for "Wewena and his fellows believe Mumbo Jumbo to be invisibly enthroned upon a black stone", and in this expanded form the quasi-name "Mumbo Jumbo" again occurs only in intentional-object position. So long as "Mumbo Jumbo" is used as a quasi-name, not as a name, it is not available for use as a subject of predication; and to shift it without notice to a name is equivocation. Let me remind you that it would anyhow be a mistake to raise the question: What about the use of "Mumbo Jumbo" *by Wewena and the others* as a subject of predications? For our supposition is that "Mumbo Jumbo" is a quasi-name used by contemptuous outsiders to describe Wewena's worship, not a word that Wewena himself purports to use as a name of a God.

It follows from this discussion that a statement like "Smith believes this ancient hill-fort was built by Arthur" is liable to a special sort of ambiguity. The speaker may intend to use both "Smith" and "Arthur" as proper names, or he may mean to use only "Smith" as a name and "Arthur" as a quasi-name. In one case, "Arthur" will link up this proposition with other predications meant to be all about the same man; in the other case, when the speaker uses the name "Arthur", what he himself will intend to refer to is not a man, but only other people's intentions to refer to a man. One proposition is related, via repeated uses of "Arthur" as a name, to a use of "one and the same man" that is meant to convey real identity; the other proposition is related, via repeated uses of "Arthur" as a quasi-name, to uses of "the same man" as expressing merely intentional identity—as when one says "Smith believes a certain man to have reigned over Britain, and Jones believes the very same man to have built this hill-fort", using the Buridan convention of word order.

Names and quasi-names are of course grammatically proper nouns. I suppose I need to say something about the contemporary idea that proper nouns do not really possess a meaning, are not words in a language, etc. For I have argued that the sentence "Smith believes that the hill-fort was built by Arthur" must be being used equivocally by two speakers when one means "Arthur" as a name and the other as a quasi-name. If "Arthur" is not a word with meaning anyhow, because it is a proper noun, then of course it can't be used equivocally, or univocally for that matter. In my view this objection is terribly silly; to those of my readers who would agree, I apologize for raising the matter.

The arguments for the view on which the objection rests seem to me to be worthless. One of these arguments uses the premiss that proper nouns are not given in dictionaries. This would be irrelevant if it were true, and is in any event false; the well-known English-German/German-English dictionary Muret-Saunders, for example, contains lots of proper nouns. Another argument is that a man who knows the Chinese name "Chiang Kai-shek" may yet truly be said not to know a word of Chinese, so "Chiang Kai-shek" cannot be a word of the Chinese language. But of course in this idiomatic sense of "not knowing a word of the language" a physicist may be truly said not to know a word of Latin although in fact he knows a score of Latin words—"*nucleus*", "*quantum*", "*a priori*", "*prima facie*", etc. And how can, e.g.,

"Warszawa" in Polish be truly said to be a feminine noun and have adjectives agreeing with it and undergo case-inflection and so on, if it is not a Polish word at all? Of course it is a Polish word—it's the word for Warsaw.

This last argument, on a previous occasion of its use, was met with the ploy that I hadn't proved "Warszawa" to be a Polish word, because I had supplied no rigorous definition of the word "word". But it is just a Socratic sophistry to argue that a proposition may not be accepted as plainly true unless the terms in it are defined—let alone, 'rigorously' defined. "Define your terms" is a regular move for political hecklers, for writers of letters to newspapers, for idle tosspots who argue inconsequentially over their beer; after bedevilling philosophy for centuries, the Socratic argument has found its proper level; let us keep it there.

I return to our main business. We can understand quasi-names, used as objects of intentional verbs, if we can understand the corresponding intentional-identity use of phrases like "the same poet" or "the same God". And we can understand that if we have a proper logical rationale of the distinction that Buridan marked by putting the object-expression now before, now after, the intentional verb. For of course the difference between "Smith and Brown admire the same poet" and "It is the same poet that Smith and Brown admire" will correspond to the difference between "Smith admires a poet" and "There is a poet Smith admires"; the forms in which the object-term follows the verb will cover, while those with the object-term before the verb will exclude, cases like the famous Antipodean hoax. (Two bored soldiers on a Pacific island picked out words with a pin and published the result as the posthumous work of a war hero; many critics admired this 'poet'.)

You may be expecting me to come out with a formal account of the Buridan distinction itself. This hope I must dash. I once thought I could do the trick, but a Birmingham pupil showed my idea wouldn't do and I've had no better ideas since. Those who are interested in my attempt at a formal account may consult my paper "A Medieval Discussion of Intentionality" (4. 2. in this book). May someone else be inspired to do better.

What is worse, I am not all that strongly convinced that the whole enterprise is not a wild goose chase. Suppose X and Y both worshipped the deity of the Sun. Do they or do they not worship the same God? X may have been an ancient Egyptian worshipper of a Sun-God, and Y a medieval Japanese worshipper of a Sun-Goddess! What criterion are we to apply? This is going to be a headache for us even if we are not interested in worship or religious belief; for similar difficulties will crop up in quite secular contexts. Let us go back to our Antipodean hoax: what conditions must be fulfilled if we are to say that many critics admired one and the same poet? I have not the least idea how to draw the line—even, how to get a consistent though arbitrary criterion for such intentional identity.

This is a grave and inescapable problem. A lot of what we take to be our understanding of other men's discourse consists in understanding when they are referring over and over again to one and the same object—without ourselves needing either to identify the object or to know that their intended reference succeeds. But what we claim to know when we say that all those others intend to refer to the same thing is itself yet another example of intentional identity; and so it is doubtful what our claim *means*, let alone whether it is true.[1]

It is a minor matter that, failing a satisfactory account of intentional identity, we also lack a satisfactory account of quasi-names. Quasi-names, let me insist, are not a philosopher's invention; words often are used as quasi-names in ordinary discourse, and some words have even come into use from the first as quasi-names; all that I have done is to invent the term "quasi-name" for this use of words, and to insist on the importance of parsing a word as a name or a quasi-name. (Which of those a word is depends on the speaker's intention, not on the facts; a name that is empty because the speaker has made a mistake of identification is still syntactically a name in *his* use, not a quasi-name.) So here also we lack a satisfactory logic for an area in which we commonly move around with an ill-founded confidence that we know our way about.

I have never liked the sentiment of that proverb about travelling hopefully, and do not now offer it as a solace to disappointed readers. But I hope that in the course of the discussion some truth has emerged and some confusions and fallacies have been removed.

---

[1] See my paper "Intentional Identity" (4.4. in this book), for an exposition of the severe difficulties over even logically formulating such a claim.

M

4.6. THE IDENTITY OF PROPOSITIONS

One prominent feature of Kotarbiński's philosophical work has been his vigorous argument for an ontology recognising only concrete objects, and not also numbers, functions, classes, Platonic ideas, etc., nor yet facts, events, situations, etc. In ordinary language we have nouns seeming to refer to all these kinds of non-concrete objects; but Kotarbiński sets before us a programme of showing these nouns to be mere 'onomatoids', to be a dispensable manner of speaking.

I should like to think that this programme could be carried out; but in some instances the technical difficulties are severe. Nobody has shown how to do mathematics without employing set theory; as Tarski once said, *inimicus Plato, sed magis inimica falsitas*. I do not despair of a reistic solution even here. Mathematical infinity, I am inclined to think, is not an infinity of objective *Gegenstände*, as Frege thought, but consists in the infinite (illimitable) potentialities of human language; if so, mathematical discourse would in the last resort be discourse about concrete objects, namely about what men, who make mathematics, are able to say and think. But the working out of this suggestion would require a gigantic development of modal logic, the logic that deals with potentialities. It is well known that there are formal parallels between modal logic and quantification theory; a better understanding of these might enable us to *translate* formulas containing quantifiers over sets, numbers, and the like, into formulas containing modal operators, and *vice versa*. If such a translation were technically possible, then it would be an extralogical decision whether we took the set-theoretic or the modal formulation as fundamental. Quine would regard the use of quantifiers relating to sets as intelligible, and the modal formulation as needing to be explained; my own feeling would be the other way. What I think is not to be hoped for is a satisfactory foundation of mathematics in a conceptual scheme that admits *neither* modal operators, *nor* quantifiers over an infinite domain. For the moment, anyhow, the translation of set-theoretical quantifiers into modal operators is mere programme; for the moment, set-theoretical entities are a myth not practically dispensable.

This is no reason for tender handling of discourse that can be more easily demythologized. I have elsewhere attacked the myths of facts and events; in this paper I am concerned with the myth of Propositions (conceived as what sentences "express").

In discussing this problem I shall have to use quotes frequently, so I begin by laying down conventions for their use. Following a useful suggestion by Hintikka,[1] I use single and double quotes indifferently for mention of the expressions they enclose, except when the enclosed expression contains italic letters; in this case the double quotes will work like Quine's corners—e.g. for any expression x, "x is a man" is the result of replacing the variable 'x' in 'x is a man' by x (which *may* be the variable 'x'). An expression displayed after an Arabic numeral on a new line of print is to be read as if it were in double quotes.

To describe the words and attitudes of others we may use either the *oratio obliqua* construction, as in:

(1) James believes that his wife fears that she has cancer,

or the *oratio recta* construction:

(2) James believes "My wife's fear is 'I have cancer' ".

Philosophers have a curious prejudice against the *oratio recta* form, and produce a range of arguments against the possibility of using it. It is clear in advance that these arguments are sophistical; for forms like (2) are common in all vernaculars (cf. the King James Bible) and perfectly intelligible, and translating from *oratio recta* to *oratio obliqua* and back is an easy exercise for an intelligent schoolchild, difficult as it would be to formulate exact rules for this. Indeed the arguments employed are often frivolously bad; applied to our example, they would be to the effect e.g. that (2) is correctly inferable from (1) only with the added supposition that James talks English and believes his wife does; or again, that a correct translation of (2) would leave the *oratio recta* in English, whereas a correct translation of (1) would translate the *oratio obliqua*. These deserve no answer; "God said 'Let there be light' " does not mean that God used English, and only a philosopher would argue that this is a mistranslation unless the original consisted of a quoted English sentence standing in a Hebrew context.

When very bad arguments are used for a philosophical thesis,

[1] *Knowledge and Belief*, Cornell University Press, 1962.

there is often some deep underlying prejudice that deserves un-earthing. Here, I think, the prejudice is expressible as follows: "(2) is only language about language, and thus can touch only the physical expressions of attitudes, not describe the attitudes themselves." To remove this prejudice would be a long and difficult business; here I can hope to make only a small dent in it.

This prejudice leads people to suppose that a propositional attitude, i.e., one describable by using an *oratio obliqua* construction, is an attitude directed towards a sort of abstract entity designated by *oratio obliqua* clauses. Frege called these supposed abstract entities 'thoughts' ('Gedanken'), and this term works well enough in many contexts; but the more familiar term is 'proposition'. This use of 'proposition' is objectionable because it ousts the older, linguistic, application of the word and leaves people to grope after some substitute for that—and the substitutes they lay hold of, e.g. 'sentence' and 'statement', are obviously not good ones. Under protest, I shall use 'Proposition', with an initial capital to mark off the modern use of the word.

The following theses would commonly be accepted about Propositions:

(i) Each unambiguous declarative sentence expresses (has as its sense) just one Proposition.

(ii) Synonymous expressions have the same sense.

(iii) A 'that' clause containing an unambiguous declarative sentence is a singular designation of the Proposition expressed by the sentence: "that p" designates what p expresses.

(iv) "The Proposition that p" and the 'that' clause "that p" are synonymous designations of a Proposition.

(v) "The Proposition expressed by Qp", where Qp is quotation of the sentence p, designates the same Proposition as "The Proposition that p".

Point (iv) must not be understood in the sense that "that p" can always be simply replaced by "the Proposition that p"; some twisting of the context around may be necessary, e.g. from:

(3) James fears that there are Martians hostile to men,

to:

(4) James contemplates with fear the Proposition that there are Martians hostile to men.

But this no more goes against the synonymy of "that p" and "the Proposition that p" than the fact that in "There were twelve apostles" "the number twelve" cannot take the place of "twelve" shows these not to be synonymous. I am not myself a friend of synonymy, but those who are do well not to fear such grammatical scarecrows. With regard to (v) no such troubles arise; "the Proposition that p" and "the Proposition expressed by Qp" are grammatically intersubstitutable.

Now it follows from these theses that *oratio obliqua* is always eliminable in favour of *oratio recta*. For by thesis (iv) an assertion containing "that p" can always be turned into one containing instead "the Proposition that p", as we transformed (3) to (4); and then for "the Proposition that p", *salva veritate* and *salva congruitate* (i.e. without becoming ungrammatical), we may write "the Proposition expressed by Qp"; e.g. (4) would become:

(5) James contemplates with fear the Proposition expressed by "There are Martians hostile to men".

This way of speaking is one to which the friends of Propositions are committed; and they cannot refuse us the right to abbreviate "contemplates with fear the Proposition expressed by" to "has this fear":

(6) James has this fear: "There are Martians hostile to men".

But this is the very way of speaking objection to which led to Propositions' being postulated. Moreover, whereas one who uses (5) is in no position to object to (6), one who uses (6) need not accept (5) as an expansion of it. Even if he did, this would not necessarily commit him to accepting "the Proposition expressed by Qp" as a singular designation—any more than one need accept "the sake of James's good name" as a singular designation standing for the sake of James's good name.

The theses about Propositions thus appear to me as like a false knot, which pulls out when tension is applied to the string. There is a further objection, too. By theses (i) and (ii) and (iv), if p and q are synonymous unambiguous declarative sentences, "a believes (the Proposition) that p" will have the same truth-value as "a believes (the Proposition) that q". But it is not easy to find any general criterion for sentence-synonymy which will satisfy this condition. Mutual strict implication—i.e. what is expressed by "Necessarily either both p and q or neither p nor q"—notoriously will not do; this premise does not warrant the conclusion "Anyone believes that p if and only if he believes that q". Mutual entailment has been proposed as a condition. But it is difficult to characterize in a rigorous way the logical laws for a connective "ent" such that "p ent q and q ent p" gives something stronger than mutual strict implication; it seems that to avoid a collapse of entailment into strict implication we have to deny laws of entailment that are intuitively obvious—e.g. "p ent q and q ent r" will not always yield the conclusion "p ent r"—and even at this price it is not clear how the use of "ent" can be satisfactorily characterized, at least I know of nobody who has done the trick. What is more, there are arguments showing that if from "p ent q and q ent p" we could always infer "The Proposition that p is the same as the Proposition that q", then *either* we must say that sentences formed in the same truth-functional way from sentences expressing the same Proposition may themselves express different Propositions, *or* we find that sometimes we have to concede this conjunction:

(7) The Proposition that p is the same as the Proposition that q and p ent r and it is not the case that q ent r.

I think that the upshot is that nobody really has the faintest idea what he means when he says "The Proposition that p is the same as the Proposition that q".[1]

A desperate remedy that I learn has actually been proposed is to concede "The Proposition that p is the same as the Proposition that q" only when p and q are the very same expression. This is not quite so desperate as it may seem. Although "Anybody believes (the Proposition) that p if and only if he believes (the Proposition) that q" will then never be inferable from a known identity of Propositions whose expressions, p and q, are verbally different, we may yet know that such a statement is true; Propositions' being different is nothing to prevent both from being believed or not believed together. Trouble will now arise, however, over the notion of sentences' expressing propositions. If the difference of two Propositions is no obstacle to their both

---

[1] For these difficulties, see the papers on 'Entailment' by C. Lewy and myself, Aristotelian Society Supplementary Volume 32, 1958. The paper by myself is now paper 4.7 in this collection.

being believed in the same breath by anybody who believes either, why should it be an obstacle to their always being both expressed in the same breath by anyone who utters a sentence expressing either? But then the whole conceptual apparatus of synonymy and non-ambiguity is in danger of collapse. Anyhow, if we cannot recognise the same sense in different verbal guises, there appears little point in postulating Propositions as the gold that backs the paper currency of sentences.

Double *oratio obliqua*, as in:

(8) Smith believes that James fears that there are Martians hostile to men

raises obstacles to my programme of replacing a 'that' clause by the corresponding *oratio recta*. We cannot readily assume that since (8) is the result of prefixing 'Smith believes that' to (3), we may go through steps parallel to (4), (5), (6), as follows:

(9) Smith believes that James contemplates with fear the Proposition that there are Martians hostile to men
(10) Smith believes that James contemplates with fear the Proposition expressed by 'There are Martians hostile to men'
(11) Smith believes that James has this fear: 'There are Martians hostile to men'.

If we could get from (8) to (11), then by a series of essentially similar steps we could eliminate the *oratio obliqua* construction remaining in (11), and end up with *oratio recta* within *oratio recta* instead of double *oratio obliqua*. But unfortunately the steps from (8) to (9) and from (9) to (10) are both disputable. I shall here discuss only the first difficulty.

Philosophers may deny that we may pass freely between the forms (8) and (9) on the score that if Smith is a logician who rejects Propositions, he may believe the first and disbelieve the second of the Propositions designated by:

(12) (The Proposition) that James fears that there are Martians hostile to men
(13) (The Proposition) that James contemplates with fear the Proposition that there are Martians hostile to men.

Thus it has been argued in respect of statements related like (8) and (9) that (8) could be true and (9) false. But this is incorrect. A person Robinson other than Smith and James could in no case consistently describe Smith's attitude by combining assertion of (8) and denial of (9). If Robinson accepts Propositions, he ought to regard (3) and (4) as synonymous, and consequently regard (12) and (13) as designating one and the same Proposition, by theses (ii), (iii), and (iv) above; so Robinson would contradict himself if he asserted (8) and denied (9). If Robinson rejects Propositions, then for him (9) is either a pompous variant of (8) or a piece of philosophers' nonsense; so if he asserts both (8) and the contradictory of (9), he is on his own premises either contradicting himself or talking nonsense. No view of Robinson's, then, and no attitude of Smith's can make it other than an abuse of *oratio obliqua* for Robinson to affirm (8) and deny (9). Even if Smith verbally affirms (3) but denies (4), that only shows that Smith is unclear about what (4) may mean, and still does not justify Robinson in affirming (8) but denying (9).

Brusquely as I have dismissed this objection, it raises a serious puzzle that I have no idea how to solve. In an ontological dispute, like this one about Propositions, one side or the other is not in plain error but in a muddle; and how can one describe a muddled state of mind without getting muddled in describing it? There is of course no logical requirement that the description should be muddled any more than one need get drunk to describe drunkenness; but there appears a difficulty in using either *oratio recta* or *oratio obliqua* to report a confused state of mind. *Oratio obliqua* that is coherently construable surely reports a clear, even if mistaken, attitude; and one who quotes ill-formed expressions in *oratio recta* only gives us symptoms of a muddle, and does not diagnose its nature.

The objection to free passage between the forms (9) and (10) is more serious: If Smith believes something about James and a Proposition, it surely does not follow that Smith believes something about James and a verbal expression of that Proposition, so (10) cannot follow form (9). The last obstacle considered was a mere mirage that we could drive through; this one is a road block, for we can no longer argue *ad hominem* that a friend of Propositions must accept the transition, as we could about (4) and (5). It is possible, I think, to get by along another route; but I do not as yet see a convincing *ad hominem* argument by which I could compel the friends of Propositions to follow me that way;

so I shall, as I said, leave this difficulty undiscussed for the present.

Thus far I have discussed *oratio obliqua* following so-called verbs of saying; I end with a brief discussion of the 'that' clauses relevant to modal logic—the ones following 'It is necessary', 'It is possible', etc. These also are commonly held to designate Propositions; and so are the 'that' clauses following 'It is true' and 'It is false'; for surely a mere form of words cannot be true or false, only the Proposition it serves to express can be.

This view that "necessary" and "true" are predicates of Propositions often goes with the view that a predication of "necessarily *P*" is always exponible as really predicating "necessary" of a Proposition itself expressed by predicating *P*; e.g. "Men are necessarily mortal" would not mean that a predicate "necessarily mortal" was true of each man but that "necessary" was true of the Proposition expressed by "Men are mortal". Now this combination of views is easily refutable. For since "It is necessary that *p*" and "It is necessarily true that *p*" are always equipollent, "necessary" and "necessarily true" are interchangeable as predicates of Propositions. Thus from:

(14) The Proposition which *a* thought of at time *t* is necessary,

(which would be true e.g. if the man called *a* thought then of the Proposition that twice one is two, and of no other Proposition) we could infer:

(15) The Proposition which *a* thought of at time *t* is necessarily true,

which by the view about predicates of the form "necessarily *P*" would mean:

(16) It is a necessary Proposition that the Proposition which *a* thought of at time *t* is true.

But (16) is false unless "The Proposition which *a* thought of at time *t* is true" expresses a necessary Proposition; so (16) does not follow from (14).

I regard it as unhelpful and uncalled-for to bring in Propositions to explain "necessary" and "possible". If the 'that' clauses to which these adjectives can be attached were to be treated as designations of abstract entities, then these abstract entities could not be Propositions; for mutual strict implication, which as we saw would not give a criterion of identity for Propositions, does give a sufficient condition in modal logic for clauses' being inter-substitutable *salva veritate*, and therefore would give a criterion of identity for the supposed designata of these clauses. But I see no reason to speak of such designata at all; I prefer to regard "necessarily" and "possibly" as operators like negation, which form statements from statements and predicates from predicates. This view will, I believe, make possible the construction of a coherent quantified modal logic. Allowing predicates like "necessarily *P*" commits us to denying Locke's thesis that there is nothing essential to individuals; but those who uphold this thesis, so far as I know, have little to say for it beyond bare assertion. Quine has sometimes said that quantified modal logic would commit us to Aristotelian essentialism; but why should we not be Aristotelian essentialists?

4.7.   ENTAILMENT

I must first consider the logical make-up of entailment-statements. (A *statement* is, for me, always a piece of language used in a certain way.)[1] We may assume that in an entailment-statement the verb "entails" occurs between two statements, which we may call its *antecedent* and *consequent*. But is the statement well-formed unless the antecedent and consequent are somehow dressed up? "Russell is a brother entails Russell is male" certainly looks odd, not to say ill-formed. And Quine would say it *is* ill-formed; on his view the antecedent and consequent ought to stand each in a pair of quotation marks, and the presence of the quotes would mean that the whole statement was a statement, not about Russell or about being a brother, but about the two blocks of type "Russell is a brother" and "Russell is male"; entailment would be on a level with such a relation between blocks of type as *containing a greater number of letters*. (Quine's actual word is "implies", not "entails", but in view of the way he uses the word the difference is insignificant.)[2]

Quine's way of dressing up entailment-statements is unlikely

---

[1] (*Note*, 1969). I should now prefer the term "proposition"; cf. papers 4.6 and 8.2. But in this paper such a use of the word might have caused confusion.
[2] W. van O. Quine, *Methods of Logic* (Routledge and Kegan Paul, 1951), pp. 37–8.

to tempt anyone who takes a serious interest in non-extensional formal logic (as he, of course, does not); but it seems grammatically satisfying, for a reason that is worth going into. The verb "entails" is transitive, and calls for a noun to precede it as a subject and another to follow it as an object. Now a quotation is rather noun-like, for the same reason as makes it natural (though not, I think, strictly correct) to call a quotation a name of the quoted expression; so the antecedent and consequent of an entailment-statement look grammatically more respectable when they are dressed up in quotes; Quine significantly calls the lack of quotes ungrammatical.

This is not the only way of achieving grammatical respectability; for if we write entailment-statements on the pattern "The proposition that p entails the proposition that q", where "p" and "q" go proxy for clauses (e.g. "Russell is male"), then the antecedent and consequent are dressed up in a still more noun-like guise, in fact they are used to form unimpeachable noun-phrases. But grammatical respectability need not be what we require in logic. The word "entails" as we are now considering it is a term of art, and it seems to me an open question whether the wrong part of speech was not chosen for the job. Entailment-statements might have been framed, not by borrowing a verb from the lawyers, but by reviving the obsolete conjunction "an if"; e.g., "An if Russell is a brother, then Russell is male". This form of statement is grammatically quite respectable, and offers us no temptation at all to think what we are talking about are blocks of type.

Moreover, this way of writing entailment-statements must be legitimate if it is legitimate to dress them up with "the proposition that—"; for we could then define "An if p then q" to mean what is meant by "The proposition that p entails the proposition that q". Thus anyone who accepts the latter way of writing entailment-statements cannot object to the analysis that "An if p then q" is meant to express—to treating an entailment-statement as being built out of a pair of statements, just as when statements are joined by "and" or "or".

There are, on the other hand, strong objections to dressing up entailment-statements with "the proposition that—". A phrase of the form "the proposition that p" is on the face of it a uniquely referring expression—what Frege calls an *Eigenname*—

standing for a certain proposition.[1] It would be cheap and silly to object by asking in the peculiar (anti-)metaphysical tone of voice "But what *are* propositions?" and talking about 'queer entities' and 'mysterious realms'; just as it is futile to ask "But what *are* numbers?" To know the reference of numerical *Eigennamen*, as Frege pointed out, means being able to identify and distinguish numbers, and this in turn means knowing the truth-conditions of a statement of number-identity—of "The number of *F*s is the same number as the number of *G*s" or "There are just as many *F*s as *G*s". Frege showed that those truth-conditions can be stated in a way that does not presuppose our understanding the term "number"—in purely logical terms. All this is territory once and for all conquered, from which we cannot be expelled by any rhetoric about 'queer entities'. I do not indeed defend Frege's misguided introduction of general set theory into the foundations of arithmetic; but, contrary to popular belief, Frege himself, at any rate when he wrote the *Grundlagen*, regarded this as something dubious and as of altogether secondary importance; the heart of the matter was for him the criterion of numerical identity.[2]

We may take Frege's achievement as showing what we might reasonably expect of a theory of propositions: namely, an analysis in purely logical terms, not presupposing that we understand the term "proposition", of the statement "The proposition that *p* is the same proposition as the proposition that *q*". No such analysis, however, is available as yet. Mutual entailment has been suggested as a criterion of propositional identity; but we shall see that this will not do. Lacking such a criterion, we do well to doubt whether there is such a concept as propositional identity, and whether phrases of the form "the proposition that *p*" stand for identifiable objects of thought at all. And then we do best to avoid such phrases altogether; they have no clear utility as terms of art, and to use them as mere padding for our sentences (as some people use "to the effect that" and "as to whether") would be both stylistically bad and likely to cause confusion.

---

[1] (*Note*, 1969) This word is here used not for what *I* call "propositions" elsewhere, i.e. pieces of language with a certain role, but for supposed abstract entities 'expressed by' such pieces of language.

[2] *Op. cit.* p. 117, last paragraph of §107. *Cf.* also my review-article 'Frege's *Grundlagen*', *Philosophical Review*, 1951, (paper 6.1. in this book) and Mr. Dummett's article 'Nominalism', *ibid.*, 1956.

Even if the mutual-entailment criterion of propositional identity would work, it would still be best not to treat the entailment-statements that are dressed up with "the proposition that" as being the standard form. For even if that form of entailment-statements were admissible, the "an if" form suggested above would necessarily also be admissible; so that we could express mutual entailment like this: "An if p, then q, and an if q, then p". Now we might indeed attempt offering this as an explication of: "The proposition that p is the same proposition as the proposition that q"; but it could not conform to our Fregean paradigm for such explications unless the use of "an if" required no previous understanding of the term "proposition"; just as "There is a one-one correlation of the Fs to the Gs" is a satisfactory explication of "The number of Fs is the same number as the number of Gs" only because we can understand "one-one correlation" without needing first to understand the term "number". If "An if p, then q, and an if q, then p" were intelligible only through a previous understanding of "the proposition that p", it would be disqualified as an explication of propositional identity. For we cannot start by using *Eigennamen* of propositions (say) in entailment-statements, and then go on to investigate propositional identity; on the contrary, failing an account of this, we have no warrant for introducing such *Eigennamen* at all. For they, unlike numerical *Eigennamen*, are not expressions with a well-established use, of which we are trying to give a philosophical analysis; without a criterion of propositional identity we just do not know how to use them. Thus we could not hope to find an explication of propositional identity along this road unless "an if" could be used in making entailment-statements without our previously understanding the term "proposition".

I shall therefore in the sequel avoid using *Eigennamen* like "the proposition that Russell is a brother", and even the term "proposition"—until I come back to an explicit discussion of propositional identity. I shall not, however, drop the verb "entails" in favour of "an if . . . then . . .", theoretically preferable as that would be; I merely give notice, once and for all, that as I use it "entails" is logically a conjunction, like "and" or "or", used to form a statement out of a pair of statements, and that small italic letters like "p" go proxy for statements, not for *Eigennamen* formed with "the proposition that"; I shall never use "entails" between such *Eigennamen*. Any grammatical discomfort we feel may be mitigated by using brackets, as in "(Russell is a brother) entails (Russell is male)"; these are just an aid to reading, and have no logical force except to mark the division of clauses.

In discussing Lewy's paradoxes, I shall find it convenient to use the Polish symbolism for truth-functional operators. The Polish symbols always precede the argument or arguments; I use "N" for negation, "K" for conjunction, "C" for the conditional, "E" for the biconditional. Brackets are not strictly needed in this symbolism, but I insert some for clarity.

Lewy's first paradox consists in the fact that for certain interpretations of the latters "*p*, *q*, *r*," each statement of the following set appears true, and yet the set is patently inconsistent.

1. It is contingent (*i.e.*, neither necessary nor impossible) that *p*, and also, that *q*.
2. It is necessary that *r*.
3. K*pq* entails *r*.
4. K*pr* entails *q*.
5. If it is contingent that *p* and contingent that *q* and necessary that *r*, and K*pr* entails *q*, then *p* entails *q*.
6. If *p* entails *q*, *p* entails K*pq*.
7. *p* does not entail *r*.
8. If *p* entails K*pq* and K*pq* entails *r*, then *p* entails *r*.

The inconsistency is easily shown: from 1, 2, 4, 5 we get "*p* entails *q*"; from this and 6, we get "*p* entails K*pq*"; from this, 3, and 8 we get "*p* entails *r*", which 7 contradicts. Thus at least one member of the set must be false, on any interpretation.

I now give two interpretations of the set, slightly modified from Lewy's: A. Read "*p*" as "The German sentence in Lewy's first paragraph unambiguously says that there is nobody who is a brother and is not male".

Read "*q*" as "The German sentence in Lewy's first paragraph unambiguously signifies something that is necessary".

Read "*r*" as "It is necessary that there is nobody who is a brother and is not male".

B. Taking "if and only if" truth-functionally throughout: read "*p*" as "Caesar is dead if and only if Russell is a brother"; read "*q*" as "Caesar is dead if and only if Russell is a male sibling"; read "*r*" as "Russell is a brother if and only if Russell is a male sibling".

To get the point of these examples, we must consider what the sentence "A brother is a male sibling" means when it is used to express a conceptual analysis. (Of course it need not be used this way; it may be used to give information about the usage of English words—more probably about "sibling" than about "brother".) The conceptual-analysis force is to convey a thought that does not come very natural to the mass of men—*viz*., that a brother is the male of something, which a sister is the female of. That this is not a natural thought is clearly shown by the totally different etymology of the words for brother and sister in many languages; no doubt there is some sociological explanation. Now to express this thought handily we need a word for what a brother is the male of and a sister is the female of; it so happens that an old English word "sibling" is available (not, in fact, here used in its old sense), but that is of no significance; the thought is not about the English word "brother" or "sibling". It then makes sense, e.g., to speak of a man's coming to realize that necessarily there is nobody who is a brother and is not male, or that Russell is a brother if and only if Russell is a male sibling; he can do this by performing for the first time the conceptual analysis I have just discussed.

Let us now consider in order whether, on Interpretations A and B, the several statements 1 to 8 are true. 1 and 2, in which "entails" does not occur, need not detain us long. The truth of 1 will be readily admitted on either interpretation. As regards 2, once the point of the last paragraph has been grasped it will be seen to be necessary both that Russell is a brother if and only if Russell is a male sibling, and that there is nobody who is a brother and is not male; these are not contingent facts about English usage. Moreover, it is *necessarily* necessary that there is nobody who is a brother and is not male; for to say it is only contingently necessary is to say that a non-male brother, though not an actual possibility, is yet a possible possibility; and though Descartes would have asserted this (on the ground that God need not have created the necessity of a brother's being male),[1] Descartes was clearly talking great nonsense.

In order to discuss whether 3–8 are true, I must attempt to state the truth-conditions of an entailment-statement. I maintain that *p* entails *q* if and only if there is an *a priori* way of getting to

[1] *Œuvres*, ed. Adam and Tannery, vol. i, pp. 145, 149, 151.

know that Cpq which is not a way of getting to know either whether p, or whether q. (If this reads grammatically odd, remember that "p" and "q" are proxies for indicative clauses used as statements.)

The qualification "*a priori*" needed to be inserted because of the possibility that somebody might be trained to *observe* whether Cpq without specially noticing whether p or whether q.[1] The notion of an *a priori* way of knowing is of course indefinite; even the narrower notion of a logical way of knowing is inherently one with no fixed boundary, as Gödel's results show. I conclude from this, not that my account of entailment is defective, but that the word "entails" has a *family* of related uses rather than one single use. We can, however, surely dodge this difficulty by supposing (as seems to me quite reasonable) that for the course of a given discussion of a concrete case—e.g., Interpretation A or B of Lewy's first paradox—there is available a fixed stock of *a priori* ways of finding things out; on this supposition "entails" will also have a fixed meaning in the immediate context.

I might have formulated the truth-condition for "p entails q" rather differently: "There is an *a priori* way of getting to know that Cpq which is not a way of getting to know either that Np or that q". The first form (suggested to me in discussion by Professor Duncan-Jones) is easier to take in, but contains redundant parts. For it is tantamount to: "There is an *a priori* way of getting to know that Cpq which is not a way of getting to know that p, that Np, that q, or that Nq." Now any way of getting to know that Cpq which was also a way of getting to know that p would be a way of getting to know that q; so, any way of getting to know that Cpq which is not a way of getting to know that q is not a way of getting to know that p.—Similarly, any way of getting to know that Cpq which was also a way of getting to know that Nq would be a way of getting to know that Np; so, any way of getting to know that Cpq which is not a way of getting to know that Np is not a way of getting to know that Nq.—Omitting, then, the redundancies, we may state the truth-condition for "p entails q" as above: "There is an *a priori* way of getting to know that Cpq which is not a way of getting to know either that Np or that q." This differs very little from a truth-condition propounded by

[1] *Cf.* Wittgenstein, *Remarks on the Foundation of Mathematics* (Blackwell, 1957), pp. 191-2.

Professor von Wright, in what seems to me one of the best papers ever written on entailment.[1] There are, in fact, only two differences between him and me. First, he refers to methods 'of logic' rather than *a priori* methods; I chose not to do this, because I should then have excluded many 'classical' examples of entailment, e.g., "(*x* is red) entails (*x* is coloured)."[2] Secondly, he uses a modal operator where I use a quantifier—"it is *possible* to . . . " instead of "*there is* a way of . . . ing". Formally, this does not make much difference, because of the well-known parallelisms between quantificational and modal logics; but I think my form is more perspicuous. Moreover, I dodge a difficulty noticed by von Wright—namely, that use of the word "possible" suggests, and one sense of the word implies, that we might have "*p*" false and "It is possible to get to know that *p*" true; for there is a sense of "possible" for which, if there *could* be a situation in which it were true to say "*p* and I know that *p*", then in the actual situation, even if "*p*" is false, it is true to say "It is possible that one should get to know that *p*". But if there is a way of getting to know that *p*, then *p*; there is no difficulty here.

Someone might object, in the style of Quine, that my quantification 'ranges over' a 'slum' of 'abstract entities', viz., ways of getting to know things; that my irresponsible 'Platonism' has led to my assuming a highly undesirable 'existential commitment'. I should refuse to be ashamed by this accusation. I am 'Platonic' no more and no less than the schoolmaster is who tells his pupils that 'there are' three ways of doing a sum; if he is hereby taking up a new 'existential commitment' the responsibility is hardly likely to be onerous, even in a theoretical way. Of course, the existence of an *a priori* way of getting to know that *p* is not to be established by a philosophic inspection of an abstract realm, but simply by proving *a priori* that *p*.

Let us now consider 3 to 8 in order. As regards 3: a man can see *a priori* that if the sentence S unambiguously says that *s*, and S unambiguously signifies something necessary, then it is necessary that *s*; and this is independent both of his knowing what the contingent facts are about what the sentence S (the German sentence in Lewy's first paragraph) says, and of his having per-

---

[1] G. H. von Wright, *Logical Studies* (Kegan Paul, 1957), pp. 166–191.

[2] (*Note*, 1969) Under the influence of Quine, I have now become more sceptical about the existence of a clearly delimitable class of the non-logical *a priori*.

N

formed a conceptual analysis of *being a brother* so as to see that it is necessary that *s*, i.e., that necessarily there is nobody who is a brother and is not male.—Again, a man can see *a priori* that *if* (Caesar is dead if and only if Russell is a brother) and (Caesar is dead if and only if Russell is a male sibling), *then* (Russell is a brother if and only if Russell is a male sibling); and again this is independent both of his knowing the contingent facts about Caesar and Russell, and of his having performed a conceptual analysis of *being a brother* so as to see that Russell is a brother if and only if Russell is a male sibling.—Thus, on Interpretation A and B alike, K*pq* entails *r* by our criterion, and 3 is accordingly true.

We might similarly show that 4 is true; but the truth of 4, on either interpretation, will probably not be disputed.

Assuming my truth-condition for entailment-statements, 5 and 6 are provable theorems about entailment.—*Proof of* 5. We assume that K*pr* entails *q*, it is necessary that *r*, and it is contingent that *p* and again that *q*; to prove that *p* entails *q*.

Since K*pr* entails *q*, an argument with a premiss saying that K*pr* and conclusion saying that *q* is valid. But then also an argument with a premiss saying that *r* and a conclusion saying that C*pq* is valid. Since it is necessary that *r*, this latter valid argument affords us an *a priori* way of getting to know that C*pq*; and this must be independent of our knowing the contingently true answers to the questions whether *p* and whether *q*. Hence, *p* entails *q*. Q.e.d.

Proof of 6. We assume that *p* entails *q*; to prove that *p* entails K*pq*.

Since *p* entails *q*, there will be an *a priori* way of getting to know that C*pq* which is not a way of getting to know either that N*p* or that *q*. But any such *a priori* way of getting to know that C*pq* supplies an *a priori* way of getting to know that C*p*(K*pq*) which is not a way of getting to know either that N*p* or that *q*, and therefore (since anyone who knows that K*pq* knows that *q*) is not a way of getting to know either that N*p* or that K*pq*. Hence *p* entails K*pq*. Q.e.d.

As regards 7: we can show that *p* does not entail *r* if we can assert that there is no *a priori* way of getting to know that C*pr*, except by getting to know that *r*. On Interpretations A and B alike, as the reader may easily verify, this condition is clearly fulfilled. So 7 is true.

If 1–7 are all true, 8 must be false; that is, entailment cannot be unrestrictedly transitive. I think that this conclusion is paradoxical only in the sense of being surprising, and ought to be accepted. From the premisses "There is an *a priori* way of getting to know that C*pq* which is not a way of getting to know either whether *p* or whether *q*" and "There is an *a priori* way of getting to know whether C*qr* which is not a way of getting to know either whether *q* or whether *r*" we can indeed infer the conclusion "There is an *a priori* way of getting to know that C*pr*" but are not warranted in adding the clause "which is not a way of getting to know either whether *p* or whether *r*". For we shall certainly have, if the premisses are true, an *a priori* way of getting to know that C*pr*—*viz.*, syllogizing from our *a priori* knowledge that C*pq* and that C*qr*; but although finding out that C*pq* did not enable us to answer the question whether *p*, and finding out whether C*qr* did not enable us to answer the question whether *r*, finding out both together may for all we know enable us to answer one or other of these questions. So, if my truth-condition for entailment-statements is correct, we cannot in general infer "*p* entails *r*" from "*p* entails *q* and *q* entails *r*". (The reader will however easily see that we can infer this conclusion given the further premiss "It is contingent that *p* and contingent that *r*". For if it is contingent which is the true answer to the questions whether *p* and whether *r*, our *a priori* knowledge that C*pr* will not supply the answers.)

Entailment, then, is not unrestrictedly transitive; and we can in fact see clearly why it should not be transitive in the sort of case to which Lewy's first paradox relates. What we have, on Interpretations A and B alike, is (i) an *a priori* way of getting to know that C(K*pq*)*r* which is not a way of getting to know that *r* and (ii) an *a priori* way of getting to know that C*p*(K*pq*). But our knowledge that C*p*(K*pq*) depends on our knowledge that *r*; for example, taking Interpretation A, we know *a priori* that if the sentence S unambiguously says that there is nobody who is a brother and is not male, then (the sentence S unambiguously says this, and the sentence S unambiguously signifies something that is necessary), only in virtue of knowing *a priori* that it is necessary that there is nobody who is a brother and is not male. So there is no reason whatever to believe that we have any means of knowing *a priori* that both C*p*(K*pq*) and C(K*pq*)*r*, and thus that C*pr*, except in virtue of *a priori* knowledge that r; that is, there is no reason to think p entails r.

So far as I can see, this draws the sting of Lewy's first paradox, without our needing either to bring in different varieties of entailment, or to say that necessarily true statements cannot occur as antecedents or consequents of true entailment-statements. This unforced solution surely confirms my account of the truth-condition of entailment-statements.

Though entailment is not unrestrictedly transitive, valid proof is; a confusion of the two may account for resistance to my solution. A chain of proof is indeed only as strong as its weakest link, but equally you cannot construct a weak chain by forging together links that are severally strong. The matter just does not admit of dispute; we can only discuss why some people have oddly thought valid proof need not be transitive. Fitch denies that it is unrestrictedly transitive in order to resolve the paradoxes of set theory,[1] but of all the counter-intuitive and *ad hoc* solutions proposed, this must be the worst.

But could not a proof be invalidated because though each step is valid, the proof as a whole is circular? Not at all; argument in a circle is not logically fallacious. It is no doubt reprehensible to deceive yourself or others into thinking you have not already assumed your conclusion, in another guise, as one of your premises; but that does not mean the conclusion does not follow —it does. A circular argument does not get you any for'arder; but neither does it get you anywhere you have no right to be. A schoolboy unskilled in algebra who is trying to solve an equation may go through a series of steps that bring him back to the original equation: a futile procedure, but not a breach of algebraical rules. So even a proof that yields one of its premises over again as a conclusion is not thereby invalidated. Still less is a proof invalidated by yielding as a conclusion a formulation of one of the steps of inference in the proof. There is no fallacy in proving "$C(Kp(Cpq))q$" by *modus ponens* in a logistic system; for knowing how to frame a *modus ponens* argument is logically prior to knowing that $C(Kp(Cpq))q$.

We may perhaps reasonably require of a valid proof that each stage correspond to an entailment; it makes no essential difference

[1] F. B. Fitch, *Symbolic Logic* (The Ronald Press Co., New York, 1952), pp. vi, 109, 125.

whether a given stretch of the proof is direct or inverse, since p entails q if and only if Nq entails Np (as is easily proved on my theory). But it is an unfounded prejudice to think entailment must hold from the beginning to the end of a proof.

In a case Lewy refers to there is a more striking failure of transitiveness. As we saw in discussing 7 above, if it is necessary that q and contingent that p, p may not entail q—our *a priori* knowledge that Cpq may be derived entirely from our *a priori* knowledge that q. But in this case p will entail Kpq; for we shall have *a priori* knowledge that Cpq which does not tell us the (contingent) answers to the questions whether p and whether Kpq; and from this we can get *a priori* knowledge that Cp(Kpq). Kpq certainly entails q. Transitiveness fails here for much the same reason as in Lewy's paradox. Lewy finds it counter-intuitive that in this sort of case we should have p entailing Kpq; but since we cannot here infer that p entails q, I think there is no ground to suspect the result.

Lewy's *second* paradox relates to propositional identity. As before, I shall first set out the inconsistent assumptions schematically and then give an interpretation.

9. The proposition that p is the same proposition as the proposition that q.

10. If the proposition that p is the same proposition as the proposition that q, then the proposition that K(Erp) (Erp) is the same proposition as the proposition that K(Erp) (Erq).

11. If the proposition that K(Erp) (Erp) is the same proposition as the proposition that K(Erp) (Erq), then, if K(Erp) (Erq) entails Epq, K(Erp) (Erp) entails Epq.

12. K(Erp) (Erq) entails Epq.

13. K(Erp) (Erp) does not entail Epq.

Interpretation. Read "p" as "Russell is a brother"; "q" as "Russell is a male sibling"; "r" as "Caesar is dead."

The inconsistency of the set is patent. If someone has hopes of reaching a coherent doctrine of propositional identity, the assumption he had best choose to drop is 9. He would certainly be most ill-advised to drop 10 or 11. If he is prepared to say that the same proposition may not be expressed by sentences formed in an identical truth-functional way from sentences expressing the same proposition; or again, that the same proposition may be expressed by clauses that are not mutually substitutable *salva veritate* in the antecedent (or, for that matter, the consequent) of an entailment-statement; then he may as well admit that the jig is up—that he really has not the faintest idea what he means by "the same proposition".

Under our present interpretation of the letters, "p, q, r", 12 comes out the very same statement word for word as 3 above under Interpretation B; and 13 comes out as a negated entailment-statement differing from 7 under Interpretation B only by having as its antecedent, instead of "Caesar is dead if and only if Russell is a brother", the conjunction of this biconditional with itself over again. So we have the same grounds for accepting 12 and 13 as for accepting 3 and 7 under Interpretation B. Thus anyone who wants to defend propositional identity had best accept 10 to 13 and reject 9.

This seems the best choice for the advocate of propositional identity; but, as Lewy is well aware, bad is the best. To deny (in our example) that the proposition that Russell is a brother is the same proposition as the proposition that Russell is a male sibling involves dropping the mutual-entailment criterion of propositional identity, with nothing to put in its place; it also involves denying that when one sentence serves to analyse what another says, they both express the same proposition. The meaning of "the same proposition" is thus made quite obscure. My own solution, as I said before, is to reject this expression, along with the pretended *Eigennamen* of propositions, and construe entailment-statements in a way independent of these dubious notions.

4.8. ENTAILMENT AGAIN

In a recent paper[1] Jonathan Bennett has defended the notorious 'proof' given by C. I. Lewis that a contradictory conjunction entails anything; in the course of his defence, he has assailed the theory of entailment sketched by von Wright and me, which would show the 'proof' to be invalid. If there were any substance to Bennett's arguments, he would have managed to show that a formalization of the von Wright-Geach theory[2] runs into difficulties even within propositional logic; for that is all that is used

---

[1] "Entailment" *Philosophical Review*, LXVIII (1969), 197.
[2] See G. H. von Wright, *Logical Studies* (London 1957), p. 174.

in the Lewis 'proof'. I shall here show that, on the contrary, a certain formal system of propositional logic with entailment, tailor-made to capture the intuitions that our papers sought to express, in fact is a decidable system and therefore cannot break down.

Consider a logical system S, with a class of wffs and a class of theorems. I characterize the *entailment extension* of S, ES, as follows. ES contains one extra primitive symbol "W" (suggested by Polish "*wynika z*", "follows from"), and the wffs of ES are characterized thus:

(*i*) Any wff of S is a wff of ES.

(*ii*) If **A**, **B** are wffs of S, then ⌐W**AB**⌐ is a wff of ES.

(*iii*) There are no wffs except as provided in (*i*) and (*ii*).

As regards theoremhood:

(*iv*) Any theorem of S is a theorem of ES.

(*v*) If ⌐C**AB**⌐ is a theorem of S, and neither ⌐**NA**⌐ nor **B** is a theorem of S, then ⌐W**AB**⌐ is a theorem of ES. ("C" expresses the truth-functional hypothetical.)

(*vi*) Any substitution instance of a theorem of ES is a theorem of ES.

(*vii*) No wff of ES is a theorem of ES except as provided in (*iv*), (*v*), (*vi*).

The rules giving the wffs of ES allow "W" to occur in a wff only initially, as the main functor. In further work on this type of theory one would wish to remove this restriction, but it is convenient for present purposes. Clause (*v*) in the rules of theoremhood embodies our basic intuition: that the entailment expressed by ⌐W**AB**⌐ must hold solely in virtue of the internal logical relation of **A** and **B**, not in virtue of the modal value or theoremhood of ⌐**NA**⌐ by itself or **B** by itself. Clause (*vi*) is anyhow required in an ordinary formal system.

It is now easy to prove the following metatheorem:

If there is a decision procedure for S, there is a decision procedure for ES.

For take any wff **D** of ES. If **D** does not begin with "W" it is a wff of S, and we can decide whether it is a theorem of ES by deciding whether it is a theorem of S. If **D** begins with "W" all wffs of *ES* of which **D** is a substitution instance begin with "*W*"; and there is a *finite* class **K** of wffs of *ES* such that any wff of *ES* of which **D** is a substitution instance either belongs to **K** or is a mere relettering of a member of **K**. Each member of **K** can be tested for theoremhood under clause (*v*). **D** will then be a theorem of *ES* iff: *either* **D** itself is a theorem under clause (*v*), which is decidable; *or* **D** is a substitution instance of a member of **K**, and this is a theorem under clause (*v*)—which again is decidable.

Propositional calculus (*PC*) is decidable; so its entailment extension is also decidable. Let us then consider those wffs of this extension, *EPC*, which figure in the Lewis argument:

(1) *WKpNpp*
(2) *WKpNpNp*
(3) *WpApq*
(4) *WKApqNpq*
(5) *WKpNpq*

(1) and (2) are theorems of *EPC*, being respectively substitution instances of "*WKpqp*" and "*WKpqq*", whose theoremhood is readily established under clause (*v*). (3) is already a theorem of *EPC* under clause (*v*), and so is (4). (5) is not a substitution instance of any theorem of *EPC*; and "*NKpNp*" is a theorem of *PC*, and therefore (5) cannot be shown to be a theorem of *EPC* under clause (*v*); so (5) is a non-theorem of *EPC*. Naturally this is nowise in conflict with the theoremhood of (1) and (2), which are substitution instances of (5); *all* theorems of *EPC* are substitution instances of the non-theorem "*p*". But *EPC* contains no non-theorems that are substitution instances of theorems.

Obviously this makes entailment nontransitive; but why not? So long as each link in a chain of proof answers to an entailment, the whole chain is sound; we need no further test of whether the big leap 'from first to last' is also, on its own, justified by a direct entailment. Moreover, when the original premises and the final conclusion are logically contingent, entailment *is* transitive.

5

Quotation and Semantics

DESIGNATION AND TRUTH

In a recent article[1] Max Black considers the following formula, which I shall call (A):

For all x and y, if x is a sentence, and y uniquely designates x, then y is true $\equiv x$.[2]

It is not clear whether Black regards (A) as significant; he certainly suggests this, by calling (A) "a sentence of the meta-meta-language".[3] It is easy, however, to show that (A) cannot be significant; and our proof will use the same distinction (between a sentence and its name or designation) as occurs in (A) itself.

Consider the sentence "Tom loves Mary"; I shall call this "Hob". Hob, then, is a sentence—the sentence "Tom loves Mary"; "Hob" on the other hand (by the usual convention for inverted commas) is not a sentence, but the name or designation of a sentence. Let us now make the proper substitutions in (A):

(B) If Hob is a sentence, and "Hob" uniquely designates Hob, then "Hob" is true $\equiv$ Hob.

But this result is nonsense, and therefore (A) is nonsense. For, in the first place, the clause ' "Hob" is true ' is nonsense; since it is Hob, not "Hob", that is a sentence, it makes no sense to call "Hob" true. Secondly, Black intends us to read "$\equiv$" as synonymous with "if and only if".[4] This reading of "$\equiv$" requires that the

---

[1] Max Black, 'The Semantic Definition of Truth', *Analysis* 8. 4, March 1948. I shall refer to this as SDT.
[2] SDT, p. 51.   [3] SDT, p. 52.
[4] SDT, p. 51, note 6.

sense of (B) should be completed by our writing a *sentence* after
"≡"; it makes nonsense if we end (B) with "≡ Hob", in which
"≡" is followed merely by "Hob", the *name* of a sentence. For
the endings "if and only if Hob is true", "if and only if Hob is
commonly said", are perfectly legitimate, but not the ending "if
and only if Hob".

Two things may hinder our seeing this second objection.
First, we may have the impression that in "≡ Hob", or "if and
only if Hob", the conjunction *is* followed by a sentence—the
sentence Hob. This is quite wrong; the actual sentence Hob no
more follows "≡" in "≡ Hob" than a real live elephant follows
the words "Jumbo is" in "Jumbo is an elephant". Secondly,
"≡" is often read as "is materially equivalent to"; and one might
quite well have the ending ". . . is materially equivalent to Hob".
But "is materially equivalent to " is *not* synonymous with "if and
only if"; the substitutions that are allowable in "$p≡q$" are
different, according as we read "≡" one way or the other. Let us
call the sentence "Mary loves Tom" by the name "Nob". Then

    (C_1) Hob≡Nob; (C_2) "Tom loves Mary" ≡ "Mary loves
Tom";

are significant if "≡" is read as "is materially equivalent to",
but not if it is read as "if and only if". On the other hand,

    (D) Tom loves Mary ≡ Mary loves Tom

is significant only if "≡" is read as "if and only if", not if it is
read as "is materially equivalent to". In (C_1) and (C_2) the sign
"≡" conjoins *designations* of the sentences Hob and Nob, in (D)
it conjoins Hob and Nob *themselves*.

If we try to correct (A), the result is rather surprising. I shall
use "DES (L) . . ." as an abbreviation for the phrase: "that which
has in the language L the designation . . .". Thus, DES (English)
"red" is red, DES (French) "l'eau" is water, and so on. I assume
the legitimacy of talking about what *sentences* designate, as well as
what *names* designate; that is, I assume such expressions as these
to be significant: 'DES (French) "La lune est ronde", 'DES
(English) "Chicago is a large city" . (This extended concept of
designation should be familiar from Carnap's *Introduction to
Semantics*.)[1] Now consider the formula:

    (E) For all x, x is true in L ≡ DES (L) x.

This offers us a definition of "true in L" in terms of "designation

[1] Pp. 49–55.

in L". (E) belongs, as it should, to the meta-language in which we talk about the language L.

We may see, by performing the proper substitutions, that (E) is significant and adequate. We require of a definition of truth such results as the following:

(F) "Mon crayon est noir" is true in French ≡ my pencil is black.

By direct substitution in (E), what we get is:

(G) "Mon crayon est noir" is true in French ≡ DES (French) "mon crayon est noir".

So what we have to show is that (G) is significant and has the same truth-value as (F). It is quite easy to do this. 'DES (French) "mon crayon" ' stands for the same thing as "mon crayon"; and again, for the same thing as "my pencil", the English translation of "mon crayon"; namely, for my pencil. Further 'DES (French) "noir" ' stands for the same thing as "noir"; and again, for the same thing as "black", the English translation of "noir"; namely, for black. So the following two sentences have the same truth-value:

(H₁) DES (French) "mon crayon" is DES (French) "noir".

(H₂) My pencil is black.

Similarly, 'DES (French) "mon crayon est noir" ' stands for the same thing as "Mon crayon est noir", and again, for the same thing as "My pencil is black", the English translation of "Mon crayon est noir". So (F) and (G), like (H₁) and (H₂), must have the same truth-value; and *a fortiori* (G) must be significant.

Thus in any particular instance we can show that (E) gives the correct result. A general proof that (E) is an adequate definition of truth would be faced with serious difficulties.[1] But I think the reader should *grasp* its adequacy by 'intuitive induction' from instances like (G).

An odd result follows; 'DES(French) "mon crayon est noir" ' must be held to be a *complete sentence*—like "Mon crayon est noir", which 'stands for the same thing'. This leads to an awkwardness as regards ordinary English syntax; one might expect 'that which has in French the designation "Mon crayon est noir" ' to be only the subject of a sentence, not a complete sentence. But this should not worry us; it just means that in this

---

[1] For the difficulties of generalisation, *cf*. Black's remarks on the formula (Θ)— SDT p. 51.

context you do not arrive at natural English by reading "DES (French)" as "that which has in French the designation . . .". And although 'that which has in French the designation "Mon crayon est noir" ' is not grammatically a complete sentence, it is so logically; in fact, it means—according to the definition (E)—the same as: ' "Mon crayon est noir" is true in French'. If we make a grammatically complete sentence by adding a predicate such as "is a proposition" or "is a fact", we get nonsense; just as we do by adding "is a rose" to the sentence "A rose is a rose".

The same censure applies to what Carnap would say:[1]

(I) That which has in English the designation "Chicago is a large city" is: Chicago is a large city.

Carnap is at least not mentally dominated by correct English; he would insist that we must *not* understand what follows the colon in (I) to be a quotation; and if we were to replace the colon by the conjunction "that", he would regard this as a concession to euphony, *not* as a sign of 'reported speech'. But if we are thus allowed to disregard the suggestions of English grammar, then, although 'that which has in English the designation "Chicago is a large city" ' (i.e. 'DES (English) "Chicago is a large city" ') is not a sentence for a grammarian, it may in logic be a complete sentence.

This eliminates problems about 'the designata of sentences' and 'the relation of designation'. Since 'DES (English) "Chicago is a large city" ' is a complete sentence, "DES (English)" is not a relational sign. And 'that which has in English the designation "Chicago is a large city" ' does not become a significant question if we prefix "What is . . . ?"; the result is like: "What is it is raining?"

The definition (E) shows *on its own account* what substitutions for "*x*" are allowed. It would be a mistake to add the proviso "if *x* is a sentence in L"; that would not prevent our getting nonsense from improper substitution.[2] For if we substitute for "*x*" "Tom" or ' "Tom" '—Tom being the piper's son—the suggested proviso has the following effect:

(J₁) [If Tom is an English sentence, then] Tom is true in English if and only if that which has in English the designation Tom.

[1] *Op. cit.*, p. 52.
[2] Wittgenstein, *Tractatus Logico-Philosophicus*, 5.5351 (the English version is here untrustworthy), and 4.1272.

(J_2) [If "Tom" is an English sentence, then] "Tom" is true in English if and only if that which has in English the designation "Tom".

But we get nonsense whether the words in square brackets are inserted or left out; so the proviso does not help us at all. This is no objection to (E); *any* sentence *shows* what substitutions can be made for its variables, but none can *say* this about itself.[1]

5.2. DESIGNATION AND TRUTH—A REPLY

Professor R. M. Martin's criticism[1] of my article 'Designation and Truth'[2] rests on his not having observed that I was attempting a *reductio ad absurdum*. I argued, in fact, as follows. Suppose we try to interpret expressions like:

(i) that which is designated in French by "Mon crayon est noir"

on the model of expressions like:

(ii) that which is designated in French by "mon crayon".

In that case we must say that just as (ii) stands for the same thing as (the name) "my pencil", so (i) stands for the same thing as (the sentence) "My pencil is black". We can do this if we like, by interpreting "that which is designated in French by—", in contexts like (i), in the (highly unnatural) sense "— is true in French"; i.e. by using the definition (E) of my article. But if we do this, then expressions like (i) are *sentences*, not names; and questions like 'What is that which is designated in French by "Mon crayon est noir" '? make no more sense than the results of prefixing "What is . . . ?" to other sentences—"What is it is raining?", "What is a mouse spins?" The purpose of introducing expressions like (i) was to talk about the designata of sentences; but it turns out that the only sense we can give to (i) by analogy with (ii) is one that makes such talk nonsensical.

Professor Martin thinks I 'assume' that there are designata of sentences, not just for argument's sake, but as my own view. Further comment on his criticisms is therefore unnecessary. I wish, however, to withdraw the last passage of my article, from the words "The definition (E) shows .. . .", p. 96, to the end; it is certainly obscure, and very likely quite wrong.[3]

---

[1] (*Note* 1969) I feel quite uncertain whether my first or my second thoughts were better, so I leave the matter to the reader's judgment.
[2] *Analysis*, 10.3, January 1950.
[3] Article 5.1 above.

5.3. *IFS* AND *ANDS*

(1) I shall first consider a misunderstanding in Lewis and Langford's *Symbolic Logic* (p. 227). They begin by saying: "Whatever more it may be, the matrix method at least is a kind of game which we play with recognisable marks, according to certain rules". All that this really tells us is that in doing logic we write down definite symbols in an orderly way; which throws no light at all upon the nature of logic. But the natural suggestion of the word "game" is that logic is something like noughts-and-crosses; I do not know if this was intended by the authors.

Lewis and Langford use the symbol "pIq" to mean "the hypothetical with p as antecedent and q as consequent". Their next remarks have reference to the following extract from the truth table for pIq (which is given on p. 203, with "$p \supset q$" instead of "pIq"):

$$
\begin{array}{ccc}
p & q & p\mathrm{I}q \\
1 & 1 & 1 \\
1 & 0 & 0
\end{array}
$$

They rightly assert that such tables need not have 'any "logical" significance'; p and q may be "any kind of things". What is required on their view is that in some game or other there should be "an operation or move, pIq, which according to the rules can be taken, when p has the property A, only if q also has the property A"; in that case the table will tell us that if p has A, and pIq is an allowable move, then q must have A. The logical interpretation will then consist in taking the property A, expressed by the figure "1", to be truth, and the property expressed by the figure "0" to be falsehood, and reading "pIq" in the way I explained above.

But there is an inconsistency here in the interpretation of the figure "1", if p and q may be "any kind of things". As regards p and q, the figure "1" is taken to stand for the property A; but as regards pIq it is taken to stand for the property of being an allowable move in a certain game. This is inconsistent, unless A *is* the property of being an allowable move; and of course that is not necessary. We see this clearly if we take a simple non-logical interpretation of the table. Let the figures "1" and "0" connote the presence and the absence of an hereditary property A, and let "pIq" mean "offspring by p out of q". Then the table will have no reference to moves in any game; it will tell us that the trait A is present in the offspring, when it is present in the sire, if and only if it is also present in the dam.

We are indeed at liberty to take the figures "1" and "0" to mean that moves in a game are respectively allowed and forbidden; but in that case p and q cannot be "any kind of things", but must be moves in the game, like pIq. The table will then be equivalent to the following sentence: "If p is an allowable move, then q is an allowable move if and only if pIq is also". And here the sign "I" does not belong to the terminology of any special game, like "Kt" in chess; it expresses what we may fittingly call a logical relation of the move pIq to the moves p and q; so that the significance of "pIq" is after all 'logical'.

I think the source of these confusions is the authors' habitual carelessness over the use of quotation marks. Whatever sort of things p and q may be, the printed sign "pIq" is a move in "a kind of game which we play with recognisable marks"—if you choose to abuse the word "game" that way. But it is not the case that, however the table is read, pIq must be taken to be a move in a game; for pIq need not be a printed sign, as "pIq" is; in the non-logical interpretation I gave above, pIq was an animal.

(2) In some many-valued logics, there is a truth-value such that if p has it, then $-p$ has it; I shall use "X" as a sign for this truth-value.[1] Lewis and Langford suggest as interpretations of "p has the truth-value X" the ordinary English expressions "p is doubtful" and "p is as probable as not" (*op. cit.* pp. 223, 230). Similarly, some Polish logicians have ascribed the truth-value X to assertions about future contingencies, e.g. the weather; the contradictories "It will rain to-morrow" and "It will not rain to-morrow" have on their view the same truth-value.

It is easy to show that this sort of interpretation will not do. If p and q have the same truth-value, then $p.q$ has the same truth-value as $p.p$. This depends merely on the fact that $p.q$ is a truth-function of p and q; it does not depend on our choice of a truth-table for $p.q$, nor yet on whether our logic is two-valued or many-valued. Again, $p.p$ must have the same truth-value as p has.

[1] (*Note*, 1969) I use italic letters, in this part of the article, as metalinguistic variables. Thus "$-p$" is to be read as "the negation of p", not as "It is not the case that p"; and similarly "$p.q$" as "the simultaneous affirmation of p and q", not as "(It is the case that) both p and q".

This is so because "$p.p$" is short for "the simultaneous affirmation of p and p"; a truth-table that did not always give $p.p$ the same truth-value as p would simply not be defining the right truth-function. It follows that if p and q both have the same truth-value, then $p.q$ must likewise have that truth-value; so if p has the truth-value X, -p also has the truth-value X, and $p.$-p likewise has this truth-value. Thus if we admit the truth-value X, the law of contradiction is not a tautology.

This shows no inconsistency in many-valued logics; their consistency has been fully proved. Nor does it show the inapplicability of the idea of contradictories in many-valued logics. The contradictory of p is a sentence that is true if and only if p is false, and false if and only if p is true; in three-valued logic there is just one matrix that defines such a truth-function, viz.:

p	T	X	F
-p	F	X	T

But what does follow is that the suggested interpretations are ruled out. In ordinary English we may truly say "It will rain tomorrow as likely as not " or "It is doubtful if it will rain tomorrow". But this cannot be taken to imply that "It will rain to-morrow" has the truth-value X; for in that case "It will both rain and not rain to-morrow" would have the truth-value X; and clearly its truth-value is in fact falsehood.

(3) According to Lewis and Langford (*op. cit.* p. 228), any of the following four truth-tables defines an implication adequate for the *modus ponens*—"If p is true, and pIq is true, then q is true":

p	q	(i)	(ii)	(iii)	(iv)
T	T	T	T	T	T
T	F	F	F	F	F
F	T	F	T	F	T
F	F	F	F	T	T

We see at once, however, that the 'implications' (i) and (ii) are hopeless claimants for the title. With either truth-table, pIq would be assertible only if q were so; hence there would be no tautologous 'implications', not even pIq; and the formula of the *modus ponens*, pI((pIq)Iq), would hold only if q held. The authors recognise in a footnote that some of their 'implications' have this property; but they do not see that this makes the term inappropriate. (iii) and (iv) agree far better with our natural idea of implication; we readily verify that with either truth-table

$pI((pIq)Iq)$ is a tautology. With (iii), however, $(pIq)I(qIp)$ is also a tautology; and this does not accord with the logic of the *modus ponens*, in which it is notoriously a fallacy to 'affirm the consequent'. Thus only *one* truth-function in two-valued logic is satisfactory for the *modus ponens*; viz (iv), ordinary material implication. I could likewise show that in three-valued logic the satisfactory implications are far fewer than the 2,916 that the authors say there are.

Similar criticisms apply to Reichenbach's three-valued logic in *Philosophic Foundations of Quantum Mechanics*. He defines a 'quasi-implication' by the following truth-table; I use my sign "X" instead of his "I" to stand for the third truth-value—that of sentences which are neither true nor false but 'indeterminate'. (*Op. cit.* pp. 151–2).

p	T	T	T	X	X	X	F	F	F
q	T	X	F	T	X	F	T	X	F
pIq	T	X	F	X	X	X	X	X	X

This truth-function has some, but not all, of the properties we expect in an implication; we see, in fact, that with this truth-table pIq is assertible only if q is, and that pIp is not a tautology, but holds only if p holds; that is why Reichenbach calls this "*quasi*-implication". So far, there is nothing to quarrel over; but we can tell in advance, without having to know quantum theory, that quasi-implication is bound to be scientifically useless. We can know that pIq, with this truth-table, holds, only when we already know that q holds; and why should we trouble in that case to assert q conditionally upon p, when we can assert q unconditionally? The only singular hypotheticals useful in science are those that we can know to hold *without* first establishing the truth of the consequent.

Our expectation is confirmed when we see for what sort of hypotheticals Reichenbach proposes this truth-table; viz for hypotheticals of the form "If a measurement M_p is made, the indicator will show the value q_1" (*op. cit.* pp. 166–8). It seems doubtful, for various reasons, whether this sort of "if . . . then . . ." is a truth-function of any sort. But Reichenbach's matrix certainly will not do; for, with that, the above assertion could be made only when we had verified that the indicator *did* show the value q_1, and would thus be scientifically useless. Moreover, we should reach the absurd result that "if this measurement is

o

made, then it is made" is not tautologous, but holds good only if the measurement *is* made. Even a hypothetical that is not a truth-function at all is tautologous when its antecedent and consequent are identical.

5.4. ON RIGOUR IN SEMANTICS

There is a prevailing impression that the formal study of semantics, as it is now carried on by Carnap and his disciples, is an extremely rigorous discipline. This impression is no doubt produced by the apparatus of numbered theorems, special symbols, new terminology, and so on. But rigour is something quite different. Much of Frege's work in semantics maintains very high standards of rigour without any of this apparatus. On the other hand the use of such apparatus does not prevent blunders; I shall illustrate this from Carnap's *Logical Syntax of Language* (*LS*), *Introduction to Semantics* (*IS*), and *Meaning and Necessity* (*MN*).[1]

(1) Both in *IS* and in *MN* Carnap uses dots and dashes, which he calls "blanks", as a way of speaking about expressions in general. Now there need be nothing wrong with the use of blanks, especially in informal exposition. Thus, there is nothing wrong with saying that "∼ (   )" means "not (   )"; or, for that matter, that "∼ (. . .)" means "not (— — —)". But Carnap makes quite a different use of blanks. For instance, he gives the following two expressions as the respective paradigms of a sentence containing a definite description and of its exposition by means of Russell's theory:

7.2. '— —($\imath x$) (. . x . .)— —'

7.4. '($\exists y$)[(x) (. . x . . ≡ (x ≡ y)) ●— — y — —]' (*MN* pp. 32–4).

Now here the correspondence of the dots and dashes in 7.4 to those in 7.2 is part of the syntax. In fact, the dots and dashes function here as *variables*; they differ only typographically from the italics or Greek letters more commonly used. But Carnap really thinks that by *calling* them "blanks" he gets over any difficulties that would arise from the use of variables. For later on he

---

[1] (*Note*, 1969) Inside any actual extract from these works of Carnap's I have followed his use of quotation marks and not imposed my own style.

modifies Russell's contextual definition of the class-symbol as follows:

$$33.2. \ `. . \hat{z}(f\chi) . . \text{' for '}(\exists g) \ [(g \equiv f) \ \bullet \ . . . g \ . .]\text{'}$$

and adds in the footnote: 'The context is indicated only by dots instead of by a second-level variable, in order to make the definition applicable also to systems not containing such variables' (*MN* p. 147). But these dots *are* a sort of variable; only, it is left obscure whether they are, after all, a second-level variable of the object-language, or are rather a variable of the meta-language. Either reading would get us into difficulties; but these ought to be faced, not evaded by a sleight of hand.

(2) In *LS* Carnap begins a 'rigorous' account of variables by distinguishing strictly between genuine variables and constants of undetermined meaning (pp. 189–190). I am inclined to accept this distinction; but Carnap has not made it out.

> In a name-language, in addition to names with deter-mined meanings, such as 'Prague', names with undetermined meanings, such as 'a' and 'b', may also be used. If 'Q' is a constant pr (whether of determined or undetermined mean-ing makes no difference), then from 'Q(x)' the sentences 'Q(Prague)', 'Q(a)', 'Q(b)', and so on are derivable. . . .

But what does " 'Q' " stand for in the second sentence? A constant pr 'Q'? Hardly; a constant pr may or may not have a determined meaning, but a phrase like: "whether of determined or undetermined meaning *makes no difference*" (my italics) shows that " 'Q' " is being used as a variable. The sentence might have begun: "For all 'Q', if 'Q' is a constant pr, whether of determined meaning or not, then from 'Q(x)' . . ."[1] But now we have a variable " 'Q' " containing inverted commas as part of itself; how is this syntactically related to "Q(x)" and so on, which contain only the letter "Q", *not* the letter "Q" in inverted commas? We could of course escape this difficulty by correcting the sentence thus: " 'Q' is a constant pr, of undetermined meaning; so from 'Q(x)' . . ."[1]. But Carnap certainly is not clear in his own mind about the distinction he is trying to draw.

The same fact comes out in the example that Carnap says (*loc. cit.*) brings out the distinction 'especially clearly':

> We must write. . . : "If 'A' is false, then for any 'B',

---

[1] (*Note*, 1969) Since this sentence proposes a correction of what Carnap says, I have followed his style with quotation marks in the proposed correction.

'A ⊃ B' is true", where 'A' and 'B' are abbreviating constants of the object-language . . . (*LS* p. 159).

For how are we to construe the expression "for any 'B' "? It looks like a quantifier; and in any ordinary symbolism quantifiers contain *variables*. On the other hand "B" is expressly stated to be a *constant*; and whether it is or not, Carnap's name for "B", namely " 'B' ", is certainly a constant, and it is " 'B' " that occurs in "for any 'B' ". Carnap does indeed mention later a queer symbolism suggested by Quine, in which there are no variables, and constants are written in quantifiers; e.g., "(0) 0=0" instead of "(*x*) *x*=*x*". But it would be charitable indeed to suppose that a symbolism first mentioned on p. 190 was what Carnap had in mind on p. 159; anyhow, if it was, he ought to have said so. Moreover, even in Quine's suggested notation the constant contained in the quantifier recurs so as to be 'bound' by it; but " 'A ⊃ B' is true" does not contain " 'B' ", *i.e.*, "B" immediately enclosed in single inverted commas. And these difficulties occur in a passage where Carnap is insisting on the need for accuracy in the use of quotation marks!

(3) There is a well-known convention in mathematics whereby 'the least' or 'the only' number fulfilling a condition is deemed to be zero if there is in fact *no* number thus uniquely described. This has technical advantages; *every* definite description has just one designatum, which simplifies the rules of substitution. Carnap proposes an allegedly similar convention for language about physical objects—for such descriptions as "the King of France in 1948":

> It is possible . . . to count among the things also the *null thing* . . . characterised as that thing which is part of every thing. Let us take 'a_0' as the name for the null thing . . . a_0 seems a natural and convenient choice as descriptum for those descriptions which do not satisfy the uniqueness condition. —*MN* pp. 36–37.

Now a really similar mathematical convention would be something like this:

> It is possible to count among natural numbers also the *standard number*, characterised as that finite integer which is the least common multiple of all natural numbers. Let us take "X" as the name of the standard number; X seems (etc.).

Further, the null thing is described as corresponding 'to the null class of space-time points'—or, in plain English, as existing nowhen and nowhere![1]

I could give a good many more examples of inaccuracy; and more than one, of absurdity. But these ought to be enough. Now what reliance can we put on the higher developments of Carnap's formal semantics if this is what the definitions are like? We certainly cannot take Carnap's word for it that his results are valid; and does the very great labour of checking them seem likely to be worth while? Perhaps after all it is not so foolish to undertake 'direct analysis' in language everybody can read.

5.5. 'NECESSARY PROPOSITIONS AND ENTAILMENT STATEMENTS'

One main criticism of P. F. Strawson's article (*Mind*, April, 1948) is that his use of quotation marks with variables continually produces expressions that have not, strictly speaking, any meaning at all.

We must begin by considering the rules governing the use of quotation marks with variables. In the following expression:

(A) In "*x* is a man" "*x*" is a free variable

"*x*" does *not* occur as a free variable; for, just because "*x*" does occur as a free variable in "*x* is a man", the expression (A) is a *true assertion*; whereas if (A) contained a free variable, it would be a *function* and not an assertion at all. The very possibility of talking about the variable "*x*" presupposes the rule: If a variable, not otherwise bound, occurs in a quotation, it is *ipso facto* bound by the sign of quotation. Without this rule, any expression that tried to assert something about the variable "*x*" would contain "*x*" as a free variable, and so would not be an assertion at all.

Let us now consider, in the light of this rule, how we ought to interpret an expression that Strawson uses twice on page 189. (What Strawson wants it to mean is another matter.)

(B) " '*p*' entails '*q*' " is a statement of higher order than "*p*" or than "*q*".

By our rule (B) contains no free variables, and is thus not a function. It looks like an assertion; but I doubt whether it is

---

[1] (Note, 1969) A friend of Carnap's rejected the explanaton. Since the null class is included in every class, perhaps one ought rather to say that the null thing exists always and everywhere! I do not know if this was the point.

significant at all. " '*p*' entails '*q*' " could only be an assertion that the variable "*p*" entails the variable "*q*", which is surely nonsense; and (B) could only be an assertion that *this* absurd expression is 'a statement of higher order' than either the variable "*p*" or the variable "*q*"—which also should seem to be nonsense.

The context in which Strawson uses (B) is as follows:

(C) For all *p* and *q* " '*p*' entails '*q*' " is a statement of higher order than "*p*" or than "*q*".

But (B), which is used in (C), should seem to be nonsense. And in any case the variables in (B) are not free variables, and (B) is not a function; so it is no more legitimate to try to bind the variables in (B) by a quantifier than to write:

(D) *For some x*, "*x*" in "*x* is a man" is a free variable.

Thus (C) is in any case nonsense.

We can, perhaps, make out what Strawson is trying to say. He wants (C) to be a generalisation of such sentences as:

(E) ' "Your parents have another child" entails "you are a sibling" ' is a statement of a higher order than "your parents have another child" or than "you are a sibling".

It will be clearest to show step by step how we first transform and then generalise (E).

(E') ' "Your parents have another child" ' followed by "entails" followed by ' "you are a sibling" ' is a statement of a higher order than "your parents have another child" or than "you are a sibling".

(E'') The proper name of the sentence "your parents have another child", followed by "entails", followed by the proper name of the sentence "you are a sibling", is a statement of higher order than "your parents have another child" or than "you are a sibling".

(F) For all P, Q, the proper name of P followed by "entails" followed by the proper name of Q is a statement of higher order than P or than Q.

The variables in (F) are such that *names* of sentences can be substituted for them; this is shown by the structure of (F).

All this may sound pedantic; but Strawson was aiming (*cf.* p. 185) at a *consistent* way of showing the difference between the 'mention' and the 'use' of expressions—or, as I should say, between an expression and its name. His aim was precision; it is a just criticism to show that he has not attained it. Nor could he plead that at least I can make out what he is after; I cannot always do so. For instance, I should not like to try to unravel the following (on pp. 193–194):

(G) "a possible argument (or what is expressed by a possible argument) of the function ' "p" entails "q" ' " (*sic*).

(G) as it stands is nonsense; for as we have seen, ' "p" entails "q" ' is not a function, and should seem not to be even significant. And I have no idea how I should correct (G); especially in view of the parenthesis.

A simple means of avoiding the entangled quotation marks would be a convention by which: (i) when two sentences are joined with "$\supset$", the name of the compound sentence may be formed by joining the *names* of those two sentences with "$\supset$"; (ii) when one sentence is formed from another by prefixing "$\sim$", the name of the first may be formed from the *name* of the second by prefixing "$\sim$". Thus, ' "your parents have another child" $\supset$ "you are a sibling" ' is the name of the sentence "your parents have another child $\supset$ you are a sibling"; and "$\sim$ "you are a sibling" ' is the name of the sentence "$\sim$ (you are a sibling)". I then use variables "P", "Q", for which the possible substitutions are *names* of sentences.

5.6. ON NAMES OF EXPRESSIONS

One way of naming an expression is to put the expression itself in quotation marks. In that case, the expression is being at once mentioned and used: it is mentioned, or named, by the combination of itself with a pair of encircling quotation marks, and it is used as a part of this complex expression. While it is always necessary to distinguish between an expression and its name, it is a mistake to oppose mention and use as though mention of an expression could never include use of it.

According to the ordinary convention for use of quotation marks, we obtain the name even of an expression containing a free variable by putting it in quotation marks: thus although "the capital of x" is not a name, ' "x is a man" ' is a name of one definite expression. Since the variable "x" is used in the name ' "x is a man" ', we must say that it is here a bound variable, as it is in "the x such that x is a human father but not anybody's child"; and since in the function "x is a man" the variable is free, we must say that in the name ' "x is a man" ' the variable is bound by the added quotation marks, just as in "for some x, x is man" it is bound by the added quantifier "for some x".

If "P" and "Q" are (short for) sentences, and "A" and "B" are the respective names of these sentences, we may have a convention by which "$A \supset B$" is the name of the sentence (abbreviated to) "$P \supset Q$". Carnap would say that in "$A \supset B$" the sign "$\supset$" is used 'autonymously', i.e. as a name of the sign "$\supset$" in "$P \supset Q$". This is a mistake; both in "$A \supset B$" and in "$P \supset Q$", the sign "$\supset$" is a connective, not a name; in "$P \supset Q$" it conjoins two (abbreviations for) *sentences* to form (an abbreviation for) a third *sentence*, and in "$A \supset B$" it conjoins two *names* of sentences to form a third *name* —*viz*.,the name of the sentence (abbreviated to) "$P \supset Q$". Whichever use of the sign we are speaking of, we should say 'the sign "$\supset$" ', not "the sign $\supset$". The ambiguity of the sign is quite harmless if the context shows which connective use is intended.

5.7. IS IT RIGHT TO SAY OR IS A CONJUNCTION?

(In this discussion of sentences containing quoted words, I take an example in which the quoted word occurs without quotation marks. Carnap would call this way of using words in quotation the *autonymous*, i.e. self-naming, use; the appropriateness of this expression is one of the things called in question by my puzzle.)

Consider this string of words:

A.   or is a conjunction.

B. A may very easily be read as a sentence.

C.   In that case, the statement that A would ordinarily be being used to convey is true.

D.   It is natural to suppose that the first word of A is then being used as a logical subject of predication.

E.   If so, then the statement which A, used as a sentence, would ordinarily be read as conveying is true if and only if what is predicated in A is truly predicable of what the first word of A is then being used to designate.

F.   I.e., this statement is true if and only if what the first word of A is being used to designate is truly a conjunction.

G.   Now the first word of A is a conjunction in A only if A occurs in such a context as:

H. The German word *sondern*, whenever it occurs, either is a verb or is a conjunction.

I. In a context like *H*, the first word of *A* designates nothing, and *A* conveys no statement at all.

J. Hence, when *A* is used to convey a statement, its first word is not a conjunction, but what its first word designates is a conjunction.

K. The first word of *A* is thus not a designation of itself, when *A* is used to convey a statement; and still less when *A* is not used to convey a statement.

L. Thus in no case is the first word of *A* used in *A* autonymously.

M. We might try rejecting *D* and saying that the first word of *A* is not a subject of predication but a sample of what the predicate applies to.[1]

N. This explanation would fit such cases as: or is printed in lower-case Roman letters—if the string of words between the colon and the dash is read as conveying a statement.

O. But, as was said before, the first word of *A* is *not* a sample of what the predicate of *A* applies to, i.e. of a conjunction, unless *A* occurs in a context like *H*, where *A* is not being used to convey a statement.

P. Hence, when *A* is used to convey a statement, the explanation given in *M* does not fit it.

5.8.   QUOTATION AND QUANTIFICATION

Shakespeare tells us that a rose by any other name would smell as sweet; I shall speak of the context of "*x*" in "*x* smells sweet" as a Shakespearean context. I think the assumption that "For some *x*, . . . *x* . . ." must mean "There is an object *x* such that . . . *x* . . ." runs us into trouble even for some Shakespearean contexts. For example, if we take:

(1) Cicero was a great orator, and "Cicero" is the only proper name of any Roman that occurs in "Cicero was more honest than Demosthenes"

as the context for a threefold occurrence of "Cicero", then obviously this context is Shakespearean—"Cicero" is replaceable

[1] Compare C. H. Whiteley, 'Names of Words', *Analysis* 17.5 (April 1957).

salva veritate, at all three places together, by any other name of the man Cicero. But if we try to pass from (1) to:

(2) For some x, x was a great orator, and "x" is the only proper name of any Roman that occurs in "x was more honest than Demosthenes"

then by the ordinary conventions about quotes (2) does not follow from (1), since (2) would falsely imply that "x" is a proper name of a Roman, whereas "x" in (2) is a variable.

However, these ordinary conventions of quotation are not the only possible ones, though logicians sometimes write as though they were. To allay scruples, we had better introduce a new style of quotes—let us say, the 'corners' of Quine's quasi-quotation.[1] ⌜Cicero⌝ and ⌜Cicero was more honest than Demosthenes⌝ would then simply be the expressions "Cicero" and "Cicero was more honest than Demosthenes"; but ⌜x⌝ would not necessarily be (though it might be) the variable "x", and ⌜x was more honest than Demosthenes⌝ would be the result of replacing "x" in "x was more honest than Demosthenes" by whichever expression ⌜x⌝ was. It would thus not make any essential difference to (1) if it were rewritten with 'corners' instead of quotes; I shall refer to the modified (1) as (1)'. We must now consider if we may pass from (1)' to:

(3) For some x, x was a great orator, and ⌜x⌝ is the only proper name of any Roman that occurs in ⌜x was more honest than Demosthenes⌝.

(3) looks like a dreadful conflation of the two formulas:

(4) For some x, x was a great orator

(5) For some x, ⌜x⌝ is the only proper name of any Roman that occurs in ⌜x was more honest than Demosthenes⌝.

(4) and (5) are each construable by taking "For some x" to mean "There is an object x such that"; specifically, (5) could be read as if it had begun "There is an expression x such that"—and Quine would allow such a quantifier to reach inside quasi-quotation. But on the face of things, if we dock (3) and (4) and (5) of their initial quantifiers, then an object x satisfying the end part of (4) must be a person, and an object x satisfying the end part of (5) must be an expression; and no object x can satisfy the

---

[1] (*Note*, 1969) An attentive reader will observe that I do not use or explain this notation *exactly* in Quine's way; in particular, Quine makes ⌜x⌝ and x the same for all x, but I do not.

end part of (3) unless we imagine some *outré* situation (something like chess with live pieces) in which a person *is* an expression; so (3) cannot be validly inferable from (1)′.

We can however interpret (3) on quite other lines: a proposition (abbreviated as) "For some x, Fx" would then be true iff each free occurrence of "x" in the context (abbreviated as) "Fx" *could* be so replaced by one and the same proper name as to yield a true result. On this interpretation, (3) would after all be validly inferable from (1)′.

There are strong objections to this procedure. Some will protest that I have no more right to speak of quoted occurrences of "Cicero" or of "x" than of the occurrence of "x" in "*six*": a quotation, including the quotes, being logically one indivisible sign. I can only say that this dogma seems to me unfounded; a decent care over the use of quotes does not commit one to it. In the lines of Edward Lear's poem:

> Pussy said to the Owl "O elegant fowl!
> How charmingly sweet you sing . . . "

there is (just) one occurrence of the word "fowl", and this is not merely a 'buried' occurrence like the 'buried' occurrence of "owl" in "fowl". The quotation of the Pussy-cat's words in Lear goes on for a couple more lines than appear above; according to the dogma, this quotation is a logically unstructured name, regardless of length; from this it would follow that I have used the dots to replace part of a single word—which is clearly untrue. The dogma evinces a lack of historical sense; words are recognisable as the words they are whether they are dressed up with quotes or not, and quotes are only a very recent device to mark out certain uses of words.

Medieval logicians held that the signification of an (unequivocal) word was conventionally assigned and logically prior to use in a given proposition; the reference or *suppositio* of a word could on the other hand be affected by the special predicate attached to the word in a given context, and one variety of *suppositio* was *suppositio materialis*, the use of a word to refer to that word itself. To use modern language, the predicable used in:

(6) ⌜Cicero⌝ is a proper name
or alternatively: "Cicero" is a proper name
must be counted as including the pair of 'corners' or quotes;

these must be considered, not as a sort of functor that forms from "Cicero" a name of that expression, but as showing an (intentional) argument-place into which "Cicero" is inserted. On this reading of quotes, iterated quotes will be unconstruable; in fact:

(7) ' "Cicero" ' is the name of a proper name

will have no more place in our logic than *Nom d'un nom*! One can indeed *give* a name, say "Tonk", to the name "Cicero"; the predicate in "Tonk is a proper name" will then be construable in terms of the more basic predicable used in (6). "Tonk is a proper name" will be exponible as:

(8) For some x, ⌜Tonk⌝ is a name of ⌜x⌝ and ⌜x⌝ is a proper name.

By our account of quantifiers, (8) is true iff some substitution of a proper name for "x" in (8) shorn of its quantifier *could* yield a true proposition; as, of course, the substitution of "Cicero" *does*. The context of "Tonk" in "Tonk is a proper name" is obviously Shakespearean—whether something is a proper name does not depend on what name it itself is given—so the context of "Tonk" in (8) ought to be Shakespearean, as it obviously is. (8) gives us a paradigm: in general, a predicable which takes into an (intentional) argument-place *the actual expressions* concerning which it is predicated can be used to define a corresponding, derived, predicable whose argument-place is open rather for *names* of the expressions concerning which it is predicated, to the same overall effect—as e.g. "Tonk is a proper name" is tantamount to ' "Cicero" is a proper name'.

We should observe that in (8) " ⌜Tonk⌝ is a name of ⌜x⌝" cannot be simplified to "Tonk = ⌜x⌝"; for if we allowed this, we should also have to allow "Tonk = ⌜Cicero⌝" or 'Tonk = "Cicero" ', and this would amount to reading a (quasi-) quotation as a name of the expression there enclosed in quotes or "corners". Notice also that "is a name of" in " ⌜Tully⌝ is a name of Cicero" and in " ⌜Tonk⌝ is a name of ⌜Cicero⌝" are quite different two-place predicables—one has only one intentional argument-place, the other has two.

My ideas on quotation have been largely shaped by K. Reach's work.[1] Reach used square brackets as I have used 'corners'. He did not, however, realize that these square

---

[1] 'The name relation and the syntactical antinomies', *Journal of Symbolic Logic*, vol. 3 (1938), pp. 97–111.

brackets could be construed as a kind of quotes, or that quotes could be taken as signs of intentional argument-places. There are in fact passages in Reach's paper to indicate that he held the conventional idea of quotations, as names of the expressions displayed within quotes.

It would be a large and difficult undertaking to reconstruct the logic of quotation on the lines here sketched. We should have difficulties, for example, over the quotation of an isolated connective; what type of argument-place could be open for such an argument?[1] Fortunately such difficulties do not here concern us; the only intentional argument-places that occur in our numbered examples are places for names (or name-variables).

5.9. ON *INSOLUBILIA*

The usual *insolubilia* (semantical paradoxes) essentially involve negation; the proof ends with a line of the form: "Ergo, p if and only if not-p, which is absurd". Now this *is* absurd only because in ordinary logic we can derive any arbitrary statement from "p if and only if not-p"; a game in which *any* move is allowed is unplayable. One might therefore hope to avoid *insolubilia* by using a logical system in which "p if and only if not-p" were a theorem for some interpretations of "p" without our being able to infer thence any arbitrary statement; or one that simply lacked negation. I shall here show that there exist negation-free *insolubilia*, which afford us a direct means of deriving an arbitrary statement "q"; for these, the remedies just mentioned are insufficient.

Our construction begins with the formula:

(1) The result of replacing W in w by quotation of w itself is true only if q.

"W" here is a proper name of the variable "w", and is used instead of ' "w" ' to avoid complications about 'use and mention'. The interpretation of "q" is to be arbitrary, but constant. From (1) we now form:

(2) The result of replacing W in (1) by quotation of (1) itself is true only if q.

Now (2) is the result of replacing W (i.e. "w") in (1) by "(1)",

---

[1] (*Note* 1969) Cf. papers 5.6, 5.7, in this collection.

which is short for actual quotation of (1); so (2) is short for the result of replacing W in (1) by quotation of (1) itself.

On the naive view of truth, we are always entitled to assert what we get from "If P is true, then p" and "If p, then P is true" when we substitute a designation of a statement for "P" and an abbreviation of the same statement for "p". Hence, if we replace "P" by the designation "the result of replacing W in (1) by quotation of (1) itself", we may replace "p" by (2), an abbreviation of the statement thus designated. The naive view of truth thus commits us to the assertions:

(3) If the result of replacing W in (1) by quotation of (1) itself is true, then the result of replacing W in (1) by quotation of (1) itself is true only if q.

(4) If the result of replacing W in (1) by quotation of (1) itself is true only if q, then the result of replacing W in (1) by quotation of (1) itself is true.

In drawing inferences from the premises (3) and (4), I use just two forms of inference: *modus ponens* (schema: "p, if p then r, ergo r" or: "p, p only if r, ergo r") and absorption (schema: "If p, then p only if r; ergo, p only if r").

We see first of all that if we apply the rule of absorption to (3), we are enabled to *assert* (2). But (2) is the antecedent of (4); and (2) and (4) yield by *modus ponens*:

(5) The result of replacing W in (1) by quotation of (1) itself is true.

Finally, (5) and (2) yield by *modus ponens*: (6) q.

We thus have a method of proving any arbitrary statement; which is absurd.

It is of course not essential to the deduction of this paradox that we bring in quotation as a means of designating expressions; we might instead use the familiar Goedelian devices, and these may be available even in a negation-free system.

Our proof is formally very similar to the derivation of the Curry paradox in set theory[1]; the one and the other cannot be resolved merely by adopting a system that contains a queer sort of negation or is negation-free; if we want to retain the naive view of truth, or the naive view of classes (that x is a member of the class of Fs if and only if x is an F), then we must modify the

---

[1] Cf. an instructive article by Moh Shaw-kwei in the *Journal of Symbolic Logic*, March 1954.

elementary rules of inference relating to "if". In Fitch's system, since he is estopped from modifying the rule of absorption (which is implicit in his 'method of subordinate proofs'), the general validity of *modus ponens* is abandoned.[1] This seems far too high a price to pay for a naive view of classes or of truth. Moreover, the particular restriction by which Fitch resolves Curry's paradox (and could likewise resolve ours) makes the validity of inference depend on how the premises themselves were proved: which seems to me to jeopardize the very notion of a formal proof. It might, however, be worth consideration whether the rule of absorption should be modified; after all, the form "If *p*, then *p* only if *r*" never occurs in ordinary discourse, and we might have a wrong idea of its logical force.[2]

[1] Cf. his *Symbolic Logic*, section 18.
[2] This way out is partly explored by Moh Shaw-kwei, *op. cit.*

6

Set Theory

6.1. FREGE'S *GRUNDLAGEN*[1]

Frege's "logico-mathematical enquiry into the concept of number", now reissued together with an English translation, is mainly concerned with the sort of number that he calls *Anzahl*—cardinal number. When I speak of a number in this review I shall always mean a cardinal number. (Austin renders "*Anzahl*" by "Number", "*Zahl*" by "number"; this does a lot towards making the English text run smoothly.)

Frege first gives his reasons, which seem to me decisive, for rejecting Mill's view that numbers are physical properties. These still need to be emphasized, for this sort of view is still put forward. Only recently two eminent logicians proposed to analyze "There are more cats than dogs" as meaning that if you take a bit of every cat you get a bigger physical aggregate than if you take an equal bit of every dog! Such an analysis will not do even for very simple observation statements like "This solid has fewer corners than edges" or "The clock struck more times than I have fingers on my hands". The notion of number is in fact applicable wherever we have things that can be identified, and discriminated from other things in the same field of thought; we can as easily speak of three sounds, three syllogisms, or three numbers, as of three cats or three dogs. If "three" stood for a

[1] Gottlob Frege, *The Foundations of Arithmetic*: *A Logicomathematical Enquiry into the Concept of Number*, translated by J. L. Austin, (New York, Philosophical Library, 1950), pp. i–xii, I–XI, 1–119, and parallel pages vie–xiiie, ie–xie, 1e–119e.

physical attribute, like "blue", such ways of talking would be nonsense, or at best farfetched metaphors.

Again, a number cannot be uniquely ascribed to a physical object. A pile of playing cards has a definite weight but not a definite number; "How heavy is this?" makes sense as it stands, but "How many is this?" does not make sense without some added word, expressed or understood—"how many *packs*?" or "how many *cards*?" or "how many *suits*?" And the answer will be quite different according to the word supplied; the same physical object is, e.g., two whist packs, eight complete suits, and 104 cards; none of these numbers, then, can be attributed to the physical object *simpliciter*.

Finally, Mill's sort of view altogether breaks down over 0 and 1. The numerals "0" and "1" are allowable answers to the question "how many?" on the same footing as "2", "3", etc. But 0 and 1 certainly are not physical properties; and where the number 0 can rightly be assigned (e.g., when we say "The number of moons of Venus is 0") there is no physical object to *be* noughtish. Perhaps one may feel inclined to compare "0" and "1" as answers to "how many?" with "nobody" as an answer to the question "who?". But this comparison will not do. As Frege pointed out in controversy with Husserl, the use of "0" and "1" in arithmetic according to the same general rules as other numerals does not lead to any such paradoxes as would arise from treating "nobody" as the proper name of a person. We must unequivocally recognize 0 and 1 as numbers; a theory of number that fails to fit them in is hopeless.

Frege fails, however, to see the fact that makes Mill's sort 4f view attractive. In spite of Frege's denial (Sec. 24, 58), there *is* a recognizable physical property common to the *four* face of a die and the four of diamonds and four pennies and the four sides of a square and a plate broken in four; we could learn to use the word "four" whenever we met with this attribute. When a plate breaks in four, a certain sample of china changes from being *in one piece* to being *in four pieces*; the words in italics stand for different species of a certain generic physical property. This generic property must however be sharply distinguished from number; for number is not restricted to what is spatial, as this property is, but applies to everything thinkable. In particular, the number one must be sharply distinguished from the physical property

P

expressed by "in one piece". When we say that the number of the Earth's satellites is 1, we are not saying of the Moon that it is all in one piece—an attribute, as Frege says, in which the Moon nowise excels the *four* moons of Jupiter.

A popular rival to Mill's sort of view is the view that we ascribe numbers to things in accordance with subjective associations. Frege dismisses this briefly and with the contempt it deserves. We get a typical expression of this view in William James's explanation of the term "number" as signifying primarily "the strokes of our attention in discriminating things" (*Principles of Psychology*, II, 653). The number of men in a regiment would thus presumably be a lot of strokes of attention performed by the commanding officer at a parade, or by an Army pay clerk.

Frege next gives us a brilliant and devastating criticism of the idea that the addition of numbers is a putting together of units— e.g., that the number 3 consists of 3 units put together. Frege shows that people who talk this way are simply playing fast and loose with the word "unit"—taking it to stand now for the number 1, now for a single countable object. (Austin is surely wrong in suggesting [p. 39[e],n.] that any peculiarity of the German word *"Einheit"* is here specially important. As Frege's quotations show, the same fallacies are committed just as often over the Greek and English words for a unit, which, unlike the word *"Einheit"*, are not derived from the words for one in the respective languages.) How is it that "one and one" makes sense, unlike "the Moon and the Moon"? This cannot be answered by saying that "one and one" means "one and *another* one"; arithmetic does not allow us to speak of *ones*, but only of *the* number one. It is senseless to ask which of the 1's in the number 3 we mean when we say that 3—1=2, or to qualify "(2—1)—1=0" by the proviso that the 1's mentioned here must be different. "+" between numerals does not express any putting together, like putting three eggs with two eggs. Plato expressed this by saying that units are uncombinable; Aristotle's lengthy criticism of this doctrine in the *Metaphysics* is an *ignoratio elenchi*—he cannot see there are not two ones in the number two. (People who translate ἀσύμβλητοί by "unaddable" commit the very mistake that Plato sought to rule out by using the word—the confusion between adding numbers and putting things together.)

We now come to Frege's positive account of number statements. In "There are *n* . . .", or "The number of . . . is *n*", the blank cannot be filled up with a possible logical subject—with a name of an object, or a list of objects. We can truly say "There is one Pope in 1940" or "There are two Martian moons"; and here "Pope in 1940" is truly predicable just of Pius XII and "Martian moons" just of Deimos and Phobos. But these expressions are not being used to *name* the objects of which they are predicable; if we substitute proper names of the objects, we get the nonsense sentences "There is one Pius XII" and "There are two Deimos and Phobos". We must never confuse a predicate that applies to an object with a name of the object, as the old logic does in speaking of a *term* that *denotes* an object. In "There are *n As*" the grammatical subject "*As*" is not being used to name certain *As*; it is logically predicative. Frege calls such a predicative expression a *concept word* (*Begriffswort*); Austin's rendering "general term" is unsatisfactory, for it is associated with a logic that Frege repudiates.

A concept word is so called because it stands for a concept (*bedeutet einen Begriff*). A concept, in Frege's sense, is that of which we express our apprehension by using a logical predicate; our apprehension belongs to the subject matter of psychology, but the concept itself does not. "*x* falls under the concept *man*" means simply "*x* is a man" and has no reference to a conceiving mind. In "There are *n As*", "*A*", being used predicatively, stands for the concept of an *A*; here we are not asserting or denying that certain specified objects are *As* or fall under the concept of an *A*, but rather ascribing a property to the concept itself—saying how often it is realized, whether many times or only once or not at all. And the number of times a concept is realized cannot be a mark (*Merkmal*) of the concept itself. The marks of a concept are properties of the objects that fall under it; but unity and plurality cannot be significantly ascribed to any object; it does not make sense to ask concerning an object whether it occurs once or more often, whether there is one or many of it. Unity and plurality can be ascribed only to concepts under which objects fall, i.e., to properties of objects, expressible by predicates. (Aquinas seems to have grasped this; *Summa Theologica*, Ia, q. 13, art. 9, has a strongly Fregean ring.)

To understand what Frege says about the concept, we must read his essay 'Ueber Begriff und Gegenstand' ('On Concept and Object'). Frege there asserts that the concept is essentially predicative and incomplete. A logical predicate is in need of completion and can be completed by adding the name of an object (which then becomes a logical subject); Frege holds that *only* expressions with this sort of incompleteness *can* stand for concepts. Even if we want to make an assertion *about* the concept (as opposed to asserting or denying the concept of an object), we cannot have as the logical subject of our assertion an expression for the concept itself.

Abstract expressions like "redness" or "the property of being red" or "the concept *red*" certainly seem to be used as logical subjects; but none of these (not even the last) can stand for a concept. The predicates "is red" and "falls under the concept *red*" alike stand for a certain concept; but "the concept *red*" does not stand for this concept—it is not a concept word like the adjective "red". Frege admits the odd look of this result, but holds that some such oddity must arise in any symbolism, because the incomplete nature of the concept must express itself somehow or other. I think Frege is here fundamentally right. It seems to me, indeed, that a phrase like "the redness *of* . . ." can stand for a concept, although it is not a logical predicate; such phrases, however, have the same incompleteness as predicates; "the redness *of* . . ." is completable in just the same way as ". . . is red" —by adding the name of an object.

Abstract expressions like "the property of being red" or "the concept *red*" are to be avoided whenever possible; they are stylistically clumsy and philosophically dangerous. It is unfortunate that Frege so often needlessly resorts to them; as we shall see later, he is thus led to give false analyses. Here are some examples:

"falls under the concept F"   instead of: "is an F"
"stands in the relation ϕ to"   instead of: "is a ϕ of"
"the Number that applies to   instead of: "the Number of Fs"
    the concept F"
"the extension of the concept   instead of: "the class of all Fs"
    F"
"the concept F is equal-in-   instead of: "there are just as
    number to the concept G"   many Fs as Gs."

In the last instance Austin mitigates the clumsiness by using "equal" for the made-up German word "*gleichzahlig*", "equal-in-number"; he can do this because he consistently renders "*gleich*" not as "equal" but as "identical".

Frege's next point is that in mathematics we speak as if each number were an identifiable object, to which properties can be ascribed, and which can have a definite description: we say e.g., that the number 2 has the property of primeness, or that 2 is the even prime number. Frege does not see how this way of speaking can be justified unless numbers *are* objects. What he means by an object is by no means made clear in the *Grundlagen*; but light is thrown on the question by his essay 'Function und Begriff'. Here the distinctive feature of objects is said to be that expressions for them lack the incompleteness that belongs, as we saw, to concept words (e.g., ". . . breathes"), and belongs also to expressions for relations (e.g., ". . . loves . . .") and for functions (e.g., "the capital of . . ."); names of objects, like "Caesar", can rather be used to fill the blanks in such incomplete expressions.

Now a numeral like "2" seems to behave like a name; compare "2 is prime", "3 is greater than 2", "the square 2", with: "Caesar is bald", "Brutus is nobler than Caesar", "the father of Caesar". Such appearances are not indeed always to be trusted; "nothing" and "nobody" likewise have a prima facie similarity to names of objects. But there is no decisive proof that we are wrong in assimilating "2" to names of objects; whereas an attempt to treat "nobody" and "nothing" as names would land us in contradictions almost at once. We do indeed get paradoxes if we treat classes as objects; but that is quite a different thing. And nobody has shown how ostensible references to numbers as objects can be analyzed without assuming such objects. Russell claimed to have done so, but his attempt will not bear close examination; his use of the term "propositional function" is hopelessly confused and inconsistent, and at a critical point he uses a symbolism of capped variables (e.g. "$\phi \hat{x}$") without even vaguely formulating the rules of formation and of inference.

If a number is an object, we shall need a criterion of identity for it. Frege accordingly considers how to analyze "There are just as many *F*s as *G*s." (As he points out, this can consistently be transformed into "the same object is both the number of *F*s and the number of *G*s" only if we always have: If there are just as many *F*s and *G*s, and just as many *G*s as *K*s, then there are just as many *F*s as *K*s.) As is well known, Frege gives the analysis:

"There is one-one correspondence of the *F*s to the *G*s." This analysis does not involve that "the *F*s" or "the *G*s" refers to a single object—a class. The relation *being a φ of* sets up one-one correspondence of the *F*s to the *G*s provided that

(i) if any object *x* is an *F*, then of some object *y* that is a *G* it is true that *x* is *the* object that is a *φ* of *y*;

(ii) if any object *y* is a *G*, then of some object *x* that is an *F* it is true that *y* is *the* object of which *x* is a *φ*

Thus, to use Frege's own example, the waiter knows he has put out just as many knives as plates because

(i) for every plate *x* there is a knife *y* that is *the* object directly to the right of *x*;

(ii) for every knife *y* there is a plate *x* which is *the* object that *y* is directly to the right of.

And there is no mention here of a class of knives or of plates.

We use here the notion of a relation between objects. Such relations, for Frege, are on the same level as concepts under which objects fall; only, whereas a concept word needs only a single name (a logical subject) to complete its sense, the sense of a relation word requires two such names of objects to be supplied. Quantification over relations, as in: "There is a relation that sets up one-one correspondence between *F*s and *G*s" is radically different from quantification over objects. If we generalize "Solomon is a son of David, and David a son of Jesse" to "There is something that Solomon is to David and David is to Jesse", it would obviously be senseless to replace "something" by "some object".

I think Frege is wrong in treating identity as a relation between objects. The predicate "is *the A*" must *not* be analyzed as meaning "has identity with the *A*", where "the *A*" is used to name an object (cf. p. 77, n. 2). This comes out most clearly when we say "Nothing is the *A*"; we are then not using "the *A*" as if it named an object and denying that anything has identity with this object; on the contrary, we are using "the *A*" predicatively to stand for a concept and denying that anything falls under the concept. Frege practically gives this explanation for "Nothing is the greatest proper fraction" (pp. 87–88, n.). Whenever "is *an A*" stands for a well-defined concept, so also does "is *the A*". Admittedly the latter concept cannot have more than one object falling under it and may have none at all; but Frege himself points out that no concept can be disqualified on such grounds. The equation "the *A* is the *B*" or "the *A* = the *B*" should be taken not as asserting a relation between named objects, but as saying that the concept expressed by "both is *the A*, and is *the B*" has some object falling under it.

Only small changes would be needed in the *Grundlagen* in order to get rid of the alleged relation of identity. For example, we should have to analyze "There are just as many *F*s as *G*s" as follows: "Either any given object is an *F* if and only if it is a *G*, or there is a relation that sets up a one-one correspondence of the *F*s to the *G*s"; for we may not use identity to establish a one-one correspondence of the *F*s to the *F*s. But the symbolism of the *Grundgesetze* would need drastic repairs.

Frege generates the infinite series of finite numbers by appealing to the fact that the finite number *n* is always immediately followed by the number of numbers from 0 to *n* inclusive. I think this procedure is valid. Difficulties might indeed arise if we regarded the number 2 as a member of pairs which were in their turn members of the number 2; but we are not committed to this by using numbers in order to count numbers. Russell's Axiom of Infinity lies open to his own taunt about the advantages of theft over honest toil; and it is surely incredible that mathematical truths should depend on empirical facts about how many things there are.

The main results we have so far considered seem to me solidly established. We still have to discuss Frege's view that numbers are classes—extensions of concepts. He himself attached only secondary importance to this (Sec. 107); rejection of it would ruin the symbolic structure of his *Grundgesetze*, but not shake the foundations of arithmetic laid down in the *Grundlagen*.

Frege holds, as we saw, that we may pass from "There are just as many *A*s as *B*s" to "Some object is at once the number of *A*s and the number of *B*s" and vice versa. His aim in treating numbers as classes is to reduce this way of recognizing a logical object to a simpler and more general one; he holds that we may pass in general from "Any given object is an *F* if and only if it is a *G*" to "Some object is at once the class of all *F*s and the class of all *G*s" and vice versa. The more general assumption, however, involves a difficulty that does not arise for its supposed special case. This may be shown as follows. Let us define "x is a K" to mean: "For some F, x is the number of Fs, and x is not an F." Then the number of Ks is itself a K; for if it is not, then it is the number of Ks and is not a K; consequently, for some F, it is the number of Fs and is not an F—i.e., it is after all a K. Therefore, by the definition of "is a K", we have: "For some F, the number of Ks is the number of Fs and is not an F." Thus the same object is both the number of Ks and the number of Fs, although some object (viz., *this* object) is a K without being an F. This conclusion is no paradox. But if now we define "x is an M" to mean "For some G, x is the class of all Gs, and x is not itself a G" we may prove by precisely similar reasoning that, for some G, the same object is both the class of Ms and the class of Gs, although some object (viz., *this* object) is an M without being a G. This proof, given by Frege himself in the appendix to Volume II of the *Grundgesetze*, shows that the ordinary idea of a class involves a contradiction and therefore cannot be used to explain what numbers are; in fact, Frege found he must recant.

To see how Frege was led to believe in such objects as classes, we must consider again his essay 'Ueber Begriff und Gegenstand' (in conjunction with *Grundlagen*, p. 80, n.). Frege holds not merely that the abstract expression "the concept *man*" does not stand for a concept, but also that it does stand for an object; he is inclined to think that "the extension of the concept *man*" or "the class of all men" stands for the same object. But Frege's inference:

"The concept *man*" does not stand for a concept;

Ergo, the concept *man* is not a concept but an object

contains just the same fallacy as the inference:

"Some man" does not stand for any definite man;

Ergo, some man is not any definite man, but is an indefinite man.

In the latter case Frege has himself pointed out the mistake. Sentences with "some man" as their grammatical subject are not assertions about something named by "some man"; otherwise "Some man is wise" and "Some man is not wise" would be contradictories, since contradictory predicates would relate to the same subject. Logically "some man" is not a unit at all, and it is senseless to ask what it stands for; "Some man is wise" logically breaks up into "man" and "some . . . is wise", and this last complex predicate must be replaced by its contradictory "no . . . is wise" if we want to negate the whole sentence. Similarly, "the concept *man*" stands neither for a concept nor for an object; where it is legitimately used, its apparent unity breaks up under logical analysis. For example, "The concept *man* is realized" does not assert of some object that it is realized; an attempt to assert that an object, e.g., Julius Caesar, is realized leads not to a falsehood (as Frege thinks) but to nonsense. Really the sentence splits up into "man" and "the concept . . . is realized"; the latter is a circumlocution for "something is a. . . .". Sentences not exponible in some such innocent way (e.g., "the concept *man* is timeless") may be regarded as nonsensical.

Frege rejected the analysis of "*x* is a man" by which "is a" stands for a logical relation between *x* and an object (a class) called "man". With a sound view of concept and object, there is no place for a copula; a concept word no more needs a copula to join it to a logical subject than a relation word needs a pair of copulas to join it to the names of the related objects. But before his recantation Frege did allow the transformation of "*x* is a man" into "*x* falls under the concept *man*" or "belongs to the class *man*" and conversely, and took "falls under" or "belongs to" to express a logical relation between *x* and the object called "the concept *man*" or "the class *man*". Now surely this rule of transformation does not substantially differ from the rule of interpretation that Frege rejects—from taking "is a" to mean "belongs to" and "man" to mean "the class *man*". If we want a sharp distinction between concept and object, we must reject such a rule of transformation.

Frege defines the Number that belongs to the concept *G*, as being the class of everything that is equal (*gleichzahlig*) to the concept *G*. Now this is legitimate only if we may take "The concept *F* is equal to the concept *G*" as asserting that an *object* called "the concept *F*" is equal to the concept *G*; and "the concept *G*" in "the Number that belongs to the concept *G*" will also, on Frege's view, stand for an object. Frege thus slips back into regarding a number as the number of an *object*. In his *Grundgesetze* he expressly defines the symbol answering to "the Number of . . ." so that the blank must be filled with the name of an object; moreover, he there throws off his reluctance to say definitely that the object a number belongs to is a class; "the number of *As*" is taken to mean "the number of the class of all *As*". As against this we must re-emphasize Frege's own results. In "the number of . . . ", or "how many . . . are there?" the blank can be filled only with a concept word (in the plural), not with a name of an object nor even a list of objects. Moreover, Frege argued in his recantation that the only tenable view of classes as objects would be such that the class of *As* may be the same as the class of *Bs* although something is an *A* without being a *B*; and this surely rules out the idea that the number of *As* is the number of the *class* of *As*, for the number of *Bs* may be different when the class is the same. (Cf. *Grundgesetze*, II, 264, col. 2.)

6.2.　QUINE ON CLASSES AND PROPERTIES

On page 120 of Quine's *Mathematical Logic* we find the relation between classes and properties stated thus:

Once classes are freed . . . of any deceptive hint of tangibility, there is little reason to distinguish them from *properties*. It matters little whether we read "$x \in y$" as "*x* is a member of the class *y*" or "*x* has the property *y*". If there is any difference between classes and properties, it is merely this: classes are the same when their members are the same, whereas it is not universally conceded that properties are the same when possessed by the same objects. . . . But classes may be thought of as properties if the latter notion is so qualified that properties become identical when their instances are identical. Classes may be thought of as properties in abstraction from any differences which are not reflected in differences of instances.

Quine here uses the strange notion of abstraction so often criticized by Frege. How do things or properties *become* identical merely because somebody chooses to *abstract from*, i.e., ignore, the differences between them? His account of how classes stand in relation to properties looks intelligible only because the notion of a class is so familiar. Suppose, however, that I introduced a new term "surman" (plural "surmen") and explained its relation to the term "man" as follows:

There is little reason to distinguish surmen from men; it matters

little whether we say "Smith is a surman" or "Smith is a man". If
there is any difference between surmen and men, it is merely this:
surmen are the same when their surnames are the same, whereas
it is not universally conceded that men are the same when they
have the same surname. But surmen may be thought of as men if
the latter notion is so qualified that men become identical when
their surnames are identical. Surmen may be thought of as men
in abstraction from any differences which are not reflected in
differences of surname.

Would this is any way serve to explain how the word "surman"
is meant to be used? Would it even be justifiable, to use the term
"surman" at all, if this were the way it had been introduced? I
hardly think so. Possibly Quine would object that my term
"surman" is not really parallel to his term "class"—that there is a
difference as regards *tangibility*. Classes are to be intangible;
whereas men are tangible, and presumably remain tangible even
when thought of as surmen, i.e., in abstraction from any difference
not reflected in difference of surname. But I do not understand
the importance Quine seems to attach to tangibility. The notion
is indeed used in schoolboy explanations of the difference between
concrete and abstract nouns:

> Abstract nouns in -io call
> *Feminina* one and all;
> Masculine will only be
> Things that you can touch or see;

but in logic I do not think it has even expository value.

It may be admitted that the term "property" would have little
value if we were so using it that expressions like "redness" or "the
property of being red" were uniquely referring names of properties. Properties so regarded would involve all the difficulties that
arise over classes; for instance, the property of being a property
that does not belong to itself would involve a difficulty parallel to
that about Russell's class of all classes that are not members of
themselves; and there would be the added problem how properties
were related to classes. But if we use "property" (as Frege used
Begriff) in the sense "what a logical predicate stands for", then
these abstract expressions are not names of properties; nor can
any paradox like Russell's be generated as regards properties thus
understood as *Begriffe*.

Of course, this notion of a property has difficulties of its own. When I say that a predicate stands for a property, is not this just a euphemism for its *naming* the property? This objection would have force if I regarded a predicate as an actual expression occurr-. ing in sentences. But in fact I should rather regard it as a common property of sentences; thus, I should say that "Smith loves Smith" and "Jones loves Jones" were sentences formed from a common predicate by supplying the respective subjects "Smith" and "Jones". In this instance, though we readily discern the common predicate, it is plainly not something that can be extracted from the sentences and displayed between quotes all by itself. The distinction between thing and property comes out in the distinction between name and predicate just because a name is an actual expression whereas a predicate is rather a common property of expressions.

Again, how can one know whether or not two predicates stand for the same property? Here I must admit partial defeat; I can suggest no necessary and sufficient criterion for such identity of reference; I am, however, prepared to state a necessary condition for it. If one predicate applies to an object and another does not, they certainly do not stand for one and the same property; for otherwise this property would both belong to the object and not belong to it. Sameness of application is therefore a necessary condition for two predicates' having the same property as their reference. This last common-sense consideration is enough to expose Quine's mistake in identifying properties with classes. For Quine's own way of escaping Russell's paradox is to hold that two predicates may have the same class as their extension though they do *not* apply to the same objects. E.g., the predicates "—is a class not belonging to itself" and "—is a class that belongs to some class but not to itself" have the same class as their extension; but there is a class—viz., this common extension itself—that satisfies only the first of these predicates, not the second, so they do not stand for the same property.

This last sentence may appear inconsistent with my previous statement that a predicate cannot be displayed by itself within quotes. In fact there is no inconsistency; the actual expressions occurring within quotes after "the predicates" are not themselves predicates, but serve to indicate predicates. To take a simpler predicate as an example: when I say that "Booth shot Lincoln" and "Booth shot Booth" contain the common predicate "Booth shot—", I do not mean that the expression last quoted occurs in both sentences; plainly it does not, for neither sentence contains a dash. What I mean is that the two sentences have the common property of being related in the same way to the expression "Booth shot—"; viz., each of them is obtained by substituting a uniquely referring name for the dash in this expression; and this common property *is* the common predicate.

I have no objection to Quine's type of solution; Frege himself sketched one on similar lines in the Appendix to his *Grundgesetze*. It does however involve a sharp distinction between class and property; for in this instance we have *ex hypothesi* the same class, and we cannot have the same property, because the application of the two predicates differs. (It is remarkable that in the earlier parts of his *Methods of Logic* Quine is content to assume that two "open sentences" have the same class for their extension if and only if they come out true for the same objects; he does not tell us that the solution of Russell's paradox he is going to suggest will involve a restriction on this equivalence; nor, having once propounded that solution, does he indicate how matters shall be straightened out.) No amount of 'abstraction' will serve to remove the difference.

A further proof of the need for our distinction may be got by considering numbers. I hold that a question of number is a question how many things there are of a certain *kind* or *nature*; the words "kind" and "nature" here are just variant expressions for my "property" or Frege's *Begriff*. Now it is easy to slide from this view into the view that a number belongs to a class. But the idea of a class as many—the many having, in Russell's words, "just so much unity as is required to make them many, and not enough to prevent them from remaining many"[1]—is I think radically incoherent. When we try to attach a number to a class a, we are really attaching it to the property expressed by "—is a member of a". This is not a trivial point; for when we attach a number to a property, the property is usually not expressed in the above form; and Russell's paradox seems to show that not all properties are expressible in that form.

As regards Quine's *Mathematical Logic* special difficulties arise; we can show that the formulae he takes to express number-

[1] *Principles of Mathematics*, p. 69.

statements will not serve that purpose. This does not, of course, mean that they are senseless or lead to contradiction, but only that Quine suggests a wrong way of reading them. An adequate symbolism for number-statements would have the effect that, no matter how "F" were interpreted, the formula read "The number of Fs is 0" would be true if and only if there were no Fs, and the formula read "The number of Fs is 1" would be true if and only if there were something that was *the* F. Let us now interpret "*x* is an F" as follows:

For any class α, α is a member of *x* if and only if α is a member of some class and is not a member of α.

It is then easy to prove in Quine's system all of the theorems that may be put in words as follows:

(1) Some class is *the* F. (There is a class α such that any class β is identical with α if and only if β is an F.)

(2) The class of all Fs is a member of 0.

(3) The class of all Fs is not a member of 1.

As I said, this involves no inconsistency within the system; but it does mean that reading a formula as "The class of all Fs is a member of 0" is not always consistent with reading it as "The number of Fs is 0", and reading a formula as "The class of all Fs is a member of 1" is not always consistent with reading it as "The number of Fs is 1". This difficulty, I think, would not be peculiar to Quine's system; I think it is no less absurd to read "the number of Fs" as "the number of the class of Fs", than to read "the class of Fs" as "the class of the class of Fs". In both forms of phrase, the plural noun is used predicatively, to express a property; the class and the number alike are specified by mentioning the property. As Frege would say: *sie haben an dem Begriff selbst und nur an diesem ihren Halt.*

6.3. CLASS AND CONCEPT

A good many philosophers, following Carnap, take both the Fregean distinction between sense and reference, and that between a concept and its extension, to be pretty much the same as the traditional distinction between intension and extension. This interpretation can, I think, be decisively refuted. First, Frege held a purely extensional view of concepts. He adopted the mathematician's attitude toward definitions—that it does not much matter which definition you choose, so long as the same objects come under it; and he expressly says that, though proper identity holds only between objects, the analogue of identity for concepts holds if and only if concepts are coextensive, i.e., have the same objects falling under them.[1] Secondly, the Fregean distinction of sense and reference is founded on quite a different feature of language from that used in old-fashioned discussions about intension and extension (as also by Carnap), viz., the contrasting pairs of concrete and abstract nouns. Thus, "humanity" is related to "men" as abstract to concrete; one would refer to an intension as "the property (of) humanity" and to the corresponding extension as "the class of men". Frege, on the other hand, says that the sense of a name like "the class of men" is itself referred to (not by an abstract noun like "humanity" but) either by the use of that very name in an indirect-speech construction ("Aristotle thought that the class of men had no first member")[2] or, in non-oblique contexts, by an expression of the form 'the sense of "A" '—e.g., 'the sense of "the class of men" '.[3] And so, thirdly, we can show that a concept is not, for Frege, the sense of the name of the corresponding class. For a concept is the reference of a predicate, e.g., of the predicate ". . . is a man";[4] and plainly this has quite a different reference from 'the sense of "the class of men" ', since the two expressions are never interchangeable *salva veritate* (Frege's test for identity of reference.)

Why then distinguish between a concept extensionally regarded and a class or extension? Frege says that extensions are objects and concepts are not.[5] But what then makes concepts not to be objects? Frege replies: *Ungesättigtheit*—unsaturatedness. But I shall not try to explain and defend this part of his doctrine, sound as I believe it to be; we should be led too far, over an obscure and debated territory.

Let us try again with another of his explanations—that a concept is the reference of a predicate, what a predicate stands for. We may well be tempted to ask what are the relations expressed by "reference of" and "stands for" and how they differ from other

[1] *Philosophical Writings of Gottlob Frege*, ed. and trans. by P. Geach and M. Black (Oxford, Blackwell, 1952), p. 80. The original sources and paginations are stated in this edition.
[2] *Ibid.*, pp. 59, 67.
[3] *Ibid.*, p. 59.
[4] *Ibid.*, p. 43, footnote.
[5] *Ibid.*, p. 32.

semantical relations; if we yield, we shall lose ourselves in the wilderness of modern 'rigorous' semantics. But we can go another way from here: If A and B are both red, then *there is something*, referred to by the common predicate, *that A and B both are*. Here the important thing is not the words "referred to" but the existential quantification contained in "there is something that . . ."; as Quine has often urged, what commits one to making predicates stand for concepts, to holding that *there are* concepts, is this replacement of predicates by existential quantification.

'But if you say the predicate "red" stands for something, and call what it stands for a concept, then you are treating it as if it were a proper name; you cannot escape this by using the verb "stand for" instead of "name", or by saying "red" is an incomplete, *ungesättigt*, expression. Like Frege, you are blurring out again the distinction he rightly made between a concept word and a name; concept words are after all names, naming a queer sort of entities. This is just like saying that "some man" stands for some man, only not for any definite man but for an indefinite man. No wonder we find in Frege such tangles about the *Ungesättigtheit* of concepts!'

This criticism breaks down because when we recognize a common predicate, replaceable by an existential quantifier, there need not be even the appearance of our wrongly making out something to be a name. "Smith cut Smith's throat" and "Jones cut Jones' throat" have a recognizable common predicate, and we can say that there is something that Smith and Jones and Castlereagh all are. (Of course "that [they] all *did*" would be a more idiomatic expression; but this is just because "did" is more natural than "are" as grammatical proxy for a predicate formed with a verb in the past tense rather than with "is" followed by a noun or adjective.) But this in no way looks like taking some word or phrase in the two sentences as a proper name of a concept. Similarly, the common predicate in "*A* is red" and "*B* is red" is not just "red" or "is red" but consists in the two sentences' both being formed by writing "is red" after a proper name.

Now if we allow every predicate of objects to stand for a concept, we have to go on and make a sharp distinction between concept and object. For let us suppose that a concept is an object, and can accordingly be given a proper name. From the proper names of concepts we can now form predicates in the following uniform way: That an object falls under the concept whose proper name is "D" is to be expressed by writing the name of that object in brackets after "D". We may speak of the predicate "$D(\ )$": remembering, in accordance with what we saw just now, that the occurrence of this predicate in a sentence does not consist merely in there being a "$D($" followed after an interval by a ")" but also requires that there shall come between the brackets a proper name or a proxy for one. Now in the statements "not $D(D)$", "not $P(P)$", etc., we can recognize, besides the predicates "$D(\ )$", "$P(\ )$", etc., just introduced, a common predicate as well; for clearly "not $D(D)$" is the same predication about the concept D as "not $P(P)$" is about the concept P. If every common predicate stands for a concept, this one will; and on our present supposition we may give this concept a proper name, "W". From this again we may construct a predicate "$W(\ )$" as above explained. Thus "$W(\ )$" will mean the same as the common predicate in "not $D(D)$" and "not $P(P)$", so that "$W(D)$", "$W(P)$". mean the same as "not $D(D)$", "not $P(P)$". But if so, what will "$W(W)$" mean? The same as "not $W(W)$", which is absurd. To escape this absurdity, we must deny that any concept is an object or can have a proper name; and the two sorts of quantification that answer to proper names and to predicates must be strictly distinguished.

This requirement is not hard to fulfil in a symbolic language; and observe that if we use two styles of quantifier, as Frege did in his *Grundgesetze*, we are not thereby obliged to accept an unending hierarchy of types like Russell's. But it is easy to be misled by phrases like "the concept Man" in philosophical language. Frege himself held that such phrases are proper names, and on that very account stand not for concepts but for objects.[1] I think he went wrong here. Just as "some man" would have to stand for some man if it had any reference at all, so "the concept Man" would have to stand for a concept if it had reference. But "some man" cannot stand for some man, since the question "which man?" has no answer; and "the concept Man" cannot stand for a concept, for then a concept would have a proper name. We must just not treat these expressions as forming logical units in the sentences where they occur—no more than "Napoleon was a great general" occurs as a logical unit in "The man who finally defeated Napoleon was a great general". "Some man is wise" is

[1] *Ibid.*, pp. 45, 46, 49, 50, 54–55.

Q

an instance not of the simple predicate ". . . is wise", but of a derivative predicate "some . . . is wise", whose contradictory is "no . . . is wise"; and similarly in "The concept Man applies to Socrates" what goes together is "The concept . . . applies to Socrates", which just means "Socrates is (a) . . . ." Sentences from which "the concept Man" cannot be thus eliminated, like "The concept Man is an abstract entity", may well be treated as meaningless; *vile damnum*. *General* remarks about concepts, on the other hand, answer to the use of a *quantifier* relating to concepts in a symbolic language.

We had to bring out the necessity in logic for the distinction between concept and object before introducing classes as objects. If there are two predicates neither of which is true of any object that the other is not true of, it seems natural to say that there is an extension common to them both, regarding this as an object; predicates that are true of different things will have differing extensions. (In particular, all predicates true of nothing at all have the same extension.) Thus two predicates that stand for the same concept always determine the same extension, regardless of their wording or sense; it is the concept itself that determines their extension, and we may speak, as Frege does, of the extension *of* a concept. In specifying a particular extension we may accordingly mention a concept whose extension it is, using a predicate to stand for this concept; I shall use as a name for the extension determined (say) by the predicate ". . . cut . . .'s throat" the phrase "the range of *x* for which *x* cut *x*'s throat". We have here a paradigm for constructing a name of an extension from any predicate. ("Range" is not meant as a translation of Frege's "*Wertverlauf*".)

Why use a newfangled phrase instead of the Fregean expression "the extension of the concept: *x* cut *x*'s throat" or the familiar expression "the class (set) of all *x*s such that *x* cut *x*'s throat"? The Fregean way of speaking makes use of the pseudo-name "the concept: *x* cut *x*'s throat"; such pseudo-names are to be avoided whenever possible, lest we forget that a concept cannot have a proper name. In my way of speaking, we refer to the concept by using a predicate, and there is nothing that looks like a proper name of the concept.

The familiar way of speaking about classes is even more misleading; it has the look of describing a class by its relation to its members—"that class of which an object is a member if and only if . . ."; the concept comes in only secondarily, because we happen to specify the members as falling under it, and would not have to be mentioned at all if we could list the members by name. Now if a class is constituted as having certain members, how can we arrive at one with no members, such as the extension of an empty concept must be? The null class was introduced into logic by Boole and Schroeder with false identity papers, as the class we are referring to when we use the word "nothing"; and modern logic books too often get over the difficulty with a mixture of sophistry and bluff. If we use "class" and "member" in their ordinary senses, there can be no null class devoid of members. My logic class has as its members the undergraduates whom I teach logic; I could not justifiably enter on my timetable a Hegel class at 9 a.m. every weekday, on the score that the class of people to whom I explain Hegel's philosophy is the same as the class of people I teach at 9 a.m. every weekday, namely the null class.

In point of fact, the familiar senses of "class" and "member" are of no logical importance. The extension of a predicate must be an object correlated with that predicate and with just such other predicates as are true of the same objects; but it is altogether indifferent for logic which object this is. You may think you know which object is called "Geach's logic class of October 1952" and what sort of object this is; but your supposed knowledge is quite useless in set theory, and there is no reason in that theory to identify the range of x for which x is an undergraduate taught logic by Geach in October 1952 with this object that you think you know, rather than with Geach himself or the moon. (This has a bearing on the view that physical objects can be analyzed away by treating them as classes of more fundamental entities. Given that we know what sense-data are, we can treat the extension of a predicate that is true only of certain sense-data as identical with a certain physical object. But this does not reduce the physical object to a logical construction out of the sense-data; no more than I am reduced to a logical construction out of certain undergraduates, if the object that is the extension of a predicate applying to the undergraduates is taken to be myself.)

We may define "x belongs to y" as meaning: "for some F, y is the range of z for which $F(z)$, and $F(x)$". We can show that if x

belongs to y, and y is the range of z for which $G(z)$, then $G(x)$. For if y is both the range of z for which $F(z)$ and the range of z for which $G(z)$, then we have, for any z, $F(z)$ if and only if $G(z)$; otherwise the predicates "$F(\ )$" and "$G(\ )$" would have the same extension y although they were not true of just the same objects, which goes against the meaning of "extension". Now if x belongs to y and y is the range of z for which $G(z)$, then we have by the definition of "belongs to": For some F, y is both the range of z for which $G(z)$ and that for which $F(z)$, and $F(x)$. And from this there follows, by our previous result: For some F, $F(x)$, and, for any z, $F(z)$ if and only if $G(z)$; from which in turn we get: $G(x)$. Q.e.d.

We thus see that, if there is such an object as the range of z for which $F(z)$, then x will belong to that range if and only if $F(x)$.

The question whether a range or extension belongs to itself can thus have a perfectly good sense. For, e.g., the range of x for which x is an undergraduate taught logic by Geach in October 1952 may quite well be a human being; and the question whether that range belongs to itself will then be answered by finding out whether that human being was taught logic as an undergraduate by Geach in October 1952. Some logicians who claim to know that it *cannot* make sense to ask whether an extension belongs to itself are making two assumptions: first, that given the objects belonging to A, we can (at least in simple cases) discern an object that is the class of them all, and must identify A with this; secondly, that no predicate can be used without equivocation both for a class so understood and for its members, and that therefore the predicate "member of the class A" cannot be used without equivocation for the class A itself. Even the second assumption is very doubtful; may I not say alike of my logic class taken collectively and of its several members that they were in my room at a certain time? Perhaps I shall be called naïve, and regaled with scholastic subtleties to make me see that the predication is here not univocal. But since I rejected the first assumption as well, I shall not be interested.

Since the predicate ". . . is an extension not belonging to itself" makes good sense, it is natural to ask what *its* extension is. But now we find that no object can be its extension—be the range of z for which z is an extension not belonging to itself. For if x were this range, x would belong to x, and thus be an extension belonging to itself, if and only if x were an extension not belonging to itself: Russell's paradox. If we always assign the same extension to coextensive predicates, and different extensions to predicates that are not coextensive, then to certain specifiable predicates we cannot assign any objects as their extensions. There are not enough objects to go round.

The best that we can hope for is to find a certain set of predicates that can all have extensions assigned to them without inconsistency. I would suggest as a basis for set theory the assumption that a predicate has an extension whenever (1) it is expressed wholly by means of truth-functional connectives, quantification over objects, and the symbol for "belongs to"; (2) it is what Quine in *Mathematical Logic* calls "stratified". We need no such restriction on the predicates that are to be taken as standing for concepts.

The theory here sketched is strictly equipollent to Quine's *Mathematical Logic*; quantification over concepts answers to his quantification over Classes, and quantification over objects or extensions answers to his quantification over Elements. (I use capitals to distinguish words given a special sense in Quine's system.) The Members of a Class are what we should call the objects falling under a concept; the Members of an Element are the objects belonging to an extension. Every predicate determines a Class whose Members are (a concept under which there fall) just those Elements (objects) of which the predicate is true. A predicate determines an Element whose Members are just those Elements (a range to which belong just those objects) of which it is true, if it is stratified and Normal, i.e., has all quantifications restricted to Elements (objects); this requirement is a mere different wording of ours. There is an apparent divergence between the two systems in that we sharply distinguish objects and concepts, whereas for Quine every Element is identical with a Class. But an Element's being Identical with a Class means just that they have the same Members; for every Element x there is a Class F such that any Element z is a Member of x if and only if it is a Member of F. This means in our terminology: For every extension x there is an F such that any object z belongs to x if and only if $F(z)$; which is unexceptionable. (It is assumed here tacitly, and explicitly by Quine, that all the objects or Elements over which we quantify are extensions. This leads to no difficulty;

for our trouble is that at best there are not enough objects to serve as extensions, not that some objects are unemployed.)

Our system, then, is essentially just a reformulation of Quine's, and can benefit by the same (relative) consistency proofs. On points of interpretation we of course differ from Quine, since he thinks the distinction between concept and object is unnecessary in logic. I hold with Frege that this distinction is founded in the nature of things, and that a logical system will either express it somehow or turn out inconsistent. In Quine's system the apparently artificial distinction between Class and Element is just the Fregean distinction under a new and misleading guise.

One last point arises about "having enough objects to go round" as extensions. If our set theory is not to be completely trivial, there must be an infinity (at least denumerable) of objects to serve as extensions. But how are we to get this infinity? To prove if predicates formed according to a certain rule all have extensions, then these extensions will all be distinct, does not yet *give* us all those distinct objects. And I think it is cheating to assume the necessary infinity without proving that *any* infinity in fact exists. But how prove that there is an infinity except by means of a set theory?

I think this difficulty can be overcome. I hold that we can and must recognize numbers as objects apart from any treatment of extensions in general; we have to bring concepts into our account of numbers, but not their extensions. If so, and we can legitimately use numbers to count numbers, we have an infinity independent of any special set theory; for the number of numbers from 0 up to a natural number n is $n+1$, and the number of natural numbers is greater than any natural number. We can then dismiss our suspicion that our chosen set theory must be wrong somewhere because it brings in infinity; and within the theory we can identify the numbers as the extensions of certain predicates. But this would have been quite illegitimate if we had not got the numbers already; this identification is not a recognition of what the numbers, which we could so far only name, really are, but is a conferment of new titles on old friends, whom we already know by sight. (And which number we identify with which extension is arbitrary.) Frege was not misled in this matter; he recognized that identifying numbers with certain extensions was both open to question and, as regards the nature of number, of altogether secondary importance.[1] The lure others have felt toward regarding numbers as classes of classes arises from an idea that you can start with concrete objects, out of these build groups, and out of like-numbered groups built those super-groups which are numbers—at no point bringing in anything mysterious and nonphysical. But the view that an extension can be built up out of the objects belong to it is a crude error that I have already exposed; those objects are related to the extension only indirectly, as falling under the concept whose extension it is.

NOTE

There is an important difference between the paradox developed on p. 229 and Russell's paradox as expounded on p. 232f. In Russell's paradox we have a predicate "$W(\ )$" such that "W[the range of x for which $W(x)$]" would have the same *truth-value* as "not W [the range of x for which $W(x)$]"; the paradox is to be resolved not by rejecting the predicate as senseless, but by denying that it has an extension that can be called "the range of x for which $W(x)$". In the other paradox we *seem* to have a predicate "$W(\ )$" such that "$W(W)$" and "not $W(W)$" would have the same *sense*, not just the same *truth-value*; this apparent predicate must therefore really be senseless.

6.4. ON FREGE'S WAY OUT

In this note I shall give a generalized form of Leśniewski's proof that Frege's way out of Russell's Paradox only generates new contradictions. Frege turns out to have been wrong even in supposing that there was only one 'exceptional case' for each predicate "F"; for the supposition

$$(y):y\epsilon\hat{x}(Fx)\equiv.y\neq \mathrm{Ex}\ \hat{x}(Fx).Fy, \qquad (1)$$

where "Ex" stands for a specifiable function that has a value for any class as argument, leads to a contradiction, except on the absurd supposition that the universal class $\hat{x}(x=x)$ is a unit class $\hat{x}(x=y)$. (Henceforth I write, as is usual, "V" for "$\hat{x}(x=x)$" and "ιy" for "$\hat{x}(x=y)$".)

From (1) we easily prove that

$$(y).y\epsilon\ \mathrm{V}\ \mathrm{v}\ y=\mathrm{Ex}\ \mathrm{V} \qquad (2)$$

$$(x)(y): x\epsilon\ \iota y.\equiv.x\neq \mathrm{Ex}\ \iota y.x=y \qquad (3)$$

[1] *Grundlagen der Arithmetik*, p. 117.

$$(x)(y): \iota x = \iota y . \equiv . x = y \tag{4}$$

$$(x)(y): x \in \iota y \supset .x = y \tag{5}$$

We now define a function θ to satisfy the following conditions:

If Ex $x \neq \iota x$, $\theta x = \iota x$.

If Ex $x = \iota x$ and x is a unit class, $\theta x = V$. $\left.\right\}$ (6)

If Ex $x = \iota x$ and x is not a unit class, $\theta x = x$.

On Frege's principles, this function is legitimately introduced; its value is specified (provided that the value of the Ex-function is) for all possible arguments.

We now easily see, since V cannot be a unit class, that

$$(x) . \theta x \neq \text{Ex } x \tag{7}$$

By (7) and (1) we have:

$$\theta \hat{x}(Fx) \in \hat{x}(Fx) . \equiv . F(\theta \hat{x}(Fx)) \tag{8}$$

Again, we can prove that:

$$(x)(y): \theta x = \theta y . \theta x \neq V . \supset x = y \tag{9}$$

For if $\theta x = \theta y$ and is not a unit class and not V, we must have: $\theta x = x$, $\theta y = y$, $x = y$. And if $\theta x = \theta y$ is a unit class, then, since V is not a unit class, we must have $\theta x = \iota x$ and $\theta y = \iota y$, and therefore $\iota x = \iota y$ and $x = y$ by (4).

We now write "W" for "$\hat{x}(y)(x = \theta y \supset \sim(x \in y))$". We have, by (8):

$$\theta W \in W \equiv (y)(\theta W = \theta y \supset \sim(\theta W \in y)) \tag{10}$$

Hence: $\qquad \sim(\theta W \in W): (\exists y)(\theta W = \theta y . \theta W \in y) \tag{11}$

By (9), however, unless $\theta W = V$, we can never have $\theta W = \theta y$ and $W \neq y$. So we have:

$$\theta W = V \tag{12}$$

Since $\theta V \neq \text{Ex} V$, by (7), $\theta V \in V$, by (2).

So, since $\sim(\theta W \in W)$, $W \neq V$[1].

But $\theta W = V$; so we must have Ex $W = \iota W$, and W must be a unit class.

$$\text{Ex } W = \iota W . (\exists z) (W = \iota z) \tag{13}$$

From (1), (4), (5), and (13), we easily derive:

$$(x)(x \neq \iota W . \iota x \neq W . \supset (\exists y)(x = \theta y . x \in y)) \tag{14}$$

Now put "w" for "x" in (14) and use (4). This gives:

$$(v)(v \neq W . \iota w \neq W . \supset (\exists y)(w = \theta y . w \in y)) \tag{15}$$

But θy is a unit class w only if $\theta y = \iota y = w$ and $v = y$. So we have:

$$(v)(v \neq W . \iota w \neq W . \supset w \in v) \tag{16}$$

Now since $V \neq \iota V$, $\sim(\iota V \in \iota V)$, by (5); so, writing "$\iota V$" for

---

[1] This simple proof that $W \neq V$ was suggested to me by Michael Dummett.

"v" in (16), we get:

$$\iota \, V = W \, v \, \iota \, \iota \, \iota \, V = W \tag{17}$$

Again, since $\iota \, V \neq \iota \, \iota \, \iota \, V, \sim (\iota \, \iota \, \iota \, V \, \epsilon \, \iota \, \iota \, V)$, by (5); so, writing "$\iota \, \iota \, V$" for "$v$" in (16), we get:

$$\iota \, \iota \, V = W \, v \, \iota \, \iota \, \iota \, \iota \, V = W. \tag{18}$$

But since V is not a unit class, by (4) the classes $\iota \, V, \iota \, \iota \, V, \iota \, \iota \, \iota \, V, \iota \, \iota \, \iota \, \iota \, V$, are all distinct: so (17) and (18) cannot both be true.

If, as Frege supposed, $Ex \, x$ is always x itself, we could reach contradiction more simply by considering the consequences of "$\iota U \epsilon U$", when $U = \hat{x}(y)(x = \iota y \supset \sim (x \epsilon y))$. This was essentially Leśniewski's way.

7

Identity Theory

7.1. IDENTITY

I am arguing for the thesis that identity is relative. When one says "*x* is identical with *y*", this, I hold, is an incomplete expression; it is short for "*x* is the same *A* as *y*", where "*A*" represents some count noun understood from the context of utterance—or else, it is just a vague expression of a half-formed thought. Frege emphasized that "*x* is *one*" is an incomplete way of saying "*x* is one *A*, a single *A*", or else has no clear sense; since the connection of the concepts *one* and identity comes out just as much in the German "*ein und dasselbe*" as in the English "one and the same", it has always surprised me that Frege did not similarly maintain the parallel doctrine of relativized identity, which I have just briefly stated. On the contrary, Frege actually enunciated with all vigour a doctrine that identity cannot be relativized: "Identity is a relation given to us in such a specific form that it is inconceivable that various forms of it should occur" (*Grundgesetze*, Vol. II, p. 254).

Absolute identity seems at first sight to be presupposed in the branch of formal logic called identity theory. Classical identity theory may be obtained by adjoining a single schema to ordinary quantification theory (for bound name-variables):

$$\vdash Fa \leftrightarrow \forall x(Fx \wedge x = a). \tag{1}$$

Quine in his *Set Theory and its Logic* attributes to Hao Wang (p. 13) the recognition that (1) will serve as a single axiom schema for identity theory. In the vernacular we may intuitively express the content of (1) by saying: Whatever is true of something identical with an object a is true of a, and conversely.

We readily derive from schema (1) the Law of Self-Identity, "$\vdash a = a$". For if we take "$F\xi$" to be "$\xi \neq a$", then schema (1) gives us:

$$\vdash (a \neq a) \leftrightarrow \forall x (x \neq a \wedge x = a), \tag{2}$$

which of course yields "$\vdash a = a$". And there are equally easy proofs of what has been called (I believe by Quine) the Indiscernibility of Identicals:

$$\vdash Fb \wedge b = a \rightarrow Fa \tag{3}$$

and of theorems asserting the symmetry and transitiveness of identity as a relation. The logical system got by adjoining schema (1) to classical quantification theory is a system with a complete proof procedure; moreover, its interpretation is categorical, in the following sense: If we try to introduce *two* two-place predicables, each separately conforming to schema (1), they turn out to coincide in application. (In this paper, as in my book *Reference and Generality*, I use "predicables" as a term for the verbal expressions called "predicates" by other logicians; I reserve the term "predicate" for a predicable actually being used as the main functor in a given proposition.)

In face of these well-known results, it may seem an enterprise worthy of a circle-squarer to challenge the classical theory of identity. All the same, it has an Achilles' heel, as I hope to show. I must first introduce the notion of a *I-predicable*. Consider a theory T with interpreted terms. What are we to take as the substitution-instances of the "F" used in stating schema (1)? It will not be enough to allow replacement of "F" by one-place predicables actually constructible in T. For suppose "$G\xi\theta\zeta$" represents a three-place predicable that can be constructed in T; then if we consider the results of filling up all but one empty place in such a predicable with name-variables, e.g., "$Gvau$", we shall certainly want the closure of the formula:

$$Gvaw \leftrightarrow \forall x (Gvxw \wedge x = a) \tag{4}$$

to count as holding good by schema (1). Similarly for other many-place predicables of T. We shall say that a two-place predicable in a theory T is an I-predicable in T if it satisfies schema (1) for all constructible expressions of T—the formulas just described being here counted as instances of schema (1).

A two-place predicable is an I-predicable, not absolutely, but in relation to a given theory T. But so far this is no ground whatever for asserting the relativity of identity; for this so far amounts to no more than the fact that what an expression signifies is relative to the language we are using. For all that I have said so far, it might be true that if a predicable is an I-predicable in a theory T, then what it expresses in that theory is strict, absolute, unqualified identity.

However, if we consider a moment, we see that an I-predicable in a given theory T *need not* express strict, absolute, unqualified identity; it need mean no more than that two objects are indiscernible by the predicables that form the descriptive resources of the theory—the *ideology* of the theory, to borrow Quine's handy term. "For real identity", we may wish to say, "we need not bring in the ideology of a definite theory T. For real identity, *whatever* is true of something identical with a is true of a and conversely, regardless of which theory this can be expressed in; and a two-place predicable signifying real identity must be an I-predicable no matter what other predicables occur along with it in the theory." But if we wish to talk this way, we shall soon fall into contradictions; such unrestrained language about "whatever is true of a", not made relative to the definite ideology of a theory T, will land us in such notorious paradoxes as Grelling's and Richard's. If, however, we restrict ourselves to the ideology of a theory T, then, as I said, an I-predicable need not express strict identity, but only indiscernibility within the ideology of T.

Nor is this all. Objects that are indiscernible when we are confined to the ideology of T may perfectly well be discernible in the ideology of a theory T^1 of which T is a fragment, given that T^1 contains more predicables than T. Of course this means that a predicable of T that is an I-predicable in T is no longer an I-predicable with regard to T^1; there is no logical difficulty about this, since the allowable substitutions for the schematic letter "F" in schema (1) will no longer be the same in T^1 as they were in T.

This abstract argument is readily illustrated by a simple example. Let the theory T be a theory about the expressions of a given natural language; let the range of T's quantifiers be *token* expressions of that language; but let the ideology of T be so restricted that in T we cannot give different descriptions for two tokens of the same type-word. Then if a predicable of T, say "$E\xi\theta$" signifies "ξ is equiform with θ", it will be an I-predicable in theory T. But now let us add to T's ideology just one predicable that discriminates between equiform tokens; in the enlarged theory T^1, we can express something that is true of a token a but not true of an equiform token b; so in T^1 the predicable "$E\xi\theta$" is not an I-predicable any longer.

But now where have we got to? It looked as though satisfaction of schema (1) gave us a necessary and sufficient condition for a predicable's expressing strict identity. But the naive reading of schema (1), by which we should speak quite unrestrictedly of "whatever is true of so-and-so", is inadmissible because of the semantic paradoxes. If instead we consider a predicable that is an I-predicable *relative to a theory* T, then this need only express indiscernibility relative to the ideology of T, and need not express strict unqualified identity. Moreover, an I-predicable of T, while remaining one and the same unambiguous predicable, may be no longer an I-predicable in a wider theory T^1 containing T as a proper part; but we certainly cannot say that this predicable, although it does not change its sense when T is expanded to T^1, expresses strict unqualified identity in T but no longer does so in T^1. We thought we had a criterion for a predicable's expressing strict identity; but the thing has come apart in our hands; and no alternative rigorous criterion that could replace this one has thus far been suggested. I urged initially on intuitive grounds that there just is no such notion as unqualified identity; it now looks as though my intuition was reliable. I might say: the prosceution rests.

Quine, however, can supply a strong argument for the defence of strict identity. His starting-point is this: Whether we interpret a two-place predicable in a theory T as expressing identity goes along with the way we interpret the quantifiers in T. His point is certainly well taken; we may see this from the theoretical possibility of modifying the usual reading of nested quantifiers so as to avoid altogether the use of a special identity sign—a device sketched out in the *Tractatus*, and further developed in recent articles by Hintikka. So we may, and indeed should, consider quantification theory and identity theory as being like two cogwheels that mesh together and move together.

Quine now proposes that if we find an I-predicable in a theory T, we should construe the range of the quantifiers in T as a class of objects for which the I-predicable expresses absolute identity, and construe the other predicables of T correspondingly. In a wider system T^1 the range of the quantifiers may on this principle turn out to be different; and then, although each complete sentence of T will survive unchanged in T^1 with the same truth-conditions as before, the *parts* of each sentence will need reconstruing in certain definite ways.

We can grasp Quine's proposal better if we take a concrete example. Let us consider the letters and words in a particular volume on my bookshelves at Leeds. (This example enables us to avoid problems about identity's surviving change; the letters and words in a book are not changeless entities, but for present purposes the changes they undergo may be ignored.) Suppose that the quantifiers of a theory T range over these letters and words and that the ideology of T does not discriminate between two token-words that are instances of the same type-word. Let "$E\xi\theta$" be an I-predicable for the theory T. Then at first sight we have a choice between two interpretations: we may treat the quantifiers of T as ranging over the token letters and words in my book and read "Exy" as meaning "x is a token equiform with y"; or on the other hand we may treat the quantifiers as ranging over the type-letters and type-words in my book, and read "Exy" as meaning simply "x is identical with y", as expressing absolute identity. Quine would have us accept this second interpretation, and construe other predicables of T accordingly. For example, '—contains two occurrences of "e" ' would not be construed as '—contains two letter "e"s'—for if we follow Quine, we are not allowed *in* T to quantify over token letters like this—but will rather be construed (in the style of his *Mathematical Logic*) as '—contains two initial segments ending with *the* letter "e" '. I here allow myself to interject a comment on the unholy mixture of Nominalist and Realist ways of talking that we get in a sentence like 'The word "teeth" contains two "e"s'. Of course we know what is intended, just as we do when someone says 'A donkey is an animal beginning with "d" '; but as Aquinas says about the more dubious texts of the Fathers, such remarks are to be charitably construed and on no account imitated.)

Let us now suppose that we add to the vocabulary of T a predicable or two enabling us to discriminate between different tokens of the same word or letter. In the enlarged system T^1, each full sentence of T will occur with just the same truth-conditions as it had in T; but the import of subordinate expressions in sentences will be radically changed. The quantifiers will now range over token-words of my volume, not over type-words; and a clause "Exy" will now mean not "x is identical with y" but only "x is a token equiform with y". Similarly, if the one-place predicable "F" means '—contains two occurrences of "e",' this will be spelled out as '—contains two token letter "e"s', and no longer as '—contains two initial segments each of which ends with *the* letter "e" '. Let us now consider the formula:

$$VxVy(Fx \wedge Fy \wedge \mathbf{1}Exy)$$

In T this will be read as: 'There are in Geach's volume two non-identical type-words x and y, and x as well as y is such that two of its initial segments end with *the* letter "e"'. In T^1 it will be read as 'There are in Geach's volume two non-equiform token-words x and y, and x as well as y contains two letter "e"s.' If we think it out, the changes of import for the bits of the formula cancel out, and the truth-condition of the whole remains unchanged.

As you might expect, I have no knock-down logical answer to this; Quine is hardly going to be caught out in a straightforward logical mistake. But I can show, I think, that this way of interpreting quantifiers so as to get an absolute identity involves a sin against a highly intuitive methodological programme, clearly enunciated by Quine himself—and obviously Quine himself ought to be worried by this objection. The programme is that as our knowledge expands we should unhesitatingly expand our ideology, our stock of predicables, but should be much more wary about altering our ontology, the interpretation of our bound name-variables. I now quote Quine's own clear statement. "But ontology is, pending revision, more clearly in hand than what may be called *ideology* —the question of admissible predicates. . . . That the ontology should be relatively definite, pending revision, is required by the mere presence of quantifiers in the language of science; for quantifiers may be said to have been interpreted and understood only in so far as we have settled the range of their variables. And that the fund of predicates should be forever subject to supplementation is implicit in a theorem of metamathematics; for it is known that for any theory, however rich, there are classes which are not the extensions of any of its sentences" (*The Ways of Paradox*, New York, 1966, p. 232).

An admirable aim; but one that we cannot attain by Quine's

device of reading strict identity into I-predicables and construing other expressions in a theory correspondingly. Let us consider a theory T, whose quantifiers are assigned a certain range by Quine's method: if T is a rich theory, we may find within T a number of predicables E^1, E^2, E^3, . . . , each of which is an I-predicable in relation to some corresponding sub-theory T^1, T^2, T^3, . . . , and none of which has the same application *in* T as any other. On Quine's view, E^1 will express strict identity in T^1, and E^2 in T^2, and E^3 in T^3, . . . ; and the quantifiers of the theories T^1, T^2, T^3, . . . , must accordingly be reconstrued as having different ranges in each case. We wanted to keep our ontology comparatively fixed while allowing changes in our ideology; but now some quite trivial shifts in ideology—the mere omission of some predicables from a theory—will result in quite large additions to our ontology, to the realm our quantifiers are supposed to range over.

Let us go back to the universe of discourse I introduced to you a little while ago—the words in a given volume on my shelves. There are various ways of counting these words: as John Austin remarked, in a rare flash of perceptiveness, type-words and token-words are just two among many ways of counting words. We may, for example, count the dictionary-entry words in a book; in this case "theism" meaning belief in just one God and "theism" meaning addiction to tea will count, although equiform, as two words; but on the other hand in an article on the philosophy of religion the singular "theism", the plural "theisms", and the possessive "theism's", as in "theism's fundamental mistake", will all count as one word. Now we can find a suitably restricted theory for each of the predicables "—is the same token-word as—", "—is a token equiform with—", "—has the same dictionary entry as—", and ever so many other predicables, so that in the appropriate theory the predicable will be an I-predicable; e.g., for the predicable "—has the same dictionary entry as—" we need only assume that the theory's descriptive resources are too meagre to distinguish between two words to which the same dictionary entry corresponds. If now we choose to follow Quine, there will be *in rerum natura* ever so many different domains of words, just in one volume on my shelves at Leeds.

This is only one illustration of the way that shifts of ideology lead to an indecent pullulation of entities in our ontology. Take another example. As I remarked years ago when critizing Quine, there is a certain set of predicables that are true of men but do not discriminate between two men of the same surname. If the ideology of a theory T is restricted to such predicables, the ontology of T calls into being a universe of androids (as science fiction fans say) who differ from men just in this respect, that two different ones cannot share the same surname. I call these androids surmen; a surman is in many ways very much like a man, e.g., he has brains in his skull and a heart in his breast and guts in his belly, for in these respects two men of the same surname do not differ.

The universe now shows itself as a baroque Meinongian structure, which hardly suits Quine's expressed preference for desert landscapes. We surely need Ockham's razor to cut through this tangle; and it is not too hard to see where to make the cut. We reject absolute identity, but admit as many as we need of two-place predicables of the form "—is the same A as—"where "A" is some count noun. The words in my book (say) will constitute just *one* universe of discourse; but criteria of relative identity, all applying with equal right within this universe, will be given by different two-place predicables, e.g., "— is the same token-word as —", "—is the same type-word as —", "—is the same dictionary-entry word as —". Similarly, we can count the men in Leeds, or, with a different result, the surmen in Leeds; but Leeds does not contain androids as well as men on that account. It is just that we are numbering the inhabitants of Leeds in two different ways; it is just a different predicable—now the predicable "—is the same *man* as —", and now the predicable "— is the same *surman* as —" (and this means, simply, "— is a man with the same surname as —, who is also a man"), —that is serving as our criterion to keep us from counting *the same one* twice over. Our ontology is now firmly under control; only our ideology is liable to expand—we cannot tell in advance how many such identity-predicables we are going to need. (We may observe that one theory may contain many such predicables not coinciding in application; though they will not then all be I-predicables in the theory.) But there could not be any objection in principle to an expandable ideology; that is inevitable anyhow—on logical grounds, not just because we happen to live in a surprising world.

R

I end this paper with an *amende honorable* to the shade of John Locke. For Locke got over the fundamental thesis of this paper pretty clearly in his *Essay*; admittedly he used, here as elsewhere, the murky jargon of "ideas", but it is very easy to transpose his sentences into a new key and talk about count nouns, as I have done. Locke's way of posing the problem of personal identity may be rephrased thus: Even if every man is a person and every person is a man, we still cannot infer that the predicable "— is the same person as —" and "— is the same man as —" coincide in application; this conclusion needs for its support an elaborate argument in the philosophy of mind, not a little logical manipulation in identity theory. Locke with his contempt for formal logic would have been left unimpressed by a formal 'proof' that in that case the same man just is the same person and conversely; his reason for rejecting the 'proof' would by my lights have been bad, but I think the rejection is right. I am not here saying whether the same man *is* the same person, and vice versa; all I am saying is that Locke was right in not allowing this to be settled easily, even on the supposition that there are no impersonal men and no non-human persons. On my own view "Every man is a person" is tantamount to "Every man is the same person as something or other"; and similarly for "Every person is a man" (*Reference and Generality*, p. 191). The bearing of this in mind may mitigate the paradox; for on this analysis the argument Locke would reject becomes inconclusive or circular.

To make this clear, let us suppose that each Leeds man has just one surname. Then each Leeds man is the same surman as himself, by the explanation of "surman"; so each Leeds man is a surman. On the other hand, since "— is the same man as himself", if true of any man, is true of any other man with the same surname as he, each Leeds surman is the same man as himself, i.e., is a man. (I have argued, *loc. cit.*, that it does not make sense to ask *which* man he is the same as.) But it does not follow that, in the case supposed, the predicables "— is the same man as —" and "— is the same surman as —" would in Leeds be coincident in application. Nor are there surmen *as well as* men in Leeds; "surmen" and "men" simply give two ways of counting the inhabitants. Just so it *might* be with "man" and "person", as Locke held.

To be sure, Locke also held that there was no special way an individual named by a proper name had to be self-identical. This view must be false if his other view is true; for by keeping on using a proper name, we mean to refer over and over again to the same 'thing'; but if this is not an intention to keep on referring to the same A, for some definite interpretation of "A" as a count noun, then, as lawyers say, the intention is void for uncertainty, and we have not managed to refer at all. Locke's error on this point has been enormously influential, and I do not repent of my repeated criticism of him in print for the error; but I ought in justice to have added that Locke himself shows the fly the way out of Locke's fly-bottle. But then, Locke's *Essay* is like a mail-order catalogue, and you buy what suits you. To switch to a communication-theory metaphor, the trouble is to make out which part is message and which is noise.

7.2. IDENTITY—A REPLY

Restricting the interpretation of "A" in "is the same A as" to count nouns was a slip of the pen on my part; I allowed mass terms as well to be such interpretations in my book *Reference and Generality*, section 31, and I had no intention of recanting this doctrine.

I carefully avoided examples with definite descriptions flanking the identity sign. The problem of identity was tough by itself, and I did not want problems about definite descriptions on my hands as well. (For the record, I hold, and have elsewhere said, that the "is" of "is the husband of Xanthippe" is *not* an identity sign, but a bare copula of predication: *Reference and Generality*, sections 36 and 75.)

I put into the mouth of an absolute-identity man the following thesis:

(T) x is identical with y if whatever is true of x is true of y and conversely.

My objection to this thesis T is that the two-place predicable "is true of" is dubiously intelligible, in view of the semantic paradoxes. The classical solution of the paradoxes is to say that "is true of" is to be understood as defined for the predicables of some definite language L, but as itself belonging not to the vocabulary of L, but to that of a metalanguage M. This solution would imply that this thesis just given, connecting "is identical with" and "is true of", indeed is unintelligible as it stands, for lack of necessary relativizations.

We must not think of the relation between a larger and a smaller language in temporal terms: we are not to imagine some poor devil with a very meagre vocabulary, who then learns a greater stock of words and can discriminate things that before were linguistically indiscernible. The relation is, of course, not temporal but set-theoretical; the words (sentences) of the sub-language are a proper sub-set of words (sentences) of the language. Moreover, whatever sentences are true in the language will still be true in the sub-language; from this it follows that all existential commitments of sentences in the sub-language are commitments retained in the language itself.

So much to remove misunderstandings. There remain two points of substance. First, given the timelessness of the relation between a language and a sub-language, what *is* my argument about indecently burgeoning existential commitments? Secondly, how does one recognize an identity predicable, on the relative-identity view?

My argument was directed, *ad hominem*, at a proposal of Quine's: namely that the quantifiers in a language L be construed as ranging over objects for which the I-predictable of L gives a criterion of *absolute* identity. From this I drew a consequence possibly unwelcome to a lover of desert landscapes: namely, that since a rich language L may allow for our carving many sub-languages, $L_1, L_2, L_3, \ldots$, out of it, users of L are committed to the existence, not only of a realm of objects for which the I-predicable of L itself gives the criterion of absolute identity, but also, for each of these possible sub-languages L_n, of a distinct realm of objects for which the I-predicable of L_n gives the criterion of absolute identity. The bizarre consequences of this, in concrete instances, were already developed in my article; and I think I need not repeat the illustrations or invent others. What I must again now emphasize, in view of misunderstanding, is that on Quine's account of the matter it must follow that these strange existential commitments would be logical commitments of the rich language we actually speak; not provisional personal commitments that we may imagine someone taking on when he spoke only a meagre language, and repudiating like a minor's debts when he learned to speak a richer one.

As for our recognizing relative-identity predicables: any equivalence relation, any relation that is non-empty, reflexive in its field, transitive, and symmetrical, can be used to specify a criterion of relative identity. The procedure is common enough in mathematics: e.g., there is a certain equivalence relation between ordered pairs of integers by virtue of which we may say that *x* and *y*, though distinct ordered pairs, are *one and the same* rational number. Absolute-identity theorists regard this procedure as unrigorous: but on a relative-identity view it is fully rigorous, and has the advantage of lightening a theory's set-theoretical burdens. (In our present example, we need not bring *infinite sets* of ordered pairs of integers into the theory of rationals.)

In such cases we have a clear and well-known way of defining the equivalence relation. The equivalence relation corresponding to "is the same man as" is, as we all know, a matter of protracted philosophical argument; I do not think the argument can be cut short by abstract considerations from the philosophy of logic. Since "man" is not a logical, nor even a mathematical, term, it is no business of logic or the philosophy of logic to supply a criterion of identity for man. What philosophy of logic can do is to rule out some false theories: an account of "is the same man as" which made identity for man non-symmetrical or non-transitive would not deserve further discussion.

Expressions like "is the same so-and-so as" are part of our language, and stand in no apparent need of justification; I need no excuse for preferring them to other suggested relativizations of "the same", "is the same in language *L*", or "is the same for Mr. Iksinski", which are expressions I do not yet understand. Logic is concerned only with general rules of inference for sentences containing identity expressions; criteria of identity obviously depend on what you are identifying. Some reader perhaps thinks that "the same" is always the same, and criteria of identity are just a matter of psychology; if so, I may here quote Wittgenstein's parody: "High pitch is high pitch—it's merely a psychological matter whether you hear it" (like the pitch of a scream) "or see it" (like the pitch of a roof). The relation expressed by "of higher pitch than" has in fact the same logical properties in both cases; but that does not mean there is just one relation, which we happen to learn about by two different avenues of sense; and the like, I maintain, holds for identity relations.

8

Assertion

8.1. ASCRIPTIVISM

The statement that an act x was voluntary, or intentional, or done with intent, or the like, on the part of an agent A has often been analyzed as a causal statement that x was initiated by some act of A's mind that was an act of bare will—a volition, or an act of A's setting himself to do x, or an act of intending to do x, or the like. Latterly there has been a reaction against this type of analysis; it has been held (in my opinion, quite rightly) that the attempt to identify and characterize these supposed acts of bare will always runs into insuperable difficulties. To avoid such difficulties, some Oxford philosophers, whom I shall call Ascriptivists, have resorted to denying that to call an act voluntary, intentional, and so forth, is any sort of causal statement, or indeed any statement at all. In this note I shall try to expound and to refute Ascriptivism.

Ascriptivists hold that to say an action x was voluntary on the part of an agent A is not to *de*scribe the act x as caused in a certain way, but to *a*scribe it to A, to hold A responsible for it. Now holding a man responsible is a moral or quasi-moral attitude; and so, Ascriptivists argue, there is no question here of truth or falsehood, any more than there is for moral judgments. If B agrees or disagrees with C's ascription of an act to A, B is himself taking up a quasi-moral attitude toward A. Facts may support or go against such a quasi-moral attitude, but can never *force* us to adopt it. Further, the Ascriptivists would say, there is no risk of an antinomy, because ascription of an act to an agent can never conflict with a scientific account of how the act came about; for the scientific account is *de*scriptive, and *de*scriptive language is in quite a different logical realm from *a*scriptive language. Though it has not had the world-wide popularity of the distinction between *de*scriptive and *pre*scriptive language, the Ascriptivist theory has had quite a vogue, as is very natural in the present climate of opinion.

Now as regards hundreds of our voluntary or intentional acts, it would in fact be absurdly solemn, not to say melodramatic, to talk of imputation and exoneration and excuse, or for that matter of praise and reward. Ascribing an action to an agent just does not *in general* mean taking up a quasi-legal or quasi-moral attitude, and only a bad choice of examples could make one think otherwise. (As Wittgenstein said, when put on an unbalanced diet of examples philosophy suffers from deficiency diseases.)

Again, even when imputation and blame are in question, they can yet be distinguished from the judgment that so-and-so was a voluntary act. There are savage communities where even involuntary homicide carries the death penalty. In one such community, the story goes, a man fell off a coconut palm and broke a bystander's neck; the dead man's brother demanded blood for blood. With Solomonic wisdom the chief ordered the culprit to stand under the palm-tree and said to the avenger of blood, "Now you climb up and fall off and break his neck!" This suggestion proved unwelcome and the culprit went free. Though the vengeful brother may still have thought the culprit ought to have been punished, his reaction to the suggested method of execution showed that he knew as well as we do the difference between falling-off-a-tree-and-breaking-someone-else's-neck *voluntarily* or *intentionally* and just having it happen to you. To be sure, on his moral code the difference did not matter—his brother's death was still imputable to the man who fell on him—but this does not show that he had no notion of voluntariness, or even a different one from ours.

I said that Ascriptivism naturally thrives in the present climate of opinion; it is in fact constructed on a pattern common to a number of modern philosophical theories. Thus there is a theory that to say "What the policeman said is true" is not to describe or characterize what the policeman said but to corroborate it; and a theory that to say "It is bad to get drunk" is not to describe or characterize drunkenness but to condemn it. It is really quite easy to devise theories on this pattern; here is a new one that has occurred to me. 'To call a man happy is not to characterize or describe his condition; macarizing a man' (that is, calling him happy; the words "macarize" and "macarism" are in the O.E.D.) 'is a special non-descriptive use of language. If we consider such typical examples of macarism as the Beatitudes, or again such proverbial expressions as "Happy is the bride that the sun shines on; happy are the dead that the rain rains on", we can surely see that these sentences are not used to convey propositions. How disconcerting and inappropriate was the reply, "Yes, that's true", that a friend of mine got who cited "Happy are the dead that the rain rains on" at a funeral on a rainy day! The great error of the Utilitarians was to suppose that "the greatest happiness of the greatest number" was a descriptive characterization of a state of affairs that one could aim at; but in fact the term "happiness" is not a descriptive term: to speak of people's happiness is to macarize them, not to describe their state. Of course "happy" has a secondary descriptive force; in a society where the rich were generally macarized, "happy" would come to connote wealth; and then someone whose own standards of macarism were different from those current in his society might use "happy", in scare-quotes so to say, to mean "what most people count happy, that is rich" . . .' There you are; I make a free gift of the idea to anybody who likes it.

There is a radical flaw in this whole pattern of philosophizing. What is being attempted in each case is to account for the use of a term "P" concerning a thing as being a performance of some other nature than describing the thing. But what is regularly ignored is the distinction between calling a thing "P" and predicating "P" of a thing. A term "P" may be predicated of a thing in an *if* or *then* clause, or in a clause of a disjunctive proposition, without the thing's being thereby called "P". To say, "If the policeman's statement is true, the motorist touched 60 mph" is not to *call* the policeman's statement true; to say, "If gambling is bad, inviting people to gamble is bad" is not to *call* either gambling or invitations to gamble "bad". Now the theories of non-descriptive performances regularly take into account only the use of a term "P" to *call* something "P"; the corroboration theory of truth, for example, considers only the use of "true" to *call* a statement true, and the condemnation theory of the term "bad" considers only the way it is used to *call* something bad; predications of "true" and "bad" in *if* or *then* clauses, or in clauses of a disjunction, are just ignored. One could not write off such uses of the terms, as calling for a different explanation from their use to *call* things true or bad; for that would mean that arguments of the pattern "if *x* is true (if *w* is bad), then *p*; but *x* *is* true (*w* *is* bad); *ergo p*" contained a fallacy of equivocation, whereas they are in fact clearly valid.

This whole subject is obscured by a centuries-old confusion over predication embodied in such phrases as "a predicate is *asserted of* a subject". Frege demonstrated the need to make an absolute distinction between predication and assertion; here as elsewhere people have not learned from his work as much as they should. In order that the use of a sentence in which "*P*" is predicated of a thing may count as an act of *calling* the thing "*P*", the sentence must be used assertively; and this is something quite distinct from the predication, for, as we have remarked, "*P*" may still be predicated of the thing even in a sentence used non-assertively as a clause within another sentence. Hence, calling a thing "*P*" has to be explained in terms of predicating "*P*" of the thing, not the other way round. For example, condemning a thing by calling it "bad" has to be explained through the more general notion of predicating "bad" of a thing, and such predicating may be done without any condemnation; for example, even if I utter with full conviction the sentence, "If gambling is bad, inviting people to gamble is bad", I do not thereby condemn either gambling or invitations to gamble, though I do predicate "bad" of these kinds of act. It is therefore hopeless to try to explain the use of the term "bad" in terms of non-descriptive acts of condemnation; and, I maintain, by parity of reasoning it is hopeless to try to explain the use of the terms "done on purpose", "intentional", or the like, in terms of non-descriptive acts of ascription or imputation.

With this I shall dismiss Ascriptivism; I adopt instead the natural view that to ascribe an act to an agent is a causal description of the act. Such statements are indeed paradigm cases of causal statements: cf. the connection in Greek between αἰτία ("cause") and αἴτιος ("responsible"). Let us recollect the definition of will given by Hume: "the internal impression we feel and are conscious of when we knowingly give rise to any new motion of our body or new perception of our mind." Having offered this definition of will, Hume concentrates on the supposed 'internal impression' and deals with the causal relation between this and the 'new motion' or 'new perception' on the same lines as other causal relations between successive events. Like a conjurer, Hume diverts our attention; he makes us forget the words "knowingly give rise to", which are indispensable if his definition is to have the least plausibility. If Hume had begun by saying, "There is a peculiar, characteristic, internal impression which we are sometimes aware *arises in us* before a new perception or new bodily motion; we call this volition or will", then his account would have had a fishy look from the outset. To say we *knowingly give rise to* a motion of mind and body is already to introduce the whole notion of the voluntary; an 'internal impression' need not be brought into the account, and is anyhow, I believe, a myth. But without the 'internal impression' Hume's account of causality cannot be fitted to voluntary causality; without it we no longer have *two* sorts of event occurring in succession, but only, on each occasion, *one* event to which 'we knowingly give rise'—words that express a non-Humian sort of causality.

For an adequate account of voluntary causality, however, we should need an adequate account of causality in general; and I am far from thinking that I can supply one. To develop one properly would require a synoptic view of the methods and results of the strict scientific disciplines—a labour of Hercules that far exceeds my powers; and it would take a better man than I am to see far through the dust that Hume has raised. All I have tried to do here is to make it seem worthwhile to investigate non-Humian ideas of causality in analyzing the voluntary, instead of desperately denying, as Ascriptivists do, that voluntariness is a causal concept.

8.2. ASSERTION[1]

A thought may have just the same content whether you assent to its truth or not; a proposition may occur in discourse now asserted, now unasserted, and yet be recognizably the same

[1] Delivered as a Howison Lecture at the University of California in Berkeley in 1963 and to the Philosophical Society of the University of Warsaw in the same year. I thank my kind hosts in both places.

proposition. This may appear so obviously true as to be hardly worth saying; but we shall see it *is* worth saying, by contrast with erroneous theories of assertion, and also because a right view of assertion is fatal to well-known philosophical views on certain other topics.

I shall call this point about assertion *the Frege point*, after the logician who was the first (so far as I know) to make the point clearly and emphatically. In some of Frege's writings the point is made in the course of his expounding some highly disputable theories, about sense and reference and about propositions' being complex names of logical objects called "truth-values". But the dubiousness of these theories does not carry over to the Frege point itself. Admitting the Frege point does not logically commit us to these theories; as a matter of history, Frege already made the point in his youthful work, *Begriffsschrift*, many years before he had developed his theories of sense and reference. Those theories are more defensible than some philosophers allow; but to discuss them here would only obscure the main issue.

When I use the term "proposition", as I did just now, I mean a form of words in which something is propounded, put forward for consideration; it is surely clear that what is then put forward neither is *ipso facto* asserted nor gets altered in content by being asserted. Unfortunately, this use of "proposition", formerly a well-established one, has become liable to be misconstrued, for the word has been appropriated by certain theorists for a supposed realm of timeless abstract 'intentional' objects, whose principle of individuation has thus far eluded capture in any clearly formulable criterion. Philosophers have weakly surrendered the term "proposition" to these theorists and cast around for some substitute; the ones they have come up with—"sentence" and "statement"—have been rather unhappy. It would be preferable to stick to the old use of "proposition", which has never quite gone out; if we need a substitute for "proposition" in the new-fangled use, it will not be difficult to find one—let us say, "propositional content".

The use of "sentence" in the sense that "proposition" used to have often calls forth rather nagging objections. What is wrong with thus using "sentence" is quite a simple matter, and one is not likely to be misled once it has been pointed out: namely, that different occurrences of what is the same sentence by grammatical criteria may be different propositions by logical criteria. More-over, the fact that "sentence" is a grammatical term makes it sound awkward as applied to logical or mathematical formulas, which could of course be naturally called "propositions". But nobody ought to plume himself on replacing "sentence" in this use by "statement"; for "statement" is a far more dangerously misleading term. It is obvious that our discourse may and does contain unasserted propositions; the notion of an unasserted statement may appear a contradiction in terms. If we want to allow for the possibility of a *statement's* being made non-assertoric-ally, we have to strive against the natural use of the expressions "statement" and "making a statement", and the natural use may be too strong—*tamen usque recurret*.

This is no imaginary danger. In his essay *If, So, and Because* Professor Ryle actually uses the paradoxical sound of "unasserted statement" as a reason for censuring as deceptive the 'code style' of the *modus ponens*: "if *p*, then *q*; but *p*, therefore *q*." The recur-rences of the letters "*p*" and "*q*" suggest that a logician can recognize something identifiable which occurs now asserted, now unasserted; a statement, Ryle argues, cannot thus have two ways of occurring. Ryle even finds it a misleading feature of ordinary modern English that the same form of words may be used now to make a statement, now in an "if" or "then" clause; surely things would be clearer if we had to alter the mood or word order of clauses in framing a hypothetical.

A hypothetical statement, Ryle argues, cannot state a relation between two statements, because the antecedent and consequent clauses are not assertoric and thus not statements; statements are neither used nor mentioned in the hypothetical. Ryle toys with an idea of Cook Wilson, who had similar worries, that a hypothetical asserts a relation between two questions; he decides against this, on the score that one who makes a hypothetical statement does not actually either pose or mention any questions. Ryle's final solution is that in a hypothetical the antecedent and consequent are indents or specifications for possible statements; they are no more themselves statements than a licence to export bicycles is itself a bicycle—only confusion is easier because these clauses, like the statements for which they are indents, consist of words.

Thus far Ryle. His argument fully illustrates the dangers of "statement" as a logical term. If we speak rather of propositions,

Ryle's difficulties vanish. What Ryle calls "making a hypothetical statement" is what I call "asserting a hypothetical proposition"; in making such an assertion the speaker is certainly putting forward the antecedent and consequent for consideration, so that they are undoubtedly propositions too, but he is of course not thus far stating or asserting them to be true.[1] He may then go on to assert the antecedent, and from this go on further to assert the consequent. This does not alter the force of either proposition; if in some languages the propositions need rewording when asserted, this is just an idiotism of idiom. The only thing that is wrong with the 'code style' of the *modus ponens*—"if p then q; but p; therefore q'—is that we might profitably follow Frege in having an explicit assertion sign "⊢ if p, then q; ⊢ p; *ergo* ⊢ q". (Here "p" and "q" are schematic propositional letters; any concrete interpretation of them as propositions yields a valid argument.)

Ryle argues that in "if p, then q; but p; therefore q" the hypothetical is not a premise co-ordinate with "p", as the 'code style' suggests, but is rather a licence to perform the inference "p, therefore q" when you have the premise "p". His argument against the more conventional two-premise account of *modus ponens* is that if we needed to supply "if p, then q" as a premise for the inference of "q" from "p", then by parity of reasoning we should need to supply "if both p and if p then q, then q" as a premise for the inference of "q" from "p" and "if p then q"— and then we should have started on a vicious regress, the one made notorious by Lewis Carroll in 'What the Tortoise Said to Achilles'.

I do not think there is anything in this. Particular readings of "p" and "q" may make "p, therefore q" into a logically valid argument; but it is not in general logically valid, and if not, then no power in heaven or earth can issue me a 'licence' that makes it logically valid. On the other hand, "if p, then q; but p; therefore q" *is* logically valid; and this means precisely that the two premises "if p then q" and "p" are sufficient to yield the conclusion "q", so

---

[1] A good instance of the tangles that the use of "statement" leads to is to be found on p. 88 of Strawson's *Introduction to Logical Theory* (London, 1952): "for each hypothetical statement", we are told, "there could be made just *one* statement which would be the antecedent"; but of course it *would not* be the antecedent if it were a statement.

that there is no place for introducing an extra premise, and a regress never gets started.

The Frege point is thus something we need to grasp in order to understand *modus ponens*; it is no less needed in the doctrine of truth-functional connectives. Thus "*p aut q*" is true if and only if just one of the propositions represented by "*p*" and "*q*" is true, and "*p vel q*" is true if and only if at least one of them is true. (I use Latin words as connectives to dodge the idiotic but seemingly perennial discussion as to the 'proper' meaning of "or" in ordinary language.) Now even if the proposition represented by "*p vel q*" or by "*p aut q*" is itself taken to be an asserted proposition, "*p*" will not be asserted in this context, and neither will "*q*"; so if we say that the truth value of the whole proposition is determined by the truth values of the disjuncts, we are committed to recognizing that the disjuncts have truth values independently of being actually asserted.

Oxford-trained philosophers often say nowadays that a sentence can have a truth value assigned to it only in that it is 'used to make a statement' in a given context. If this were literally true, then a truth-functional account of "*p vel q*" or of "*p aut q*" would be impossible: for the disjunct clauses represented by "*p*" and "*q*" would not be being 'used to make statements' in a context in which only the disjunction was asserted, and would thus not have any truth values for the truth value of the whole proposition to be a function of. This consequence is not often drawn: Strawson's *Logical Theory*, for example, does not raise this as a fundamental objection to the very idea of truth-functional logic, as on his own premises he might well do.

Nor can the idea of only statements' having truth values be reconciled with truth-functional logic by saying that the truth value of a disjunctive sentence used to make a statement in a given context is a function of the truth values that the disjuncts would have had if they had been separately used to make statements in the same context. For this is not even plausible unless we mean by "the truth values that the disjuncts would have had" those that they would have had if *without change of sense* they had been used to make statements in the given context. But if we can tell what truth values the disjuncts would have had, given the sense they actually have in the context of their occurrence, then a denial that they actually have truth values is quite empty; it just evinces a determination not to *call* unasserted propositions "true" or "false", and this is what Professor Anthony Flew has aptly called a conventionalist sulk.

The truth-functional "and" occasions another error to those who miss the Frege point. Thinking in terms of statements, they see no need to recognize a conjunctive statement "*p* and *q*" as distinct from the pair of statements "*p*", "*q*"; if you recognize conjunctive propositions as a kind of proposition, you may as well say, Mill remarked, that a team of horses is a kind of horse or a street a kind of house. But it is clear that in contexts of the kind "*p* and *q*, or else *r*" or again "if *p* and *q*, then *r*", where we have a conjunction occurring unasserted, the conjunction is a single proposition, a logical unit, not a pair of separate propositions.

In another sort of case, however, we do get a pair of assertions rather than the assertion of a conjunctive proposition. Any statement containing a phrase of the form "the fact that *p*" is exponible as a pair of assertions, one of which asserts the content of the "that" clause. For example, an assertion "Jim is aware of the fact that his wife is unfaithful" is equivalent to the pair of assertions "Jim is convinced that his wife is unfaithful" and "Jim's wife is unfaithful".

We cannot analyse such an assertion as the assertion of a single conjunctive proposition—in our case, of "Jim is convinced that his wife is unfaithful, and Jim's wife is unfaithful". For this proposition conforms, as we might expect, to the law of excluded middle; it can be substituted for "*p*" in "either *p* or it is not the case that *p*" so as to get a logical truth. But we cannot so substitute "Jim is aware of the fact that his wife is unfaithful"; since "either Jim is aware of the fact (and so forth) or it is not the case that Jim is aware of the fact (and so forth)" is not a mere instance of excluded middle, but is something that can be admitted only by one who takes it to be a fact that Jim's wife is unfaithful. Like the original assertion about Jim, this is a double-barrelled assertion; an assertion about Jim's wife gets smuggled in along with, and under cover of, an instance of the excluded middle.

This assertoric force of "the fact that" comes out even in requests, commands, questions, and so forth. If I ask "Is Jim aware of the fact that his wife is deceiving him?" I am not just asking a question; I am asserting that Jim's wife is deceiving him.

The question as I pose it cannot be properly answered "Yes" or "No" by someone who does not accept this assertion; a corresponding but unloaded question would be "Is Jim convinced that his wife is deceiving him?" In such cases, we do get a separate asserted proposition, which for clarity's sake ought to be separately enunciated; this points up the contrast with the genuine unity of a conjunctive proposition.

Negation often gets paired off with assertion as its polar opposite; this is another mistake over the Frege point—one exposed by Frege himself in his paper 'Negation'. Just as I can put forward a proposition "*s*" without asserting "*s*" as true, so I can put forward the negation of "*s*" without rejecting "*s*" as false— for example, when this negation occurs as part of a longer proposition, in a context, say, of the form "*p* and *q*, or else *r* and not *s*". Thus logic in any case demands the use of a negation sign which is not polarly opposed to the assertion sign and does not express rejection of what is negated; and when a proposition is rejected, we may equally well conceive this act as an act of asserting the negation of a proposition.

Indeed, there are serious objections to any other way of conceiving the matter. It is clear that "if not *q*, then *r*; but not *q*; therefore *r*" is a mere special case of the *modus ponens* "if *p*, then *r*; but *p*; therefore *r*". But if we regarded rejecting a proposition as different from asserting the negation of a proposition, we should have here two quite different logical forms; we might write these as follows, using Łukasiewicz' sign ⊣ for a rejection opposed to Frege's assertion ⊢ :

⊢ If not *q*, then *r*; ⊣ *q*; ergo ⊣ *r*.
⊢ If *p*, then *r*; ⊢ *p*; ergo ⊢ *r*.

Plainly this is a futile complication. All we need in logic for assertion and negation is two signs—the assertion sign, and a negation which does *not* convey rejection (as in "if not *q* . . ."); whatever is more than these, as Frege says, cometh of evil.

Frege's logical doctrine suggests a parallel doctrine in the psychology of belief. Christians and Muslims have called each other unbelievers; but this does not mean that there are two polarly opposed activities or attitudes, believing and unbelieving, and that the point at issue is which side goes in for which; it is just that what Christians believe is opposed to what Muslims

believe. Believing, like seeing, has no polar opposite, though
contrary dogmas may be believed, as contrary colours may be seen.
An incredulous man is not a man who goes in for unbelieving,
but a man who believes the contrary of what people tell him.

On this view of beliefs, there will be a sharp difference between
belief and appetitive or emotional attitudes; for love and hate,
desire and aversion, pleasure and pain, are opposite as attitudes,
not by being attitudes toward opposite objects. The distinction
of 'pro' and 'contra', of favourable and unfavourable attitudes,
has its place only in the realm of appetite, will, and passion, not in
that of belief; this shows the error in treating religious beliefs as
some sort of favourable attitude toward something.

I was speaking just now about assertoric sentences containing
a phrase "the fact that p", which are to be expounded as pairs of
asserted propositions, not as single propositions. A similar complication occurs in some other cases: thus, an assertoric sentence
of the form "A has pointed out that p" is exponible as the double-
barreled assertion of "A has maintained that p" and of "p" itself.
Again (an example of Frege's), "A fancies that p" is exponible as
the double-barreled assertion of "A thinks that p" and of "it is
not the case that p". Assertions thus exponible will certainly
retain part of their assertoric force when put, for example, into
an "if" clause; thus, one who asserts "If A is under the illusion
that p, then q", does not mean "If A is under the impression that
p, but it is not the case that p, then q"—rather, he both asserts
"It is not the case that p" and asserts "If A is under the impression that p, then q". Notice that no such complication arises for
the verb "know". Use of the expression ". . . knows that p"
does not commit the speaker to asserting "p"; to adapt an
example of Hintikka's, one who asserted in 1916 "If Russell
knows that Wittgenstein is dead, then Wittgenstein is dead"
would not himself be asserting "Wittgenstein is dead".

In these special cases, we have an expression that endows a
clause within a sentence (or the negation of such a clause) with an
assertoric force that is, so to speak, inalienable and is not can-
celled even by prefixing an "if" to the whole sentence in which
the clause occurs. Apart from these special cases, which for
simplicity's sake I shall henceforth ignore, there is no expression
in ordinary language that regularly conveys assertoric force. The
conjunction "if", which generally cancels all assertoric force in

s

the "if" clause, can grammatically be prefixed to any sentence of assertoric form without altering its grammatical structure or even the way if sounds; somebody who fails to hear the first word of my "if" clause may actually mistake what I say for an assertion, so that like Alice I have to explain 'I only said "if" '.

In written or printed language, however, there is something of a clue to what is meant assertorically. There is a certain presumption—though of course it can be upset in various ways—that an author of a non-fictional work intends a sentence to be read as an assertion if it stands by itself between full stops and grammatically can be read as an assertion. The assertoric force of a sentence is thus shown by its *not* being enclosed in the context of a longer sentence.

Possibly there is something corresponding to this in the realm of thoughts; possibly a thought is assertoric in character unless it loses this character by occurring only as an element in a more complicated thought. In Spinoza's example, the boy whose mind is wholly occupied with the thought of a winged horse, and who lacks the adult background knowledge that rules out there being such a thing, cannot but assent to the thought of there being a winged horse. This would be a neat solution to the problem of how thought is related to judgment, but I do not insist on it; there may be fatal objections. Anyhow, if this theory is true, I need not recant anything I have so far said; it would still be true that a thought may occur now unasserted, now asserted, without change of content. But if I had to choose between this theory and the Frege point, this is what I would reject.

There have been a number of attempts to treat some expression of ordinary language as carrying with it the assertoric force. I think these attempts all miscarry; apart from the exceptional cases of double-barreled assertions, previously mentioned, there is no naturally used sign of assertion, but only the negative clue to assertoric force that I have just been discussing. That is why Frege had to devise a special sign.

Let us consider some attempts to read assertoric force into some ordinary expression. We want our assertions to be true, or to be taken for true; so it is natural to cast "it is true that . . ." for the role of assertion sign. But this will not do, for this expression may come in an unasserted clause without any change of meaning; nor is there any equivocation in an argument "It is true that p;

and if it is true that p, then q; ergo q". Indeed, whether asserted
or not, "It is true that p" is scarcely to be distinguished from the
plain "p". This does not mean that "true" is a useless sign, for it
is not always trivially eliminable—not, for example, from "What
the policeman said is true" nor from "There is many a true word
spoken in jest". But the identification of the assertoric force with
the meaning of "it is true that . . . " is just a mistake.

Oddly enough, Frege himself committed a similar mistake in
his *Begriffsschrift*. He regarded an unasserted proposition as a sign
for the circumstance (*Umstand*) that so-and-so, and called his assertion sign a "common predicate" in all assertions—one predicating
of the relevant circumstance that it actually obtains. But "The
circumstance that p is one that actually obtains", like "It is true
that p", hardly differs from plain "p", and any such proposition
may unequivocally occur now asserted, now unasserted. In later
works Frege saw his mistake, and give up any attempt to explain
the assertion sign by classifying it as a predicate, or as any other
sort of sign; it is necessarily *sui generis*. For any other logical sign,
if not superfluous, somehow modifies the content of a proposition;
whereas this does not modify the content, but shows the proposition is being asserted.

Another concept often confused with assertoric force is the
concept of existence. To be sure, people guilty of this confusion
would say it is improper to speak of the concept of existence; for
the assertion sign adds no concept, so their very confusion makes
them deny that the verb "exists" or "there is" adds a concept
either. What "there is an A" or "an A exists" adds over and
above the bare term "an A" is not a concept, they say; rather,
there is a transition from the bare concept of an A to a judgment,
and it is the act of judgment that mirrors existence (or, they would
perhaps prefer to say, being).

In recent philosophy the best-known advocate of this view is
Gilson. Gilson fathers it on Aquinas; but I really do not see how
it can be extracted from Aquinas' text. (Aquinas says a judgment
is true when it says a thing is as it is; I suppose Gilson would read
Aquinas as saying that a judgment is true when a thing IS as the
judgment says the thing IS.) The actual provenance of Gilson's
view seems to me to be different: he knowledges an anticipation
of it by Brentano, and there is an even clearer anticipation in
Hume. "It is far from being true, that in every judgment which

we form, we unite two different ideas; since in that proposition, *God is*, or indeed, any other, which regards existence, the idea of existence is no distinct idea, which we unite with that of the object. . . . The act of the mind exceeds not a single conception; and the only remarkable difference, which occurs on this occasion, is, when we join belief to the conception, and are persuaded of the truth of what we conceive" (*Treatise*, Book I, Section vii).

Be the doctrine whose it may, it is hopelessly erroneous. For one thing, an existential proposition, like any other proposition, may occur unasserted without change of content; we get this in such propositions as "Either there is a Loch Ness monster or many observers have been unreliable", or again, "If there are canals on Mars then Mars is inhabited." An existential proposition need not express a *judgment* of existence. And let no one retort that in such cases, just because there is no judgment, there is no existential proposition; for even the unasserted proposition "there is an *A*" is quite different in content from the bare term "an *A*". As Frege pointed out, we cannot substitute "there is a house" for "a house", in "Priam lived in a house of timber"; we cannot even substitute "there being a house". Again, as Aristotle pointed out, "goat-stag" by itself gives us nothing true or false, but "There is a goat-stag" does give us something false; and, we may add, the falsity of this proposition in no way depends on anybody's asserting it, or else we could not assert with truth "It is false that there is a goat-stag", if nobody ever asserted there is.

In Buridan's *Sophismata* the point I have been making is brought out in an elegant ontological disproof of God's existence. Buridan points out that if I just say "a God" or "a horse" I have not yet said anything true or false, but if I add the verb "exists", then I have said something true or false; therefore, "a God exists" must signify something more than the bare term "a God" signifies. But, on the orthodox view, only after the world was created was there something more than God for the proposition "a God exists" to signify; therefore before the creation it did not signify anything more; therefore it was not true; therefore God did not then exist!

Of course, Buridan did not mean us to take this very seriously; there is in fact a patent equivocation in the use of "something more". Before the world was created, there would not be "something more" than God that could be signified by a name; but the sense in which "exists" in "a God exists" or "a horse exists" signifies "something more" than the grammatical subject is clearly not that it names another object. All the same, it does signify something more, in the sense of introducting a new *ratio* or concept into the proposition, whether the proposition is asserted or not.

The Hume-Brentano-Gilson thesis cannot be intelligibly stated if it is true; it claims that existence is unconceptualizable and can be grasped only in existential judgments, but this very claim is not an existential judgment and treats existence as conceptualizable. This suicide of a thesis might be called *Ludwig's self-mate*; but Wittgenstein at least ended his *Tractatus* by saying that now he must shut up, and he was fairly brief in coming to that conclusion.

Just as the "is" of existence has been supposed to carry assertoric force, so has the "is" of predication (which some people, two thousand years and more after Plato's *Sophist*, will wantonly confuse with the existential "is"). I can be brief about this; since the copulative verb "is" occurs in unasserted clauses, it cannot carry assertoric force. In fact, I should agree with Frege that the "is" of predication, *die blosse Copula*, has no force at all. There is no logical difference between the predicates "surpasses Frank at chess" and "better at chess than Frank"; the requirement of the latter for an "is" is mere idiom, and there is no such requirement in Russian nor in classical Greek (so that Aristotle can say casually that a predication is formed with or without the verb εἶναι "to be").

A more important and pervasive error has been the idea that the predicate itself carries the assertoric force: a predicate is often explained as what is *asserted* of something in a proposition. To be sure, someone who talks this way need not be ascribing assertoric force to the predicate; his "asserted" may be the German "*ausgesagt*" rather than "*behauptet*"; but his way of talking is ill-advised and will certainly confuse people (as I found before I mended my own ways in the matter). And in many writers there is actual error on the point; here, indeed, one might well fear lest 'mountainous error be too highly heapt for truth to overpeer'. I shall not here try to state a correct view of predication; it is enough to point out that since one and the same unambiguous predicate may occur now in an asserted proposition, now in an unasserted clause, the predicate cannot have any inherent assertoric force. Again, if predicates have assertoric force, how can they ever be used in questions?

A recent example of this error about predicates may be found in Strawson's work *Individuals*. Rightly supposing that there is something important underlying the old distinction of subject and predicate, Strawson tries to explain the predicate as the term whose insertion into a proposition conveys assertoric force (in his own words: the term that is "introduced" in "the assertive or propositional style"). Strawson does indeed recognize that there are nonasserted occurrences of propositions; but he regards these as derivative, the asserted occurrences as primary, and is thus still able to think predicates can be characterized as the terms to which propositions in their primary occurrence owe their assertoric force.

Accepting the Frege point, we know that no term of any proposition gives the proposition assertoric force; for the same term might occur without any change of sense in an unasserted occurrence of the proposition. For predicates, the matter is especially clear: any predicate may be negatively predicated, and then, even if the proposition is asserted, the predicate is not being asserted of anything. Nor can negative predication be called a secondary use or occurrence of a predicate; "*P*" and "not *P*" are grasped together, and one is no more prior to the other than one side of a boundary line you draw is logically prior to the other side; as medievals said, *eadem est scientia oppositorum*.

What distinguishes predicates from subjects, I suggest, is not that they are assertoric in force, but that by negating a predicate we can get the negation of the proposition in which it was originally predicated (plainly, there is nothing analogous for subject terms). This feature of predicates was already brought out very clearly by Aristotle, but is wholly ignored by Strawson. All the same, it may be just because predicates are negatable that Strawson (with many others) came to think of them as bearing the assertoric force; if, as is often fancied, assertion and negation are Siamese twins, then they must share a home.

Predicates of a philosophically exciting sort have been badly misconstrued because assertoric force has been supposed to inhere in them. Theory after theory has been put forward to the effect that predicating some term "*P*"—which is always taken to mean: predicating "*P*" assertorically—is not describing an object as being *P* but some other 'performance'; and the contrary view is labelled "the Descriptive Fallacy". All these theories are constructed on the same pattern and admit, as we shall see, of the same refutation.

The briefest statement of some of these theories ought to suffice. To call a kind of act bad is not to characterize or describe that kind of act but to condemn it. To say a proposition is true is not to describe it but to confirm or concede it. To say "He hit her" is not to state what happened, but to ascribe the act to him as a matter of legal or moral responsibility; and such an ascription is a verdict, not a statement, about him. To say "That looks red" is not to describe how a thing looks but to assert tentatively that it is red. Or again, the difference between a set of statements of sensible appearance and a statement that there is now, for example, an orange on the mantelpiece is supposed to be illuminated by considering a difference between a jury's accepting that all the evidence points to guilt and their actually delivering a verdict. To say "I know that p" is no statement about my own mental capacities, but is an act of warranting my hearer that p. And so on and so on.

Each of these theories is devised for a certain class of assertoric sentences; very often we find the theory will not even fit all of the class it was meant for. Thus, whatever plausibility there may be in analyzing "I know that Smith is the murderer" as "Smith is the murderer—I warrant you that", no such analysis will fit "I know who is the murderer"; for here I do not even tell you, still less give you my warranty, who the murderer is. Again, "He hit her" is a very loaded example—what a swine to hit a woman!—but suppose 'she' were a lioness that he shot? In that case, "He hit her" could be a mere bit of narrative and undoubtedly propositional in character; are we to suppose that the logical character of the utterance, its being or not being propositional at all, is radically affected if 'she' is not a lioness but a woman?

But these particular objections are of minor interest. In all the kinds of case I have mentioned, the very same sentence can occur in an "if" clause; and to such occurrences the anti-descriptive theories will not apply. For example, in saying "If what the policeman said is true, then . . .", I am not confirming or agreeing with what the policeman said; in saying "If he hit her, then . . .", I am not ascribing the act to him, and still less giving some moral or legal verdict about him; in saying "If that looks red, then . . .", I am not even tentatively asserting that the thing is red.

Of course, the anti-descriptive theorist will reply that his theory was not meant to cover such cases—that the same form of words, after all, may have different uses on different occasions. This possibility of varying use, however, cannot be appealed to in cases where an ostensibly assertoric utterance "*p*" and "If *p*, then *q*" can be teamed up as premises for a *modus ponens*. Here, the two occurrences of "*p*", by itself and in the "if" clause, must have the same sense if the *modus ponens* is not to be vitiated by equivocation; and if any theorist alleges that at its ostensibly assertoric occurrence "*p*" is really no proposition at all, it is up to him to give an account of the role of "*p*" that will allow of its standing as a premise.

This task is pretty consistently shirked. For example, Austin would maintain that if I say assertorically, "I know Smith's Vermeer is a forgery", this is not an asserted proposition about me, but an act of warranting my hearers that the picture is a forgery. Austin never observed that this alleged nonproposition could function as a premise obeying ordinary logical rules, in inferences like this:

I know Smith's Vermeer is a forgery.
I am no art expert.
If I know Smith's Vermeer is a forgery, and I am no art expert,
    then Smith's Vermeer is a very clumsy forgery.
Ergo, Smith's Vermeer is a very clumsy forgery.

Still less did Austin discuss *how* a nonproposition could be a premise. But failing such discussion, Austin's account of "I know" is valueless.

The theory that to call a kind of act "bad" is not to describe but to condemn it is open to similar objections. Let us consider this piece of moral reasoning:

If doing a thing is bad, getting your little brother to do it is bad.
Tormenting the cat is bad.
Ergo, getting your little brother to torment the cat is bad.

The whole nerve of the reasoning is that "bad" should mean exactly the same at all four occurrences—should not, for example, shift from an evaluative to a descriptive or conventional or inverted-commas use. But in the major premise the speaker (a father, let us suppose) is certainly not uttering acts of condemnation: one could hardly take him to be condemning just *doing a thing*.

Here it is only fair to mention one exception to the bad practice of anti-descriptive theorists that I have just censured; for R. M. Hare does offer some sort of account of how acts of condemnation, though they are not propositions, can serve as premises. Hare argues forcibly that there is a logic of imperatives, although imperatives are not propositions; and he holds that condemnations like "Tormenting the cat is bad" and imperatives like "Do not torment the cat" are alike in being species of prescriptive or action-guiding language. But we need not go into details of this; for Hare has offered us no imperative-logic model that even looks likely to yield an account of such moral reasoning as occurs in my example; and the fourfold unequivocal occurrence of "bad" in that example is enough to refute the act-of-condemnation theory.

Of course an *asserted* proposition in which "bad" is predicated may be *called* an act of condemnation. But this is of no philosophical interest; for then being an act of condemnation is nothing that can be put forward as an *alternative* to being a proposition. Moreover, this holds good only of asserted propositions, whereas "bad" may be predicated without change of force in unasserted clauses. The assertoric force attaches no more to "bad" than to other predicates.

The magnitude and variety of philosophical errors that result from not seeing the Frege point justifies a missionary zeal in the matter. When philosophers fail to see the Frege point, the reason, all too often, is that they have in general little regard for formal logic as a philosophical instrument; and this comes out in other ways too—as in M. Gilson's assertion that formal logic cannot cope with existential judgments, or in some Oxford philosophers' assertion that formal logic cannot cope with ordinary language. For myself, I think logicians have an all-purpose utility, as accountants have for all kinds of business; and resentment at an accountant's inquiries is not a healthy sign in any business. When a philosopher manifests annoyance at someone's counterexamples to a theory that runs smoothly enough for the philosopher's own chosen examples, he acts like a delinquent clerk: "Why should the accountant meddle with *that* book, when these other books are all right?" But logicians, like accountants, are paid to look out for discrepancies.

9

Imperatives and Practical Reasoning

9.1. IMPERATIVE AND DEONTIC LOGIC

How fallacious it is to judge of the nature of things by the ordinary and incon-
stant use of words appeareth in nothing more than in the confusion of counsels and
commands, arising from the imperative manner of speaking in them both and in
many other occasions besides.

HOBBES, *Leviathan*, c.xxv.

Moral utterances are sometimes regarded as being a kind of
imperative, or at least as resembling imperatives in their logic.
In fact, the two sorts of utterance have essentially different logical
features; in particular, as regards negation. Of course the contradictory of a moral utterance is itself a moral utterance, just as the
contradictory of an imperative is itself an imperative; but that is
as far as the resemblance goes. Let "P" represent the contem-
plated act of a given agent in given circumstances. In answer to a
request for orders, "Am I to do P?", only two answers are
possible—"Do P" and "Do not do P", which are contradictories.
No other order is a direct answer to the question; and to say "You
may either do P or not" would not be an answer but a refusal to
answer—I was asked for an order and I refuse to give any.[1] But
there are three relevant answers to the moral enquiry "Ought I to
do P?"

[1] This 'two-valued' character of plain imperatives is pointed out by Hare in his
Language of Morals (hereafter *LM*), p. 23; his explanation of the consequent difference
between them and deontic utterances is considered later. I am very grateful for his
comments on an earlier draft of this paper.

(A) It is your duty to do P.

(B) It is all right for you to do P, and also all right for you not to do P;

(C) It is your duty not to do P.

(B) is the conjunction of the negations of (C) and (A), which themselves are not contradictories and do not even appear to be. If, however, I had written "You ought" instead of "It is your duty" in (A) and (C), they would have looked like contradictories; this is a trivial linguistic fact (contrast German "ich muß", "ich muß nicht", which can be genuine contradictory forms), but I suspect that it fosters confusion, and would suggest to writers on ethics that they use "duty" rather than "ought". (B) is not a refusal to give moral advice, as "You may either do P or not" would be refusal to give an order in the matter; it expresses a definite moral attitude.

It might be suggested that in giving moral advice I am not just enunciating an imperative for the particular case but appealing to a general moral precept, and that the general precepts by which (A) and (C) would be supported would be not contradictory but contrary; this would explain why (A) and (C) themselves are contraries, although the corresponding plain imperatives are contradictories. (Cf, *LM*, pp. 191–2). I am inclined to agree that a moral utterance about an individual act does need to be backed up by a general moral principle; but this goes for utterances like (B) as well; they need to be backed up by general *permissive* principles, of the form "For anybody satisfying the conditions C, it is all right to do P (or: not to do P)". Now whereas general moral precepts can with some plausibility be regarded as something like imperatives, general permissive principles cannot; here again deontic logic extends beyond the limits of imperative logic.

(It may perhaps be helpful to give a concrete example of moral reasoning from general permissive principles. A counsellor says to his sovereign: "This traitor's life is at your Majesty's disposal; you have the right to pardon him, for it is right for a king to pardon penitent offenders of his free grace; but you also have the right to punish him severely, for it is right for a king to punish ringleaders in rebellion." The counsellor is appealing to general permissive principles that he accepts; on these principles the King may pardon or punish the traitor as he chooses; it is not a matter of the King's having to resolve a conflict of obligations.)

A thoroughgoing reduction of deontic to imperative logic would require Procrustean amputations: perhaps not of possibility (B), but certainly of general permissive principles. I have not come across any moral philosopher hardy enough to propose the former amputation; but I think writers have often not drawn enough attention to possibility (B), nor to the dangerous ambiguity of "it is right to . . . " as between "it is *all* right to . . ." and "it is *the* right thing (a duty) to . . .". (Hare has explicitly mentioned this ambiguity—LM p. 182.) General permissive principles, on the other hand, are practically ignored by many moral philosophers; and I think that this may well come about from their assimilating moral utterances to commands (even if only implicitly).

The other way of assimilating imperative and deontic logic would be to treat plain imperatives as a special case of deontic utterances. This would involve introducing possibility (B) into the logic of ordinary imperatives; and I have already argued against this.

The logic of proper imperatives is, I think, fairly trivial. For every proper imperative, there is a future-tense statement whose 'coming true' is identical with the fulfilment of the imperative. This is the source of everything that can be said about the inferability, incompatibility, etc. of imperatives; their being imperatives does not affect these logical interrelations. There are indeed serious logical problems about the 'coming true' of future-tense statements;[1] but when moral philosophers have recourse to the logic of imperatives, they show no interest in these—for instance, Hare so little regards the restriction of imperatives to the future tense as logically important that he thinks ordinary language could be 'enriched' with past-tense and tenseless imperatives (LM p. 188).

We can easily imagine ourselves using a language that entirely lacked proper imperatives without suffering any practical inconvenience; we could just use the plain future tense to give orders, as the military authorities sometimes do. The same utterance of

---

[1] Cf. Professor Prior's John Locke lectures *Time and Modality* (Oxford, at the Clarendon Press, 1957); especially chaps. ix and x.

the sentence "The patient will go down to the operating theatre" may be at once an expression of the surgeon's intention, an order to the nurse, and a piece of information to the patient; but it is not on that account an ambiguous utterance, like a two-edged remark that means different things to different hearers. One and the same state of affairs would be the fulfilment of the surgeon's intentions and the nurse's instructions and the patient's expectations; the logician is interested only in the fulfilment as such, not in the differences between intending, being commanded, and being forewarned; for logic, the differences between the three roles of the utterance are irrelevant.

There are, indeed, some highly interesting philosophical questions about the special role of imperatives; one that occurs to me is the question why we find it natural that the verbs "can", "können", "pouvoir", etc. should all lack an imperative mood. The answer, I think, is roughly that such an imperative would *necessarily* be useless. My telling you to be something is pointless unless you are able to; so my telling you *to be able* to do P is pointless unless you are able *to be able* to do P. But that just means: unless you are able to do P; and if you are already able to do P, it is again pointless for me to tell you to be able.

Are there, however, special logical principles for the imperative mood; or can arguments involving proper imperatives be assessed for validity by simply substituting for the imperatives the corresponding plain futures? Hare thinks there are such special principles, and has formulated two of them (*LM* p. 28):

(1) No indicative conclusion can be validly drawn from a set of premises which cannot be validly drawn from the indicatives among them alone;

(2) No imperative conclusion can be validly drawn from a set of premises which does not contain at least one imperative.

I regard these principles as mistaken, and shall produce clearly valid arguments which contravene them. (These arguments will in fact all pass the test I have just suggested for the validity of arguments that contain imperatives; but in the sequel I do not assume the correctness of this test.)

To refute Rule (1): Imagine a king knighting a subject of doubtful loyalty and saying: "If you are a faithful subject, then rise up, Sir George!—But do not rise; stay on your knees, fellow!" The conclusion of this *modus tollens* is obvious; moreover, it is one to which the King is logically committed; his two imperatives are reconcilable only on the assumption that George is no true subject.

The use of a ritual imperative as an example may look like cheating, so let me take another example. The games master says to the cricket captain at 12.45: "If the 12.55 weather forecast says it will be showery, cancel this afternoon's match." At 1.15 he sees him again and says: "Don't cancel the match." Here again, the games master is logically committed to the assertion that the 12.55 weather forecast did not say it would be showery. "Unless he has changed his mind!" That is a possibility logic is bound to ignore, for indicatives as well; a man could always evade the logical commitments of a pair of premises by saying that he changed his mind between uttering one and uttering the other.

In discussing Rule (2) I shall first introduce the Stoic logicians' notion of *themata*. A *thema* is a rule whereby, given one valid inference, we may derive another. For example: 'if "p", "q", "r", are so read that "p, q, ergo r" is a valid inference, then with the same interpretation "p; ergo if q, then r" is a valid inference'. We may write this *thema*, which is clearly a correct rule if "p", "q", "r" are all indicative, in the following way:

Thema I. p, q, ergo r || p; ergo if q, then r.

Hare does not use the term "*thema*"; but clearly what he is trying to do on *LM* pp. 34–5 is to apply *Thema* I to the following inference, which by his rules (and in plain fact) is valid:

> Grimbly Hughes is the largest grocer in Oxford;
> Go to the largest grocer in Oxford;
> *Ergo*, go to Grimbly Hughes.

Now here he runs up against a difficulty; in this case "p" is indicative, but "q" and "r" are imperative, so how do we frame "if q, then r" at all? An imperative will not (grammatically) go into an "if" clause. On the view that an imperative differs only in its practical functioning, and not logically, from a plain future, the solution would be easy: use a plain future in the "if" clause instead of an imperative. Application of *Thema* I would then yield the following inference as valid:

> Grimbly Hughes is the largest grocer in Oxford;

Ergo, if you are going to go to the largest grocer in Oxford, go to Grimbly Hughes.

(But that does not look quite right; and in any case I said I would not here assume the correctness of that view.) Hare's solution is quite different:

Grimbly Hughes is the largest grocer in Oxford;
Ergo, if you want to go to the largest grocer in Oxford, go to Grimbly Hughes.

I am afraid I have not understood what force he wished to give to the word "want" here. He does not intend its sense to be psychological; for then, as he would allow, the above inference could not be justified by *Thema* I; since no psychological term occurs in the premise "q" of the original inference, i.e. in "Go to the largest grocer in Oxford", none may be introduced into the antecedent of "if q, then r" in the derived inference. What he says (*LM* p. 34) is that "want" is here a logical sign; later on we are told that it is a disguised imperative neustic (*LM* p. 37).

So far as I can follow Hare's explanations, an imperative neustic would be something for imperatives analogous to what Frege thought the assertion-sign was for indicatives (*LM* pp. 17–19). But this does not help us at all. An assertion-sign so conceived could not stand in an "if" clause, since "if" removes assertoric force from the clause that follows it. Similarly, a performatory utterance like "I give you this book" no longer has performatory force in an "if" clause.[1] I do not understand, therefore—since the imperative neustic is conceived as analogous to Frege's assertion-sign—how "want" could be a disguise for an imperative neustic in an "if" clause. Hare himself describes this matter of hypotheticals as "still very dark" (*LM* p. 38).

It seems to me that at least some 'hypothetical imperatives' beginning "if you want . . ." are genuinely imperative, but only grammatically hypothetical (and therefore, of course, do not qualify as cases of "if p then q" in *Thema* I). They are, surely, like a sort of grammatically hypothetical statement that I have heard Professor Austin discuss: as when your host says "If you want a cigarette, there are some in the silver box". What your host says is true if and only if there are cigarettes in the silver box;

[1] See papers 8.1. and 8.2. and in this collection.

your wanting a cigarette has nothing to do with its truth. He might have said without change of meaning: "Do you want a cigarette? There are some in the silver box", Similarly, I think, Hare's 'hypothetical imperative' could be replaced without change of meaning by: "You want to go to the largest grocer in Oxford? Go to Grimbly Hughes." What your host tells you, in the one case, or what someone tells you to do, in the other case, has nothing hypothetical about it; but if you happen not to want what is mentioned, the information or direction you are given will not interest you, and the speaker is implying that you may then ignore it; this, of course, is a practical, not a logical, consideration.

Hare, however, regards

> If you want to go to the largest grocer in Oxford, go to Grimbly Hughes

as a genuinely hypothetical imperative; he escapes from the possible charge of having violated his own Rule (2) in allowing the inference of this from.

> Grimbly Hughes is the largest grocer in Oxford

by denying that the conclusion has any content *qua* imperative; it has, he holds, only the force of the indicative premise from which it was inferred (*LM* p. 37).

It is not possible, however, to deal with all violations of Rule (2) in this way. To show this, I shall need to establish the validity of the following inference:

> Grimbly Hughes is the largest grocer in Oxford;
> *Ergo*, either[1] do not go to the largest grocer in Oxford or[1] go to Grimbly Hughes.

The conclusion here is undoubtedly imperative. It may indeed seem to be vacuous as an imperative, because, as things are in Oxford, you cannot help fulfilling it, whatever you do; and so it may seem to have the content merely of the indicative premise. But an utterance does not become vacuous *qua* imperative merely because, as the facts are, it cannot but be fulfilled; the relevant meaning of "vacuous" is logical vacuousness, not

---

[1] Here and in the following discussion I use "either . . . or . . ." in a nonexclusive sense.

practical futility. And to somebody unfamiliar with Oxford the conclusion does not even seem to give the information that Grimbly Hughes is the largest grocer in Oxford; any more than

> Either do not go to the largest grocer in Oxford or go to Blackwells

is an utterance vacuous as an imperative, but serving to give the mendacious information that Blackwells is the largest grocer in Oxford.

It is not even correct to say that an imperative inferred in this way from an indicative premise must be practically futile. Clearly if the imperative conclusion "either not q or r" logically follows from the indicative premise "p", it will be practically futile (because not disobeyable) if we can do nothing about the truth of "p"; but this is not in general the case. (A logician determined to show, by disobeying the "Grimbly Hughes" imperative, that it was not practically futile could do so by getting a friend in the I.R.A. to blow up Grimbly Hughes, and then visiting the *then* largest grocer in Oxford but not the ruins of Grimbly Hughes.)

Thus, if the above inference is valid, it is a clear counter-example to Rule (2). Its validity can in fact be established in two ways. *First proof*:

Thema II. p, q, ergo r // p; ergo, either not q or r.

This *thema* gives us no such trouble as *Thema* I gave when we wanted to apply it to a case in which "p" is indicative but "q" and "r" are imperatives; for "either not q or r" is then readily constructible and interpretable as an imperative. If now we apply this *thema* to the inference to which we were just now trying to apply *Thema* I, we get the result we wanted. (I do not think that in allowing such applications of *Thema* II I am committed to saying that imperative and future-indicative inferences must *always* run on parallel lines.)

Second proof:
Thema III. Either not p or p; q; ergo r // q, ergo r.

This *thema* licenses the dropping of a vacuous premise. Now Hare would certainly have to allow the validity of the following inference:

T

> Either do not go to Grimbly Hughes or go to Grimbly
> Hughes;
> Grimbly Hughes is the largest grocer in Oxford;
> *Ergo*, either do not go to the largest grocer in Oxford or
> go to Grimbly Hughes.

If we apply *Thema* III to this inference, we again get the result we wanted.

I may be wrong about the dispensability of imperatives in favour of plain futures, and I am uncertain about there not being special principles of imperative logic; but Hare at least has failed to formulate such principles. And even if his Rules (1) and (2) were correct, they cannot have the importance he gives them, as regards the relation between moral and factual utterances (*LM* pp. 29–31); for in any case deontic logic is not related as he thinks it is to imperative logic.

9.2. IMPERATIVE INFERENCE

Mr. Williams attacks the notion of imperative inference—of somebody's passing from imperative premisses to an imperative conclusion—but he admits without demur that a set of imperatives may be logically inconsistent. This notion deserves examination; I shall therefore begin with a general discussion of inconsistency, taking Strawson's account[1] as a peg to hang the discussion on.

Strawson says that a charge of inconsistency is an "internal criticism" of a piece of discourse—one that "does not refer to anything outside the statements a man makes" but simply to "the way his statements hang together". Now if indeed it were possible to allege inconsistency without referring "beyond the words and sentences a man uses to that in the world about which he talks", the man need not worry much about the allegation; he might well retort "Do I contradict myself? Very well then, I contradict myself. I am large, I contain multitudes". Strawson's rejoinder might be, in his own words, that "the standard purpose of speech, the intention to communicate something, is frustrated by self-contradiction. Contradicting oneself is like writing something down and then erasing it, or putting a line through it. A contradiction cancels itself and leaves nothing". But the man

---

[1] P. F. Strawson, *Introduction to Logical Theory* (Methuen, 1952), pp. 1–3.

accused of inconsistency could escape this criticism by adopting the useful technique of keeping well apart in his discourse the inconsistent ('complementary') propositions each of which he was prepared to assert, and carefully avoiding the transition from the fruitful assertion of P and Q severally to the self-stultifying assertion of P and Q together. No doubt Strawson would regard this as sophistical double-talk, no less than I do; but his theory of inconsistency does not, I think, afford grounds for such condemnation.

The allegation of inconsistency is in truth not a mere internal criticism of discourse. The trouble about inconsistency is that if our factual statements are inconsistent, one or other of them is going to be false, and we often wish statements made by or to ourselves to be true. Similarly for commands: we wish the commands we give to be obeyed, and if they are inconsistent one or other of them is not going to be obeyed. We seek to avoid inconsistency precisely because, and precisely where, our discourse does relate to the world outside our discourse. In fiction, where, as Frege put it, we are content with a thought and do not try to go on to a truth-value, inconsistency need not matter: the value of Trollope's novels is not affected by the result of Ronald Knox's investigation as to whether one can draw a consistent map of Barsetshire.

Again, Strawson's account would at best apply only to patent inconsistency, whereas what most interests a logician is latent inconsistency. The perpetration of a latent inconsistency is not in the least like writing down a proposition and then erasing or cancelling it. Somebody once tried to convert an atheistic pupil of mine by the argument: "Everything is caused by something else; therefore, there is something by which everything else is caused, and this is God". Now so far from being a logical consequence of the premise "Everything is caused by something else", the conclusion "There is something by which everything else is caused " is actually inconsistent with the premise —at least if we assume our naive theist to have intended "caused by" to stand for an asymmetrical relation. This, however, is a latent inconsistency, which can be brought out only by a particular proof; and the theist was not just cancelling his premise in drawing his conclusion.

In fact, in logically interesting cases R is inconsistent with P

and Q, not because it is patently inconsistent with P by itself or with Q by itself, but because its contradictory follows from P and Q together, or because from P and Q and R together as premises there follow both S and the contradictory of S. It is thus not arbitrary whether we choose to explain inferability in terms of inconsistency or the other way about; whether to explain "R follows from P and Q" as meaning "P and Q and the contradictory of R are inconsistent", or rather to explain "R is inconsistent with P and Q" as meaning "From P and Q there follows the contradictory of R". Except for trivial cases, inconsistency has to be explained in terms of inferability, not the other way about. (Again, non-trivial inferences are possible in formal systems that contain no negation; and here we cannot explain the inferability of a conclusion as the inconsistency of its contradictory opposite with the premises, for this contradictory is not expressible in the formal system.)

All that I have said here applies to commands as well as to statements. Now it would hardly be said that only patently inconsistent commands count as inconsistent; and if anyone were perverse enough to say so, it would not alter the fact that even if a set of commands has only what I call latent inconsistency, one or other of the set is not going to be obeyed. But if we admit that a set of commands may be latently inconsistent, we cannot reject the notion of one command's logically following from another. For if R is latently inconsistent with P and Q, this means that the contradictory of R follows from P and Q, or that a patently inconsistent pair follows from P and Q and R; and the contradictory of a command is itself a command, one that would be obeyed if and only if the original command were not obeyed.

Williams raises a puzzle about who can, who is in a position to, deduce the imperative conclusion that follows from imperative premisses. Even if a new order promulgated by an authority follows from orders previously given, and even if the authority is aware of this implication and was moved by a desire to make the implication plain, even so it seems odd to speak of the authority's having inferred its later order from earlier ones. And neither, Williams argues, can the person who is to obey the orders be said to derive an imperative conclusion from imperative premisses; surely what he infers is a conclusion "I am ordered to do so-and-so" from premisses of the form "I am ordered to do such-and-such", and these are not imperatives but statements about imperatives. Similarly, a third party could only infer a conclusion "He is ordered to do so-and-so" from premisses of the form "He is ordered to do such-and-such". How then can we say that an imperative conclusion is inferable from imperative premisses, if nobody could actually be said to make that inference?

As Hobbes pointed out, however, imperatives are used to express counsel as well as command;[1] and with regard to counsel it seems pretty clear that a series of imperatives may constitute a passage from premisses to conclusion on the part of the counsellor. "Either do x or do y" says the counsellor; I give him my objections to doing x; "Very well then", he goes on "don't do x; do y". It would be hard to deny that here the counsel "Do y" not only logically follows, but was actually inferred by the counsellor, from the pieces of counsel "Either do x or do y" and "Don't do x" as premisses.

Even where orders are concerned, Williams surely exaggerates the difference between the authority's "Do x" and the subject's "I must do x"; the difference between "You are to do x" and "I am to do x" looks much less—in fact it looks like, and I think is, the very same difference as that between "You are doing x" and "I am doing x". In the one case the speaker gives and the hearer accepts the same description of the hearer's action; in the other case, we may say, the authority gives and the subject accepts the same *directive as to* the subject's action. In a previous article I quite mistakenly suggested that a man's following a directive is much the same as his action's conforming to a (future-tensed) description;[2] Miss Anscombe has well brought out the different roles of the shopping list used by a man (a directive to him) and the list of the man's purchases made by a detective who follows him (a description of his activities).[3] But as regards the logical relations of directives among themselves, the provenance of the directives is no more important than is the provenance of statements as regards *their* mutual logical relations. As Miss Anscombe remarks, the role of the shopping list as a directive to a man is just the same whether the list originates with his wife, as a command, or with himself, as an expression of intention; and

[1] *Leviathan*, c.xxv.
[2] Paper 9.1 above.
[3] *Intention*, §32.

similarly the logical relations of orders among themselves, and their relations to the acts that fulfil them, are quite unaffected by whether we consider them as orders issued by A or as orders accepted by B. We may thus turn round Williams's objection that a conclusion cannot really be inferable from premisses if nobody could actually be said to make that inference; for if anybody at all can make a valid inference, the conclusion certainly is inferable from the premisses; so if the subject B can infer a directive R addressed to him from directives P and Q which are addressed to him and which he accepts, then the inference from P and Q to R is valid, even if the authority A who promulgates P, Q, and R as orders could hardly be said to infer R from P and Q.[1] And if no imperative conclusion can be got from imperative premisses, how could we speak of a man as commanding something by implication—as in any sense commanding anything that he has not commanded in so many words?

The logical analysis of arguments in the imperative mood runs into many difficulties, even when the premisses are very simple in logical form; to make a beginning I shall here consider the logical structure of disjunctive and hypothetical imperatives. Whereas the simple command "Do x" can be otherwise expressed with a performative use of "I command" as "I command you to x", "Do x or do y" cannot be re-expressed as "I command you to do x or I command you to do y", for here the occurrences of "I command" cannot be performative. But equally, an assertion "p or q" cannot be re-expressed as "I assert that p or I assert that q". That the clauses of a disjunctive command are not commands is no more of a puzzle than that the clauses of a disjunctive assertion are not assertions.

The only hope of clarity here lies in making the distinction that Hare has made with his terms "phrastic" and "neustic". "Do x or do y" and "You will do x or do y" would in Hare's style of paraphrase come to have an identical phrastic, "Your future doing of either x or y", to which would then be added the imperative neustic "please" or the assertoric neustic "yes".[2] The disjunctive structure belongs to the phrastic; the neustic attaches

---

[1] Williams's argument to show that in any event the authority could not be said to infer one command from another may well be valid; but I am unfortunately too uncertain about the relations of permission to command to be able to discuss it at present.

[2] Cf. R. M. Hare, *The Language of Morals* (O.U.P., 1952), pp. 17–19.

to the phrastic as a whole, not to either disjunct separately. To be sure, in "Do *x* or do *y*" either clause is grammatically imperative on its own account; but we must not let this bit of grammar mislead us.

Similarly, the imperative "If you do *x*, do *y*", and on the other hand "If you do *x*, you will do *y*", would come out as having an identical phrastic "Your doing *y* on condition of your doing *x*"; and again only the phrastic as a whole would have "yes" or "please" attached to it. The grammatical difference between the indicative antecedent and the imperative consequent of the hypothetical imperative is, I believe, of no logical significance. The imperative neustic attaches only to the whole phrastic, not to the part "Your doing *y*" that corresponds to the consequent clause.

There is, however, a further complication about hypothetical imperatives. If we employ a performative "I command" or "I advise" to spell out the force of "If *p*, then do *x*", we get two possible interpretations:

(i) I command (advise) that, if *p*, you should do *x*.
(ii) If it is the case that *p*, then I command (advise) that you should do *x*.

(i) is another way of expressing what Hare would express somewhat as follows: "Your doing *x* on condition of its being the case that *p*, please". On interpretation (ii), what is conditional is not the phrastic of the imperative, but rather the act of counselling or commanding. If it is the case that *p*, then I have given you a command or a piece of advice to suit that contingency; and if it is not the case, then, so far as this utterance of mine goes, I have given you no command or advice at all. We may compare the conditional form of bet, "If *p*, then I bet you £5 that *q*". If it turns out not to be the case that *p*, then so far as this utterance goes I have not yet risked my money.

Imperatives of the form "If you want to do *x*, do *y*" should, I think, be analysed in the second way. As Hobbes says (*loc. cit.*) "He that giveth counsel pretendeth only, whatsoever he intendeth, the good of him to whom he giveth it"; so the form "If you want . . ." suits counsel rather than command. What is hypothetical in these instances is not the content of the advice but the giving of it; conditionally upon the hearer's having certain wishes and preferences, he is counselled to do so-and-so, and if his wishes should be otherwise no counsel has so far been given him.

This analysis incidentally fits very well such examples as Hare's "If you want to break your springs, go on driving as you are at present". Spelled out with a performatory expression, this becomes: "Upon the supposition that you want to break your springs, my advice to you is that you should go on driving as you are at present". The speaker well knows that he is not really giving advice, for the act of advising is conditional upon a wish of the hearer's which the speaker presumes not to exist in fact. (The sarcastic tone must simply be transferred from the sentence analysed to the longer sentence offered as an analysis.)

The account I gave in my earlier article[1] of hypothetical imperatives beginning "If you want . . ." now strikes me as unplausible; as Hare remarked to me, it will not fit the sarcastic examples. Hare's own account, however, strikes me as even less plausible. He argues that in "If you want to do x, do y" the word "want" is used in a non-psychological sense, to form a periphrasis for the grammatically impossible but logically desirable use of an imperative in an *if* clause.[2] Now the imperative "Do x" comes out in the Hare analysis as "Your doing x, please". So if we take "you want to do x" after "if" to be a disguised imperative, "Do y if you want to do x" will work out as "(Your doing y conditionally upon: your doing x, please) please", and here the phrastic is surely ill-formed. Hare speaks of the imperative neustic's getting inside the *if* clause; but this idea is very obscure —I cannot accept a neustic-phrastic analysis unless it is laid down that the neustic shall apply only to the phrastic as a whole. The sarcastic examples of this form 'tempt' Hare to offer a metalinguistic analysis in terms of statements about the inferability of imperatives;[3] but one can certainly understand such sarcasms without ever having thought about the validity of imperative inferences, though of course not without being able to perform them.

The view I have now reached would require some alterations in the views I put forward earlier about imperative inferences— particularly, in my views about inferences where the premisses and conclusion are neither all assertions nor all imperatives. But I have no space to develop this new account; and having once

[1] *Op. cit.* p. 54.   [2] *Op. cit.* p. 27.   [3] *Ibid.* p. 38.

fallen into serious mistakes, I would rather put forward these foundations for imperative logic with a view to critical inspection, than venture once more to build on what may be shaky.

9.3. KENNY ON PRACTICAL REASONING

A first reaction to Dr. Kenny's theory[1]—it was my own—may well be that this can't be right, that theoretical and practical reasoning are surely not as different as all that. I think this first impression can be removed by carefully considering Kenny's arguments and examples.

An essential feature of inference, shared by theoretical and practical reasoning, is a certain asymmetry between premises and conclusions. A set of premises may well yield a single conclusion that could not be reached from any one premise separately; any system of logic must contain some rule governing inferences of this character. On the other hand, a set of conclusions follow from a single premise only if each single conclusion in the set follows. (Carnap and Kneale have devised technical dodges for removing this asymmetry; but I think it is perverse to wish to remove it.) It must be emphasized that this asymmetry holds good in Kenny's account of practical inference. This rules out a suggestion which, if correct, would trivialize Kenny's account: namely, that Kenny is just using the familiar rules of inference to find practical premises from which a given practical conclusion follows, rather than to find which conclusions follow from premises; that he has just paradoxically switched the terms "conclusion" and "premise". For if we made such a switch, then there would be cases where a set of 'conclusions' were derivable from a 'premise' although no member of the set was severally derivable from the 'premise'; and no such case arises on Kenny's theory.

In what follows I attempt to give formal rules for practical inferences conceived in Kenny's way; whatever its defects may be, this formulation is definite enough to serve as a basis for any improved one.

The essential rule is I think the following. From a set of fiats $\mathfrak{F}q, \mathfrak{F}r, \mathfrak{F}s, \ldots$, one may infer a conclusion $\mathfrak{F}t$ provided that the phrastic of the conclusion *entails* the phrastic of one premise and

[1] 'Practical Inference,' *Analysis* 26. 3, 1966.

is consistent with those of all the other premises: e.g. if *t* entails *q* and the conjunction K*t*K*r*K*s* . . . is consistent. (The object of deliberation is to find a way of satisfying one want consistently with other wants.) It follows at once that no practical conclusion can be drawn from an inconsistent set of fiats; if K*q*K*r*K*s* . . . is an inconsistent conjunction and *t* entails *q*, then K*t*K*r*K*s* . . . is inconsistent and ℑ*t* is not validly inferable from the set ℑ*q*,ℑ*r*,ℑ*s*, . . . This result might have been expected: there can be no deliberation as to how to satisfy inconsistent requirements.

A further result is that practical inference is *defeasible* in a way that theoretical inference is not. In indicative inference, the addition of a premise cannot invalidate a previously valid inference; it ℭ*t* is inferable from ℭ*p*, ℭ*q*, then ℭ*t* is inferable from ℭ*p*, ℭ*q*, ℭ*r*. But if ℑ*t* is derivable from ℑ*p*, ℑ*q*, this means that ℑ*t* gives a means of satisfying one of these fiats consistently with satisfying the other; and thus ℑ*t* may no longer be derivable from ℑ*p*, ℑ*q*, ℑ*r*. For we may may have *t* entailing *p* and K*t*q consistent without having K*r*K*t*q consistent; and then the inference of ℑ*t* from ℑ*p* and ℑ*q* will be valid, but the inference of ℑ*t* from ℑ*p*, ℑ*q*, ℑ*r* will be invalid.

Some years ago I read a letter in a political weekly to some such effect as this. "I do not dispute Col. Bogey's premises, nor the logic of his inference. But even if a conclusion is validly drawn from acceptable premises, we are not obliged to accept it if those premises are incomplete; and unfortunately there is a vital premise missing from the Colonel's argument—the existence of Communist China." I do not know what Col. Bogey's original argument had been; whether this criticism of it could be apt depends on whether it was a piece of indicative or of practical reasoning. Indicative reasoning from a set of premises, if valid, could of course not be invalidated because there is a premise 'missing' from the set. But a piece of practical reasoning from a set of premises can be invalidated thus: your opponent produces a fiat you have to accept, and the addition of this to the fiats you have already accepted yields a combination with which your conclusion is inconsistent.

The correspondent alleged that Col. Bogey's 'missing premise' was the existence of Communist China. Kenny seems to me essentially right as regards the way such factual premises should be handled in practical inference. Any deliberation has as its background certain relevant facts of the situation, facts that one takes for granted and is not proposing to alter; any such facts should be represented by a premise-fiat whose phrastic expresses the fact. This corresponds to the prudential maxim "Don't run your head up against a brick wall"; one's deliberations will clearly be futile if their conclusions are not consistent with such facts. Col. Bogey would have to allow his critic to add to the set of premises the fiat "$\mathfrak{F}$ (there being a Communist China)"— unless indeed the Colonel's deliberations did not take this fact as part of the given background, because e.g. it was for him an open question of policy whether Communist China should continue to exist or should be annihilated.

In view of the defeasibility of practical reasoning by added premises, there may seem to be a threat to what Peripatetic logicians called "the synthetic theorem"—the principle that if a conclusion t follows from a set of premises P, and if P plus t in turn yield the conclusion v, then the premises P yield v. Only if the synthetic theorem holds do we get a *chain* of inferences linking the original premises to the final conclusion—which is clearly needed in practical as in theoretical inferences. We can in fact show that Kenny's doctrine does secure the synthetic theorem.

We said before that on Kenny's theory a conclusion $\mathfrak{F}t$ is correctly drawn from a set of fiats provided that its phrastic t entails the phrastic v of one of these fiats and is consistently conjoinable with the phrastics of all the *other* fiats in the set. It would have been possible to omit the word "other" in stating this condition; for if t entails v, $KtKpKqKr$ . . . is a consistent conjunction iff $KtKvKpKqKr$ . . . is consistent. In the proof that follows, we assume the criterion of validity in this handy equivalent form.

We are to show, then, that form:

(1) $\mathfrak{F}t$ is inferable from $\mathfrak{F}p$, $\mathfrak{F}q$, $\mathfrak{F}r$ . . .

and

(2) $\mathfrak{F}v$ is inferable from $\mathfrak{F}t$, $\mathfrak{F}p$, $\mathfrak{F}q$, $\mathfrak{F}r$ . . .

it follows that

(3) $\mathfrak{F}v$ is inferable from $\mathfrak{F}p$, $\mathfrak{F}q$, $\mathfrak{F}r$ . . .

(1) will hold iff t entails one of the phrastics p, q, r, . . . and the

conjunction KtKpKqKr . . . is consistent. Without loss of generality, we may assume that t entails p. Now (2) will hold iff v entails one of the phrastics t, p, q, r, . . . and the conjunction KvKtKpKqKr . . . is consistent. But if v entails t, then since t entails p, by (1), v entails p; and so whether v entails t or entails one of p, q, r, . . . , v will in any case entail one of p, q, r, ... Again, if KvKtKpKqKr . . . is a consistent conjunction, so is KvKpKqKr . . . ; so v entails one of p, q, r, . . . and KvKpKqKr . . . is a consistent conjunction: so (3) holds. Q.E.D.

Further, although *modus ponens* will be defeasible by added premises, a conclusion by *modus ponens* will stand as valid unless overthrown by an added premise. For we get no conclusion at all, as we saw, from inconsistent practical premises. But if p and Cpq are consistent, so are p and q; so Kpq will be consistent; and q will entail Cpq; but then $\mathfrak{F}q$ is a correct conclusion from $\mathfrak{F}p$ and $\mathfrak{F}$Cpq.

A more surprising result of Kenny's theory is that in practical reasoning the fiat $\mathfrak{F}$Kpq is not deductively equivalent to the pair of fiats $\mathfrak{F}p$, $\mathfrak{F}q$ (whereas in indicative reasoning $\mathfrak{F}$Kpq is equivalent to the pair $\mathfrak{E}p$, $\mathfrak{E}q$). This is not really a paradox; the equivalence supposed would lead to an absurd result. For by parity of reasoning the set $\mathfrak{F}p$, $\mathfrak{F}q$, $\mathfrak{F}r$, . . . would be deductively equivalent to $\mathfrak{F}$KpKqKr. . . . But this last fiat could be fulfilled only by a policy guaranteed to satisfy all our wants at once (expressed in a fiat $\mathfrak{F}t$ such that t entailed KpKqKr . . .). What the failure of this equivalence means is that we shall need special care in stating further inference-rules for practical reasoning.

10

Logic in Metaphysics and Theology[1]

10.1. NOMINALISM

Although this is not just one more piece on 'the problem of universals", I need not make much apology for my title. I shall not make much of the fact that some leading exponents of the theory I shall be attacking, like Buridan, Ockham and Hobbes, have commonly been called Nominalists: what is much more important is that this theory is a theory attaching a pre-eminent importance to names, and that its mistake, as I shall argue, lies precisely in thinking just of names and what they name, in cases where actually we need to consider some other logical category than that of names.

The theory I want to attack is the two-name theory of predication: namely, that in an affirmative predication the subject is a name and so is the predicate, and the predication is true if and only if the subject-name and the predicate-name stand for the same thing or things. On this view, the simplest form of predication will be the traditional "*SiP*", "Some *S* is *P*", which will come out true just in the case where there is something named "*S*" and also named "*P*". It is an interesting fact that the two-name theory has recently had a great revival in Poland, under the odd name of "ontology"; and in one way of axiomatizing

[1] (*Note*, 1969) Originally read to the Priests' Philosophical Group, London. See the Preface.

ontology, *"SiP"* is taken as the primitive form of proposition, though this particular form of presentation is not essential. In any event the distinction between subject and predicate is of no particular logical significance if both are names; the unimportance of the distinction is specially clear if *"SiP"*, which is simply convertible to *"PiS"*, is taken as the simplest form of proposition.

The origins of the two-name theory may fairly be traced back to Aristotle; Aristotle was Logic's Adam, and his doctrine of terms was Adam's Fall, with ruinous consequences for his posterity. In his days of original justice, Aristotle had held quite a different view, which we find in the *De Interpretatione*. Here, the very simplest form of predication contains not two names, but a name and a verb; and names and verbs are assigned essentially different characteristics. A name is always tenseless (*aneu chronou*); a verb is, or may be, tensed. A name is a possible logical subject; a verb is essentially predicative (*aei tōn kath heterou legomenōn semeion*). A predication may be negated by negating the verb, never by negating the name that is the logical subject. Both names and verbs, however, are supposed to be syntactically simple—to contain no significant parts of which logic need take account. This theory and terminology may be found in all essentials in Plato's *Sophist*; and I see no reason to doubt that in his state of original justice Aristotle would have accepted what Plato there explicitly says—that you cannot get a predication by combining two names or two verbs, but only by combining a name and a verb.

Except in one particular, I believe this *De Interpretatione* theory to have been thoroughly sound. The point to which I must demur is the requirement that verbs should be syntactically simple. Aristotle's corresponding requirement about names is entirely reasonable: complex names are a chimerical category. For the role of a name is simply to stand for the thing named; and then a name must signify its bearer directly, and not *via* other signs in the language, as any complex sign would have to do. But there is no reason at all why the predicative part of a proposition should be syntactically simple; what you say about a named object may have to be very complex. It looks as though when he wrote *De Interpretatione* Aristotle had a programme of analysing complex propositions as molecular combinations of atomic, one-name one-verb, propositions. He must, however, have soon satisfied himself that this programme would not work out.

In the *Prior Analytics* we get a different and irreconcilable story. The simplest form of proposition is still the subject-predicate form; but we find no mention of the distinction between name and verb. Instead, a proposition may be split up into two terms (*horoi*); in the proposition, one will be subject and the other predicate, but neither is essentially predicative; the very same term that in one proposition is a predicate may, without any change of meaning, be a subject in another proposition. The requirement of syntactical simplicity is altogether dropped. The schematic letters in a syllogism "If A applies to every B and B applies to every C, then A applies to every C" need not be interpreted by single words nor even by expressions that are grammatically namelike: to use Aristotle's own example we may take "There is one science of any contraries" as an instance of the schema "A applies to any B", taking "B" to mean "(pair of) contraries" and "A" to mean "there being one science of them", and here the interpretation of "A" is neither a single word nor namelike phrase.

The doctrine of terms appears to me to be one of the worst disasters in the history of logic. It was a *felix culpa* in that it probably helped Aristotle to grasp the idea of a general logical form expressible with schematic letters—without this idea formal logic could hardly exist—and also in that it freed him from the mistaken restriction of 'verbs' or predicates to syntactically simple words. But the price to be paid was heavy: by dropping the requirement of syntactical simplicity for names as well, the distinctive notion of a name became obscured. The distinctive notion of a predicate became still more obscured, by dropping the requirement that a 'verb' should be *essentially* predicative, and requiring that any predicate could in some other proposition be a subject; I am convinced, on the contrary, that the class of 'terms' which can be indifferently subjects and predicates is in fact empty.

Aristotle's false doctrine of terms made it easy to commit a further confusion: to confuse the relation of a name to what it names with the relation of a predicate to what it applies to or is truly predicable of. Aristotle, I think, never expressly made this identification. If we do make it, we fall into the two-name theory almost at once. For if we waive some details, not of present concern, about the quantifiers "every" and "some", we may say that the truth of an affirmative predication consists in the predicate's being true of, or applying to, what the subject names: if now we confound the relation of applying to with the relation of naming, we get the two-name theory, that truth consists in having a subject-term and a predicate-term that name the same thing. And then, since a predicate that is not a noun-phrase (or at least an adjective!) does not look much like a name, we get the requirement, explicitly rejected by Aristotle, that a proposition must come in the guise of two such name-like terms joined by a part of the verb "to be"—otherwise it is logically not properly dressed. A further development along this line is the idea that tense must be shoved onto one of the terms, not left in the copula: e.g. "Peter will be a sinner" is to be turned into "Peter is a future sinner". I shall not discuss this development, which is not found in the medieval formulations of the two-name theory.

I have elaborated elsewhere an attack on the Aristotelian doctrine of terms, and its sequel the two-name theory of predication, from the point of view of a formal logician. My task here is rather different: I shall argue that the two-name theory leads inevitably to grave distortions of Catholic dogma, and is therefore not a relatively harmless speculative error. Since I have found some manuals of logic used in courses of philosophy for seminarians to be heavily infected with the errors of the two-name theory, the importance of the matter is obvious.

My manner of refuting the two-name theory will be to show that arguments that would be valid by the two-name theory lead from true premises to false and heretical conclusions; particularly in relation to the dogmas of the Trinity and the Incarnation. This shows that the arguments in question are logically invalid, and therefore that the two-name theory is false. A refutation of this form does not, indeed, show just *what* is wrong with the two-name theory; but it does show *that* it is wrong, and wrong in an area where error is particularly to be avoided; and this may stimulate people to scrutinize the theory for fallacies that might otherwise go unsuspected.

While nobody here would say that an argument with true premises and a heretical conclusion is logically valid, I am not sure that everyone would infer that such an argument must contain an ordinary logical fallacy, which we can detect and expose if only we are clever enough. If all the arguments against a mystery of faith can be cleared up, then surely, people may object, the mystery ceases to be a mystery. This objection is confused. What I am maintaining is that for each single argument against faith there is a refutation, in terms of ordinary logic; not that there is some one general technique for refuting all arguments against faith, or even all arguments against a particular dogma of faith.

I do not claim that we can prove, or even clearly see, that the propositions expressing mysteries of faith are consistent. Modern logicians like Church and Gödel have shown what a severe requirement the demand for a general consistency proof is; as regards many theories, the demand is demonstrably unreasonable. And as regards the doctrine of the Trinity in particular we can see that a demand for a consistency proof could never be satisfied. For the propositions expressing this dogma, relating as they do to the inner life of God without bringing in any actual or possible creatures, cannot be only possibly true; if they are possibly true, they are necessarily true. So a proof that the doctrine is consistent would be a proof of its truth, which is certainly impossible. What I do claim about this and every other dogma is that in any given proof that an adversary sets up against it there is some fallacy to be found if one is sharp enough: *manifestatum est probationes quae contra fidem inducuntur non esse demonstrationes sed solubilia argumenta.*

The exponent of the two-name theory whom I am going to study in some detail is William of Ockham; I have chosen him because he is so consequent and clear in following out the theory's implications. We shall see that in the end he avoids open heresy only by the most arbitrary means; as regards the Trinity, by declaring the ordinary laws of logic inapplicable; as regards the Incarnation, by an unacceptable redefinition of the term "man".

The logical strain that the doctrine of the Trinity puts upon the two-name theory does not come about merely from the mysteriousness of the doctrine. Any doctrine in which relative terms essentially occur is bound to strain the two-name theory. It is clear in the first place that on a two-name theory there can be no relations—no *res* answering specially to relative terms. For take a proposition affirming relation, like "The cat is on the mat": if the word "on" answers to something *in rebus*, a relation, then clearly this *res* is neither named by "cat" nor by "mat", and these terms do not name the same thing as one another; so we have an

U

affirmative proposition whose truth is not accounted for by the two-name theory. It is thus natural that Ockham should deny the existence of relations: there are only relative terms, and these are names of the things related, e.g. "father" or "father of Solomon" would be a name of David. This, of course, raises new problems. What sort of term is "of Solomon"? We can hardly say that in "pater Salomonis" two names of David are put in apposition, for then how would "pater Salomonis, Isai filius" differ from "pater Isai, Salomonis filius"? Should we not have, each time, the same four names of David stuck together? Ockham in fact is content to say that a relative term is one that e.g. a genitive congruously goes with; he does not explain the mode of significance of the genitive.

I shall not pursue this, but go straight on to the special Trinitarian puzzles. Rejecting as he does the idea of relations *in rebus*, Ockham cannot remove the appearance of contradiction that arises if we say that one single simple thing is each and all of three distinct things. Aquinas can and does say that the term *"res"*, "thing", is a transcendental or category-jumping term, which applies both to *res absolutae*, non-relative realities, and to relations. The Blessed Trinity is one *res* or three *res* according as we are speaking of *res absolutae* or of relations. We do not find ourselves forced to say that one single and simple *res absoluta* is at the same time three *res absolutae*—these are only three distinct *relations*. This is not, of course, the end of puzzles: we now have to ask how and in what sense a *res absoluta* can 'be' a relation. But if Aquinas is still in check, Ockham has already been checkmated; and this he himself recognizes in effect. The line he takes is this: certain arguments about the Persons of the Trinity are invalid, although other arguments of the same logical form are valid; the only decision procedure we can apply is to see whether the premises and the contradictory of the conclusion are all guaranteed true by some text of Scripture or decision of the Church—or, Ockham adds, by some 'evident syllogism' from premises of this kind! Ostensibly valid syllogisms not thus ruled out by authority are 'universally valid'; so we need not worry about applying the rules of logic, such as the *dictum de omni*, in the domain of creatures, where the Church does not require us to believe one thing is each and all of three different things; but syllogisms about the Divine Persons are subject to ecclesiastical censorship.

The difficulties about the Trinity arose over relative terms; the difficulties about the Incarnation arise, for one thing, over abstract terms, like "humanity" or "human nature". It will not, however, be necessary for the moment to discuss either the general difficulties of abstract terms or the special difficulties of the term "nature" in the theology of the Incarnation; for we can show up the predicament of the two-name theory by shifting to another mode of expression. Instead of saying "Christ's human nature was passible, his divine nature impassible", we may say "Christ as man was passible, Christ as God is impassible": and so in other cases. But the feasibility of this depends, as Aquinas pointed out, on taking seriously the distinction of subject and predicate. The term after "as" occurs predicatively—"Christ as man" means "Christ in so far as he is a man"; if we take the subject-predicate distinction seriously, we may therefore distinguish between what is predicable with truth of the subject "the man Christ" and what is predicable of "Christ as man". Such distinctions are indispensable in the theology of the Incarnation. For example, "Christ as man is God" is false, and "Christ as man began to exist" is true; but on the contrary "The man Christ is God" is true, and "The man Christ began to exist" is false (*Summa*, III, xvi).

For a two-name theory no distinction like this can make sense. A term like "man" or "God", in subject or predicate position, is just a name, and is a name of the same thing in either position. There can be no distinction between what is true of Christ as man and what is true of the man Christ. Ockham has indeed a logical theory of this reduplicative construction "*A* qua *B* is *C*", but one of no use for present concerns; for he expounds the form by a conjunction "*A* is *B*, and *A* is *C*, and every *B* is *C*, and if anything is *B* it is *C*". This form of exposition is surprisingly redundant —both "*A* is *C*" and "every *B* is *C*" are superfluous given the other clauses—but anyhow it is useless for present purposes, since it would give e.g. "If anyone is a man, he is sinless" as part of what is meant by "Christ as man is sinless".

Ockham's view as to the logical character of propositions about the Incarnation is obscured by a sort of logical thimble-rigging with the terms "man", "humanity", and "*suppositum*". The term "humanity" as used by Ockham has only the outward guise of an abstract noun: it is no more a genuine abstract noun than "Majesty"—the humanity of Socrates just is Socrates, as the King's Majesty just is the King. A humanity is a concrete thing consisting of body and soul; the humanity which is Socrates could be assumed by a divine person and go on existing, and the humanity which now is sustained by the Son of God could be laid down by him and go on existing. We can indeed say that Christ is a man and Christ's humanity is not a man: this is because the definition of the term "man", *exprimens quid nominis*, is a disjunction—"either a humanity or a *suppositum* sustaining a humanity". The first half of this disjunction applies to any man other than Christ; the second half, to Christ alone, since an ordinary man is a humanity, and is not a *suppositum* sustaining a humanity, because he does not sustain himself. And thus if the humanity that is Socrates were assumed by the divine *suppositum* that is the Son of God, it would by definition no longer be a man; and the humanity now sustained by Christ is not a man but would forthwith and *eo ipso* become a man if Christ merely laid it down.

The meaning of Ockham's doctrine may escape us because he talks in a way familiar to us of Christ's assuming or sustaining or laying down his humanity (the last expression has of course no actual application except for the *triduum mortis*). But when we talk this way, if we know what we are doing, we are using "humanity" with these verbs the way that a genuine abstract noun is used: as when we speak of a man's assuming or sustaining or laying down a mayoralty. It would be manifest nonsense to say that the mayoralty a man assumes could go on existing after he had laid it down and would then forthwith and *eo ipso* be a Lord Mayor. Of course the cases are not the same; but the difference between them arises because of the category-difference between the concrete terms "Lord Mayor" and "man", not because in its relation to the corresponding concrete term "mayoralty" is any different from "humanity". If Ockham were using "humanity" as a proper abstract noun, what he says would be as much nonsense as my nonsense about a mayoralty becoming a Lord Mayor.

It is pretty clear, though, that in fact this doctrine is not nonsense but thinly disguised Nestorian heresy. Ockham thinks, as the Nestorians thought, that what was assumed to some sort of union with the Word of God was a human creature existing independently of such union. He merely writes "humanitas" where an outspoken Nestorian would write "homo"; this no more alters the force of his propositions than writing "the King's Majesty" instead of "the King". And though he can claim that his definition of "homo" makes it unequivocally true of Christ and other men, this too is a mere subterfuge; for Christ is not *verus homo* as we are, if "homo" applies to him and us only because one half of the disjunctive definition applies to him and the other half to us. Moreover, this definition of "homo" would certainly not have been in the mind of any Latin-speaking contemporary of Christ; so on Ockham's showing Pilate will have erred in saying "Ecce Homo", since what Pilate meant by "homo" will not on Ockham's showing have been true of Christ.

I think the sort of troubles which arise for Ockham are inevitable for any consequent thinker who holds the two-name theory. Medieval two-name theorists are in general liable to say about some abstract logical rule, "Haec regula habet instantiam (i.e. has a counter-example) in mysterio SS Trinitatis/Incarnationis". To my mind, the need to say such a thing about the rule simply shows that the rule is wrongly formulated and that we must try for an unexceptionable reformulation of it. And this reformulation must not contain a saving-clause that actually cites the theological cases as ones to which the rule shall be inapplicable; that would be contrary to the nature of logical science—no particular terms of first intention, whether theological or geological or what you will, can come in for special mention in logical rules; a logical rule must contain only syncategorematic words and second-intention terms.

There is a confusion about the way that logic is *de secundis intentionibus* which I ought perhaps to mention here: one sometimes encounters it in print—I have read a cleric's attempt to rule out of court a logical objection to the IIIa Via, on the score that St. Thomas was thinking on an ontological level and not on the second-intention level of abstract logic. Suppose a man gave a narrative of his past life that was not only implausible but positively inconsistent, it would not lie in his mouth to reject a protest against his inconsistency, on the score that he had been talking on the ontological level of action and not on the second-intention level at which there arise questions of inconsistency between propositions. This would be mere impertinence; it is no less impertinent to reject logical criticism of an argument on the score that the argument itself is not *de secundis intentionibus*. And the similar objection that one cannot infer the invalidity of an argument-form from the material truth of premises and falsity of conclusion in some instance of the form is equally not to be listened to.

All the same, it can never be the case that the *only* way to refute an incorrect logical rule is to cite a concrete counter-example from theology, i.e. a theological argument of the suspected form with true premises and a false conclusion. Even if, having our eye on the theological counter-example, we framed our rule so as to avoid trouble over the example without expressly bringing theological terms into the rule: even so the position would be unsatisfactory, and an unbeliever could be excused for suspecting that logic had been bent *ad hoc* to meet the needs of theology. It is a tasteless and dubious procedure on Ockham's part when he cites *only* theological counter-examples to some invalid syllogistic forms. The procedure is all the more objectionable because some of Ockham's alleged theological truths are in fact Nestorian heresies; but it would be objectionable anyhow. A theological counter-example shows that a form of argument is invalid; but it does not show why it is invalid; and the same of course would hold about a counter-example from geology or botany or physics.

To make the role of counter-examples clear, let us consider Aristotle's use of them in the *Prior Analytics*. His invariable way of refuting an invalid syllogistic form is to find a set of three concrete first-intention terms which he thinks make the premises true and the conclusion false. For example, he refutes the form "If no *C* is *B* and some *B* is not *A* some *C* is *A*" by the counter-example that "No swan is a horse" and "Some horse is not white" are true, but "Some swan is not white" is false. Unfortunately, "Some swan is not white" is true, so the refutation fails in this instance; and is it not unworthy of logic to have to worry about black swans turning up, even if they never do?

Saccheri ingeniously overcame this difficulty by constructing for each invalid mood a counter-example belonging to logic itself and using only second-intention terms. Thus, the invalidity of the mood *AEO* in the first figure is shown by the following example of the mood: "Any instance of *Barbara* is valid; no instance of *AEO* in the first figure is an instance of *Barbara*; ergo, some instance of *AEO* in the first figure is invalid". If this instance of *AEO* in the first figure is valid, we cannot infer that *AEO* in the first figure is a valid form; for though a valid form cannot have invalid instances, an invalid form may well have some valid instances (ones that are also instances of some other, valid form). We can on the contrary say that if this particular instance of this *AEO* form is valid, then, since its premises are true, its conclusion is true, namely that not every instance of this form is valid; and thus *AEO* in the first figure will be an invalid form. If, on the other hand, this instance of *AEO* in the first figure is invalid, then obviously the form *AEO* in the first figure is invalid.

Saccheri's procedure, brilliantly original and thoroughly sound as it is, is by no means necessary to remove the defect of Aristotle's refutation method. We may for example convince ourselves by a Lewis Carroll diagram of the general possibility that there should be terms "*A, B, C*" such that "No *C* is *B*" and "Some *B* is not *A*" are true and "Some *C* is *A*" is false: this method does not require any actual interpretation of the letters, not even one using second-intention terms.

When we prove that a logical form is invalid by citing an actual instance, using first-intention terms, in which it fails, this may be a perfectly logical proof in the sense of being a valid argument with true premises; but for all that it will not be the sort of proof for a logical result that a logician ought to put in a logic book, for qua logician he ought not to appeal to the actual truth of premises, nor to the actual falsehood of a conclusion, containing first-intention terms. The thesis that a logical form is invalid is certainly true if some instance of that form has true premises and a false conclusion; but this logical thesis does not itself specially relate to one or other instance of the invalid form; and if we know a form to be invalid, it can only be through lack of ingenuity that we fail to find a counter-example to it outside a specific subject-matter, since logic applies to all subject-matters alike.

Let me sum up the three theses for which I have just been arguing.

I. If an argument has true premises and a heretical conclusion, then a logical rule that would make it out formally valid is simply a bad bit of logic.

II. A statement of a logical rule will not be correct if it is vitiated by a theological counter-example; nor, in order to avoid this, will the rule expressly advert to theological propositions.

III. Whenever a logical form is shown to be invalid by a theological counter-example, we could if we were clever enough construct a non-theological counter-example.

To meet these requirements, it is clear that a lot of hard work in logic will have to be done. Some indications of the lines on which we should work are to be found in Aquinas. He was not much interested in formal logic for its own sake, as many medieval philosophers were; he never bothered to finish his commentary on the *De Interpretatione* (and what there is of his commentary is of little intrinsic interest, apart from the passage on future contingents) and he never commented on the *Prior Analytics* at all. But in the practice of theological argument he was well aware of the need for having sharp logical tools and a good stock of them; and some of the logical distinctions he finds it necessary to draw, in e.g. his treatises on the Trinity and the Incarnation, are of an importance that could hardly be exaggerated.

First, Aquinas explicitly rejects the two-name theory of predication and truth. Subject and predicate terms have different roles: a subject relates to a *suppositum*, a predicate to a form or nature, and the truth of an affirmative predication consists in con-formity—the form that exists intentionally in the mind, signified by the predicate, answers to the form in the thing (*indicat rem ita se habere sicut est forma quam de re apprehendit*). Taking the subject-predicate distinction seriously gets him over shoals on which two-name theorists like Ockham came to grief: e.g. he is readily able to distinguish pairs like "Christ came to be a man" (true) and "The man Christ came to be" (false) or "Christ in so far as he is a man is a creature" (true) and "The man Christ is a creature" (false). For "man" in subject position is a name— here, in apposition to the name "Christ", it is a name of the eternal *suppositum*; "man" in predicate position relates rather to the nature by which Christ is a man. Two-name theorists treat this distinction as an idle one at their peril. Nor need one resort to theological examples to bring out the point. With regard to "Christ became a man" one may be tempted to ask "which man?"; but the nonsensicality of this sort of question is glaringly apparent in the parallel case of "The present Prime Minister only recently became Prime Minister". It would be nonsense to ask which Prime Minister he became; even though it happens to be true that he only recently became Sir Alec Douglas-Home, this is not giving a name of the Prime Minister that the Earl of Home became. In "became Prime Minister" the noun is not used to name a Prime Minister but to refer to that which formally constitutes someone Prime Minister.

Ockham's attempt to bring "becomes" propositions within the scope of the two-name theory is a desperate one. He begins by expanding "Socrates became a philosopher" into "First of all Socrates was not a philosopher and then he was a philosopher": fair enough. But then he says that of this expanded form the first clause is true because of all the contemporary philosophers that Socrates wasn't, and the second half because of the philosopher that he eventually was, namely Socrates; and this is manifest nonsense.

Another point where the two-name theory is at fault is over the thesis that if two terms apply to just one thing, then as logical subjects they admit of the same predications. A two-name theorist is committed to this thesis by his view of truth. Aquinas states this thesis (Ia, q. 40, art. 1, 3) but only to reject it. What can be truly predicated depends not only on what the subject-term signifies but also on the *modus significandi* of the subject-term. In view of the many headaches that the nominalist principle about identity has caused in modern logic, a modern logician need not be so confident of its truth as to be sure Aquinas was wrong to reject it. Aquinas here attaches particular importance to the distinction between concrete and abstract terms, even *in divinis* when there is no question of any real distinction between God and Deity, or between the Father and his paternity; for example, predicates expressing acts like begetting or creating can be truly attached only to concrete terms as logical subjects.

There are various other important logical distinctions emphasized by Aquinas, for which there is no room in the two-name theory: for example, the distinction between substantival and adjectival terms. But I hope I have said enough to show how important it is for theology to have a subtle and complex logic of terms; learning a bad, crude doctrine in the logic course may make things easy for the time, but will assuredly lead to confusion and darkness later on in dogmatic theology.

10.2. SOME PROBLEMS ABOUT TIME

When I was invited to give this philosophical lecture and was considering which subject to talk about, I found my mind turning towards a great philosopher, a Fellow of this Academy, who died just forty years ago: John Ellis McTaggart. I consider myself very lucky to have been introduced to McTaggart's work early in my philosophical life; McTaggart sets high standards of clarity, rigour, and seriousness for a young philosopher to try to live up to. I suppose McTaggart is little read nowadays; he was a metaphysician, and metaphysics is not in fashion; even those who stridently call out for metaphysics to be done do not produce any themselves, and ignore the one British metaphysical work of genius in this century. But I make bold to put into McTaggart's mouth the words of one of his favourite poets:

> But after, they will know me. If I stoop
> Into a dark tremendous sea of cloud,
> It is but for a time; I press God's lamp
> Close to my breast; its splendour, soon or late,
> Will pierce the gloom: I shall emerge one day.
>
> (Browning's *Paracelsus*)

I shall be talking about a subject that was of central concern for McTaggart—the problems of time. I begin by examining a view of time that is now widely held in one form or another. In its crudest form, this view makes time out to be simply one of the dimensions in which bodies are extended; bodies have not three dimensions but four. An instantaneous solid is as much a mere artificially abstracted aspect of a concrete thing as a surface without depth is; photographs of a man at different ages represent different three-dimensional cross-sections of a four-dimensional whole. Time is only subjectively and relatively distinct from the other dimensions in which things are extended. We may illustrate this by the simile of horizontal and vertical; though at any given point on the Earth's surface a unique vertical direction can be picked out, there is no cosmic distinction of horizontal and vertical, and people at different places on the Earth will take different directions to be vertical. Or again, as Quine says: "Just as forward and backward are distinguishable only relative to an orientation, so, according to Einstein's relativity principle, space and time are distinguishable only relative to a velocity"; and he speaks of "an hour-thick slice of the four-dimensional material world . . . perpendicular to the time axis".[1]

Since Einstein, indeed, this sort of view has been very popular with philosophers who try to understand physics and physicists who try to do philosophy. Some of the arguments used in its favour are decidedly odd. Thus, it is supposed to be supported by the fact that we can represent local motion in a graph with axes representing space and time; the line drawn on the graph-paper is taken to represent a 'world line' or 'four-dimensional worm' stretching through a 'space-time continuum'. We might as well be asked to believe that the use of temperature charts requires the physical existence of 'world lines' in a 'temperature-time continuum'. Obviously the two axes of a graph, though themselves magnitudes of the same sort, may represent quite heterogeneous magnitudes.

Another odd argument is that modern formal logic, in particular quantification theory, can be applied to propositions about physical objects only if these objects are regarded as four-dimensional. This is not at all true. In Quine's *Methods of Logic,* for example, we learn from his precept and practice how to apply modern formal logic to propositions of ordinary language; there is no obstacle to such application, he points out, in the sort of ambiguity that is resoluble by considering "circumstances of the argument as a whole—speaker, hearer, scene, date, and underlying problem and purpose"; all that we really need is that the sense and reference of expressions should "stay the same throughout the space of the argument" (op. cit., p. 43). In a later work, *Word and Object,* Quine does indeed pay lip service to the need of four-dimensional talk; but the parts of his book essentially involving such talk could easily be cut out; the great majority of the sentences given as logical examples are in a streamlined version of English, not in four-dimension-ese; and Quine's discussions almost all relate to the mode of significance of terms and the structure of propositions in this near-vernacular language. Thus it is not open to Quine to maintain that if we are to be "serious about applying modern logic to temporal entities", in particular if we are so to apply quantification theory, then we

[1] *Word and Object,* p. 172.

need "the four-dimensional view" as "part and parcel" of what we are doing.[1]

Logic would not be much use for arguments about concrete realities if we had to hold that, outside pure mathematics, logic applied only to a language yet to be constructed, one that nobody talks or writes. Logic was a going concern, and was applied to inferences about concrete matters, long before anyone ever dreamed up four-dimensional language. If all these past applications of logic had to be written off as misconceived, we could not have high hopes for future applications to an as yet non-existent language. Quine is certainly not himself prepared to write off so much of logic's past.

Nor ought any logician to try to accommodate his doctrines to demands made in the name of contemporary physics. Logic must be kept rigid, come what may in the way of physical theories; for only so can it serve as a crowbar to overthrow unsatisfactory theories. Lavoisier remarked that the phlogistonists ascribed different and indeed incompatible properties to phlogiston in order to explain different experimental results; what a good thing there were not then logicians prepared to bend logic in the interests of the phlogiston theory—to say that these were 'complementary' accounts of phlogiston, both true so long as you did not combine them!

The view that time is merely a fourth dimension in which things extend is in any event quite untenable. On this view, the variation of a poker's temperature with time would simply mean that there were different temperatures at different positions along the poker's time-axis. But this, as McTaggart remarked, would no more be a *change* in temperature than a variation of temperature along the poker's length would be.[2] Similarly for other sorts of change. A man's growth would be regarded as the tapering of a four-dimensional body along its time-axis from later to earlier; but this again would no more be a change than is a poker's tapering along its length towards its point. We thus have a view that really abolishes change, by reducing change to a mere variation of attributes between different parts of a whole. But, as McTaggart again remarked, no change, no time; the view we are

[1] 'Mr. Strawson on Logical Theory', *Mind*, October 1953, p. 443. On the previous page of the same article, Quine had quoted the very passage from his own *Methods of Logic* that I quoted just now!

[2] *The Nature of Existence*, vol. ii, sections 315–16.

discussing countenances talk of a *time* axis, but such talk is inappropriate on these premisses.

The view really commits us to saying that time is an illusion. In Absolute Reality there is a changeless arrangement of four-dimensional solids; in Present Experience certain aspects of this arrangement appear to our perceptions as changes of three-dimensional bodies. McTaggart too thought that time was an illusion—though he had a very different account to give of the Absolute Reality that we misperceive as changeable bodies. But time cannot be an illusion; and certain arguments of McTaggart's own, ironically enough, are readily adapted to prove this.

The arguments in question show that certain features other than time in our experience cannot possibly be illusory. Thus, there really must be error in the universe; for there appears to be error, and if this appearance is false, then again there is error.[1] Parmenides and Mrs. Eddy alike are in a quandary what to say about the 'error of mortal mind'. Again (as mention of Mrs. Eddy reminds me) there is plain incoherence in the optimistic doctrine that misery is only an 'error of mortal mind': if my 'mortal mind' thinks I am miserable, then I am miserable, and it is not an illusion that I am miserable.[2] (Of course, so far as this goes, it might still be true that our misery would vanish if we all perceived things without illusions; McTaggart could consistently hold that, as he in fact did.) But now, quite similarly, even if my distinction between past, present and future aspects of physical things is a fragmentary misperception of changeless realities, it remains true that I have various and uncombinable illusions as to which realities are present. I must therefore have these illusions not simultaneously but one after another; and then there is after all real time and real change.

One might perhaps hold that time and change are only in the mind, in the sense that only a mind lives through time and undergoes change; in this sense, misery is 'only in the mind'. But this sense of the phrase must be sharply distinguished from the sense in which a thing's being 'only in the mind' implies its unreality. A man can no more 'only think' he has changing impressions of the world than he can 'only think' he is unhappy.

McTaggart tried to show that there was a difference between

---

[1] *The Nature of Existence*, vol. ii, section 510.
[2] *Ibid.*, section 857.

error and misery, on the one hand, and time on the other. A state of error or misery cannot be just illusory, because to be under such an illusion would be a state of real error or misery; but a state of self-consciousness that presents itself as temporal need not, he argued, be on that account really temporal.[1] This distinction is sound, so far as it goes; however, it misses the point that temporal appearance requires the existence of diverse *and uncombinable* impressions as to what is present. I am not arguing that *each single* state of self-consciousness must really be temporal because it presents itself as temporal; I am arguing that the *variety* of states each person experiences must really be, as it appears to be, a change in his experience, because these states are combinable only in succession, and not simultaneously.

However, we might try modifying the view of a four-dimensional and changeless *physical* reality by allowing that there is real change in the world of experience. There would then be a set of observing minds each of which continuously 'moved on' from one part of the four-dimensional physical world to another; though the ordered cross-sections of four-dimensional bodies would then appear to an observing mind as earlier and later, they would not really stand in temporal relations—only in the experiences of the observing minds would there be real time and change.

To make this story consistent, the observing minds must be supposed incorporeal and physically dimensionless; otherwise there would, contrary to hypothesis, be real change in the physical world. How then can mind be said to *move*? We need not make heavy weather of this; a simple analogy may help us out. The order of printed words on a page is an unchanging spatial order; but it appears as a temporal order to a reader whose attention moves on from word to word and from line to line— and surely nobody will have felt a difficulty over my use of "moves on" in this context.

The theory I have just sketched is *one* theory of time to be found in the opening discourse of the Time Traveller in Wells; and it is a theory that lends itself to speculative developments. Why should we assume that an observing mind's attention must always travel on in one direction like that of a slow, plodding, reader? Even normal minds may sometimes slip back to a part

[1] *Op. cit.*, section 511.

of the physical continuum that their attention has already scanned; Wells in fact gives us this 'explanation' of vivid reminiscence. And why should not a practised observer learn a skill like that of the practised reader, of looking before and after, seeing, for example, by anticipation those parts of the physical continuum that he would observe only later on by the normal movement of his focus of observation?

This whole theory, though, is open to the gravest objections. It incorporates an extreme form of Cartesian dualism: the human body is a changeless four-dimensional solid, the human mind a changeable dimensionless entity that reads off data for its *cogitationes* along one dimension of this solid. The theory is thus exposed to all the general arguments against Cartesian dualism; and also, to certain special objections. Though admitting an inability to understand the mind's power to move the body, Descartes did not venture to deny this power; even the Occasionalist disciples of Descartes, who did deny such a power to the mind, held that God would miraculously tamper with our normally automatic bodily machinery so that within limits it should move as we wish. On the theory we are now considering, there is no time or change except in minds; the four-dimensional physical world is an absolutely fixed order, not to be altered by any will, human or divine. The mind just cannot interfere with what will physically come to be; in fact, the very phrase I just used is only a loose manner of referring to those regions of the changeless four-dimensional world which a given mind is next going to observe.

Such a view would reduce the will of man to an impotent chimera, buzzing in a void and feeding upon second intentions (in the words of the perhaps legendary medieval conundrum). It may be beneath the dignity of philosophy to say "We know our will is free, Sir, and there's an end on't"; but we do know that our plans and purposes radically alter our physical environment, and there's an end on't; any contrary theory, however plausibly argued, just has to be false.

The view that our decisions cannot bring about physical changes may be called *fatalism*. Fatalism has a bad name among philosophers, like solipsism; arguments in favour of either will be dismissed as ingenious sophistries, and a reduction of a thesis to either counts as checkmate in the philosophical game. Determinists are mostly anxious to repudiate fatalism: to maintain only that human designs are predictable from causes, not that they do not have effects. I think this defence is open only to some varieties of determinist; other determinists evade fatalism only by a sort of doublethink; indeed, it sometimes looks as though doublethink were being deliberately advocated as a way out of free-will puzzles. Be that as it may, fatalism naked and undisguised has a strong imaginative and emotional appeal for many people. John Buchan was such a person; in his admirable novel *The Gap in the Curtain* he worked out the consequences of that purely mental 'time-travel' into the future which, as we just saw, would be allowed as a theoretical possibility by the theory of mental observers' scanning an unchanging physical world. I will not spoil this novel, for those of you who have not read it, by giving away the plot; I will just remark that the fatalism is consistently upheld. Buchan's characters merely get a glimpse of the future, with no power to change it; as in Oriental tales of Fate, what is to be comes to pass regardless of man's designs.

We find it easy to imagine the future as a country into which we are travelling and which is there before we travel into it; a country of which we might get a Pisgah sight through a break in the clouds before we actually get there. Here it is interesting to notice the change of meaning that has happened to the phrases "the next world" or "the world to come". They originally meant the *age* to come, *vitam venturi saeculi*, which is to follow the return of Messiah; nowadays, to many people, they suggest some other *place*, as when one calls Mars "another world".

The fundamental difficulty about this picture is quite different from the obvious one. At the price of adopting dualistic fatalism, one can, as I have shown, make some kind of sense out of this talk about travelling; it is not the travelling that raises the real difficulty, but the destination. What *is* (say) the England of 1984? Is there really such an object *in rerum natura*, distinct from the England of 1965?

It is very natural to talk this way: very natural to think of the successive phrases in an object's history as ordered parts of the object itself—somehow like the segments of a worm's body. I shall here borrow an example from McTaggart; he, of course, did not believe in Time, but his example suits well enough for recent statements of this view, for example, by Quine and J. J. C.

Smart. The phrase "St. Paul's in the nineteenth century" would designate an individual, and so would, for example, "St. Paul's in 1801"; and these must be two distinct individuals, for many predications that are true of St. Paul's in (the whole of) the nineteenth century are false of St. Paul's in 1801 and vice versa. Moreover, "St. Paul's in 1801" will designate a part of the whole designated by "St. Paul's in the nineetenth century"; and if we take the individuals designated by "St. Paul's in 1801", "St. Paul's in 1802", up to "St. Paul's in 1900", they will together include all the content of the individual designated by "St. Paul's in the nineteenth century".[1]

I think this account involves an erroneous analysis of propositions into subject and predicate. Let us consider one sort of predications that might be used to discriminate the individuals designated by phrases like "St. Paul's in 1856": if you were answering the question "How many visitors were there?" you might have to give a different answer for each year of the nineteenth century and of course a different answer again for the century as a whole. We can certainly consider a proposition: "There were *n* visitors to St. Paul's in 1856", as a predication about St. Paul's; I have chosen this example to show that the problem I am raising does not arise from superficial grammatical considerations, for here we have in any case a logical subject of predication that is not a grammatical subject.[2] The question is whether we can also analyse the same proposition as a predication about St. Paul's in 1856; as attaching to the subject "St. Paul's in 1856" the predicate: "There were *n* visitors to . . ." This analysis is not excluded because the other is possible; we may surely analyse "Queen Anne's hat was red" equally well as predicating of Queen Anne's hat that it was red and as predicating of Queen Anne that she had a red hat; similarly, it could be argued, our example *both* predicates something of St. Paul's *and* predicates something of St. Paul's in 1856. But I think the second analysis

---

[1] *The Nature of Existence*, vol. i, section 163. It is of no present concern that McTaggart chose to use the word "substance" where I use "individual". He was clearly assuming that the Christian era begins on 1 January A.D. 1, so that the nineteenth century runs from 1 January 1801 to 31 December 1900.

[2] Anyone disturbed by this sort of subject-predicate analysis may be reminded that it has an Aristotelian precedent. Aristotle analyses "There is a single science of (a pair of) contraries" into subject "(pair of) contraries", predicate "there being a single science of them"; and he explains this as meaning, not that contraries *are* there being a single science of them, but that *it is true to say of them* that there is a single science of them. (*Analytica Priora* 48b 4 ff.)

V

can be excluded on other grounds; phrases like "St. Paul's in 1856" cannot be taken as logical subjects at all.

Let us shift to another example: "McTaggart in 1901 was a philosopher holding Hegel's dialectic to be valid, and McTaggart in 1921 was a philosopher not holding Hegel's dialectic to be valid". If we regarded "McTaggart in 1901" and "McTaggart in 1921" as designating two individuals, then we must also say they designate two philosophers: one philosopher believing Hegel's dialectic to be valid, and another philosopher believing Hegel's dialectic not to be valid. To be sure, on the view I am criticizing the phrases "McTaggart in 1901" and "McTaggart in 1921" would not designate two philosophers, but two temporal slices of one philosopher. But just that is the trouble: for a predicate like "philosopher believing so-and-so" can of course be true only of a philosopher, not of a temporal slice of a philosopher. So if our example, which is a plain and true[1] empirical proposition, were construed as a conjunction of two predications about temporal slices of McTaggart, then it would turn out necessarily false; which is an absurd result. The absurdity does not come about just for my chosen example; it arises equally for Quine's example "Tabby at t is eating mice";[2] for a cat can eat mice at time t, but a temporal slice of a cat, Tabby-at-t, cannot eat mice anyhow.

The friends of temporal slices will no doubt here pray leave to amend the examples so that they contain predicates fitting temporal slices, instead of predicates like "philosopher believing so-and-so" or "cat eating mice", which fit living beings and not temporal slices of living beings. But we ought not to grant them leave to amend. The whole ground for treating, for example, "McTaggart in 1901" and "McTaggart in 1921" as designating two distinct individuals was that we seemed to find predicates true of the one and false of the other. But now we find that such predicates as appear in ordinary empirical propositions are often of a kind that could not be true of temporal slices; so the ground for recognizing temporal slices as distinct individuals has been undercut; and we ought to reject temporal slices from our ontology, rather than cast around for new-fashioned predicates to distinguish them by.

---

[1] Cf. The Nature of Existence, vol. i, sections 48–50.
[2] Word and Object, p. 173.

I conclude that temporal slices are merely 'dreams of our language'. It is no less a mistake to treat "McTaggart in 1901" and "McTaggart in 1921" as designating individuals than it would be so to treat "nobody" or "somebody". If we take the name "McTaggart" as logical subject of both clauses in our example, no such troubles arise; for, on the face of it, the predicates we are attaching to this subject are a compatible pair, namely "philosopher believing in 1901 that Hegel's dialectic is valid" and "philosopher not believing in 1921 that Hegel's dialectic is valid".

Predicates of this sort, in which dates are mentioned, are a long way above the most fundamental level of temporal discourse. Our ability to keep track of the date and the time of day depends on a set of enormously complicated natural phenomena; such phenomena, serving "for signs and for seasons and for days and for years", might easily not have been available. We can easily imagine rational beings, living on a cloud-bound planet like Venus, who had no ready means of keeping dates or telling the time, and were too well endowed by Nature with the necessities and amenities of life to feel any need to contrive such means. Clearly, such creatures might still speak of one thing's happening at the same time as another, or after another, and might have past, present, and future tenses in their language. This is grass-roots temporal discourse; it is perverse to try to analyse it by means of the vastly more complex notions that are involved in saying "in 1901" or "at time *t*".

In particular, it is definitely wrong to analyse an unsophisticated simultaneity proposition, like "Peter was writing a letter and (at the same time) Jenny was practising the piano", in terms of what happened at some one time *t*—"For some time *t*, Peter was writing a letter at *t* and Jenny was practising the piano at *t*". Such a use of "at the same time" as we have here does not involve any reference to an apparatus or technique for telling the time (and still less, a reference to Absolute Time). On the contrary, telling the time depends on knowing some of these primitive simultaneity propositions to be true. Telling the time by an ordinary clock involves observing that the long hand points (say) to the 12 and the short hand *at the same time* points to the 6; clearly we do not need another clock to verify that it *is* at the same time. A physicist may protest that he simply cannot understand "at the same time" except via elaborate stipulations about observing instruments; his protest may be dismissed out of hand, for he could not describe the set-up of any apparatus except by certain conditions' having to be fulfilled *together*, i.e. simultaneously, by the parts of the apparatus.

Simultaneity is involved in empirical statements; but it is not an empirical relation like neighbourhood in space. The natural expression for simultaneity is not a relative term like "simultaneous with", but a conjunction like "while" joining clauses; it is an accident of English idiom that "at the same time" seems to refer to a certain *time* that has to be *the same*, and the words for "at the same time" in other languages—Latin *simul*, Greek ἅμα, Polish *razem*—have no such suggestion.

These conjunctions joining clauses no more stand for a proper relation than, for example, "or" does. If I say I can see with my myopic eyes something over there that is *either* a hawk *or* a hand-saw, I do not claim to observe a hawk in the act of being an alternative to a hand-saw; to try to conceive a relation of alternativeness between such concrete objects would soon land us in paradoxes. Like alternativeness, simultaneity is not a relational concept, but is one of those concepts called transcendental by the medievals, formal in Wittgenstein's *Tractatus*, and topic-neutral by Ryle; the last term is the most informative of the three—it shows us that these concepts are not departmental but crop up in discourse generally.

Because of this topic-neutrality, "at the same time" belongs not to a special science but to logic; its laws are logical laws, like the so-called De Morgan laws for "or". Physicists may have interesting things to tell us about the physical possibilities of synchronizing clocks by the transmission of electromagnetic signals; but this information is wholly irrelevant to the logic of basic simultaneity propositions. Our practical grasp of this logic is not to be called in question on account of recondite physics; for without such a practical grasp we could not understand even elementary propositions in physics, so a physicist who casts doubt upon it is sawing off the branch he sits upon. And a theoretical account of this logic must be given not by physicists but by logicians.

I remarked just now that the natural, primitive, way to speak of simultaneity is to use a conjunction joining clauses, rather than a relational term like "simultaneous with". In general, I think we need to get events expressed in a propositional style, rather than by using name-like phrases (what Kotarbiński has called "onomatoids"). We need, that is to say, propositions like "Wellington fought Napoleon at Waterloo after George III first went mad", rather than "George III's first attack of madness is earlier than the Battle of Waterloo".

Some years ago philosophers were all the while talking of people and things as being 'logical constructions out of events'. This was a topsy-turvy view: nobody ever has talked or is going to talk a language containing no names of people or things but only names of events, and the claim that our language could in principle be replaced by such a language is perfectly idle. On the other hand, any sentence in which an event is represented by a noun-phrase like "Queen Anne's death" appears to be easily replaceable by an equivalent one in which this onomatoid is paraphrased away; we could use instead a clause attaching some part of the verb "to die" to the subject "Queen Anne". Any ordinary sentence, that is, will allow of such paraphrase; philo-sophical sentences like "Queen Anne's death is a particular" may resist translation, but we can get on very well without them. On the other hand, "Queen Anne's death is a past event" goes over into "Queen Anne has died" (or "is dead"), and "The news of Queen Anne's death made Lord Bolingbroke swear" goes over into "Lord Bolingbroke swore because he heard Queen Anne had died". Cutting out the onomatoids in this way, we get a manner of speaking in which persons and things are mentioned but events do not even appear to be mentioned; so far from its being people and things that are logical constructions out of events, events are logical constructions out of people and things.

McTaggart's proof that time is unreal has often been criticized on the score that it essentially depends on treating "past", "present", and "future" as logical predicates in propositions like "Queen Anne's death is past". I think I could show that this is too easy a way of dismissing McTaggart; some at least of his arguments could be restated so as to avoid the criticism. Anyhow, the critics have oddly failed to see that if the ostensible predicate "past" in "Queen Anne's death is past" is not to be parsed as a logical predicate, then equally the phrase "Queen Anne's death" is not to be regarded as being, or even going proxy for, a logical subject.

In his lectures on Logical Atomism, Bertrand Russell forcibly argued that a phrase like "the Kaiser's death" is not even a description, let alone a name, of an object nameable by a proper name, but rather goes proxy for the corresponding proposition "The Kaiser is dead". For example, people might in 1918 assert or deny or doubt the Kaiser's death; this shows that the onomatoid "the Kaiser's death" goes proxy for a clause "The Kaiser is dead". (Observe that it would be nonsense to speak of asserting or denying the Kaiser's *spiked helmet*—this phrase *is* a description of a nameable object.)

To be sure, later on in the same course of lectures Russell tells us that a person or thing is "a series of classes of particulars, and therefore a logical fiction".[1] This often happens with a work of Russell's: you pays your money and you takes your pick. I have no hesitation which of the two views I should pick. For the first, there are sound logical reasons; for the second, there is only an ontological prejudice of Russell's—"the things that are really real last a very short time".[2]

There is more than this wrong with Russell's treatment of persons. He is trying to ride two theories of classes at once: the no-class theory (that classes are fictions) and what we may call the composition theory (that classes are composed of their members and series of their terms). Only the composition theory, *plus* the segmented-worm idea of a person's temporal parts, can make it plausible that a series of classes is what a person is; Russell then concludes that, being a series of classes, a person is a fiction, by jumping over to the no-class theory. I doubt the staying power of either horse; to try to ride both at once is really desperate.

If my own arguments are sound, time-order and space-order are radically different. We can indeed verbally use such forms as "*A* is between *B* and *C*" for either sort of order; but I think this only leads to confusion. Spatial order relates individual objects: Bill is between Tom and Joe. We can get grammatically similar sentences about time-order by using onomatoids like "the Battle of Waterloo"; but the logically perspicuous way to represent

[1] *Logic and Knowledge* (Allen and Unwin, 1956), pp. 186–9.
[2] *Ibid.*, p. 274.

time-order is a complex sentence whose sub-clauses *report* (not name) events, these clauses being joined by temporal conjunctions like "and then", "and at the same time", "while", etc. Such conjunctions, which form narrative propositions out of simpler ones, are of course quite different in category from relative terms that form propositions out of names or name-substitutes; and time 'relations' are not to be spoken of in the same logical tone of voice as space relations.

If in "*x* adjoins *y*" we replace the schematic letters by names or descriptions of bodies, the resulting proposition will not be even a description, let alone a name, of something that can itself adjoin a body. On the other hand, if we replace the letters in "*p* and then *q*" by narrative propositions like "Queen Anne died" or "Wellington defeated Napoleon", the result is again a narrative proposition reporting a course of events; and this can be used to build up more complex narrative propositions, of such forms as "while *r*, (*p* and then *q*)". Nothing analogous to this is possible for propositions describing spatial order: "*x* is between (*y* is above *w*) and *z*" gives us mere gibberish if we replace the schematic letters by names.

Miss Anscombe has raised an interesting objection to this argument. She rightly remarked that from a grammatical point of view "where" will serve as a conjunction forming sentences out of sentences just as well as "when" will. To give an example: we may join "The Dome of the Rock was built" and "Solomon's Temple was built" either with "when" or with "where" so as to make sense; the "when" proposition is of course false, but that is no objection to it as a logical example. Some medieval logicians did in fact class both conjunctions as means of forming 'hypotheticals', i.e. complex propositions, out of simpler propositions; there were temporal hypotheticals and local hypotheticals. But without going into the analysis of local hypotheticals, we can quickly see that their logic does not run at all parallel to that of temporal hypotheticals. For, as I just now remarked, a temporal hypothetical "*p* and then *q*" can be used as a clause in a more complex one such as "while *r*, (*p* and then *q*)". We can play no similar tricks with local hypotheticals: "where *r*, (*p* to the south-east of where *q*)"—e.g. "Where the Dome of the Rock was built, (the Pyramids were built to the south-east of where the Parthenon was built)"—is just not an intelligible build-up for a proposition. The Pyramids just *were* built to the south-east of where the Parthenon was built; this just *is* so, and there's no sense in trying to say *where* it was so. The more we try to assimilate space and time, the more we shall find ourselves logically impeded from doing so.

I am strongly inclined to maintain that the rules for our grass-roots employment of temporal conjunctions—not only "at the same time", but also "before" and "after"—belong to the domain of formal logic. This claim is highly disputable, and I can here only sketch my reasons for it. They derive from the branch of logic called modal logic—the logic of necessity and possibility. Tie-ups between modal logic and our elementary temporal discourse might well have been suspected; for is not the future precisely the domain of unrealized possibility? Arthur Prior was a pioneer in these researches, and further work has been done by a band of younger logicians, including Hintikka, Dummett, Lemmon, and Kripke. The March 1965 number of the *Journal of Symbolic Logic* contains an important article on the adequacy of certain modal-logic calculi for dealing with temporal order.[1] I feel confident that much progress will be made in these researches; I am not invoking anyone's authority, but you can see that the idea of clearing up time problems with tools of modal logic is not just a programme vaguely sketched by me here and now. Nor would it be fair to say that calling these researches "logic" is an arbitrary bit of nomenclature; modal logic is traditionally a part of logic, from Aristotle onwards; and the systems now being used in tense logic are based on modal systems originally devised by Lewis and Langford with no such application in mind.

People have long felt inclined to ascribe to some truths about time the same necessity as logical truths have: one could as easily describe a world in which *modus ponens* broke down as a world in which time was two-dimensional or the past was changeable. If I turn out to have been right in my conjecture about the possibility of reducing to modal logic the rules that govern temporal discourse, then this feeling will have been a divination of the truth. Geometrical truths, as is well known, are not necessary in this way; we can describe without contradiction a world whose geometry is non-Euclidean just as well as a Euclidean world. But if these basic truths about time are logical,

---

[1] R. A. Bull, 'An Algebraic Study of Diodorean Modal Systems'.

then a world differing from ours in regard to them is a mere chimera.

However this may be, it is certain that there is a category-difference between space and time order, between events and individuals; and this can be brought out in quite ordinary language. But sometimes important things are too close to us to be clearly visible, or are concealed like faces in a puzzle picture; the labour of bringing them into plain view is then not wasted. And mistakes and confusions about this sort of thing are both common—witness the reams of nonsense about time you can find in bookshops—and of some practical importance. Squandering vast sums on foolish enterprises is an everyday occurrence; we may yet be witnesses of a 'time race' between East and West. Will the U.S. time explorer get back and eliminate Lenin before his Russian rival gets back even earlier and eliminates George Washington? In a few years the world may be anxiously waiting for the answer. If such spectacular folly once gets under way because governments have been convinced of some nonsensical theory, a logician will not waste effort on protests that will certainly go unheeded; he need not, after all, lose any sleep about who is going to succeed, and he could be glad that destructive efforts were directed where they would only squander human resources in a silly way.

One does what one can, though, against the Kingdom of Darkness; and perhaps less spectacular follies can be cured by exposing them to the light. Let me just instance a sophistry often used on one side of a current controversy. Some people are wont to say that it cannot make any significant moral difference whether you avoid something you wish to avoid by interposing a spatial barrier or by interposing a temporal barrier. If we do not let ourselves be fooled by the merely verbal assimilation of temporal and spatial barriers, the principle is really not a bit plausible; we need only test it on a case that rouses nobody's passions.

Let us suppose that it is my duty to organize a meeting in Cambridge. I fix a date for the meeting; then I suddenly realize that that ass Smith, whose presence would be disastrous, is coming to Cambridge for the day on that date, and will certainly attend given this opportunity. I may avoid this disaster either by changing the date of the meeting—'interposing a temporal barrier'—or by locking Smith in his hotel room—'interposing a spatial barrier'. It really is not morally indifferent which of these methods I adopt.

When we find writers copying from one another the false moral principle I have just attacked—particularly when we find one of them supporting it with talk of 'space-time'—we may be pretty confident what the trouble is; here we have, to use Hobbes's phrase, Darkness from Vain Philosophy. It is not for me here and now to enter upon a discussion "of the Benefit that proceedeth from such Darkness, and to whom it accrueth".

10.3. GOD'S RELATION TO THE WORLD

It is a well-known thesis of Thomistic theology that the relations of creatures of God are 'real' but the relations of God to creatures are not 'real'. This is a systematically misleading expression, to borrow Ryle's term, if ever there was one; for of course we cannot suppose that among the relations that *there are*, only certain ones *are real*. I can see no hope of making the Thomistic thesis intelligible unless we paraphrase it by using language about language: we must take it as a way of saying that some relational *propositions* latch on to reality in a way that others do not. This difference would have to hold between *true* relational propositions, and even between pairs of logically equivalent true propositions; for clearly "God providentially governs the world" is logically equivalent to "The world is providentially governed by God", but by the Thomistic theory only the second of these propositions predicates a 'real' relation, though both are true.

In saying that both are true, I am deliberately flouting a muddled scholastic tradition which, if taken seriously, would mean that not both are true. This tradition, to be found in scholastic manuals, is a misconstruction of Aquinas's sound doctrine that the way our mind works need not be the same as the way things are—that our mind in thinking need not, as Wittgenstein once believed, mirror the structure of the world. The doctrine in the manuals is rather the doctrine that a thought of things *as being, as if they were*, what they are not, may both be inescapable for minds like ours and *not* be false thought. (For example, our thought may by this doctrine represent nonentities as entities, or attributes as subjects of inherence, without ceasing to be true thought.) In that case our minds could inescapably represent *all* relations as having converses although in reality there are relations without converses. This doctrine is sheer muddle and inconsistency. A thought that represents things *as being* what they are not *is* a false thought—that is precisely what falsity is—and to deny this is mere confusion. It seems to me that Aquinas himself clearly saw the distinction between saying that a true thought need not *be* the way that the situation thought of is, and saying that a true thought need not *represent a situation to be* the way that situation is; and that he rejected the second view as erroneous. This is a matter of interpretation; I would ask my readers to look at passages like Ia q. 13 art. 12 ad 3um and Ia q. 85 art. 1 ad 1um and to judge for themselves. If I am right in my reading of Aquinas, he did not fall into the error of the scholastic manuals; at least sometimes, he saw and avoided it. But even if he could fairly be cited against me on this issue— *magis amica veritas.*

Some philosophers have held, though nobody is likely to ascribe to Aquinas, the view that our way of thinking 'in present experience' is inescapably erroneous in certain fundamental ways; and Bradley in particular held that our thinking is both inescapably relational in character and on that very account inescapably erroneous. I gladly leave to others the defence of such a position; I shall here simply take for granted that our ordinary relational thought is sometimes quite true, and *therefore* represents things as being what they in fact are.

As I have said, the question of 'real' relations is a question of *how* a true relational proposition latches on to reality. I must begin by refuting a false view as to the logical syntax of relational propositions: the view that such propositions do not admit of subject-predicate analysis. This is a narrowly logical point to make; but the acceptance of such a view would prevent us from accepting or even understanding the Thomistic doctrine of 'real' relations. If a relational proposition indeed made no predications about A or B, but only affirmed a relation 'between' them, then it would be quite unintelligible how, if true, the proposition could correspond to a reality in A rather than to a reality in B; and of the two converse relations, alike holding 'between' A and B, one could not very well be more 'real' than the other. So we need to see why the 'between' account of relations is wrong.

The account has been widely accepted because it is believed to follow from modern formal logic; Russell himself may very well have given this impression in his more popular and polemical writings, and certainly it has been propagated as a truth of modern logic by some of Russell's epigoni. But in fact the logical system of *Principia Mathematica* positively requires that propositions of the form "*Φab*" be treated as particular examples of the form "*Ψa*": that is, that a proposition saying how *A* is related to *B* be treated as a particular sort of predication about *A*.

To make this important matter perfectly clear, I take a concrete example of relational argument (from Quine's *Methods of Logic*). Given the premises:

(1) Edith envies everybody luckier than Edith

(2) Herbert is not luckier than anybody who envies Herbert

to prove:

Herbert is not luckier than Edith.
One easy proof uses a combination of dilemma and syllogism; we can prove that the addition to the premises of either (3), "Edith envies Herbert", or (4), "Edith does not envy Herbert", yields our conclusion by a valid syllogism. For with (3) and (2) we get Syllogism (A):

(2) Herbert is not luckier than anybody who envies Herbert

(3) Edith envies Herbert

Ergo: Herbert is not luckier than Edith.

And with (4) and (1) we get Syllogism (B):

(1) Edith envies everybody luckier than Edith

(4) Edith does not envy Herbert

Ergo: Herbert is not luckier than Edith.

This method of proof is formally valid by modern logical standards, and indeed must count as valid by any reasonable standards. But now let us notice that in Syllogism (A) we took "envies Herbert" as a term, and in Syllogism (B) we took "luckier than Edith" as a term. This would be quite illegitimate if we took seriously the view that relational propositions do not admit of subject-predicate analysis; for then out of a proposition like "Edith envies Herbert" or "Herbert is (not) luckier than Edith" we could not isolate the end piece as a logical unit, a predicable term; the sense of the binary relative term "envies" or "is luckier than" would be completable only by adding the two names simultaneously, as an 'ordered pair', and it would not combine with *one* of the names to form a predicate. Since this would break the back of even such simple and clearly valid inferences as I have given, the non-predicative view of relations may safely be rejected.

If we may after all regard a relational proposition as making predications about the related things *A* and *B*, then it will make sense (whether it is true or not) to suppose that when we take the proposition as a predication about *A*, there is some actuality in *A* answering to the predication, but that when we take the same (or a logically equivalent) proposition as a predication about *B* there is no actuality in *B* answering to the predication. And in concrete examples we can make it plausible that this is true. Take "Edith envies Herbert", for example: if Edith comes to envy Herbert, it is natural to regard this as a change in Edith rather than a change in Herbert (his 'coming to be envied'); and it is very natural to regard a state of envy as an actual condition of Edith, but very unnatural to regard a 'state of being envied' as an actual condition of Herbert. This gives a plausible content to the statement that, when Edith envies Herbert, this involves a 'real' relation on Edith's side but not on Herbert's.

I have thus tied up 'real' relations with 'real' changes. I have written about the problem of 'real' changes elsewhere (cf. the index to my recent collection *God and the Soul*, Routledge and Kegan Paul); I have urged that we need to distinguish 'real' changes, processes that actually go on in a given individual, from among 'Cambridge' changes. The great Cambridge philosophical works published in the early years of this century, like Russell's *Principles of Mathematics* and McTaggart's *Nature of Existence*, explained change as simply a matter of contradictory attributes' holding good of individuals at different times. Clearly any change logically implies a 'Cambridge' change, but the converse is surely not true; there is a sense of "change", hard to explicate, in which it is *false* to say that Socrates changes by coming to be shorter than Theaetetus when the boy grows up, or that the butter changes by rising in price, or that Herbert changes by 'becoming an object of envy to Edith'; in these cases, 'Cambridge' change of an object(Socrates, the butter, Herbert) makes no 'real' change in that object. Now the denial that God is 'really' related to creatures is quite traditionally bound up with the denial that God undergoes change. This latter denial can be true only if we are thinking of 'real' change; for all things are subject to 'Cambridge' changes—even a timeless abstract entity like a number is subject to a 'Cambridge' change if it comes to be thought of by A, or ceases to be the number of B's living children.

As with other theses of traditional theology, there has been some 'rethinking' about the changelessness of God; I have heard Catholics defending a 'Biblical' view that God is so far from changeless that he is liable to frustration by men's misdeeds. (It reminds me not of the Bible but of the Iliad—Zeus futilely lamenting the death of Sarpedon.) What I am going to say about the matter will doubtless not impress the sort of reader who will swallow the remark that the theological application of a developed formal logic, and the burning of witches, were two signs of degeneracy in the Church of the late Middle Ages (see the Dutch Catechism, English version, p. 220). Anyhow, what makes it necessary to regard God as changeless is that otherwise we cannot consistently regard God as cause of the world.

If God is changeless, then we may dismiss the question "Who made God?"—the question of a cause for A does not arise if A is changeless. But if God is changed by the changes of creatures, then God will only be one more ingredient in that aggregate of changeable beings which we call the world, and will not be the Maker of the world. Even if we could consistently think of such a God as causing *all the rest* of the world (as I do not believe we could, not consistently), even then the causal questions that arise about other changeable beings could rightly be raised about such a changeable God; as Schopenhauer said, you cannot pick up an argument like a cab and pay it off when it has taken you as far as you want to go. So this God would not be God after all, since he, like his so-called creatures, would have to have a cause. So I dismiss any 'rethinking' of God's changelessness; it can lead only to an alien and incoherent view of the Divine.

Those true propositions about God which seem to involve a change in him (and do involve a change in him, if we stick to the

Cambridge criterion of change) are traditionally explained away as involving a 'real' change only in creatures, not in God. This is not too difficult to understand if we consider causal propositions; God's 'becoming' Creator or Lord of a new creature involves a 'real' change only in the created world, not in God. But severe difficulties arise as regards the Divine knowledge and will.

(1) If we, who have to speak about God at different times, are to speak the truth about God, we shall certainly have to enunciate different propositions at different times about what God knows or wills. "God wills to bring it about that so-and-so" will no longer be a true thing to say when so-and-so has already been brought about; nor is it true any longer to say "God knows that Socrates is sitting down" after Socrates has got up. How then can God's mind be 'really' changeless in so far as he is concerned with creatures?

(2) Knowledge and will are, in the old jargon, immanent acts: to know or will is an actuality in the knowing or willing person, and does not consist in an action upon an object like kicking or biting; to be the object of knowledge or will is not something that 'really' happens to an individual. This doubly threatens the Thomistic doctrine: it is hard to see how the object of God's knowledge and will can be 'really' related to him, and equally hard to see how God can fail to be 'really' related to the objects of his knowledge and will.

However, merely to speak of "objects of knowledge and will" —as though *individuals* could be such objects—is to use a misleading expression. A proposition affirming that something is known or willed just does not affirm a binary relation of two individuals, whether or not one of the individuals is God. As regards knowledge, the point was made long ago in the *Theaetetus* (in a theory Socrates feigns to have heard in a dream); what one knows is not nameable, like an individual, but only expressible in a *logos*, a proposition. I can learn or assert *that* Jones is such-and-such; it is nonsense to say "I learned Jones" or "I asserted Jones". With the verb "to know" the matter is not so clear; unfortunately in English we *can* say "I know Jones" as well as "I know that Jones is a rascal". But this only shows that the natural selection of words is not so uniformly beneficent as John Austin perhaps supposed. It is just our bad luck that in current English we do not say "I ken John Peel" and "I wot that John

Peel keeps a pack of hounds"; the distinction that used to be marked by a pair of verbs in English still is so marked in many languages (as it was in Greek).

Philosophers have misconstrued knowing-*that* as a binary relation by *inventing* objects of knowing, such as timeless Propositions:[1] "I know that Jones drinks" would be short for "I know the Proposition that Jones drinks", and this Proposition here referred to by a complex phrase "the Proposition that Jones drinks" would be an individual, a nameable entity, which could also be the object of belief, doubt, assertion, etc. But this is nonsense: "I've just asserted Fido" (or "learned Fido") is nonsignificant if "Fido" is a proper name of *any* individual—that is the whole point of the 'dream' theory in Plato. (Calling the alleged entity a "fact" or a "situation" instead of a Proposition naturally makes no difference.)

As regards will, the same point can be made, and fortunately is less obscured by philosophical theories. I will *that* so-and-so, e.g. that Jones shall be punished; it would be nonsensical to say "I will Jones".

It is thus a mistake from the outset to treat what is known or willed as one term of a two-term relation, the other term being the person who knows or wills. Following Aristotle, Aquinas often speaks as though we had a two-term relation here; whenever he does so, *pietas* must not hide it from us that his logical apparatus is inadequate and his language misleading.

Another mistake we tend to fall into is to regard God's knowledge of creatures as contemplative. But it is an old doctrine that this knowledge is practical; *scientia Dei, causa rerum*; it is analogous not to our observational knowledge but to our knowledge of our own skilled performances. We could better assimilate this old truth if we worked towards a better understanding of what practical knowledge amounts to in human beings: Miss Anscombe's *Intention*, a pioneering investigation, among other valuable points rightly emphasizes that some of a man's knowledge of his own performances is non-observational. The glib sciolism of our time will say "It's just a matter of feedback"; but 'feedback' does not account for all of our control of our own actions; quite familiar facts show this—when a skilled musician

---

[1] I use the capital letter to distinguish this use of the word from its use to mean a piece of language with a certain logical role.

plays a passage with many short notes in rapid succession, 'feedback' certainly cannot account for his skill, because nervous conduction is too slow to give him a 'feedback' of his own playing. And very often the sensations that are supposed to give us observational knowledge of our own performances are merely postulated occurrences. We ought to try harder to understand this non-observational knowledge whereby we control our own actions; for this is the way we are made in God's image, as Aquinas says in the prologue to the Prima Secundae.

Just because man's control of his own actions is an image of God's providential control of the world; because, as Sir Leslie Stephen said, there is a great First Cause and ever so many little first causes; we must avoid representations that would make us into mere puppets of God. A parable I have found useful is this: a chess master, without looking at the board, plays a score of opponents simultaneously; his knowledge of chess is so vastly superior to theirs that he can deal with any moves they are going to make, and he has no need to improvise or deliberate. There is no evident contradiction in supposing that God's changeless knowledge thus governs the whole course of the world, whatever men may choose to do.

As regards will, what we need is a correct account of voluntary causality. The most usual account is that the will is a faculty of the soul with special acts of its own, *actus eliciti*; these are what is primarily voluntary, and whatever else is brought about is a consequence of some *actus elicitus* of the will. This account is the most common one in philosophy books and scholastic manuals; and it is *sometimes* followed by Aquinas. If we try to apply to it the Divine will, it leads to a hopeless puzzle; for happenings in the world are contingent, but they follow infallibly upon the *actus elicitus* of the Divine will; is this act, then, itself contingent or necessary? The familiar answer that this *actus elicitus* is necessary "in its entity but not in its term" is quite useless; for all that this answer tells us is that the Divine act of will is necessary, but its 'term', the happening in the world (which follows infallibly upon God's willing it!), is a contingent event; and that is just the problem, not an answer to the problem.

Fortunately, we can come to see that this puzzle arises not from the mystery of the Divine nature, but from inept philosophizing even about the human will. For there are no mental

w

states identifiable as the *actus eliciti* of the will which regularly precede voluntary actions of the mind or body. There are indeed such acts as trying, setting oneself to do something, formulating an intention, and the like; but a little thought shows that these are not the supposed *actus eliciti* of the will; for many voluntary performances are not preceded by anything like trying or setting oneself to do it or formulating an intention. And as for the 'volitions' of recent philosophy, which are supposed to trigger off the movements of muscles, they are a mere myth, devastatingly exposed by Ryle in *The Concept of Mind.* (Scholastically trained readers should notice that in modern philosophy this word is not used equivalently with "volitio" in medieval Latin.)

In Aquinas, side by side with the untenable notion of *actus elicitus*, we find a quite different account: that "nature" and "will" signify two ways in which an agent can bring about something. "A brings it about naturally (voluntarily) that so-and-so happens" does not signify that first of all A has a natural (voluntary) kind of event happening within himself, and then, as a result of this event, so-and-so happens; rather, the adverbs "naturally" and "voluntarily" serve to differentiate two ways in which the so-and-so that happens may proceed from the agent A. (Cf. e.g. Ia q. 41 art. 2)

With this account many puzzles are removed. For example, if the *actus elicitus* of the will were an actual observable event in its own right, then there would be no obvious reason why such an event could not be 'elicited' from a man by outsiders using some technique; indeed, some people believe that just this can be done by 'brainwashing'. But on the account of voluntariness we are now considering, it is simply self-contradictory to say that some issue *both* is up to A's choice *and* is decided by factors wholly outside A's control; external control of the will is an inconsistent notion (as indeed Aquinas holds—Ia IIae q. 6 art. 4). The same consideration removes the deterministic dream that 'in principle' the movements of men's bodies could be predicted independently of any mention of what men intend to do. Sometimes it is said that such a purely physical account is 'complementary' to the familiar account in terms of intentions; but "complementary" is just a way of papering over a logical inconsistency.

This account of will enables us to make sense of certain dark sayings of Aquinas:

Knowledge relates to things as they are in the knower;

will relates to things as they are in themselves. Now all other
things exist necessarily as they exist in God, but they have no
inherent absolute necessity. So God knows necessarily whatever he knows; but he does not will necessarily whatever he
wills. (Ia q 19 art. 3 ad 6um)

I have argued that the practical knowledge by which God controls
the world may be regarded as eternal and unchangeable. But to
say "God brings it about by his will that p" is to say "It comes
about, voluntarily *ex parte Dei*, that p". And as a matter of logic
this proposition will be contingently true if "p" is contingently
true.

Index